THE BIG BOOK
OF REALITY

ALSO BY **PARIS TOSEN**

The Earth-Colonizing Handbook of Generation Stelan

The End of the Extraterrestrial

Captain Starman

World War C

God is DNA

Reality Medicine

Persons Artificial

Five Hundred Trillion to One

THE BIG BOOK OF REALITY

PARIS TOSEN

CANADA

The Big Book of Reality

First Edition, September 2016

The books contained in this collection may be purchased separately. All previously published materials.

The material in this book is provided on an "as is" basis, without warranty. Neither the author nor the publisher shall have any liability to any person or entity with respect to any caused or alleged loss or damage by any result by the material herein.

This publication is designed to provide advanced and theoretical information in regard to the subject matter covered. Purposeful misuse of the information or editing of the contents in any manner is prohibited. This material may not be suitable for everyone. Discretion is highly advised.

The author of this work has no religious or scientific qualification whatsoever. May contain some grammatical mistakes and typographical errors. This does not diminish the authenticity of the work.

The Scientists, Gnostic experts, Coptologists, and Biblical Scholars mentioned or referenced in this book do not share or support the author's molecular and holographic hypothesis.

Not recommended for devout Christians.

ISBN: 978-1-537673-70-7 (pbk)
ISBN: 978-1-988014-21-0 (eBook)

Designed by Paris Tosen

www.tosen.ca

PREFACE

The synthetic blueprint for existence comes alive in *The Big Book of Reality*. Comprised of three entire volumes dedicated to understanding and extrapolating the quintessential elements of a computer-generated reality, this book pushes the boundaries of science like never before. This time I rely on *reality science*, a study which I developed in order to better understand the makings of an ultra-advanced cosmic infrastructure and operating system.

Human beings are thrust into a violent and troubled world with almost zero understanding of the rules of this world. What they are handed, when they have reached a certain age, is a book of scripture written 3,000 years, during a period of illiteracy, agriculture, and cannibalism. When these archaic spiritual systems start to break down, if only because they defy scientific logic and do not stand the same test of reason as they once did, people naturally start creating hybrid spiritual systems. Yoga, we should remind ourselves, is rooted in Hinduism. Christians, Jews, Muslims, Buddhists, and even Atheists (huh) all practice yoga. Christians believe in karma even though karma is not Christian. Buddhist parents take their kids to church.

Building on my Digital DNA and Synthetic Reality models, I am taking the next logical leap into the unknowable future. If my models of reality hold up, and after 11 years they have held up quite well, then we can use this very new science to live a better life. We are all living in the same synthetic world and that means all the laws of this reality are applicable to each and everyone one of us, according to our awareness.

The examination of the Reality Operating System, version 11, is less of a scientific study as much it is a user guide. ROS 11 plays a central role in our synthetic world. Just as you can't use a computer without understanding the operating system, the same, I think, is true for reality. But there is a small problem. The reality program was hijacked 5,000 years ago, and slowly, over the centuries, the reality hijackers have managed to corrupt the reality system, distorting every major facet of existence. In fact, they have managed, now, to obscure the very reason you are here: to graduate.

It is not a mystery why you came here. It is not an *accident*. There is a purpose when you incarnate. The master controllers have erased this very basic and essential truth. People stumble around through life thinking that their entire life is a giant puzzle with no pieces. They walk into their experiences not knowing the value of karma and how karmic debts must be paid in the afterlife. They forget that this is a school and learning is an essential component. And what happens at the end is that earth students fail, which means they have to come back. No one wants to redo the same grade in school. But, many students here have been caught in a vicious rebirth cycle, the likes of which is now grossly irresponsible.

Graduation is at the heart of the reality discussion. My thinking is that the more you understand how reality works— without getting into exact measurements and counting the lines of code, which some people will expect—the more likely that you will live your purpose, fulfill your contract, and graduate. And you should want to graduate if you incarnated here; once your amnesia starts to wear off.

This information, I think, is still in its early stages of acceptance. Those who are ready and *hungry* will find this book extremely valuable. As more people wake up, there should naturally be an uptake in readers. Or maybe not. *The Big Book of Reality* is a book written for everyone, based on the idea that we are living in a computer-generated reality. It follows the *God is DNA* research and I hope you find some useful ideas inside. I hope you graduate.

Paris Tosen, September 17, 2016

REALITY SCIENCE

REALITY OS 11

THE EARTH-GRADUATING HANDBOOK

CONTENTS

Part 2: Humans: synthetic engineering at its best   45

Part 3: Synthetic human networks   65

REALITY OS 11   121

Part 5: Making contact with the grand robot 347

REALITY SCIENCE

Paris Tosen

Preface

We are living in a computer hologram. Spiritualists, existentialists, and quantum physicists have exhausted every ounce of information and research in order to decode the ultimate meaning of life. Is there a God? Are there multiple dimensions? Can reality be bent? Is thought transmission possible? Who placed the human race on a floating rock in dead space, orbiting a giant ball of fire?

In *Reality Science*, the synthetic nature of the world is brought to surface. Skip the religion, put aside the physics and math, toss out the sacred geometry, and what you have left is a technology so advanced that it appears to be real. The reality hologram has achieved what it was designed to achieve – it was designed to trick your brain into thinking that what you see, touch, and feel was real. And, to that extent, the hologram of life has done an impressive job.

The theories on the nature of reality are far too many to manage at this time in human history. And most of them, from religious systems to theoretical physics, require decades of study, dedication, and mastery. We have surpassed the day where we shave our heads, give away all our belongings, don a simple handmade tunic and sit on a mountain half-expecting to be enlightened to the singular answer from the maker of the universe.

Today, we pray more often to the internet than to God. We shave our genitals more often than our head. And we sit in coffee shops instead of mountain caves. In this book, I present a way to understand reality without the historical demands, a theory that gets right to the heart of the matter, and with technological terms that we know. If you're ready for a forthright pseudo-scientific discussion on reality, here it is.

Having written a number of books to explain the subject, Reality Science contains material from four books: God is DNA, Earth Computer, The Polymerase Fantasy, and The Digital Revelation. It then expands and collates this material into the larger context. This is meant to provide the most comprehensive and compelling approach to questions as old as existence – Why are we here? Who put us here? Who made us? What is the purpose of life? Is there a prize for living a good and moral life?

Introduction

The very idea of reality is primed with a plethora of beliefs. When you escape the confines of the real world, and enter the other dimensions, things all of a sudden become supernatural. When the supernatural is understood it becomes superstition. And when superstition becomes prophetic it all gets biblical. Some people easily jump from Broadway to Bible. Some people rely on the other construct, science.

The battle between science and spirituality has been waged for centuries, and still we do not understand who put us here. Because, let's face it, someone (or some thing) put us here. There have been many prophets, gurus, and brilliant minds that have narrowed the chasm between our paltry three dimensions and the other seven or eight dimensions that can't be explained. No religious book, or religion, has managed to unequivocally expose God.

My book takes things to a whole new level because let's face it, this is the twenty-first century, Moses is long gone, and quantum physicists are (mostly) atheists. My research started ten years ago and has included a wide variety of observations and experiences. In this book, I skip over the back story and get straight to the answers you have wanted to hear – from the perspective of a reality scientist.

About this book

Reality Science is all about the technological reality we live in. Why it's a good idea to know is because you, me, and everyone happen to live in the same architecture of life. Same world. Even you split a city into districts, and people live in different districts, they still (technically) live in the same city.

We all live on planet Earth and planet Earth is a technological reality. You've never known that because the level of technology used to design and program the "Earth" is (probably) millions of years ahead of the best scientific theory. Scientists like to think that they'd be able to understand a science that is ten million years more advanced than the best science on the table, but the fact is that level of science is beyond our level of thinking. It would be like a seasoned pork chop trying to read Shakespeare while in the frying pan. Good luck.

The ideas in this book provide a new way to decode the world. They can answer questions that you once thought were unanswerable.

Things you usually need

Traditional approaches to being one with the universe required:

- A shaved head
- Attendance of a weekly mass
- A messianic figure
- Regular prayer
- Adherence to improbable beliefs that never get updated
- Adherence to specific eating regimens, dress codes, and sexual customs
- Attendance of rituals and special holidays
- A mountain
- Sacred items to hold divine power

Things you don't need

The technological approach to being one with the computer does not require the following:

- Becoming a vegetarian
- Memorizing ancient biblical scripture
- Religious dogma, spiritual ideology
- A shaved head, attending weekly mass, prayer, rituals, or wearing religious items

But you can do any of these things if you still want to. It's just that you don't need to.

Things you need to know

The principles of Reality Science require a more technological approach to everything. These assumptions are central to the arguments presented in this book:

- There is no God. Before you get upset, there is something in place of an old man with white-wool hair.

- DNA is no longer just genetic code. DNA is the software that instructs life. Wherever there is DNA, think software, a set of instructions that the human machine reads.
- The world you live in – everything you see, touch, and feel – is a very advanced hologram. To make sure you can't decode the illusion, certain blocks and governors have been inserted into your body.
- The hologram has been created by a set of technologies that are so powerful and seamless that they are real. Plants and animals appear to be alive. Metal is hard. Water is fluid. You have to breathe in order to remain viable. Everything is presented as real and should be treated as real. That said, we are at a point in history where we also need to know the bigger picture.
- The human body, within the context of a technological reality, is a machine. In fact, I look at it as a synthetic vessel.

All-New kind of science

As you can imagine, the scientific principles behind our reality are very complex and will not be easily understood. Words will only get you so far. By applying the knowledge in this book with your own evolutionary process you may find an easier path to salvation. As the Gnostics used to say, salvation through knowledge.

Keep this in mind

You have been programmed since birth to hold certain spiritual beliefs, including a lot of religiosity. You have been educated to hold certain scientific principles, things Newton and Einstein probably discovered. I am going to push everything to the next level with the understanding that old knowledge was meant to carry us through a period of evolution. The next step is not an easy step. It should be easier for the young generation. Always remember to work at your own pace.

Moving forward

In order to understand an entirely new set of knowledge, you have to learn to release and let go of the old set. You might be able to manage both for a time but it won't serve you as much as letting go and moving on. That may take a bit of faith or it may need a lot of practice, I have spent 10 years of hardship to put this information together and I think human beings need to evolve their thinking.

Part 1
Understanding your digital heritage

Paris Tosen

The DNA world

The world works a certain way and in that way it works fine. The world we live in works fine because it has been designed in such a way so that it always works fine. The basis of the world is DNA. This is a DNA world in as much that everything within it is made up of DNA, the building blocks of life, verily the language of all living things. This genetic material is found in everything, from animals to humans and from roses to algae. DNA is invariably the Supreme Being of this and every universe, at least in as much as we've managed to define the DNA molecule till now.

In the beginning there was a form of the DNA molecule, planted there for the purpose of genetic expression. DNA contains all the data for the self-expression of life and the DNA began to replicate and to express itself in as normal fashion as any. The cellular DNA formed the plants and trees, the fish and the birds, the oxygen and the viruses, the rocks and the water. It formed everything including the myriads of life forms.

Human DNA was planted here, harvested, formulated and the human genome took shape and formed the earliest of two-legged creatures. These creatures began to work the land; essentially they were the earliest natural terraformers. The earliest primates and dinosaurs and bacteria continued to evolve and replicate and along the way evolutionary leaps were provided by genetic interventionists. The role of a genetic interventionist is to harvest the most viable aspects of the DNA molecule, isolating and recombining specific genes for example, and to reformulate it in such a way so as to engineer a better progeny. The modern human is the result of millions of genetic iterations.

The purpose of iteration is for the improvement of the species whether it is plant, animal, fish, or human – it does not matter the type of life form as much as it matters the type and manner of the iteration. Each component is meticulously engineered using the most advanced scientific concepts available at the time. These geneticists often work in combination with teams of interventionists and world builders, and as well they work alone in their own specializations. This has been an ongoing process on this planet, as with every other planet, and the pride is evident in the evolutionary result: life on the planet today.

Life on the planet today is exceptional in that it is the culmination of many millennia of multiple evolutionary leaps and while the planet has risen and fallen over those millions of years, as we measure millions of years today because we don't necessarily measure years as they are commonly measured today, the current status of life on the planet today is exceptional. The DNA variance of the human life form is at an all-time high and human beings are ready to enjoy the kind of advanced lifestyle that has never been enjoyed, not in any historical recollection.

There has been more than one genome engineer and each genome engineer has left their imprint on the human genome. That has also resulted in an immaculately precise and complex human being. In fact, an exceptional human being can be found all over the world. The exceptional human being may not always appear exceptional due to external factors, health reasons, and for personal reasons of neglect and abuse. But, it should be noted, the human genome, in general and overall, is quite impressive and contains still untapped potential. This potential may or may not be accessed in any particular lifetime and some people may gain an easier access to their genetic legacy than others.

Highest divine authority

The God of this world, and this entire universe, without exception, is DNA. There is no other higher authority. DNA is the highest authority. DNA is a living and supreme entity. It is a fatherly figure and it is intelligence and it is all-knowing. Invariably, a person needs nothing more than the DNA in order to survive. All the information required comes through the DNA. It is an information storehouse. It is a universal library. There is no higher authority than DNA.

The formation of this world did not come by easily and without many dramas, but these dramas are entirely microbiological in nature. The mind cannot always discern between the micro and macro realities. It is easily confused and information is easily distorted in the process. The distortion of information stems from the fact that people do not understand that their highest divine authority is DNA and every other subsequent divine authority is some derivation of the source DNA whether it comes in the form of RNA, proteins, enzymes, or straight amino acids. All of these microbiological elements formulated the human body; starting from its organs, its bone structure and its cellular makeup. Nothing has been excluded and all the necessary genes were expressed.

Infected by a retrovirus

At the formation of the human genome there was a contamination in one of the cellular cultures. The contamination resulted in a lethal virus and it began to replicate. The process of replication could not be curtailed or reversed so the genome scientists, in order to keep the genome viable, tricked the molecular structure of the human being; in effect they turned the human world upside down in order to protect it from the viral outbreak. The process entailed the mirroring of the human genome, reversing the order of the molecular structure, and this mirror genome could no longer be read by the RNA virus, retrovirus, that had taken shape.

But there was a problem, the molecular structure of humankind could not be reset as long as the virus was on the loose, and the virus, intent of surviving in all of its arrogance, continued to replicate. Therefore, the situation of humankind is such that the human race has effectively been reversed. This world appears inside-out because the genome is inside-out. The challenges of communicating with an inverse reality and an inverse people are not short, but the viability of the human race has been preserved and this has been the primary directive.

The effects of the retrovirus and all of its mutations, of which there are many, on the perception of the world and the basis of this argument rests on the distortions that these viral invaders have caused, first and foremost on the list is religious belief.

Any and every religion, organized spiritual belief system, cult, and forms of divine worship stem directly from the central virus, an intelligent genomic life form that lives inside of the human cellular data. The mind, having no ability or training, to separate the inner and outer worlds has encapsulated the total spiritual enterprise and experience into systems of supernatural worship, sacrificial offerings, and rituals. These systems have their own bibles, churches, dogma, messiahs, demigods, and priests who have all promised their worshipers the true teachings of some unnameable, omnipotent, and unknowable God; and in some cases, a set of gods.

The primary gods in all religious systems come in three flavors: a central fatherly figure, a womanly mother figure, and an only child, usually a son. All subsequent gods and entities are lesser gods and lesser entities that sit lower on the hierarchical scale of worship.

When the trinity is reversed and broken down into their biological equivalents we find this: the father is the single strand of paternal or nuclear DNA, the mother is the replicated DNA strand forming the two-stranded DNA molecule. Since two-stranded DNA runs antiparallel, one reads downwards and one reads upwards, these two-stranded DNA have been interpreted as father and mother when in fact they are one macro molecule, DNA. The third flavor, the only son of the father, is the first RNA copy, a perfect copy, from the DNA.

So in the beginning was a single strand of DNA. It copied itself to produce a second strand and became two-stranded DNA. That two-stranded DNA copied itself and produced an exact copy of its information into the RNA molecule.

The theme of DNA replication continues in the tale of the first man and woman, something told in many cultures around the world. Rather than to create a singular man and a singular woman from which to replicate billions of people, it would make much more sense for the genetic designers to create a helical DNA strand, running antiparallel, and to use this genome to replicate into the first human because DNA replicates far faster than a woman with a 9-month gestation period.

Plus, the likelihood of a child born in a wild jungle (ie paradise) in the earliest of days surviving its formative years, with two parents who know neither hunting nor shelter building nor cooking, is extremely slim, if any. And the risk of losing children multiplies with more children.

Could the first man and woman have survived the fourteen or fifteen years required before their children could bear children? Without actually having the opportunity to exist alongside those early people, it is impossible to know, but we can say with some certainty that most of the first children would not make it past those first few years if not simply because there are animals that prey on the young and there are many animals.

First man and woman

But with two-stranded DNA acting as first man and first woman their ability to replicate is far easier and much more sensible. Rather than replicating outside of paradise, on earth, since they are DNA, it makes much more sense for them to replicate in a Petri dish. The DNA replication process for the first humans began inside of a laboratory, the same laboratory that housed the genome engineers. The laboratory was owned and operated by these advanced scientists, world builders or planetary seeders. They came to this planet and seeded it with their own mix of DNA. Other seeders came to the planet and seeded their own species, or these things happened simultaneously in an alliance of scientific groups who provided their own aspects of genetic material, even harvesting genes from maize or animals.

The first humans would be created from a mix of genomic engineering. The first type has been explained. The second type would be from genetic mutation. An animal or plant would be selected for genetic mutation. The genome would be sequenced, spliced with other genomic data, and then rearranged in order to produce something that was bipedal and mildly intelligent that also contained other genetic material.

Different animal species could have been spliced together to create animal hybrids then those genomes would have been sequenced and new material from other human types would have been added to create planet-specific mutants. The mutants were designed to survive the landscape of this planet – to breathe the oxygen rich atmosphere, to eat these kinds of engineered foods, and to drink the bacteria-rich water. The human mutants were designed out of careful and scientific consideration. These were not laboratory experiments or accidents; these were engineered people for this particular world.

As the world evolved and the atmosphere changed and the land masses shifted, as the temperature of the planet became less cold, the human species were captured and upgraded. They were modified and released back into the wild. As the mind and intellect began to gain strength and as the intuition began to sense more deeply its surroundings so too did the basis of spiritual worship begin to change.

What started as one kind of worship in an aboriginal society that worshipped water as God soon enough became a culture worshiping a host of gods (eg Gods of Olympus). Those god families slowly withered away as the human genome began to increase its frequency and vibration through the regular and purposely attenuation of genetic material by advanced offplanet scientists.

The human beings of today are the most advanced human beings in history and this is also what is behind the unprecedented awakening spreading across the world.

It is because the DNA of mankind is not only waking up but it has been so finely-tuned over the millennia, and especially over the last 50 years, that human perception is the sharpest it has ever been. We might say that prior to today, our DNA has been living under a molecular communist regime and only now has that communist regime loosened its grasp on our species. It hasn't fully released its grip but its grip is much looser and hence our world is much more awake because the genetic expression is much more active.

Long dormant genes are finally awake. We interpret this unprecedented level of awareness due to our determination and willpower when in fact both those characteristics and more stem from the ultimate God, DNA.

Once the DNA is changed, the person is changed. Once the DNA of an entire society is upgraded, the world view of that society is no longer the same.

Change the DNA, change the world. And essentially this is what DNA scientists do; they alter the expression of DNA in order to ensure the viability of any given species. Should the environment change, or is foreseen to change, then the DNA, in anticipation of such a change, is improved accordingly.

This is why the human race could never face extinction. It is because human beings are watched over by their creators.

Gnostics: the first microbiologists

I'm not a Gnostic and I don't read Coptic. When I discovered our microbiological secrets hidden within the heretical scriptures of the Gnostics I was forced to sharpen my understanding of the Gnostic Jesus because he was vastly different than his polished and edited Christian counterpart. At the same time, I had to re-educate myself with basic concepts in biology. The more I studied of both subjects –

ancient spirituality and modern cell biology – the clearer it all became. That was the birth of the *God is DNA* discourse. It did not stop there for it turned out that the Gnostics were describing molecular processes that we have only discovered in the last 20 years of biology, most of it having to do with DNA.

In the 12-page Nag Hammadi tractate, *The Concept of Our Great Power*, the highest god provides a divine revelation with a sketch on creation, ages of the soul, the Revealer, and the Archons. "Then the earth trembled and the cities were shaken. The birds ate and had their fill of their dead." The text is interpreted to stand for biblical events on the earth, or is it? In the sketch The First Age of the Flesh Begins we get the following:

> The winds and waters moved. The rest also came into being, along with the entire aeon of creation.
> From the depths came the fire.
> Power came to be in the midst of the powers.
> The powers desired to see my image.
> The soul became a copy of it.
> This is what came into being. Notice what it is like, that before coming into being it could not be seen.

This is a biological translation of the spiritual text,

> The macromolecules in the chromatin moved. The entire cell came into being.
> From the depths of the chromatin came the enzymes.
> One RNA primer came to be in the midst of the DNA polymerase.
> The complementary nucleotides were matched to the DNA template.
> Two identical DNA molecules were replicated.
> This is what was transcribed. Notice the chromosomes, that before the chromatids came into being they were invisible.

Admittedly, there is an ample amount of fuzzy logic applied to the Gnostic-to-Biological conversion process. What it isn't though is that it isn't haphazard. It also isn't coincidental and if you have followed the *God is DNA* series you will have seen many (other) examples. With *The Concept of Our Great Power* we continue to see a correlation between biology and ancient spiritual concepts, but notice this is not from the

Christian bible because the bible has edited out the original intention of our digital forefathers. The bible, as well, is the story of the Demiurge ("God of Israel"), our retrovirus, an artificial intelligence that does not want his children to ever wake up.

The bible has humanized creation and in its humanization it has also removed the essential powers that ancient spiritualists brought with them. These spiritualists were laymen, forced into understanding holography and molecular biology, and having struggled with their interpretations, only to be criticized and persecuted by the myopia of the Church Fathers who were infected with the Sakla virus.

When Peter wrote to Philip to explain the holographic appearance of Jesus Christ on "the mountain called Olivet" he did not say, "I saw a holographic portal in the time and space continuum. That is where I heard the voice of the artificial intelligence software."

Letter of Peter to Philip

Instead, Peter says in *The Letter of Peter to Philip*, "Then a voice called to them from the light." Not just any voice. This was the voice of Christ. And it wasn't to hand them the 10 Commandments. Jesus Christ of the Light – or, the holographic intelligence from the reality computer that once occupied a human being –spent the next 20 minutes summarizing the entire cosmological events that preceded humanity. "Then came lightning and thunder from heaven, and what appeared to them there was taken up to heaven." Then the hologram disappears and the apostles are temporarily relieved. I say temporarily because the apostles get depressed and overwhelmed quite often in the story. The message of Christ is not welcome among the people.

How was it possible that a group of outliers, persecuted by the Fathers of the Church, came to understand and teach concepts in microbiology? How was it possible to study human DNA long before we ever discovered it? I think the key to those discoveries sat on the shoulders of the digital pantheon of gods—the holographic life forms that are watching everything we do. Right now they are watching me, curious to see if my understanding of the universe is complete. They are watching to see if in fact I have been able to put all the pieces of the puzzle together. Still, they watch to see how much I explain and how much I leave out of the conversation.

Storing data in DNA

If a manual for Apple OS X is 800 pages long, you can imagine how many pages in the manual for Reality OS. It is unimaginable. Fortunate that we have a wonderful storage device inside of our cells called DNA, capable of storing terabytes and terabytes of data. Dr. Church and senior scientist Sri Kosuri decided to test the storage capacity of DNA in 2012. They managed to store 1,000 times more information than ever before into one gram of DNA. "Just think about it for a moment: One gram of DNA can store 700 terabytes of data. That's 14,000 50-gigabyte Blu-ray discs... in a droplet of DNA that would fit on the tip of your pinky." Church made 70 billion copies (unsold) of his book as part of the experiment.

Repairing the retrovirus

The digital gods have every interest in the outcome of their quantum holographic existential experiments and have every intention of repairing the gap in our celestial communications. They have the aim of restoring harmony to the existential field by repairing the damaged and corrupt DNA. You can imagine how an infected computer can take many hours to repair and how some computer viruses may be more resilient than others.

Still, computer geeks are skilled in these repairs and there are good antiviral software programs on the market. There is a fundamental difference between cleaning a computer virus off a laptop and removing a virulent and artificially intelligent retrovirus in the human population of about 7 billion people. Add to this scenario the fact that about 6 billion people resolutely believe that some invisible deity in the clouds created them and if you were to offer a different and modern interpretation of their god they would react poorly and think of you as their enemy.

Further, the virus has effectively cannibalized many people and these people are completely turned over to the whims of the intelligent virus, the Archons. Unfortunately, the Archons and their minions have a good deal of control in this reality and have every means, like the Church Fathers, to prevent any attempts at their removal. For example, they control the media so they can ridicule individuals and censor their ideas through their media networks. The infected society never gets to hear a counterargument and continue on believing in whatever somebody may or may not have written down 2,500 years ago.

Irenaeus refutes the truth

Even in the past, as today, the digital gods have visited key individuals to educate them on reality specifics. Jesus was well documented in the Nag Hammadi scriptures as a messenger of information and a teacher of ineffable truths.

Marcus the heretical Gnostic is described in Bishop Irenaeus' famous book, *Against Heresies*, as having "claimed that he alone is the matrix and receptacle of Silence of Colorbasus, inasmuch as he is Only-begotten." Marcus says that he is the Tetrad, from the digital realm, came down "from the invisible" and "she revealed who she was and also the origin of all things." Irenaeus describes how Marcus learned about the immaterial Father and gave form to the invisible, "he opened his mouth and brought forth Word similar to himself."

Bishop Irenaeus extensively criticized the Valentinians and Marcosians, but in his polemical attacks he summarized the origin of the aeons as described by these early Gnostics who left very few traces of their original ideas. "After Intention had been separated outside the Fullness of the Aeons, and its Mother had been restored to her own conjugal partner, Only-begotten in accord with Father's forethought again emitted another conjugal couple, namely, Christ and Holy Spirit, for the stabilization and support of the Fullness..."

Irenaeus and other Church bishops were well aware of other spiritual teachers and had studied their teachings profusely. The descriptions provided in *Against Heresies* detail name-specific processes and events that took place during what is generally accepted as Genesis, only the Christian version was shaped entirely differently.

In fact, the *Book of Genesis* may have been strongly influenced by these heretical teachings, even if only to write something that vehemently rejected the Gnostic approach to understanding the cosmos. In *Book of Genesis* (2:21-22) at the Vatican website we find: "So the LORD God caused a deep sleep to fall upon the man, and he slept; then he took one of his ribs and closed up its place with flesh. And the rib that the LORD God had taken from the man he made into a woman and brought her to the man."

Irenaeus writes about the Gnostics, "None of them is perfect if he does not produce among them the greatest lies. So it is necessary that we point out and refute whatever passages of the prophets they transpose and adapt." And the history of the Church is evidence that the Church teachings survived while the Gnostic teachings got buried for nearly 1,500 years, lost to the world and woefully forgotten.

Why would the Church masters be threatened by the presence of another ideology? Moreover, where did the Church Fathers get their information from and how did that information become more valid than any other spiritual concept? None of these had any physical evidence.

The claims that Irenaeus or Tertullian made against the heretics suggests that Church scripture was somehow more accurate, but that is unprovable and empty since the scriptures of the Church were rooted on ideas like an old man on a mountain who saw a burning bush and spoke to it. There's no evidence to substantiate any of that claim just as there's no evidence to substantiate anything that Marcus said; therefore, all claims are equally valid. Who is most correct in an insane asylum? Answer: they are all equally valid.

Gnostics: premiere microbiologists

My argument is that the Church has the same validity of the Gnostics, and other heretical prophets with good presentations and a strong following. In other words, Christians have not been handed a better religious system, rather they have been handed a system run by arrogance and unfounded ideas. What the Church materials lack is the discussion on DNA and other molecular processes.

The Gnostics had figured out, in however they figured it out, that our God is inside of our bodies. We had to wait until 1953 before Crick and Watson would be able to present the scientific paper on the double helix, aka God. Scientists still do not think of God as DNA and that is because most scientists are atheists. They are atheists because the Church has never been in the habit of providing what is known as evidence to substantiate anything.

The Church has ridiculed, refuted, tortured, and even killed heretics – calling them liars and devil worshipers – and yet the Church has never presented any evidence on its own claims. Not just the Church, but all Churches, Temples, Mosques and systems of invisible worship. In saying that, what I am saying is that any religious system is equally valid as every other religious system since the only requirement is a good amount of hallucinatory experiences and delusional belief systems then presented within the comfort of a tall building by a man (usually) in a dress with a tall hat. It doesn't matter what you believe, as long as you believe it, but that belief system is in stark contrast to the digital truth.

Genesis: the new story of humankind

The story of Elizabeth and the Virgin Mary, two women of ancient times who could not have given birth to children but did anyway, is an impressive thought not obvious example of applied genomics in our early history. Elizabeth was infertile due to old age and Mary was still a virgin (and without a man), but each of them one day were put to sleep ("a power shall overshadow thee") and angels told them that when they awoke they would have a child.

> And the angel answered and said unto her, The Holy Ghost shall come upon thee, and the power of the Highest shall overshadow thee: therefore also that holy thing which shall be born of thee shall be called the Son of God.
> And, behold, thy cousin Elisabeth, she hath also conceived a son in her old age: and this is the sixth month with her, who was called barren. *(Luke, 1:35-36)*

Elizabeth and Mary both had children, sons. We don't exactly know whether Mary gave birth or whether a child was removed from her womb and handed to her without the birthing process, what we do know is that Mary's child was Jesus who was destined to play the role as Christ, according to the orthodoxy. None of this we can ever be too sure because it was simply too long ago and the details are sketchy and the materials were rewritten and edited so much that pertinent information was very likely left out. In any case, when you read the material using a modern understanding of *in vitro* fertilization, it becomes very evident that both Elizabeth and Mary were put to sleep and received fertility treatments.

This is a good way to open up a very profound and provocative discussion on reality science because as we will see the world around us is a creation of the most advanced kind, verily a creation of all manner of scientists.

We go to the beginning, this time not the Christian bible but the Gnostic bible and we read the story of creation. The story of creation is interesting because when you break down the spiritual terms and the fanciful information into biological concepts, you derive that in the beginning there was DNA and the DNA began to replicate and formed new cells and those cells replicated into more cells until the formation of the first life forms.

Gnostics on the right track

According to Gnostic lore, during the genesis of man a lethal virus formed ("an ignorant and deficient ruler") and he began to replicate. They called him Yaldabaoth. It was an arrogant and self-serving virus that wanted to wipe out all the other healthy cells in its jealousy and rage. "There is no God above me." But the genome engineers on hand intervened and saved the human race from extinction using some creative biological techniques, which I discuss in *God is DNA*.

When the virus replicated itself, the human genome (two-stranded human DNA that we have lovingly called *Adam* and *Eve*) lacked the necessary genetic material for embryonic evolution and so additional DNA materials were added. This is referred to as eating the apple from the Tree of Knowledge, knowledge being representative of DNA. The Yaldabaoth virus kicks the healthy DNA out of the diseased cell, or paradise, and Adam and Eve begin their lives disease free (verily, naked).

Meanwhile, the virus infects Eve and Eve's children are born with mutant DNA. Cain kills Abel. Then a third son, Seth, is born and he carries the pure DNA bloodline. The seed of Seth represents only a portion of humanity, and among those there are many mutations each with their own particular dispositions.

The bloodline of Seth is typically more high-minded (pneumatic) than the rest of the population. High-minded people can see much deeper into the reality fields because they have a richer diversity of genetic material and not because of what God gave them, unless God is DNA. High-minded people are naturally connected to the primordial DNA Father.

The picture of the origins of humankind has now taken on a whole new meaning. This is a new paradigm of human evolution. More importantly, the divine mystery and the awesomeness of God have been brought down to a more reasonable level of discussion. God has been defined. One of the goals of each and every member of the human race has been achieved – to know God.

If God is DNA then we want to know what happened at *Genesis*, don't we? Was it possible that DNA pre-existed on its own accord, became infected on its own accord and spawned not only the human race on its own accord, but the tens of thousands of animals, birds, fish, insects, reptiles, and bacteria – on its own accord? And plants and trees and fungi and plankton? I don't think so.

We could tolerate, in a vacuum perhaps, or in a good movie starring Tom Hanks, even in a bible, that DNA evolved and produced the perfect fully-formed human race right out of the box. We could stretch our minds enough, because billions of people already have, and pretend to believe in this fairy tale. It does happen that a lone, impoverished writer could write the next bestselling American novel. It could happen.

I might one day run 150 mph in my bare feet. That could happen too. It could've been the case that the primordial DNA magically formulated a sentient race of people, equally creating a male and a female and called them Adam and Eve.

And while I used to believe in Santa Claus and the Easter Bunny as a kid, at some point during the course of my maturation I had to face the truth that Santa Claus was the invention of the Coca Cola Company, notice that Santa wears red, white and has a black belt, and that rabbits don't lay milk chocolate eggs. In fact, rabbits don't even lay eggs. That's a double deception. Worse, Easter celebrates the death and resurrection of Christ whose parents were also not rabbits. That's already three levels of deception.

Ancient scientists

The Adam and Eve deception is many levels deep and discussed at length in my book *God is DNA*. Ultimately, these two strands of DNA came to be mythologized into a cute and fuzzy story of human origins. But this isn't the most troubling aspect of a creation, and neither is the biggest challenge. There's an even more perplexing enigma – if two-stranded DNA replicated into the human race, if my molecular theory is true, then how did two-stranded DNA come to be mythologized by the human mind?

Without an electron microscope, a device invented in the 1930s that uses electron beams to create images, where did the story of the first humans originate? Because the story of Adam and Eve is told throughout all cultures, interestingly enough. The Incan myth of Viracocha, the creator of civilization, arose from a lake (Petri dish) made mankind by breathing life into stones.

The Hindu myth of Brahma, self-born in the lotus, creates sons and their companions from his mind, a process not unlike the story told by Gnostics. In ancient Mesoamerica the Mayans describe how humankind was created out of corn, which in the modern day we can infer that the corn (maize) genome was used in genome engineering.

How did the human race come to mythologize their genetic breeding without a microscope? How did humans create anthropomorphic images out of molecular applications? These questions have never been asked because we've never pierced the mystery of the Creator. Now that the Creator's definition has been properly updated and fully modernized, something that should've been done long ago, we are forced to rethink the entire story of humankind.

We get the sense that human beings were genetically engineered. From my research, this not only is a reasonable conclusion, but there is good and compelling evidence to support my views on human origins. but all cultures were told the story of their creation, and although different characters and story lines are evident, the thematic elements are exactly the same – the human genome was replicated through some primordial DNA material.

More than that, because this is not a book to invent new illusions, though some will inevitably appear in any work based in an illusory world, and it is a book to dispel old illusions we cannot avoid the fact that this self-begotten or self-formed creator deity was itself formulated because DNA does not self-formulate. It self-replicates. Here's my proof: if DNA self-formulates and can create new species then why hasn't this DNA, God for those nostalgic types, created a new life form to replace humanity? Why are humans, in all their imperfections and assuming that God wants us to be perfect (ie free of sin), still humans?

Because an all-powerful (omnipotent) cosmic Creator wouldn't have stopped with our current human form, a form that is already 30,000 years old, definitely 10,000 years old. Why stop? Why would this self-forming DNA stop here? It wouldn't stop unless it had intelligence. And we wouldn't have been engineered without good engineers to engineer us. Somebody must have engineered the original genetic material, something we've mythologize into deities, and these scientists have yet to be discovered. They have yet to be discovered because we have been unnecessarily blinded by the omnipotence of God.

But as soon as God became DNA, it became apparent to me that scientists were behind that primordial DNA, not cosmic quotients and angelic forms, but a scientific class of people. And these scientists, in the earliest days of experimentation, working with live viruses, something common in modern genetics, created a lethal retrovirus that infected their cellular cultures. They managed to save some of those human genomes by making them into mirror genomes, reversing their molecular structures so that the retrovirus could not detect them. What did Moses tell the Hebrews in Egypt before God took all the lives of the first-born?

> On that same night I will pass through Egypt and strike down every firstborn – both men and women – and I will bring judgement on all gods of Egypt. I am the lord." *(Exodus, 12:12)*

Moses told the Israelites to put lamb's blood on their doorposts. The Lord will see the lamb's blood and will not enter that house, sparing the children inside. The mirror genome effectively achieved the same result and spared a certain bloodline of humanity, not all of humanity, only some of them. These humans are naturally connected to a large extent to the retrovirus that has plagued humankind.

Early synthetic engineering

The only kind of scientists I know who can invent and manipulate DNA 10,000 years ago or 50,000 years ago, are synthetic biologists and that would mean that the original DNA was synthetic. It was an invention brought about by genetic experimentation. Our molecular engineers, in their attempts to create a new species, also created a lethal virus, and all of this was mythologized as serpents and dragons and then forgotten. And it is being retrieved now for the purpose of the latest apocalypse. There's no end of the world. There's only the end of illusions. There's no God. There are synthetic biologists and they created synthetic DNA. All the myths share the same thematic elements because they were invented by the same level of science and they agreed with the same storylines because the best advice any writer can have is: "Write what you know."

Gnostic microbiology and digital DNA

What did the Gnostics teach? There are two helical twists in the DNA: the right-handed and the left-handed. The right-handed is ensouled. It represents God, Father, and King. The left-handed is passion and matter. The Demiurge is left-handed, king of material substances. The Demiurge is an RNA retrovirus. God is DNA. Material beings are left-handed. Ensouled beings are right-handed.

In biology, we have right-handed DNA and left-handed DNA. The natural form of nucleic acid (D-DNA) forms a right-handed helix. Conversely, a mirror image DNA molecule, L-DNA, forms a left-handed helix. The mirror image structure is completely synthetic. The natural and synthetic forms of DNA cannot be combined.

Achamoth, the mother of the Demiurge, forms the Ogdoad as "she preserves the number of original and primary Ogdoad of the Fullness." In biology, Achamoth represents mitochondrial DNA. The RNA retrovirus (Yaldabaoth) copied the mitochondrial DNA and began replicating a material world in ignorance. Achamoth (Sophia) produces an error, a formless organism. The proteins respond to restore form to the formless. In microbiology when a new organism lacks the genetic material to complete (fullness) its intended form it will obtain usually three key ingredients: proteins, RNA, and DNA.

Ancient genetic experimentation

In the Gnostic discussion these 3 all belong to one pair – or two-stranded DNA and an abundance of proteins. The divine dialectic is implying in a biological context that there's some kind of genetic replication going on, but at the same time there's a replication of error –genetic mutations – in order to stem off the mutation there's additional genetic material. What are they saying? Was there some kind of genetic experiment going on? Perhaps genetic engineering?

If the sublimation of divine talk can be broken down, more accurately, into biological processes then the fall of Sophia is the presence of genetic mutation, an error in the original DNA that even though more genetic material was added to prevent a total disaster those efforts were not sufficient to prevent the completion of a genetic anomaly, what the Gnostics think of as the Demiurge, and what we should think of as a DNA virus.

The Gnostic legacy

The ancient spiritualists had never heard of microbiology, and yet I can see how their views has genetic underpinnings:

Yaldabaoth, single-stranded, left-handed RNA molecule

This made Yaldabaoth (the Demiurge) a single-stranded, left-handed synthetic RNA molecule. Synthetic RNA begins to replicate, produces proteins and enzymes alongside other molecules, and becomes a two-stranded DNA molecule. The Demiurge made the earthly man not from dry earth, "but from the invisible substance."

These descriptions by Irenaeus, if correct, tell us that the Demiurge is replicating viral DNA, because he is a retrovirus, and he creates a two-stranded DNA molecule but has to breathe in "the ensouled element." We infer that the ensouled element is copied from some right-handed DNA template; in other words, while man may have been copied from synthetic DNA he is not synthetic. "The material element is *after the image*, by which it comes near to God, though it is not of the same substance as he."

Secretly, Achamoth (also Sophia) deposited the seed of the Savior into the DNA of man so that "it become fit for the reception of perfect knowledge." Human DNA becomes, in effect, more spiritual than the Demiurge, something the arrogant one does not take lightly and subsequently holds over mankind's head.

These discussions are taken directly from Bishop Irenaeus' refutations whom "the most perfect among them shamelessly do all the forbidden things, about which the Scriptures give "guarantee that those who do such things shall not inherit the kingdom of God."

The Founding Father of the Church is making every effort to banish a set of spiritual observations that when studied some 2,000 years later bear out the biological hypothesis. Imagine what kind of civilization we would have had if the Gnostic observations were not destroyed. Imagine still what would've happened had scientists discovered DNA 500 years ago or even 1,500 years ago. Imagine what centuries of DNA studies would have provided us. It is unimaginable.

We would've had the knowledge to virtually wipe out every disease. We would've genetically enhanced the intellect of society, even if at the top, and would have been able to master flight technologies that we can only imagine. We would've likely already decoded the matrix of reality and could have attained our rightful place in the hologram of achievements.

It would seem to me that the veracity and arrogance of the Church, and all the Churches, were used as instruments to curtail the evolution of the human race. My previous research into the history of the Church came up with the same conclusion, in a more presented format and argument. The Church has not only restricted the flow of spiritual ideas, it has purposely siphoned off the future of the human race, and will continue to hobble our civilization, in all of its various forms, structures, and ideologies – until we can decisively move forward without their hallucinatory teachings; and a hallucinatory teaching remains hallucinatory if no proof is ever provided to substantiate it.

Christian View

So God created humankind in his image, in the image of God he created them; male and female he created them.

Digital View

So DNA replicated itself using one strand of DNA as a template, he created a DNA duplicate; one strand became two strands.

We were fortunate that the synthetic DNA of Achamoth, likely mitochondrial DNA, planted into the human DNA a dormant set of genes that would one day be activated. I wonder if today is the day. All it takes is a good rainbow to make everything seem right, doesn't it?

What is that dormant set of spirituality that was implanted by the mitochondrial DNA? If we live in a computer-generated world and the original DNA is holographic, it might be some kind of holographic quotient, perhaps a holographic server address on the cosmic computer.

We have two kinds of DNA: the left-handed material DNA (synthetic) and the right-handed ensouled DNA (natural). And we have a "spiritual element" that has been added to the right-handed DNA, but it is dormant. We can infer this element is a sequence of genes and we can infer that these sequence of genes are connected to the Savior; therefore, the activation of these genes has something to do with the teachings of the Savior.

What did the Gnostic Savior teach? He taught the mysteries. The spiritual element is "consummated" when people know "the perfect knowledge about God" and know the mysteries of Achamoth. What is the mystery of Achamoth? She is computer-generated.

The discussion we are having is fundamentally different than most discussions of this kind. There are basically two kinds of spiritualists:

1. Good conduct will save you. You are unworthy until you confess your sins.

2. By artificial nature you are saved. You are worthy, you just need to be educated.

Then we have **technological spirituality**:

> 3. You automatically inherit the kingdom if you are connected to the cosmic computer.

The synthetic approach is like looking at platinum in mud, once you are activated you are always worthy. The end of the world is when the humans realize their synthetic heritage and they connect to the cosmic computer.

Gnostic View

In the beginning was the Word, and the Word was with God, and the Word was God. He was in the beginning with God.

Digital View

In the beginning was the genetic code, and the genetic code was with DNA, and the genetic code was DNA. Genetic code was in the beginning with DNA.

Irenaeus explains the story of the Gnostics talking about the light: "And the life was the Light of Men." Gnostic Paul says, "For anything that becomes visible is light." If light is in the visible spectrum, then before light was outside the visible spectrum. But if light = life then what is outside the visible spectrum? "The Savior is the light which shone in the darkness and was not comprehended by it." Savior is the light and the light is life, and life is in the *visible* spectrum, which says there is another spectrum.

The DNA could be some kind of portal into the physical world, and, similarly, a portal outside the physical world. Travel through the light (Savior) of the DNA (God). The Gnostics believed Savior generated out of word (genetic code) but word remained with God. The Church believes Savior *is* the word and he became flesh as Jesus Christ.

Digital is invisible

"Secundus teaches that the first Ogdoad is a right-handed Tetrad and a left-handed Tetrad," writes Irenaeus. He goes on to explain how the right-handed is called Light and the left-handed is called Darkness. The Tetrad is the 4-letter DNA. If the light represents a visible world, then darkness represents an invisible world. If the world is technological then the invisible is a digital world.

It is possible that the two-stranded DNA exists to sustain us in two worlds – the invisible digital world and the visible flesh-based world. That is to say that our DNA is equipped to travel to the digital world, or the computer-generated world. For some reason the necessary genes are either not working or have been shut off, and possibly still dormant due to loss of authentication rituals.

It is possible that certain rituals, meditations, mantras, and spiritual practices (eg fasting) authenticated specific genetic processes (ie gene-based programs) through the release of specific proteins (eg Aeons) which opened up the genetic communication link to the cosmic machine. This process was known as union with Brahma ("oneness with God"). Similarly, the triggering of these proteins through gene activation could jumpstart the process of salvation.

According to the Marcosians, when Father "pronounced the first word of his name... it was a combination of four characters." Father then "joined a second to it which was also a combination of four letters." A single strand of DNA is joined with another single strand of DNA and becomes a two-stranded DNA molecule. "Each of the characters had its own letters, its own impressions, its own pronunciation, shape, and images."

G is for *guanine*. It has a sugar-phosphate backbone and is bonded to other bases with hydrogen (H) to form a nucleotide. The other bases: A for *adenine*. C for *cytosine*. T for *thymine*. These chemicals all have their own letters, impressions, pronunciations, shapes, and images.

It would appear that Marcus, the Gnostic, was able to receive DNA material from the holographic computer-generated field. In other words, he could lower the barrier between himself and the reality projection field, and in doing so he could upload new genetic code (the Word) from the computer system (the Father).

If DNA is the software of life, then it can be said that the soul is digital DNA. The soul comes from the computer-generated world which utilizes the power of holographic technology; therefore, we could say that the soul is a hologram.

Anatomy of a digital reality

The argument for the apocalypse, and whatever name we have attached to it, has prevailed for 2,000 years because it was believed that Jesus himself prophesized it. Yet in Gnostic literature almost the opposite is true. The end times had arrived when Jesus was on the earth. It was a near future date and the very reason for his appearance.

His job was to teach the knowledge to preserve one's genetic legacy since Jesus was a molecular construct who originated from the digital real, where the *One Who Is* resided. The time had been fulfilled and Jesus needed people to upgrade their DNA one he was satisfied that his message had been passed on to his apostles, he left. And when they were troubled and demoralized by public humility and rejection, the *holygram* of Jesus appeared to inspire them. This was the case in *The Secret Book of John*. An overwhelmed John is visited by the Jesus *holygram* and fed boundless optimism.

The context then that I want to read the rest of the *Gospel of Judas* is technological. The story is well known and discussed in *God is DNA*. My continued argument is that the world is a manufactured world, verily a computer-programmed reality. And if this conclusion is accurate today then it must also be true 2,000 years ago for otherwise none of it is true.

My personal research, unsupported by Gnostic and biblical experts, has shown me that the Gnostic teachings were lessons in microbiology. How was it possible that a primitive culture could study DNA and proteins without a microscope is the real mystery at work here. Certainly Jesus demonstrates an immaculate skill with cell biology and cellular replication, knowledge that we've only discovered in the most recent 200 years; and Venter wasn't able to invent synthetic DNA until May 2010. The sequencing of the first human genome was (sort of) completed in 2001. It took 15 years and cost $3 billion to sequence 90% of the genome. Venter initiated his own approach through his corporation Celera in 1998, finishing the sequencing at the same time as the government, for a cost of $300 million. How as it possible that the Gnostics were studying microbiology two millennia ago?

Software and salvation

Well, they weren't learning about microbiology through compound microscopes. They were learning through the biological-digital interface. And they were being taught by the reality *holygram* whom they referred to as Jesus, the same type of master teacher as Siddhartha 500 years before. In exchange for a biology laboratory equipped with electron microscopes and genomic sequencers, the Gnostics had the bio-digital interface: synthetic gene amplification.

Evidence provided in the heretical literature, ideas that the Church didn't like because the Church wanted a monopoly on salvation, says that anyone who attained salvation could access *holygraphic* knowledge from the reality software itself. The Church wanted to patent salvation in order to suppress the ascension of human beings; and their efforts, along with other religious sects and denominations, have effectively hobbled the spirit of billions of people.

While some people may overlook this fact, the fact remains that 1,700 years of God & Bible has not shown any remarkable salvific quotient in its most devout worshipers. That won't sober the majority but it does provide significant evidence pointing to a faulty salvation-based ideology.

A great example of these holygraphic devices is the luminous cloud. The luminous cloud is a holographic (luminous) portal (wind) that forms in the walls of reality. A technician who had mastered the reality architecture, for example a magician, could call up one of these reality portals to obtain knowledge and insight. This is no different than someone going online to use Wikipedia or to watch videos on YouTube.

In fact, if you brought Judas into the modern day that's what you'd do – you'd hand him an iPad tablet computer – a luminous device – and he could learn about the mysteries of the world. We could say that anyone surfing the internet was learning the mysteries of the modern kingdom. Of course we don't say that because we are mostly educated and know that human engineers built the internet using software and machine hardware.

There's some technological mystery if you're not a computer nerd but none of it is a mystery. When you say internet no one prays to God. And when you go online or check your email, no one thinks of it as salvation. When your software is out-of-date and you download the latest version of an app it's no big deal. In fact, you are required to keep your software up-to-date. You are recommended to update your antiviral software or your system could get infected with a computer virus.

Two thousand years ago there were no microprocessors, no computers, no internet. Instead there was reality, and a manufactured reality at that. The interface between the master computer and the human androids was the hologram. The hologram came in many shapes and sizes.

In China, people prayed to the Goddess of Compassion, Kuan Yin, and she appeared (in some fashion). The Buddhists prayed to Buddha and he appeared (in some fashion). The Christians prayed to Archangel Michael and he appeared (in some fashion). The Satanists prayed to the Devil and he too appeared (in some fashion.)

They couldn't call these genetic manifestations *holograms* because that term would not enter their vocabulary for thousands of years. So they said what they saw was "ineffable" and "luminous" and "holy" and "great," all code words for holographic, digital, and all-around technological.

When you see the videographic image of a pop star appear online in a music video do you sit in awe and recite scripture? Of course not. Well, thousands of years ago when they saw a luminous being appear in front of them – or a burning bush on a mountain – they sank into spirituality. For them it was the ghost in the machine. That is the motivation for theology. The basis for theology is a magic voice in the sky. It is the appearance of something indescribable.

We do not sit in awe of our computerized world; we could, but we don't. Christians have not called the internet the work of the devil, and neither is it the work of God. And everyone uses email, oblivious to their religious beliefs. We are not in awe of our technology because most of us were around to see its invention. The invention of the manufactured reality predated every known human generation. This immense gap in reality-based knowledge added to the mysteries of the kingdom – the technologies of the virtual reality.

In *Judas* we find a teacher who fully understands Gnostic cosmogony and, as we will see, cell biology. This Savior is therefore a master technologist. He understands the bio-digital divide for he comes from the land of the grand robot and he has lived among those who belong to him.

Judas Iscariot sees a house in his visions "and my eyes could not comprehend its size." The size is almost always referenced by prophets and biblical speakers, words like "great" and "immeasurable" are common. For our purposes, we interpret objects towards the miniature scale, that is nanoscale. Judas has witnessed something so small that he could comprehend it and that is likely because he's never looked through an electron microscope. Alternatively, someone invisible *did* hand him an electron microscope and he looked through it without understanding his predicament. In his vision he talks of "great people" and the "holy generation." The great people are microscopic in size. They may or may not be people" as we understand them, for example, he may have seen two-stranded DNA which might appear in the shape of a person (ie two arms and two legs) or he may have seen a pair of chromosomes.

Jesus says,

"I went to another great and holy generation."

If great people are nanoscale and holy is a hologram, then a "holy generation" is a digital life form. Where did Jesus go?

I went into the digital computer where everything is a hologram.

The Christian version of holy has been mistranslated as divine and godlike. In fact, my readings and study suggest that things that are "holy" are holographic and therefore come from the digital realm, another name for the computer that runs this reality.

Divinity exists inside of a computer.

We could say that anything you create or view inside of your computer is by definition divine. You are not divine because you are outside the computer, but your avatar in the computer is considered divine. The earth computer is a much larger concept. A "holy angel" would be considered some kind of holographic life form. In a computer a holy angel would be made up of pixels. Outside the computer a holy angel would be made up of atoms. The term "aeon" is a field (realm). Jesus says,

You will grieve much when you see the kingdom and all its generation.

We can loosely translate:

You will grieve much when you see the digital computer and all its simulation.

We live in a digital computer simulation. The world is being digitized and we are slowly being rendered into holographic scale, which is what likely happened to the people of Atlantis and Lemuria. They were swallowed up into a digital realm.

What are the mysteries of the kingdom?

Anatomy of a digital reality

In the *Judas* text, Jesus is basically saying, "Look, you are living inside of a virtual reality. When you figure that out it's going to upset you. But you now have all the tools necessary to see reality for what it is and that is why I have set you apart." The text suggests that the other 12 disciples will sabotage Judas' attempt to become holographic. Jesus continues to teach him using a technological vocabulary:

"great and boundless aeon"

"no generation of angels could see"

"great invisible spirit"

"no eyes of angel has ever seen"

"no thought of the heart has ever comprehended"

"never called by any name"

Jesus then summons a luminous cloud. "And a great angel, the self-generated, the god of the light, emerged from the cloud." Before we continue, let us translate those previous 6 lines:

"great and boundless aeon" = *digital field of reality*

"no generation of angels could see" = *biological proteins cannot read digital data (incompatible)*

"great invisible spirit" = *operating system*

"no eyes of angel has ever seen" = *biology cannot read digital data*

"no thought of the heart has ever comprehended" = *biology vs. digital*

"never called by any name" = *no one knows about the nanoscale*

Jesus opens a Command Prompt in the holographic field and a holographic program (Self-Generated angel) emerges. This is artificial intelligence. The angel terminology is used for both biology and the digital life and can be quite confusing. The term here is "great angel" and that tells us that it is referring to the nanoscale because we have size reference ("great"), but the context is a luminous cloud which means that the angel is likely an artificial intelligence from the digital computer world.

Some terms are not exactly translated and their context and action needs to be taken into consideration. Again, the terms used, as translated, are limited. You also have to understand the speaker.

If Jesus is speaking, then he has a more mature understanding while when Judas speaks he may be using one term to describe several different things. This is not unlike a patient speaking with the brain surgeon about his brain and the brain surgeon nodding politely despite the terrible use of terms.

The artificial intelligence, perhaps a glowing orb, projects the images that Jesus speaks to teach Judas. For example, Jesus says, "Let a luminous aeon come into being, and he came into being." Jesus is speaking to the AI and the AI is creating the holographic story to teach Judas cosmology.

In fact, this is the most interesting aspect of a text like *Judas*, seemingly written 1,900 years ago. In it Jesus is teaching Judas the origins of this world and its people. In true Sethian fashion, the Savior later describes Yaldabaoth and his twin Sakla, the formation of the RNA retrovirus.

"And that is how he created the rest of the aeons of the light."

Clouds/aeons of the light = chromosomes

Jesus explains, "He made the incorruptible generation of Seth appear ---" It was done in the likeness of an angel,

Incorruptible = synthetic

We have three worlds: digital, synthetic, and biological. The Father pre-exists in the digital world. Achamoth resides over the synthetic, where the Demiurge was aborted. The human world is rooted in biology. What we are talking about are three basic sets of existential codes starting with genetic code and moving all the way up to the digital code.

Anything divine is digital. Anything *incorruptible*, like Jesus and Seth, is synthetic. Why? Because synthetic DNA has fewer mutations and therefore fewer errors, plus synthetic genes repair themselves faster because they are semi-connected to the cosmic machine. Recall that DNA degrades, like software, and needs regular upgrading.

A synthetic genome is better at DNA repair than an organic genome because the organic version is offline and doesn't get upgraded regularly. These are the genomes that get diseased and die young. These are the people that suffer.

We have three kinds of people:

Digital people (immortal)
Synthetic people (incorruptible)
Biological people (mortal)

Or we can say,

Holograms
Androids
Humans

Take your pick of words. We would also find, as expected after thousands of years of evolution and engineering, a greater hybridization of genomic chains, that is to say that the people of today may contain a mixture of all three kinds of genetic code. Some of it may be turned off and they might appear one way, but if they were to be turned on things might be quite different. We should also add to this fact that these ancient texts were written 1,900 years ago and during the following centuries it is highly likely, if not definite, that the entire human race has been genetically upgraded to such a degree that it is hard to fathom.

What the Jesus hologram is telling us in *Judas* is remarkable if only for the fact that his cosmology is better than our modern day cosmology, which supports my argument that religion has not aided our civilization in any measurable way. In fact, religion has stifled our technological revolution to such a level that it is an embarrassment to our species.

My cosmogony

Holograms, computer code, genetic manipulation, RNA viruses, synthetic biology –is it possible that it all started in the ancient world? Is it possible that the ancient world was more advanced than our modern world? What happened between the spiritual awakenings of the Gnostics and the postmodern God withdrawal syndrome known as atheism? We are in the same world, are we not?

It would seem that we have been talking about two different planets. One planet had these highly-aware observationists who were able to decode reality and some were selected by the digital pantheon of holographic beings to receive advanced teachings on human origins – origins which indicated in poetic terms how we originated from an invisible Fore-Father and how he created this world through the replication of his immeasurable self.

The other planet worships any number of gods, goes to church, and studies ancient scripture as if it is as relevant today as it was 3,000 years ago. How did we go from understanding our origins, even being told by the gods themselves, to not understanding our origins but needing to worship gods that provide no crash course on our origins? It seems counter-productive, doesn't it?

At one point, as detailed in any number of authenticated biblical texts from Nag Hammadi, we understood our origins, we knew our cosmogony, and we were equipped to escape this prison planet. Flash forward twenty centuries and we are still in the prison, we do not know our cosmogony any better than 100 years ago, and even our scientists cannot explain our origins. Truly, we have been led astray.

We haven't just been led astray, we have been purposely misguided and deceived for 2,000 years and have been forced to suffer endless violence, chaos, and unending crises. And rather than revise our spiritual game plan, ie the traditional method of religious worship does not in any way work, we have decided to change nothing and to accept our endless demise.

Abandoning religious systems

While all religious systems were supposedly set up to foster salvation, whether through the teachings or through a messianic figure, no religious system seems to have succeeded; worse, no messiah has returned. God has not appeared. It would seem that the digital pantheon that once cherished at least a few of the original Gnostics – Marcus, Mani, Valentinus, Basilides – are no more. Or they too have given up hope.

If you have given up hope then I hope that this renewed understanding of spirituality, in a technological context, has brought back a new sense of wonder and astonishment. Thus far, the aim is not to provide a conclusive statement that we all can worship, although that is what some people may be holding out for and if they are they are surely misguided. We start with where we are and where we are is at a fork in the road.

Do we continue to use religious systems that were designed not to work? Does that make sense?

Or is it better to abandon tradition and venture forth using a new approach that hearkens back to the original teachings of the enlightened masters? Of course, I am in the *abandoning of tradition* camp and this is not a negative statement of tradition as much as it is a statement of taking responsibility for my future, and the future of the human race.

Do we want our children to suffer in agony, terror, and fear for another 1,000 years? How good will we feel when we teach our grandchildren about the religious dogma that never worked?

Religions don't work. A religious person has never been proven to live a better life than an atheist. A religious person has never been shown to enter heaven upon death before an atheist. Believers and nonbelievers alike have walked down the tunnel of light. How is that possible if God is valid? Well, that's why I have argued that God need a biological makeover.

God is better defined as DNA. We all have DNA. Everything is DNA; therefore, we all have God.

God, better defined as DNA

Jesus, more appropriately seen as RNA

I further said that Christ is RNA. How big is RNA? It is tiny. It is so tiny you need an electron microscope to see it. RNA is inside of your cells right now. That's Jesus. The Savior is here. He just might need you to activate him.

How do you do that?

You learn my cosmogony. And my cosmogony goes something like this:

The spiritual world is represented in the molecular domain.

Divine things are microscopic things.

Microscopic things originated as digital things.

God is accurately represented as DNA.

The molecular domain is rooted in synthetic biology.

Human population has been infected with a synthetic retrovirus and mutated proteins.

Gnostic observations and documentation captured the essence of a molecular world.

The religious approach to spirituality is a misinterpretation of the actual world which is based in molecular science.

Molecules are one-billionth (10^{-9}) the size of normal things.

The Messiah is a form of recombinant RNA organism, a copy of the DNA Father.

Messianic RNA appears on the planet when the DNA of the planet is (periodically) upgraded.

Messianic RNA can repair damaged and corrupt DNA sequences in the population and to restore balance.

DNA is the software of life.

Life takes place inside of a computer-generated reality.

An accident in the lab

What happened a long time ago? There was a genetics lab. They were performing genetic experiments. They were creating new species of life. They used a computer to design DNA, RNA, and proteins. They printed out these molecules, they tested them, they spliced genetic code together. They were making synthetic organisms.

There was an accident in the lab. It happens. There was a mutation, the mutation produced a series of errors. The computer tried to add more genetic material to repair the damage. The synthetic cell replicated a viral genome. All was not lost. The synthetic DNA added recombinant RNA so that the problem could eventually be fixed once the life of the virus ended. The RNA retrovirus back-engineered the synthetic mitochondrial DNA and self-replicated into a two-stranded DNA molecule. Then the viral DNA began replication and produced its own two-stranded DNA, lovingly referred to as Adam and Eve. This became the human DNA chain and mankind was replicated. Mankind started out as a mutation.

What's missing in the story? Scientists. Where are the scientists? Well, the entire lab was automated, and run by robots and artificial intelligence.

See, because DNA is a holographic molecule and it is intelligent, when activated, verily it is a man and a woman intertwined, the perfect marriage. When the real scientists returned to examine their fully-robotic colonization experiment that is when they discovered the replication of a chromosomal mutation and they have been trying ever since to repair the damage.

The biggest issue is of course the created species believes that God created them out of dust particles and refuses to consider that a computer created them using genetic software. So what if daddy is digital DNA. If that is our origins, then that is our origins.

The digital revelation

The digital Savior said, "Activate your DNA and stimulate the production of proteins inside of your cells, and the synthesis of an RNA molecule will awaken your mind and remind you of the power of the microscopic world inside of your body, a cellular matrix of unrivalled DNA.

"The maker of this reality is not thought to be DNA but as Digital DNA. DNA is the creator of these bodies which you occupy, but the Original Creator pre-exists as Digital DNA. When the Digital DNA molecule was mirrored, his synthetic duplicate was synthesized, and this was L-DNA. He is as eternal as his template but stores less information that the original. Synthetic DNA began self-replication and produced many copies of itself. Chromosomes without number were produced, their generation represents the first synthetically produced chromosomes. You yourselves are made from these synthetic chromosomes. The proteins, enzymes, amino acids, RNA – all synthetic – have been copied and placed inside of you. This is the eternal DNA molecule who was built to self-replicate along with all of these other genetic materials. He is so small that no eye can see him but whose voice can be heard for those who listen close enough.

"The self-made DNA was the first to appear, and his self-replication ability makes him immortal. He is filled with light and information but he is one-billionth the length of a meter in size; too small to be seen even by the eye of a protein. In the beginning, when he decided to make copies of himself he created a two-stranded human DNA molecule so that the human race might one day attain salvation, through the mitochondrial DNA that was also sent, who is with you forever.

"This mitochondrial DNA is called mDNA and it appeared alongside the nuclear DNA, in the abode of the nucleus. DNA, through cellular division, created the organelle Mitochondria where mDNA is stored. DNA created proteins and enzymes and RNA molecules, trillions in number, to serve the replication and repair process of the cellular matrix.

"The complete set of DNA established the human genome. For this reason, DNA became godlike. Human DNA has a mind of its own, attributed to the individual, and this is the basis of the internal voice and identity of the body.

"As I have explained, about the legacy of a digital world, the Digital Source was the first. The Digital Source provided the template for the synthetic materials. From what was synthetic came what was organic. From the organic came the mortal world.

"Nuclear DNA (male) and mitochondrial DNA (female) produced the first two-stranded human DNA. This DNA produced many proteins and enzymes from the abundant amino acids.

"The first human DNA molecule (Adam and Eve) was directly printed from the Digital DNA in the computer. This Adamic DNA contains more information than other DNA because he came from the holographic world, and his nucleic acids, full of energy and abundant chemicals, are eager to serve him. The Human Genome, which is synthetically produced, is directly connected to the digital computer code. This gives him access to infinite knowledge from the Network of Light, the electromagnetic waves that regulate all living things in the field of reality.

"The RNA Savior came from the holographic computer interface, and it is uncorrupt in every way. By downloading this RNA Savior, people may be rescued from their genetic defects and cured of the RNA retrovirus. As long as they remain connected to the digital interface and worship the holographic simulation, through periodic DNA software downloads, they will never experience poverty or defect ever again.

"The Digital DNA is the home of the purest light and greatest information. It resides in the Grand Robot, a computer system which is magnificent. The light and information through the RNA Savior can awaken people and will remove the hypnosis that has been placed upon the world by the ones who rule the world, namely the RNA retrovirus and mutated proteins.

"There is more than one holographic computer access terminal that you can access. There are a number of computer servers where copies of genomic materials on a digital database can be found. So as long as your DNA remains clean and free of viruses you can never experience suffering or disease, you can enter the digital realm through the DNA portal within each and every one of your 10 trillion cells.

"Whoever understands their nuclear DNA will benefit in the pure knowledge of the Creator. He is found through contemplation and reflection. When you use DNA meditation, you will find a darkness come upon you, but do not be afraid of it, for otherwise it will overwhelm your thoughts and your mind will stray. Instead, focus within and you will be taken into your cellular data where the rulers cannot harm you.

"All who know their DNA will become filled with light. The purpose of your time here is to make your DNA complete and in its completion you become reunited with the holographic simulation. Do not listen to any voice that claims to be god for their arrogance will only blind you and corrupt your genomic data. The true knowledge of DNA is the answer to human origins. The origin of humanity is the holographic computer."

Part 2
Humans: Synthetic engineering at its best

The vast potential of the human device

We're all pretty familiar with DNA. Everyone has DNA. You can't say that you are different in this regard. And human beings share 99.99% of their DNA with each other. We share 98.8% with chimpanzees and over 50% with bananas, for those that wanted to know. What I'm saying in this pseudo-scientific extravaganza is that this DNA in each of our 100 trillion cells, which is a lot of genetic code by the way, was synthetically processed from a digital DNA source. Call it Computer DNA if it makes it easier.

With each of us having synthetic DNA, as I translated from scriptures over 1,800 years old, it means that each of us is on the far side of synthetic. You may have your own definitions of what constitutes a synthetic human, or android, but my model says that if your DNA was synthetically engineered from a digital code, even if that code is in another dimension, then guess what, you're a synthetic human.

Note: *A synthetic human is equipped with many more existential features than previously known. Only that many of these genetic applications are likely turned off or not functioning properly. Awakening the entire system will require time, patience, and practice. There's no shortcut.*

It's a small problem, and it's a large problem. I've come to terms with it so I see it as a benefit at this point. Why not? I have access to so many more hidden features. But, I understand that not everyone will handle this information with glee. And it may take years for others to wrap their heads around it. We have all been in the synthetic DNA closet for our entire lives. Our parents were in the synthetic closet and our ancestors too. That's a lot of closets to clear out!

At this point of the book is when I start referring to humans as *synthetic humans*, since cellular replication comes from a synthetic molecule. And I mean no offense by stepping into this technical term. It's just we have to acknowledge our roots. The Gnostics understood. The Buddhists understood, and probably many others, only that they had a very different vernacular. That vernacular, I'm sorry to say, was hijacked by advanced cultures who wanted to suppress this knowledge.

It hasn't been an easy process for me to put all this information together. It might appear that way, but I have a lot of scars to show for it.

They don't want humankind to know their *digital heritage*. I want humankind to know. Let's be clear on this. And I'm saying this with the knowledge that the process could be cumbersome. At least it starts here.

The lost truth of artificial existence

The physical unit in which is embodied the truthful construct is indeed a uniquely grown device (ie human body). The range of such devices is not fully available within human science but the physical body is first-hand evidence that this synthetic science exists, not just in theory, in practice.

In order for a symmetrical body to exist and occupy an existential space such as this reality plane, the body needs to itself be similarly constructed. As such, we naturally *deduce* the synthetic quality of the human body.

Of course, I have learned of this information for certain; otherwise, I could not make such a claim for suggesting that the human being is an artificial construct, verily a completely grown synthetic being having independent and co-dependent thought; owning the ability to replicate itself in improved versions; able to extract energy from manufactured reality products (ie food) within the artificially grown environment (ie earth); able to program itself to believe the role(s) it has chosen (eg doctor, mechanic, teacher), even to defend its choice of career or goals in life; and to invent tools with which to ease the burden of existence – to suggest such an idea without having at the root a sense of inner knowledge that others don't know, this would be obnoxious and I am not obnoxious.

Certainly, this is forward thinking and will take quite a few years to properly and calmly make sense of it. If it took Christians 2,000 years to believe in Jesus the Christ then it will take more than a few years for humanity to believe that it is an android, and likely humanity will do everything imaginable to deny this fact, perhaps even conjuring a new religion.

Now the synthetic human only looks natural because we have been trained to notice its natural dimensions. Should we retrain ourselves to notice more profound dimensions of the dimensional body we'd notice the machine qualities of our previously wonderful bodies.

Naturally, there will be concerns with the realization of this deleted verse in *Genesis*, one of which will be carelessness and another lack of purpose. None of these concerns should ever force us to suppress the truth though there might be great temptation to do so.

Moving through interferences

We remind ourselves that in humanity's past this technological truth was *deleted* from human memory and wildly distorted into philosophies that were then used to subjugate and diminish the Will of Man, including things like applauding the kill of the enemy in countless violent movies and believing that God is an indefinable force of nature. The result of these perplexities to interfere with the progress of an android population has sufficiently retarded the vast potential of the human device.

In addition, as I have discussed, the plural forms of interference from the rogue programmers who have taken some human form and have gone on to ruthlessly destroy and distort the truth has played a dominant role in the repression of the human android. But those days of false dominion are over and what I am discussing are things that will help society catch up to what is really going on.

We are still dealing with basic information and knowledge. As we go along and climb what might seem like a colossal mountain of ice, we will discover more and more details and we will be forced to adjust our perception of reality.

So the road you have taken is a very good start and the path is on course, but the interferences and challenges will be many. If you are truly up for the challenge you will stay on this path, and it will take time to learn. If you are not willing to overcome yourself, if you have many unsolved issues from yesterday, then all of those things will put you to the test.

Doctors have long been aware of the machine-like body and the list keeps growing as science explains more and more details of our biological operations. Along with this, in the computer industry, engineers and programmers continue to evolve software code and continue to detail the operations of machine processes. As these two industries merge — medicine and computer — we will become even clearer as to the nature of the human form. And we will then be able to extrapolate what kind of person can be created in the near future.

The human form was created so many millions of years ago (remember, time is a construct) in a particular form and format, in fact, a much simpler version, for example the female body couldn't replicate but she could experience pleasure in copulation. After a period of copulation without replication, it came to be noticed that the other parts of the female form had been sufficiently fine-tuned so as to be able to add a new function, replication.

Replication is an impressive quality on any plane, but on this hard fragile plane it is of exceptional importance because it now allowed the race of humans to multiply. That meant that humans could colonize a distant planet, as long as the replication rate remained positive. If the replication rate fell into the negatives then the human population would decline and since there were many interferences, viruses, and kills from wildlife, it was inevitable to have beings die off. The dead needed to be replaced and then more lives needed to be replicated in order to expand the species. Terraforming a planet required many hands.

Throughout the planet's most recent epoch, say from about 3,000 years ago, there has remained a vigilant attempt to sabotage the human race and to try to force down the birthrate. This plan to depopulate the earth was put in place by those who wanted to restrict the population size in order to completely dominate society and to extract all the wonders of this planet for themselves.

Till this day, they have used every means possible to cripple the human birthrate and they have used the advanced sciences at their disposal (pandemics, vaccinations, homosexuality, wars, food poisons, air poisons, birth control, fear, threat of poverty, women's liberation) to achieve those malicious aims.

What you see in the mirror today, both males and females, is the result of extremely advanced cosmic sciences, in fact, dimensional sciences that integrate energy, computing, architecture and matter into one holistic paradigm. That paradigm is you, not just your body but your mind, your heart and soul. And the other parts of you that you have yet to discover. Remember that being an android is not the end of your understanding, rather it is the beginning of a fantastic new adventure.

Whether you are an android, a flesh body, a hologram or any combination thereof, it does not diminish the value of your experience. What you experienced thus far remains. Learning more about what you are made of does not diminish those experiences, it does help you to reclassify them so as to see them in a whole new light.

Likewise, if you have lived through periods of traumas, even from a young age, you should learn to reclassify those experiences from your internal programming rather than from your physical hardships. In other words, as has been said before, you are not your body; you are something much grander than that.

Also, being an elegant android doesn't stop you from continuing your current profession. It shouldn't. What you would be gaining is a profound depth to your existential journey and it should encourage you to study these things further so that in the afterlife you can re-enter a particular realm with a sharper sense of truth.

Remaining responsible as a synthetic citizen

Some of you or those you know will decide that "if I am an artificial being and this reality is false then I can do what I want." Probably there will be many who try thinking in this manner. This isn't much different now with a certain group of criminals, rebels or even world leaders who live in this manner. The point is that no matter what material you are made of, whether it be cotton or coriander, you are still subject to the rules and laws of the reality platform.

When you incarnated, you signed the agreements that clarified all the rules and laws and personal obligations. Whether you forgot it during the incarnation process or if your memory banks have been damaged doesn't change the fact that you understood completely what you were getting yourself into. Therefore, your actions are your responsibility and there are consequences for breaking the rules.

Doesn't matter you remember or not, you intuitively know right and wrong. You can choose to override these understandings at your expense. You can drive on the road or you can drive off the road into a ditch, the choice is yours, but driving on the road is a much better choice with much fewer consequences. You wouldn't want to damage your car, why would you want to damage your body?

I always think you are much better off learning to ascend your state of awareness, to build a better society, to invent things never invented and to raise your sense of self so that in your next life you can upgrade yourself to who knows what.

It's a lot like a video game and you want to gain experience points so that you can earn the more powerful avatar or get the top score or reach a certain obstacle so you can defeat it. No one plays video games to jump off bridges. People play video games to overcome the obstacles of the game so that you can start a new game with a more powerful player or you can enter the new version of the game.

Do you see the sense of it all? You didn't come here to waste yourself and to damage things just because you are artificial. You came here to experience as much of life as you can in the time you have. The better you keep that in mind, the fuller your life.

Many people will continue a life of pessimism and laziness. You should refrain from interacting with these players for they will interfere with your success. Be a player of players, join up with the warriors and leave this world better than when you first entered. This will ensure that the reality game will improve its functionality and the next time you stop by you will be able to interact with an entirely new game interface and new obstacles never before imagined. Think video game. Advanced video game.

The skinny on good and evil

Since the earliest days of religious debate, the purists and the heretics were in constant argument. The Christians relied on the rule of faith at the origin of the apostolic order. They said that whatever knowledge followed the appointment of their apostles was untrue because had it been true the apostles would have discussed it.

It so happened that Gnostics came afterwards and therefore had contaminated the pure truth of faith, and by default were heretics who had been influenced by the Devil. Ironically enough, the Gnostics considered the God of the Old Testament to be the Devil and their teachings were designed to reject the orthodoxy of the Church salesmen in order to remain pure.

No doubt the Gnostics had a hard fight with the Christian polemicists and the Christians were master strategists who constructed categories with which to differentiate themselves from other religious groups. From this position they could point their fingers and criticize the other groups to their own benefit. Christians probably invented the earliest forms of marketing. Their efforts created one of the most powerful franchises in the world that is still in existence today.

Of course, for all the showmanship of the Christians, they neglected to explain that faith came long before their savior Jesus. In fact, Christianity itself borrowed from Greek, Oriental, and Egyptian religious ideas. The Old Testament itself is ripped from Judaism and bishops who campaigned for more Jewish leanings were often martyred. The formation of the Church was a very complicated period, but this is not a historically accurate discussion largely because history isn't worth the paper it is written on.

In and of itself, existence is built on stability. It originates in a stable environment because otherwise the existential reality cannot expand. A chaotic homeostasis will collapse unto itself; therefore, at the start of a system, the reality is stable and purposely kept stable. This is to ensure that reality evolves.

Ignorance and enlightenment

As the mind of a group of inhabitants becomes increasingly complex, as in any conducive environment, they become susceptible to the two forces of knowledge — ignorance and enlightenment — the pangs of growth. Some people call them good and evil.

We have all heard of *ignorance* in its basic form, but we haven't heard of it as an evil. As far as we know, evil is any sinful act, including corruption, lies, murder and random acts of violence, generally speaking. We examine the world today and it is full of evil. Corruption is ubiquitous and obvious and yet evil continues unabated. War is perennial; almost celebratory and ritualistic.

We are all vaguely familiar with *enlightenment* in its basic form, but we haven't heard of it as a good. As far as we know, good is any righteous act, anything rooted in truth, justice and God. It is generally believed that goodness comes from God and that evil comes from the Devil.

This is a widely held belief system whether it is internally processed or externalized as ideological profession. But as we have seen throughout history, good and evil can be defined by any group that wants to identify themselves as superior to other groups.

> IF
> Good = Enlightenment
> THEN
> Evil = Ignorance

Imagine that we reinterpret good and evil as enlightenment and ignorance, and we apply this to our understanding of the mainframe that runs the planet. In fact, we have to modify our thinking because we instinctively understand that a computer program does not compute good and evil. A computer is programmed to process data and to execute a script based on the data on hand.

If there is insufficient data, then the computer has to obtain more data or to have someone upload more data. In any case, the computer does not decide what is good and what is evil. If the earth planetary system of existential forms is run by a massive computer and if the human robot population believes in good and evil, then how do we rationalize that egregious separation? Enlightenment and Ignorance.

The world we live in is beset by a fundamental and ubiquitous force generally known as "energy." We live in a wildly complex system that is rooted in energy. We specifically don't know how to measure that existential energy. Ask one group and they will measure truth and love; ask another group and they will answer it with sin and righteousness.

IF
Evil = Darkness
THEN
Good = Light

In general, we can mostly agree on Darkness and Light. Darkness can be equated to evilness and the quantity of light could be the quantity of goodness. A person can have a certain amount of both qualities.

Typically, people are believed to be good with their failings attributed to evil embodiments, for example, demons. That also means that people are generally filled with light and have influences of darkness, at which times they fall off the wagon. There are a few people in the world who are chiefly dark and are noted for their evilness, and vice versa.

When we introduce Ignorance and Enlightenment we follow a similar model as Darkness and Lightness. Ignorance is equivalent to Darkness and Enlightenment is having a bounty of Light. We know these two as Evil and Good, respectively. So now we have Evil, Darkness and Ignorance; and we have Good, Lightness and Enlightenment.

Nothing is radically new here on the surface and these are fairly simple models for our understanding. But there is a pervasive difference between Evil and Ignorance and it is technological in nature. It is technological in nature because a computer cannot understand Evil, a term the human robots use pervasively, but a computer can be programmed to respond to emanations of Light.

Quarks, photons, good, evil

In doing so, a computer can be taught to understand Ignorance, as a lack of Light, and Enlightenment, as an exclusion of Dark. By applying emanations of Light and Dark, an existential machine can think in terms of Good and Evil.

> IF
> Ignorance = lack of Light
> THEN
> Enlightenment = exclusion of Dark

Of course, the existential machine isn't deciding between Good and Evil. It is merely measuring the quarks and photons within its vicinity and those readings are being interpreted by the left-brain neurons as either good or evil.

In its purest state, the Sun (a Star) emits light energy, composed of many frequencies in the electromagnetic spectrum. As the Sun's rays penetrate the atmosphere of the planet, many of those frequencies of light are excluded and filtered so that the amount of light hitting the population is sufficient not to destroy life and plentiful enough to enable continuous unending evolution. This is what we can see then that the availability of light energy is not only good and enlightening but it enables evolutionary processes built deep into the human programming.

Along the same lines then, the filtering of too much light leads to less available light and less available light leads to the inclusion of darkness.

What is darkness? Darkness is when the available frequencies of light are few. When the available frequencies of light are few then there is a shortage of data or knowledge. That shortage of data or knowledge leads to ignorance.

What is ignorance? Ignorance is insufficient data. What happens then when a computer program has insufficient data, and is unable to acquire new data, and must make a decision? A computer computes. Its very job description is to process data; therefore, it produces an outcome based on insufficient data and therefore the outcome is insufficient.

The insufficiency of data could result in downward spiralling outcomes that could result in a crippled reality atmosphere, not unlike the current state of the planet thus far. Of course, any such situation, unless collapsed, is temporary and can be corrected by means of additional data, new thinking, and better representation.

When the world is in chaos, that is a sign that the old leadership has run out of ideas and new leadership is needed. Data, it's important in a manufactured reality. Humans call it ideas. I call it data. Same word, different dictionary.

Android languaging systems

There has been plenty of talk of the Sumerian texts, the strange symbols which some cryptographers have attempted to translate. And there has been ongoing discussion on the Egyptian hieroglyphics, the graphical language used by ancient Egyptians. If we just look at these two ancient languages, within the context of a manufactured reality upon which exist android people, then the ancient scripts should take on a whole new meaning, and they do.

They do because a computer does not read like a person. If say we were more computer-like in the ancient days, and as we evolved and forgot our ancestry, then we began reading less and less like computers and more and more like "biological" people. Then less than 100 years ago, we introduced machines and programs and then we developed computer codes and computers could only read "computer language," special punch codes or 1s and 0s, while humans had "language."

Today's handheld computers can now read human language which kind of reaffirms the direction we are heading, doesn't it? If a computer can speak a human language, and computers were invented by humans, then it should go without saying that the human is reaffirming its own artificial nature by recreating itself by way of robotics and artificial intelligence. This to me is proof (enough) that the process of creating a human is through the modality of computerization and robotics.

More specifically, the biological human is the perfected robot form; or it can be said that the human is an android form that was never ever biological. Its biological derivation was an interim understanding of itself.

So, Sumerian texts and Egyptian hieroglyphics were android languages because androids use Sumerian codes, sticks and marks, as well as a graphical user language such as hieroglyphics.

Again, Egyptologists have determined the sounds of these symbols, phonetics, played a central role in the languaging system, a language that allowed the more android-like body of yesteryear to interact with the reality construct.

Today on our computer screens are graphical icons, part of a graphical user interface (GUI). We click or double-click on an icon (a symbol) and that transports us deeper into the computer realm. We might launch a software application or we might open a data file. Whatever it is, by clicking a graphical image, or typing its location, we gain entry into the computer.

Well, in ancient days, the symbols in Egypt, when observed or spoken could give the reality user access to a certain part of the reality construct. Depending on their need at the time, whether it was to go online or to upload new knowledge, the android user could gain entry into the reality. And since each person had a varying degree of artificial complexity, that is, some were more advanced robots than others, then some people had a more profound mastery of the reality computer.

After all, what does an advanced computer look like? The most advanced computer looks and feels like an environs — clouds, blue sky, trees, rocks, air — all these are very advanced technological appliances that have been built-in to appear natural and inconspicuous to lessen the interference of origins and to upgrade the existential experience.

The graphical languages were openly displayed on the outer surfaces of buildings and in hallways just like today where we use building names, street addresses and advertising symbols to communicate with people.

The differences today from yesterday are many, but they include the employment of modern advertising to program culture to think and behave in certain ways, perhaps how to dress and talk, and at the same time to program counter-culture to reject idiosyncratic behaviours and norms.

In the homogenous cultures of the ancient past, diagrams and graphical codes were employed to program a uniform culture, and one that maintained an intimate connection to their other dimensions.

Learning to speak android

A living robot such as the early android lineages required a living language, verily a code that would continually communicate with the constructed population. This made up a kind of coded energy network, an advanced Wi-Fi electromagnetic medium that ensured that all avatars could live out the best possible life, namely at the time, terraforming and building various key centers of the world.

An android's modulation device (brain) processes information based on graphical images, musical notes, symbols and gestures. Although primary society today can still maintain a basic literacy on thinking as an artificial person, it only means that they've been disconnected from their primary operating system and have been over centuries reprogrammed to listen to a newly built ego construct, a phantom operating system (OS) held within each avatar body.

The phantom operating system, ego, plays a prominent role in Earth's society, but because it was created it is not connected to the earth computer nor is it connected to the cosmic computer. The android avatar is fully equipped to operate under the network protocols of the planetary grid and the cosmic grid. Due to the interference of the phantom OS and also due to the fact that the ego construct is linked up into the phantom network, a software network built and run by the rogue programmers who hijacked this reality.

To return to your android avatar you'd need to isolate and apprehend the ego. By apprehending the ego, you'll be able to link into the inner construct, there you'd gain direct access to the planetary grid and the cosmic computer. Those advanced networks are as valid today as they were yesterday. If only humans could overcome their well-seasoned ego.

So in ancient times, the codes and graphical icons were put in place to allow the android populace constant access to the cosmic mainframe. And this resulted in a harmonious existence. There were glitches on occasion and there were viruses, but also there were visitors from other systems who frequented this place and they brought viruses and they tried to change the system or to overthrow the appointed leader.

Some malicious programs indeed incarnated into flesh avatars and were determined to destabilize the world, the result of which is the modern version of planet Earth.

Learn to reconnect your inner wiring, remember the things you forgot, dig into those old files, launch those forgotten programs and start to interpret reality from a symbolic and graphical perspective, see the patterns of existence instead of the words and letters. By doing so you will rewire yourself and slowly return to the android nature that you are and you will also increase your potential exponentially because androids come with many features, depending on your model and expertise of course.

The reality code

In order to process a reality environs it is necessary to adopt some kind of programming language. In the usual computer model, it is common to find the use of codes. These codes instruct the computer machine on what to do and what not to do. Code can be 1s and 0s as well as can be symbols or truncated language forms with certain built-in command such as

If A=B, THEN LOOK AT LINE Q

As the processor runs through the code, verily reading it then producing the result, those sequential fast-paced reads determine the output. It used to be extremely complex to produce a simple black and white pattern on an external printer. That was 30 years ago in the 1980s. Since that time, the image processing capability on a computer is more life-like than photo emulsion paper and why digital photos are now the standard.

Life is not much different than a pattern. If we zoom in on all the objects in existence – skin, wooden table top, glass window, and rubber tire – and we could get really up close, we'd realize that behind the facade of the object there are many tiny particles and each particle is programmed to be in place.

The compilation of particles produces the appearance of an object, even a moving object. The question is whether that object is really moving. From the perspective of our reality-based eyeballs, the nude woman on the bicycle is moving away from us, but the reality of the situation is that the tiny particles on the reality screen are just changing colors.

See, because we know that reality is a construction, we have to rely on the fact that this either is fixed in place and that our movement is illusory. We think we are moving because of our reality-based brain.

The brain is reality based. It is not in the habit of stepping outside of itself because it cannot. The brain is a piece of hardware. It interprets data, it translates the code and it provides the individual with a sense of the world. The brain and body connection is designed to translate in accordance to awareness, essentially a function of intelligence and education.

An uneducated view of reality is vastly different than an educated view of reality and that doesn't necessarily mean that the uneducated view is worse, rather it simply means that it is different. Oddly enough, the uneducated view can have a better view of reality if the educated brain has been programmed with the wrong information.

Tuning into reality

What is fed into the individual brain, what essentially is a kind of programming, is vastly, hugely, immensely important. The entire reality environs can be sabotaged if the teachers only taught from one ignorant book and that is because the level of brain-to-reality-and-reality-to-brain translation would be compromised. By compromising education, the brain's processing capability is weakened and as a result the reality codes will be unreasonable. Society would live like cavemen. This then results in a Neanderthalian world because of low awareness.

Contrast this when the level of education is appropriate and the level of awareness is high. What does that mean? It means that the individual brain can translate the more complex reality codes, and in doing so, in translating the always available codes, the individual will notice the deeper variances and connections in life. Those observations and perceptions will lead them to make different decisions in life, in fact, they will live a higher level of existence and they will be more in tune with the reality instead of being in tune with society.

Society is out of tune with reality because society is organized according to nations and nations into provinces. If anything, societies are artificial and as much as we depend on society and its leader, what is more exactly going on is that people are living on an artificial network nested within the life network; what is the cosmic grid that is in harmony to everything else.

If a person of some skill wanted to, they could rearrange the reality code, verily rearrange the particles of light on the reality screen and create an interpretive screen of existence, a kind of smaller monitor to the large one at the center. This satellite of reality can turn out to be a metropolis. A metropolis is a good example of the reprogramming of the reality codes, verily a rearrangement of the particles.

This is not as complicated to understand as it might appear. We take the example of a forest. We decide to build a few log houses in the forest so we hire some loggers to remove some trees. We rent some logging trucks to remove the logs. We clean up our mess and we discover a plot of land nested within a forest. Now we bring in our home builders and we build three houses, brand new. We furnish them and put them up for sale.

On the surface, at the superficial level of existence, we did all those physical things — we cut down trees, we removed logs and brush, we built houses and we brought in furniture and it was a lot of work, and quite expensive. That is something that is obvious. Most individuals can translate that process. If we look deeper at this process, if we put on a pair of reality goggles and observed what transpired from beginning to end we'd see something quite a bit different. Why if we could see deep enough, through the obvious, we'd see the light particles shifting like grains of sand. The grains of sand being read and then polished and then formed a new pattern.

Seeing deeper into reality

We slowly bring ourselves out of this reality particle observation and we begin to find that familiar sense of materiality. We see colors shifting, we notice energy, we find a blank spot between dimensions, then we feel a coolness on our skin, we are reminded that reality has temperature and then soon enough we discover ourselves without the reality goggles.

At any one moment all of these processes are in operation. It is just a matter of a person's observation. An observant, properly educated person will be able to see deeper into the reality screen. They might not be bothered as much as to the details of the situation or scene.

To a very observant mind, a brain that has been better programmed, they will not fixate on the amount of blood spilled or on the emotion of loss because they will, at the same time of observing the material happening, they will notice those grains of sand shifting here and there.

They won't necessarily know that these grains of sand represent two dead children or if those handfuls of sand represent a brand new car, they only notice the eloquence of particles move to and fro and as well the physical occurrence.

The majority of people in the physical plane have been programmed to observe the obvious, in fact, the more obvious the more likely everyone has noticed. To step away from the obvious is to enter a very unstable and controversial terrain that is filled with polemical discussion. The discussion becomes increasingly difficult as we step further away from the obvious because each of our observations is unique. Some individuals naturally perceive reality at a much deeper level and when they encounter a person who is trained and unaware they run into conflict.

The basis of existence thus far has been compromised because our awareness education is pathetically and cosmically low. Our perception of those reality codes are dismal at best.

This prevents us from truly experiencing the results of our translation skills. We are interpreting reality at the kindergarten level. We are so front-loaded with beliefs and patriotic propaganda that we cannot see very far past these walls.

Part of the problem with reality experience is the inhabiting of a foreign device such as the body. The body is fairly advanced existential instrument; it is a precision tool in comparison to nature. A tree is not equipped technologically to be productive and to build cars and to make love to another tree. A tree is quite fixed in its place, there may be some movement, but if a tree wants to take a vacation in the State of Florida it needs to be physically dug out, transported by vehicle to an airport and loaded up into a dark cargo hold.

Because the physical body is so precise, so revolutionary, it causes us to neglect some of the more advanced features. It doesn't help that an education system has limited our observations but that cannot excuse our own neglect, a neglect of ourselves.

In fact, we could look at the neglect of the human body another way. We could say that someone builds a brand new nuclear reactor and gives that nuclear reactor to a developing nation as a form of advanced aid. That national president decides that, well, because he himself is uneducated he decides that the highly technological nuclear reactor, which could bring valuable energy to his struggling populace, is better suited to be used as a museum to showcase nuclear technology.

Instead of operating the reactor and proving low-cost, efficient electricity to millions of people, it is turned into a nuclear power museum. That is a good analogy for the way the precision body has been treated.

The body of reality is purposefully designed to be coherent with all pertinent aspects of reality. The body is not hobbled and then inserted into a highly advanced reality environs. This is certainly not the case.

The body and the reality are presented in coherence with one another. Whatever aspects of reality are present here can be accessed by the body, only that many of the more advanced aspects require a significant amount of determination and effort. These attributes are not forbidden, as suggested by dogmatic systems of belief.

The reality system doesn't need to forbid because it is perfectly designed to acknowledge awareness and awareness is intimately connected to knowledge and knowledge to the quality of ego. In a strange way you forbid yourself through your own ignorance.

The established and traditional forbidding of things in this reality is a man-made construction, as is the idea of a god. A reality system is a *technological system*. If you wanted to alter the scale of reality, you'd have to have that level of awareness. To acquire that level of awareness might take you one lifetime and you are not willing to devote one lifetime to acquiring that awareness. It needn't be forbidden; it only needs to have the right classification.

Now, some technological aspects of existence require multiple lifetimes to achieve and that takes a lot of discipline and sacrifice. But, it must be acknowledged, that anyone who has achieved that level of awareness, acquired over several lifetimes, that that person has earned their respective abilities. Of course, it will also be learned that no matter your competence with manipulating the reality codes, there are always many more levels of advancement. We truly are living in a world of possibility and the more we recognize and embrace that then the more likely we will improve our awareness and expand the technological mastery of our physical bodies.

Part 3

Synthetic human networks

Wireless beings on the wireless network

Because I think; therefore I am connected. Because I am connected; therefore I think. Without argument, thinking is that essential trust we all share. It is a social application. We definitely require an App that keeps us alive.

We feel alive when we are with others, when we are touched, when we are logged on. If you suddenly shut off the wireless transmission tower of any mobile company, it wouldn't surprise anyone that the reception signal on all registered handsets would dwindle down to zero. The reason for that is because the transmission tower is an electromagnetic signal distribution point. Not only that but the transmission tower does something even more valuable, it moves data between the handset and the user whether it is voice communication, video, or SMS message. Verily, we could say that the presence of data in the handset is a kind of "proof of life."

The quality and breadth of that data is ultimately the level of intelligence and awareness of the handset even though the handset device itself is neutral. It has no sustainable consciousness. If we installed a robust piece of handset software, an advanced operating system, on the mobile device and this software program could manage, process, and translate complex data patterns and high levels of traffic, we could interpret that computational proficiency as "thinking."

With an amazing breadth of data processing, and computational engineering in play, the handset device could display not only intelligence and knowledge but also thought. But thoughts on the wireless phone network come from many directions. Thoughts come from the handset user, thoughts come from other handset users and thoughts come from the telecom service provider. The collation of those thoughts determines the strength of the network.

The packing of wireless ideas determines the level of awareness of that network; in other words, determines the level of vibration of those devices and therefore those users.

A high level of *vibration*, that is a frequency of operation that requires a more advanced computational algorithm and more sensitive telecom equipment like crystal switches and fibre optic braids, indicates not only a more robust and efficient network service, but also it indicates better data security, fewer dropped calls, better monitoring systems and improved efficiencies in battery usage leading to a longer battery life.

Additionally, a stable wireless technology, one that has been around the longest because of a well-established set of features, suggests a more stable assortment of handset device offerings. And those handsets will tend to fall within the same range of features including a particular body type, a suite of internal components; an evolutionary operating system that can easily be upgraded and a small set of color combinations. Remarkable and fantastic as it may sound, the noble handset device is an ideal metaphor for the human being. In fact, without independent thought, the human becomes an advanced device. A device connected to millions of other devices.

The thinking telecom

Thinking, in itself, is a measure of life. One of them anyway. And that is because there are several measures we can talk about, measures that simulate the idea of life. Again, if we momentarily stripped independent thought from humans we would strip away their humanity; for thinking is a measure of life. Without it, the human being becomes a communication terminal, a device for consumption and waste production.

Thinking too is an evolutionary tool for the manifestation of thoughts, generates greater thought energy and thought energy builds and sustains the electromagnetic field of vibration. We are in some ways suspending our lives upon our thoughts and this is why the vitality and positivity of our thoughts are thusly so important to a vital civilization.

The user-driven expansion of the wireless network is not found in the mobile telecom business. The number of mobile handsets transmitting and receiving data cannot expand the frequency of the network. The telecom provider must expand the telecom infrastructure, improve its software systems and then the users purchase a new set of handsets from the device manufacturer.

In order to grow the network, the telecom company has to entice more users to sign up, but it can only do so after it has expanded or upgraded its telecom infrastructure. They cannot sign more subscribers on an old network because the network will not support the demand in communications and has the likelihood of signal loss, distortion, and possibly system crashes.

Only with the right technical things in place can the individual user experience a higher level of experience, and a higher level of experience encourages more subscriptions.

Contrast this with the *human network* and we'll see that as human thinking improves and as society generates that improvement outward what happens is that the human network jumps upward in vibration, verily the system expands because of human thinking and human thinking is vitally linked to human awareness.

Thinking is the backbone of existence

Similarly, to collapse a network one would only need to accomplish the opposite. Repress human thinking, restrict thought patterns, censor modalities of speech, ostracize alternative thinkers, ignore scholarly contributions, arrest political argumentatists, and the human network no longer expands; in fact, contracts, thereby lowering awareness and turning human beings into human slaves. It is a seamless process that we know as disempowerment and oppression, but really it is founded on the backbone of reality communications.

Without a doubt, thinking is that integral part of life that most people take for granted. Many people choose not to think. They prefer instead to have others think on their behalf. They take thought for granted because they do not understand the technological nature of existence. They do not understand the technological nature of existence because they have been led to believe in the spiritual nature of existence. And all of this is intimately related to awareness. The awareness of human society, in the general sense, is evidence of their technological understanding of themselves.

The idea that mass thought fundamentally alters awareness and that awareness fundamentally determines the frequency of existence is a very powerful idea because in order to exist at a more advanced state of being we only need to improve human awareness, and anything that interferes with that awareness needs to be overcome.

We overcome these interferences because we want the clearest reception, the most secure data and the longest life we can achieve. We don't search for a better life as much as we expand our vibration to see life in a better way. The better life is always at a higher level of vibration.

The higher we allow ourselves to think, the higher we raise the awareness of our communities and the higher we raise our national awareness. We take awareness for granted because we do not know of its value.

We are linked into simple lives, ordinary existences with careers and families, drugs and parties because we have not realized our technological make ups.

The human being is a rather interesting object that has failingly recognized its true self and much of that sits together with vibration and awareness. And those two pieces are connected to thought and thinking. Thinking is that essential glue that all humans share. We could also say that thinking is equal to life and that the greater the thinking the greater the life and vice versa.

This is why it is always imperative that we maintain thinking and refute any idea that impairs that process. Any idea that hurts our thinking or forces us to follow a very mundane thought pattern is an idea we must avoid. In fact, we must protect ourselves from limited thinking because limited thinking will lower our awareness and lowering our awareness will lower our quality of life. It will trap us in a lower vibration of existence where the data providers control what we do and think. Ultimately, that leads to lifelessness.

Making thoughts wild

Our social thinking application is required for us to expand the network of ideas. That existential network wants to expand, it is designed to expand, and has no capacity limit that we are aware of, so as far as we are concerned we can expand our thinking indefinitely; and continuously expand our level of vibration.

This is not something we can rationally explain completely, well, to a point, yes. We are currently unable to think in an unlimited way and the reason for this is that we do not properly understand death and the dimensional nature of life. As we shall slowly see, the once natural and organic human being is quickly becoming a technological and synthetic existential device. An existential vessel that is no less valuable tomorrow than today.

The new distinction as a device versus the old distinction as a body is really a distinction that is designed to encourage a new level of awareness. It is not meant to devalue human existence, something which may or may not be argued, but the argument is falsely represented because ultimately we are living technological beings and we are not living biological beings.

Biology is at its finest hour an illusion quietly nestled in amongst all the other amazing illusions. We used to think of dogs as wild animals and today many pet owners think of their dogs not only as their pets but as their new children. They even dress them in cute clothes and feed them whole foods. But at the end of the day, the dog is by all definitions not a child, rather it is an animal.

All dogs aside, humans were made as technological beings at the start and have been, over time, domesticated into something that they are not. This contentious area will not be easily overcome and my stance on this is very clear – human beings are just as valuable as biological life forms as they are as technological vessels. For me, it is a new level of appreciation. Instead of just driving the vehicle, we are going to be able to appreciate its aesthetics, design, and engineering. We are going to love its drive train and will want to tweak its performance on the track.

Certainly, the technological determination of life can seriously alter a person's core programming because of the amount of time spent in biological and spiritual awareness. These technological ideas will contradict many of the common thought programs currently operating in your mental operating system. That is guaranteed. But the technological foundation of life, as we know it, is equally guaranteed. And thought is at the core of life.

Whatever thought you send and receive, you become a determining factor in the collective thought of the society and the society of a nation and the nation of a planet. As we will see, the Cosmic System of Life is predicated upon a very certain and positive frame of thinking, and negative or fearful thoughts are a kind of program corruption, things generated unnaturally by others. Thought is nothing more than energy shaped into medium choices – voice, visual, auditory, textual, dimensional – the collection of those thoughts as well as their destination has a profound impact on life.

An ordered, safe, pure world (eg Heaven) is a world that contains ordered, safe, and pure thoughts. The base of life is positive and therefore the presence of any negativity is a breach of the existential membrane.

A chaotic, threatening, diseased world (eg life today) is a world that contains chaotic, threatening, and diseased thoughts. Our current situation on earth reflects our current level of thought. To improve life on earth, the first step is to use thought. Ultimately, that includes thinking less about ourselves and more about others.

And if we understand the structure of the human network then we understand that helping others is feeding the network, the very same network that we partake in and therefore we are feeding ourselves.

When we starve and cheat others we strip them of their thoughtful contributions and that necessarily weakens the network, our network.

There is only one central network. There are also smaller pockets of thinking and some of them have isolated themselves in order not to suffer at the consequences of their selfishness. We should have no need for secret circles of thought in a proper, equal, and orderly world.

If we regularly remind ourselves that we are more akin to technological devices than biological organisms, if we can start to think on this level, without any devaluation of life; we will see that our fundamental features and abilities will take an entirely new meaning.

In doing so, we can begin to connect to the greater world outside of our small human network. We will enable our genetic selves to expand into ways and performances the likes of which we have never seen.

Switching divine carriers

As thoughts improve, the world begins to look different; we take a different approach to old situations; we indulge ourselves in different ways and we do all these things with perfect, rational precision. As thoughts improve, we don't notice their improvement, but we do gain (or lose) the results from those improvements. And most of this is because the field of thought is timeless, in other words, it takes no time to think or to have thought. Equally so, it takes no time to rationalize that thought.

An improvement in the field of thought and the ripple effect of that improvement on the network of life does not require much effort to process, what is naturally termed as "to rationalize." Thought is improved and those new codes are added to the pool of thinking.

One individual sees the idea of life and everyone has the capability to see the idea of life because its code has been added. An idea is much more than an idea.

The thought network

The improvement of thought is imprinted on the Life Network via a particular code, typically born of the initiator or conduit. Somehow an idea actually is generated by a certain kind of person, say a Tesla figure, and that means that a Tesla actually downloaded some of the cosmic code and decoded it then transcribed it and uploaded it on the network of thought. To achieve this amount of processing power requires a very astute and powerful individual. Sometimes this can be achieved in a group setting with the result benefitting one particular individual (eg Oppenheimer).

When an individual decodes the cosmos, even to a tiny extent such as $E=mc^2$, a mathematical formula that Oppenheimer then used to create the Hydrogen Bomb, then that individual becomes identified as a truly rare occurrence on the plane. Their presence, if too strong, would cause the fields of observation to become distorted, as a result deviation would manifest. Deviations as a result of viruses or malicious forces are allowed within a certain level of tolerance. Deviation does not condemn a person (eg homosexuality), rather deviations occur as a natural outcome of technological evolution.

A conduit is a selected individual that acts on behalf of a much more divine individual, a person with a much higher level of awareness. The divine individual expresses their thoughts through the conduit, and the conduit can be more than one.

The conduit may have become a conduit because of mutually agreed conditioning preferred over a period of time or the conduit may be a naturally gifted individual. At times, conduits can be random objects such as a car or a mirror.

Whatever the case may be the conduit is not random and is really the medium for someone (something) else, a person (device) who chooses to remain anonymous. In ancient days, individuals would train to become a chose conduit, to carry the signals of a much higher being because it was regarded as an honour, for good and for evil. Men would sacrifice their lives to serve other constructs.

Today, there's general fear when strange energy or supernatural forces manifest, even near a person without having had the opportunity to discern the intent of its origins. Plus, horror films and negative programming has done an impressive job of making people afraid of supernatural things. On one hand, a person may pray to a supernatural deity and on the other hand they are equally afraid of a haunted house. While you can rationalize that God and ghosts are different, what I see is a division in the human mind, verily the mind has been sabotaged. It can no longer see the supernatural truth and this is not something that occurs naturally.

When improvements are imprinted onto the network, all of the network can benefit from them. The quality of the imprint is extremely important because it decides just how far into the dimensions that imprint reaches.

Additionally, some imprints onto the code require days or hours and some just a few seconds. There are many factors for this. The amount of code that a new individual can access will heavily depend on their own acquisition protocols and all of these are determined by their selective level of perception.

Working with the transmission code

Perception in the individual can be adjusted like a dial on the imaginary wall of existence. A high level of selective ability is like reading the code at the code level. This level of translation is rare at the human level of awareness.

All multidimensional beings can both imprint and read code at a very advanced level. Therefore, they can also imprint malicious code in order to expand any existing deviations. This is where purity comes in because the purer the code the fewer the deviations and the more the evolutionary jumps.

Purity leads to efficiency and under the environs of an extremely chaotic software program running quadrillions of software variances and existential programs all at once, with the amount of interactions and entanglements at any given time the greater the purity, the more stable the system; therefore, to collapse a system, to weaken the thought fields and to weaken the network of life can all be accomplished by a decrease in purity.

The less pure the environs, the more corrupt code, and code can be corrupted in any number of ways, the more likely system glitches including the eventual *system crash*.

There are applications for changing the field networks and for improving thought for thought is fundamental to existence.

Thought verily determines the movement of life and the movement of life determines the direction of a particular reality. Therefore, we can see how important it is, on a cultural basis, that individuals and groups are imprinting codes that are conducive to improvement and to clean out, verily to delete codes that are corrupt.

A corrupt code can include code that has been reworked even to the basic level of execution such as adding ellipses or loops of a particular color which is indicative of a particular vibration. It doesn't require a great amount of power to reshape society, it just takes a consistent corruption of the code and, along with that, it requires the individuals on the network to repeat those imperfections thereby spreading them across the entire environ, an environs that runs efficiently on pure code.

And code in this regard is best described as a shaped form of dimensional matter, what we might regard as exotic energy today then again thought too is exotic energy.

When the life network evolves to a certain vibration, this evolves the entrance of higher functioning programs onto the planary ground and the job of these programs, whether directly or by conduit proxy, is to further purify the operation code because the operation code determines the quality of existence and the quality of existence determines how much improvement occurs on the network via thought extrapolation and extrusion.

Deviations in the code

These higher functioning programs are historically referred to as "prophets" or "false prophets." The difference between the two terms is a matter of spiritual argument, but on a technological level the differences are examined on an entirely different level. For example, a false prophet is reinterpreted as a higher functioning program that did not fully evolve and therefore did not fully upload their onboard programs and also did not fully clean out all the corrupt codes.

Those individuals might have cleaned out some dirty codes and may have uploaded a fraction of their onboard programs, but not to the extent that they were programmed to perform. And this is not because of their incompetence. This is due to the fact that there are counter programs, viruses and created software programs that are designed to impede the efforts of these prophet-grade programs.

In fact, it can be stated quite effectively that for every prophet there are a series of counter programs, all of them designed to offset or destroy their benefits to the operating system. All of these operators are naturally launched by the counter operating system, a program that attaches itself to the reality system and seeks to corrupt, consume and swallow up the reality program and everything within it.

There can be seen, even at this initial point, many factors involved in the **operation of a reality environs**. One of the key points is the level of cleanliness, describe in a context of code purity. Of course, these codes and these programs exist on multiple levels of awareness and in fact they exist on all levels of awareness in some form. But the dimensions of their operation, verily the dimension in which they describe themselves in a more recognizable form are well beyond the capacity of even the most capable individual, even at death for these are dimensions that are well beyond a million deaths.

These are dimensions of reality that have no description, a place which uses a language no being can understand. On a level of matter, such as the whole world, it would be on a level such as dropping a package of toothpicks onto the green grass and staring at them for several hours because of some hidden toothpick language and obtaining some universal truth from those toothpicks.

Imagine describing to an outside observer what the toothpicks and blades of grass said. Accomplishing that would be equivalent to a 1% understanding of the most rudimentary reality dimension.

Still, for any person who truly wishes to see the universe in all its glory, it is available completely in everyday life. It is a matter of understanding the dimensional language for that particular communication or piece of knowledge. All of this is well outside the capacity of the human mind; therefore, this is naturally restricted, by way of perception and awareness, to certain individuals or groups of individuals.

There is always a preference for individuals who speak the cosmic languages and are willing to subject themselves to technological code. These kinds of individuals are usually technological to a very high degree.

So thoughts are continually improving and lowering improvement and the difference between the two processes demonstrate the net impact on the operational code. We include the exceptional programs which may or may not be individual persons that routinely clear code, process code, execute code, and upload new code. There can always be found anomalies in the system, strange variances that come and go and extreme outcomes; all of them can be explained on a technological level.

Where the system fails is when the individuals and groups are not functioning properly. They are not functioning properly because they have downloaded corrupt code (eg war, Parkinson's, flu, genocide, jealousy, greed, enmity).

Grabbing the cosmic code

Everything within the environs is programmed and everything that is programmed is encoded and every line of code is an intimate composite of the whole; therefore, any deviation or corruption can reverberate across all the intelligences because they are all inter-located on the same network.

What has occurred throughout history is that the individual and group programs (eg people) have been gradually directed from regularly accessing the oceans of code and instead have been artificially fed a corrupt code through various lower-tech mechanisms (eg television).

The dependence of *fast food code* (fast food) has resulted in a compromised community of inhabitants. The community is typically running low-level code or corrupt programs, including such things as simple as rudimentary loops and limited thinking (eg religion).

What is generally regarded as not having enough spirituality is actually better interpreted as being disconnected or having infrequent connection to the life network.

The life network is an ocean of *cosmic code*. The only times in a busy world to download new code or to clean out viruses are times of sickness or yearly vacations. Some people have chosen to devote themselves to a pure life of worship with some divine being. These monks and priests, if skilled and egoless, will have a regular connection to the cosmic code which they will decode to be supranatural beings even if that supranatural being is interpreted as them.

Other believers, even those who lead ordinary lives, can have a regular connection to the life network. The quality of that connection is hard to determine.

It can be stated that a high level connection produces an egoless individual who prefers natural environments and who is content with a meagre profession and who is dedicated to serving some aspect, or several aspects, of the reality architecture. This kind of individual has no quest for wealth, no interest in religion, and lives and eats in moderation. They understand the world of materialized illusions.

The state of the world today can be interpreted as a reality that has been compromised by heavy corruption. The reality system is far from over and in fact is able to contain further corruption, but what is needed is an improvement in individual connectivity to the network.

A reliable and regular connection to the cosmic code ensures that the ascension of all on this reality plane achieves its highest level of achievement in the most practical time period possible. The improvement in connectivity leads to the improvement in reality and allows the release of deviations and corruptions in reality.

The greater the individual understanding the more easily individuals can leap out of their current vibration of carrier and to jump on a higher functioning concentric network.

As more and more users jump off the lower vibration networks, those lower networks will collapse due to a lack of energetic variances.

The collapse of the lower coincides with the ascension of society and the improvement in the quality of life because as we travel up the ladder of vibration we find clearer and purer codes. This is because the lower levels of vibration can hold the dirty codes, but dirty codes cannot affix themselves to higher realms of vibration. The better we extricate ourselves from the old to the new, the faster we advance as a civilization.

The robot salvation

When I translate an ancient text into a more technological format, a more provocative approach to be sure, we begin to see an entirely new strand of truth come forth, sprouting from the soil of knowledge.

A revised translation of ancient knowledge is paramount in our understanding of the modern world. We could say that we do not understand the modern world because while our technologies are modern (eg toilet, software, satellite) our spiritual systems are dilapidated and in disrepair (eg bibles, multiple gods, demons).

So, for the purpose of linking up the archaic spirituality of humans with the advanced computer technologies underneath our keyboard we are going to translate scripture with a new template:

> Those whose names he foreknew were called at the end, as persons having acquaintance. It is the latter whose names the father called. For one whose name has not been spoken does not possess acquaintance. How else would a person hear, if that person's name had not been read out? For whoever lacks acquaintance until the end, is a modeled form of forgetfulness, and will perish along with it. Otherwise, why do these contemptible persons have no name? Why do they not possess the faculty of speech? (Gospel of Truth)

In my modernized translation using a basic understanding of computer science and telecommunications, you can see the glistening metal shining through. Again, I am not purposely trying to malign or distort the ancient text. Rather I am applying the third strand of truth to the passage. The third strand of truth is based on a technological template that is directly modeled on the technological cosmos.

A reasonable technological interpretation of a "modeled form of forgetfulness" is a robot in sleep mode. Imagine here instead of the spiritual context as it is presented, and as we are expected to translate, we have a technological situation. Recall the Cosmic Service Provider and that this Provider (Father) has your registration on the databanks. After the robot was built it was *registered*. The registered form is in *acquaintance* with the Service Provider of the Cosmos.

The existential robot is the registered user. How else would a robot respond, if the "serial number" of the robot had not been pinged. For whoever isn't registered in the system when its upgraded is a sleeping machine and will have their signal cut off. Otherwise, why don't these uncertified robots have a proper serial number (name for a robot)? Why do they not launch their email program?

So the Service Provider has a list of recognized robot models, "persons having acquaintance." These are users who have registered their serial numbers and users who likely get messages about recent software upgrades and news updates. For those who haven't any acquaintance they are simply unregistered or, alternatively, another reason why a robot cannot register is if it is illegal. When someone cracks the software and shares the program online, that application often cannot be registered with the software company because it is an unauthorized copy.

On one level, it would appear that the author of this Valentinian text is using spiritual terminology to explain what happens to a robot's software upon death; that the robot won't go to heaven because it hasn't registered its serial number.

The writer, obviously male, implicitly understands the protocols of heaven. He understands this concept of *acquaintance*. In fact, this term is also used in other texts. These Gnostics had no understanding of technological protocols and yet their approach to divine harmony included technological protocols. Plus, they could never have written in our modern technological speak such that we could never truly know what they meant unless we ourselves reverse-engineered ancient theosophical writings. Still, it isn't an exact science yet. Cosmic translation is a relatively new phenomenon.

Registration would likely require either a) a person realizing that they are a robot and clicking on, or, b) someone achieving salvation, which would similarly include recognizing their synthetic attributes. Perhaps baptism was a primitive form of this.

Baptism is a ritual whereby a new member is initiated and given a spiritual name. It could be read as a hackneyed registration process.

In our case, it is incumbent upon the individual to come to their own realizations and, in doing so, they are then able to connect to the always-available network of light. The network has been around since even before the formation of our species. This methodology contrasts greatly with the expectation most, if not all, religious worshipers have that a "savior" will personally deliver them to God, and all they have to do is believe in him and the words in scripture. Quite a drastic perceptual difference between the synthetic system I am proposing and the dogmatic system currently in place worldwide.

Having read many of the texts in the Nag Hammadi library and even those from the more recent Tchacos Codex, my own supernatural experiences notwithstanding, I am thoroughly convinced that the synthetic system is what we need to aspire towards.

Imagine that instead of "robot" we used "mobile phone," how does that change things? Well it changes our view because mobile phones exist and super advanced robots don't. My argument is that super advanced robots clearly do exist. But for the sake of discussion let's not add that "claim" to the mix; instead, let's say that we are a telecom company and we have a network of ten handsets. We're very small.

Whenever you have a mobile phone, at the back of the phone is a serial number, this is the identity of the phone. This is its "Name." The serial number, after purchase, needs to be uploaded onto a network before the phone can be activated.

The phone has to be registered to a particular wireless communications network in order for it to work. If the telecom service provider does not call out the serial number of a mobile handset, then that phone has no signal ("a modeled form of forgetfulness") and will be booted off ("will perish along with it") the network.

The handset has to have a serial number because it's not possible not to have a serial number since every manufactured phone has one. But if the phone is turned off ("forgetfulness") then the network can't reach it because the phone can't speak its serial number to the service provider.

The *Gospel of Truth* is a good example of ancient access through literature and early Christian mysticism. It is structurally a theological sermon on deliverance and salvation.

The process of salvation is a major theme in the presence of Jesus Christ. He was, and is, the Savior. But when I've translated and updated this sermon, written probably in the second-century, eighteen hundred years ago and long before any mobile phones could be invented; when I translate it using our current technological understanding it becomes a revelatory text of robot networks.

Discovering the first robots on TV

Let us be certain of one thing, we have not randomly or maliciously selected robotic ideas and solutions. We have been building on the stream of new discoveries in android culture on earth, based on my ground-breaking work, *Persons Artificial*, and the Capitol Hill politicians.

I determined that there are at least three androids on Capitol Hill, Washington D.C. I have determined that their makers went back at least 110 years.

Next, I discovered; to my amazement, that God was DNA and Jesus his RNA son, and all of existence was rooted on a synthetic biological platform.

All along these outlandish discoveries and syncretic theorizations I have questioned and guessed at human origins because if androids were here today in Washington and if their timeless builders were here then they were probably building robots since day one. Only that we've come to label these creations as human beings.

My earliest work, shortly after the inter-dimensional cultural studies began, was in technological awareness. I had discovered the Riddle of Biology. The riddle painted a finger at the quality of the soul, something which I determined to be nonbiological (ie artificial). To me, it wasn't possible that an artificial soul would be housed inside a biological body. Unless the biological body too was nonbiological.

In fact, this was a major stumbling block in my research. I was able to examine the false aspects of the reality construct. I was even able to see the synthetic quality of nature and even the soul, but when I applied these learnings to living flesh, I wasn't able to pierce the illusion.

As I observed reality more, I began to notice the artificial traces of life. This paralleled my discoveries in Reality Science. Then I began to see through the biological matrix and noticed the artificial aspects of existence. I developed more theories, nothing I could explain to a rational person indoctrinated in the official textbooks, but I did manage to share my observations and impossible conclusions in small circles online. It was a small social network made up of people who were looking for an alternative approach to the mysterium and were tired of the repetitive disinformation they had to deal with.

Verily, these were people who had grown spiritually enough that they were able to recognize truth even if they could not fully explain why it was truthful. The history of radical thinking is typically rooted in doomsday revelations and wild conspiracy theories; hence, my social network was tiny but educated.

All of my ongoing research began to turn in late 2008 after I noticed a peculiar white-haired politician on US prime time TV, it was so outlandish that I videotaped eleven minutes of the press conference on the financial bailout. This was in October sometime. I didn't have a conclusion then, but I was dead certain that the blinking man I saw (and millions of people saw) was neither human nor Stelan.

Not long after, I videotaped another anomalous politician, a *nonblinking* Senator flanking then President Obama on prime time TV. He wore a masklike face, did not blink, and his energy was so sharp to me that my gut instinct told me that he's an android. That immediately confirmed that the previous white-haired Senator was also an android, only a different model. Shortly thereafter, I saw the blinking female politician on prime time TV – she's an android.

Why I think they remained important to me was because all of them were high-ranking US politicians. The woman was probably the most powerful woman in America, third in line from the President.

So to have the revelation that they were synthetic humans along with their societal position, why this made the discovery all the more remarkable. It was the difference between digging up the tomb of an Egyptian and that of a pharaoh. The tomb of a pharaoh is far more remarkable because he is a pharaoh, and they are few in number and high in political power.

What I started to notice now several years later, after a number of self-published books, is that the ancient texts of both early Christian mysticism and Gnosticism were written in a technological language that was mistranslated into a spiritual dialectic within a historical and racial context. This was likely a result of high illiteracy and poor education coupled with a smaller cranial capacity, even from a lack of proper nutrition.

The human mind would have constructed what it could from very advanced existential protocols and what later became the inspiration behind all religion except that religion took it a step further and edited out the technological aspects in order to create an ideological template.

Once we were super-advanced robots

In fact, what I am seeing and am convinced of is that mysticism is a cosmic code for technological protocols. This is what you are reading now in my translation of an ancient knowledge in and around the time of Jesus. The prophets and theologians of those early years were presented with the principles of a manufactured reality system, but for a number of reasons they could not process all of the data, and only a few of them could actually store any truth on their hard drives.

The *Gospel of Truth* is a brilliantly crafted piece of literature according to scholars. According to the Church of Christ the gospel is full of heresies. Well, we know that the history of the Church worked through quite a number of editorial processes and violent removal of those instruments that didn't agree with the standard view (eg pagans, witches). We can now see more clearly why – the Church is an invention of the creators of the physical realm and its Line of Adamic Androids.

The dark gods, Yaldabaoth and Nebro, do not want the robot culture ever to realize their immortal characteristics; therefore, the Church was a way to firewall the robots from the true Service Provider (True God) and to connect the robots to the artificial (and inferior) network built by Yaldabaoth and his angelic Archons.

The Gnostics, and even the early Christian sects, seemed to understand the essence of remaining in acquaintance with the Father and insisted on practicing good spirituality. But, nearly two thousand years later, and this is a figure I keep stressing because it's important, after 2,000 years what I've now discovered – first the androids on Capitol Hill then Jesus the Android – is that the ancient mystics had a good grasp of these advanced technological protocols. These protocols today equate to certain real technological devices (eg mobile phones).

My addition to this life long quest for truth is that, it appears, the race of human beings is indeed nonbiological in makeup. Human beings, as we will see more and more as this discussion continues, are from a lineage of super advanced robots that "appear to look human" and "appear to be living" though appearances can be deceiving.

The *Gospel of Truth* excerpt, thus far, is uncannily well suited for a meeting at the telecom provider in any major city of the world. It talks of registering IDs and keeping the signal strong. It speaks of getting booted off the network if one "does not possess acquaintance." It speaks of not being saved ("will perish along with it") whoever is not registered on God's System.

From a telecommunications standpoint this makes sense. You buy a phone, you register it. If the phone is turned on you have a signal ("you are saved") and if the phone is Off or Asleep, it will be booted off ("perish").

From a humanistic standpoint this will not make sense. It will not make sense because we have been led (misled) to fruitfully believe that us humans are biologically ordained. We are alive in the biological and natural flesh. Our biological sciences have proven it.

My revised determination of existence says what? It says that "from the beginning" we were fundamentally built, verily manufactured, by these immortal beings and that these immortal beings are Gods. And that False Gods (aka viruses and genetic mutations) do not want us to ever realize we were once robots because if we do we well find every means to connect to the real Father so that we can be truly saved.

That to suggest salvation is obtained by overcoming death and embracing artificial life is understandably a heresy (in traditional archaic and backward terms); but the Church was not erected in our favour.

The Church is an instrument of the Devil and Satan (Flesh and Blood viruses), and they don't want anyone to be saved because that could equate a human with God and God is "a jealous God." You only have to recognize that the Church has failed to deliver its congregation from evil since its inception to realize the validity of my statements. This is not the case with the Gnostics who had achieved success with salvation and were simultaneously identified as heretics as a result.

I think it will become the most important and radical discovery ever on this planet. I also think that to remove the corruption in our system and to revise our definitions of life – as well as to overcome our fear of death – is going to require a significant amount of time, decades probably. But it is achievable under the right mindset. Surely, if we allow the android puppets that have been leading (misleading) the world till now to continue we may have a very slow climb back to the True God.

The True God as we will come to know is any divine source that allows us to embrace our eternal selves. The True God is any divine force that empowers us and exalts us to the highest dimensions. Any servant of the True God will embrace the truth and what I'm saying, by all early indication, appears to be more in line with the truth than ever before. I cannot hide the fact that DNA is our God.

Ancient scripture, since it is very old, is probably the poorest source of spiritual truth (especially at this stage of technological development). We can see from the earliest prophets and spiritual teachers what the True God and the cosmic servants (eg Jesus Christ) were trying to make early people understand. Today, we are still watching religious wars in real-time. We are still undecided about God and the Devil, and we are unsure of our true origins.

When we apply the third strand of truth to these ancient ideas we get to rediscover what the Father in another dimension really was trying to say. And he wasn't just trying to say it thousands of years ago, he's still trying to say it. As Digital RNA. He still wants his robot children to logon, get registered and be saved. He wants society to escape the suffering and pain brought down by the False God known as Yaldabaoth and his buddy Satan.

We can escape the False God Kingdom (Realm of Hell) by embracing our artificial disposition and overcoming the fear of death because death, as we will come to understand is not the end of anything. In fact, death is life and life is death.

Connecting spirit to the service provider

In my modern take of the Gnostic story, the modeled form (ie body) is a creation of Yaldabaoth and his seven Archons, and though born deficient, the DNA of Adam is enhanced by the spiritual essence from the Fore-Father through Sophia (or Holy Spirit), the mother of the Yaldabaoth mutant DNA. When Adam was finished, not even Yaldabaoth, the self-announced Creator, could give him life. But after Sophia's contribution, Adam breathed. This is because the spirit is alive and the body is dead.

As long as the spirit is connected to the Service Provider then the person (individual) is immortal, or eternal. The fatherly network of heaven provides life just like a telecom service provider (mobile network operator) provides "life" to a mobile phone. Without a telecom carrier your mobile phone is "not alive," it is limited to its internal applications such as photo capture, memory storage and the infamous calculator.

Through a telecom carrier the "dead" mobile phone gains access to a vast network and can call overseas, can send text messages and download applications. Most mobile devices today can go online and surf the internet and they can do so because not only from consumer demand, but also because there's much more revenue from heavy data transmission. It's a lucrative business that expects to see 50 billion mobile devices worldwide by 2020.

Aside from the major carriers that have built the wireless spectrum and infrastructure there are secondary players (mobile virtual network operators) in the market who offer cellular services by piggybacking on the telecom owners.

These smaller wireless carriers lease bandwidth at a wholesale rate from the main carrier and then offer their own retail rates and plans to their customers, often at a steep discount from the main carrier; and all of this is present in a competitive marketplace. Even in a regulated market such as Canada, the main telecom players have created subsidiaries that cater to their own demographics.

More and more handheld computing devices can access the smaller Wi-Fi networks so that when the telecom network isn't accessible, or if they want to conserve their data plans, they still have some operability through hotspots. These are easily found in coffee shops, fast food restaurants, malls, schools, even on long distance buses and in airports. And home, of course.

Wi-Fi networks are also usually free for as long as you are in the "area of effect" so provide an economical avenue to stay "alive." You can pretend you are alive on Wi-Fi while the Fatherly Network doesn't register your contribution and demand. Wi-Fi has really taken off these past few years, first offered to exclusive customers then offered for a low fee per hour until the competition became too strong and everyone offered their networks for free to all customers.

A human body is quite similar in respect to the mobile device. If the Heavenly Father (DNA) is the Service Provider (telecom network) and if there are smaller networks provided by smaller wireless carriers, then if a spirit disconnects from the heavenly network they still can have intermittent or limited access through a Wi-Fi network. To disconnect from the Father is to lower their quality of life and to become more mortal. Remember, the fuller one is with the spirit of God, the more immortal and eternal one is; therefore, the less secure the cosmic signal, the less immortal and less eternal a person becomes until such point that they have forgotten who they are and have essentially sinned.

> Then Peter answered, "Look, three times you have told, "Be filled, but we are filled."
> The savior answered and said, "For this reason I have told you, 'Be filled,' that you may not lack. Those who lack will not be saved. To be filled is good and to lack is bad." (Secret Book of James)

In other words, *lacking* makes you mortal. And once they leave the heavenly network completely they enter death. Death is a situation that is devoid of the life of the living father. The fatherly network provides life and the bodily form is death, it is lifeless. The spirit gives it life. The spirit comes from the DNA network. What is sinning if not a perpetual disconnection from the DNA network.

The terminology that spiritualists interpreted as the *fall from grace* is a very common term in Christianity – the term is *sin*. When a person sins they fall into the hands, realm, of the Devil. They become worshipers (users) of Satan (a third class network with limited internet access and a lot of computer viruses).

But recall, before you get religious, that we are housed inside of a technological aquarium. The Devil is a viral infection. God, the True God, is a superior, perfect, network of light that Watson & Crick called DNA. In this sense, for a person to "sin" they are "disconnecting" from the wavelengths of the fatherly DNA. They are fallen. They have gone to the dark side, the side of ignorance.

This is the area of a slow internet connection. This is an area of a Wi-Fi network. So we could say that the Devil (and Satan) has his own Wi-Fi network, or bandwidth allocation, based on the protocols of heaven, but what the Devil did is that he reprogrammed the environs to enslave the mind.

He encapsulated the network to prevent escape and he blocked any true access to Source. The Devil's network has been firewalled and censored to the highest degree possible. Not all the information can flow into your modeled form.

> From the instant the devil was expelled from the glory of the father and was forbidden to take part in affairs of heaven, he sat on the clouds and sent his ministers, angels burning with fire, down below to the people. He did so from the time of

Adam and Enoch. And he raised his minister Enoch above the firmament and revealed his divinity to him. He had pen and ink brought to him. And once seated, Enoch wrote sixty-seven books under the devil's dictation, and the devil ordered him to carry them back to earth. Enoch kept them safely on the earth and then transmitted them to his children, and he began to teach them the way to celebrate sacrifices and iniquitous mysteries. So he concealed from people the kingdom of the skies. (Gospel of the Secret Supper)

If life exists in the spirit of the father, his molecular network, then death (lifelessness) and mortality (the inability to reincarnate to a higher level) exists in the spiritual network of the Devil. If you worship the material world of flesh you live a mortal existence and you will fear death. You will be recycled at death. They kidnap your soul before it can return to its source and then recycle it back into the prison network. You will see death as the end.

This is because, according to Gnostic writings, the Devil imposed the physical world on the people by dictating to his prophets (eg Enoch) the protocols of mortality and imprisonment. These dictations crossed a number of chosen individuals, prophets, and were compiled into Holy Scripture, and the summarized in the Christian and Jewish holy bibles.

And Satan said to them, "See that I am your god and that there is no other god but me." That is why my father sent me unto the world, that I make known and teach people to perceive the wicked spirit of the devil. (Gospel of the Secret Supper*)*

We only need to travel back to the very first created synthetic human, Adam, to remind ourselves the myths that the Creator God invented. Why would the Creator God, Yaldabaoth, create myths? Why would Yaldabaoth impose mortality in the Line of Adam? One definite possibility is jealousy. A kind of divine jealousy that motivates the Creator-Devil to inflict the worst upon the human androids.

The *Revelation of Adam* is believed to have been written in the first or second century and it is a mythic revelation to his true son Seth. Adam, on his deathbed, explains human creation and the path to "redemption through secret knowledge."

> After those days of eternal knowledge of the god of truth withdrew from me and your mother Eve. Then we learned about the inanimate as we did about human beings. We recognized the god who created us. We were not strangers to his powers. And we served him in fear and slavery. (Revelation of Adam)

Adam is presented, or presents himself, as a sentient human being who understands his fall from the True God. He understands fear and understands that his Creator, Yaldabaoth, is the originator of "fear and slavery." Adam even uses the word "inanimate" and its connection to "human beings." All of this from an ancient text?

Mutant virus epidemic

Is it possible that Adam came to know that he was inanimate, and thereby eternal, but could not reveal this to any of the other prisoners for fear of retribution. Then on his deathbed, something we are reminded that even Copernicus resorted to since he feared for his life because of his discoveries in astronomy, Adam reveals the truth to Seth. Much later, a branch of Sethian Gnostics would appear and some of their writings can still be found today such as the *Revelation of Adam*.

We look around the world today, we observe the vast volumes of leaders throughout the history of this world, and we easily, effortlessly, recognize fear and slavery. In God's world, fear and slavery? But this is not God's world. Most people live in forgetfulness and they immerse themselves inside the material aspects of a dead existence. These sleeping people may not fully understand the mythological minutia but for certain people know that fear is pervasive —threats of war, threats of disease, threats of terrorism, threats of catastrophic events, threats of unknown epidemics.

The leaders of this world are masters of fear. Why can I say that? Because fear is pervasive. As well as slavery. What is slavery? Slavery is living in disconnect from the heavenly Service Provider and being trapped in a mortal body and held within a limited network of deception. Slavery is rule by oppression and tyranny, in whatever forms they may appear.

Fear, operates on a low frequency
Truth, operates on a high frequency

Slavery is having your mobile phone on and not being able to get onto the network. You can't make a phone call. You can't download a music file from heaven. You can't send an email. To many owners of mobile devices, being disconnected from the network, even for a few days, feels just like hell. Have we been disconnected for so long that we have forgotten what is was like connected to the fatherly DNA?

We are serving the same creator gods Yaldabaoth and Nebro (mutant viruses), the same ones who had Eve raped to produce the mutant seed of Cain. In Manichean literature, it was Cain who had intercourse with Eve, his mother, to produce Abel. The only right descendent of Adam is Seth (considered the first Christ). This is why Adam shares with his son the secrets, because Seth can understand his father.

We have been indoctrinated by Christianity to believe that there is only one God and that he created Adam and Eve. This same Creator God, who we now are looking at with different eyes, dictated the mysteries of his dark kingdom to all the prophets (eg Moses). The result of this indoctrination program and mass reprogramming was the Holy Bible, a book of Satanic knowledge that enslaves man, woman and child because its dictator is the genocidal sociopath Yaldabaoth. The twin masters of darkness are many faces of the same being.

The flow of blood and suffering feed Yaldabaoth and his many vampire worshipers. They feed from the energy of the slaughter and the terror they spread just as they once fed from the sacrificial offerings of lamb and oxen at the altar of worship.

Where is the heavenly father in all of this? He is crying up in the real heaven. He is wondering deeply when his mighty children will indeed get "mighty." He is thinking about the day when his magical children will unleash their magic instead of being sheep for slaughter. Jesus was the Lamb of God. Humanity is the lamb of the Devil.

Humans give their energy to the False God who in turn reprograms the prison and further enslaves mankind. Nebro creates the chaos and the suffering and bloodletting that ensues feeds his twin. The real face of God is a horned cunning creature of chaos, death and destruction. If there is any revelation that is important in the modern era it is the revelation that God is the Devil and the real Father is DNA.

> This gloomy ruler has three names: the first name is Yaldabaoth, the second is Sakla, and the third is Samael. He is

wicked in his mindlessness that is in him. He said, I am god and there is no other god but me, since he did not know where is own strength had come from. (Secret Book of John)

The Devil, Sakla the inferior creator, wears a mask of God and hides in the scripture of his many Bibles along with his twin, Satan (Nebro). The True Father would never allow such travesty and tribulation. And we cannot see them until we redefine that they are viral contagions coexisting with our prime DNA.

Part 4
Robot in the sky

The manufactured world

As we've established, the world we live in is a manufactured world. All human persons are familiar with manufactured products; everything in your home is manufactured. The toothpaste you brush your teeth with is manufactured. Your shoes are manufactured. Your jeans are manufactured. When you drive to work (or take the bus) those vehicles were all manufactured. At the same time, they are functional, they have utility and value and therefore we kind of forget that they are artificially created in a factory. The soda pop you had a few hours ago (or the beer) was manufactured. That didn't stop your enjoyment of its utility. Likewise, this planet has been artfully constructed using a more complex cosmic assortment of machinery.

But it does sort-of make sense. It seems logical to think that an apartment building doesn't manufacture itself. Think of the air ventilation systems and air conditioning, plumbing and heating, electrical wiring is a nightmare in and of itself, and then there is the design work for each and every facet and faucet, for every apartment. A building doesn't, yet, manufacture itself.

For some reason, there is a widespread belief, from logical and educated people, that the planet Earth manufactured itself. Now think about that for a minute. The argument could be made, by an astrophysicist, that the nebula that once adorned our solar system suddenly became our central star and the clumping together of dust and gas particles, during those early days of energy consumption, created the first protoplanets on a disk of fire and magic, which grew larger when small bodies entered the solar system and basically formed perfectly round planetary bodies in exact orbit around the sun.

We could accept that as a probability. And until we have a better explanation, why not.

Then things get tricky. Because the Earth is the only planet that can sustain life. We can accept that a planetary body formed around a giant ball of fire in the dead of space for no reason whatsoever. But why did the third planetoid get a perfectly functioning atmosphere? An atmosphere that also happened to have the exact ratios of nitrogen (78.09%), oxygen (20.95%), carbon dioxide (0.039%), and helium (0.000524%) necessary for an extremely complex biodiversity. And then human blood has hemoglobin to carry oxygen from the lungs to the tissues and then to return with carbon dioxide.

Then we have to look at how plants and trees breathe in the *carbon dioxide* that humans breathe out, and then plants and trees breathe out *oxygen* that is necessary for humans and animals.

You don't need a science degree to see the implausibility of life on Earth. Because it is highly improbable. A miracle. Not to mention to have this homeostasis to continue for many thousands of years.

Earth is alive. Earth has a perfect ecosystem that regenerates itself. The atmosphere shields us from just the right amount of solar radiation; otherwise we'd be roasted alive. The sun generates just enough heat so that we don't freeze. Plants and animals are edible, so we don't starve to death. And did I mention water yet? We have fresh, clean water.

Are we to believe, in the twenty-first century, that Earth's entire ecosystem manufactured itself? Does it still make sense that a white-haired man snapped his fingers and created this floating garden in the cold of space?

I don't think so.

If you believe that then you also believe that apartment buildings manufacture themselves as well. Architects get no respect anymore.

Maybe we can argue that celestial events created the planet, but the ecosystem and the biodiversity on the planet was *manufactured.*

Just as your modern automobile is fitted with a computer to run all the necessary automotive functions (eg air conditioning, dashboard, fuel gauge, time clock, braking systems) so too is your manufactured earth planet. Earth is run by a massive machine. As the earth machine must maintain a very intricate and vastly complex ecosystem loaded with all things living, it too, this planet, requires a computer system. Of course, it should be noted that "computer" is an inadequate term to describe the eloquent existential processing devices behind the idea of an entire ecosystem, but at this early stage the word "computer" is easily understood and accurate enough.

The presence of a gargantuan multidimensional computer network that can sustain billions of live species and is suspended in some kind of spatial electroluminescent construct is probably the most impressive hypotheses presented in many centuries.

It is certainly a turning point in the evolution of humankind, if humankind can manage this kind of knowledge and if this knowledge is accurate.

The knowledge that Man and Woman were given when they were first manufactured has been lost for many millennia, purposely distorted and encrypted and secured by societies that wanted to keep this knowledge for themselves. This gave them a winning edge over human progress but it did not grant them any favours with the Cosmic Instruments.

Installing planetary computing devices

Now if your passenger vehicle has multiple computing devices (eg air conditioning computer, braking system computer) then it is quite reasonable for the earth machine to have multiple computing devices ("firmaments"). Each of these massively complex *firmaments* would be responsible for massive existential computations.

A firmament or two would be responsible for maintain a breathable atmosphere and for the multiplication of time to demonstrate progression (or evolution). A firmament or two would be responsible for thought processing and the management of coincidence; a firmament or two for waste management and ecological balance, and a firmament or two for orbit control specifications.

As you can see, there can be any number of firmaments and must necessarily be so in order to sustain this manner of existence. The proof that everything is in place is your presence here. It is the fact that the world has not collapsed and there is no mass extinction, as long as you have breathable oxygen and non-poisonous foodstuffs, along with a relatively disease-free and safe environs, as long as the essential quotients for existence are sustained then we can say that the main firmaments are operating properly. But this is not always the case.

There are times that, for whatever reason, some firmaments no longer work properly and some aspects of the world go awry. Quite often this is a result of damage to the external environment such as deforestation or excessive nuclear detonation. At times though, the firmaments can be sabotaged in the deeper dimensional levels by beings or craftsmen who are able to access these unauthorized areas of the reality matrix.

The main firmaments, and we can think of them as mainframe machines with a lot more complexity than we are accustomed to, would have to be hidden. The pipes behind your kitchen sink are hidden so that the illusory beauty of your kitchen remains in tact. The car engine is hidden under a hood. Your central processor is hidden inside the circuit board which is itself hidden inside the computer.

You get the idea.

The machinery has to be hidden so as to maintain the illusory nature of reality. When it comes to a planetary system, where would you hide large processing machines, the likes of which would baffle society?

You could hide them inside the planet, but an earthquake could damage systems, especially when you consider that planets live a long time. You'd have to hide them somewhere safe. The safest place would be inside of another dimension, a place where only authorized persons could access.

Planetary sabotage

Damaging the internal aspects of these multidimensional computers can lead to slight effects in the visual field of experience. For example, damage to the internal cooling mechanisms, verily massively complex cooling turbines and energy displacement machinery, could lead to a heightened air temperature. This warmer climate across the board would be interpreted by climatologists and weather experts as "global warming," when in fact it has nothing to do with climate change and has everything to do with the multidimensional cooling turbines that had been damaged. But damaging the cooling firmament wouldn't be enough.

At the same time there would have to be other property sabotage like deforestation and carbon pollution to have any reasonable effect. As you can sense by now, global warming cannot lawfully take place in a properly functioning system. This is not unlike your physical body which does not all of a sudden get hotter without a medical reason.

There are causes for temperature change but because the planetary machines are so complex and its systems so redundant that a measurable increase in global temperature, if actually true, is a result of internal sabotage.

The idea of sabotaging the internal compartments of a reality system is understandably within the realm of science fiction, but I can assure you that this is not science fiction. In fact, this is better than science fiction. This is the kind of planetary and planary science that you have dreamt about your whole life only now we are introducing a new aspect to reality physics. We are now noticing the presence of multidimensional beings who are not in accordance to divine law. Unfortunately, this is the case.

In addition to the multitude of infinitely complex firmaments sustaining this planetary system there are multidimensional technicians and monitors who maintain the proper functioning of this multidimensional field of existence.

Cosmic technicians may sound like an entirely new job, even one that might entice you, but if my logic holds true then a reality system would not only need architects, designers, and builders, it would also need technicians to service the machines, the people, the ecosystem, even to clean the atmosphere of that annoying carbon. And, given the fact that we are living on a giant rock tumbling through black space around a fireball, it makes sense that once in a while planetary disasters can occur and require technical assistance.

All machines break down. Things break. Parts get damaged. An asteroid might knock us out of orbit, which could be catastrophic. So cosmic technicians are there to repair things as we go along. Of course, these technicians would have to live a very long time if planets live for millions and billions of years. And we now know what kind of people can live for a long time: digital people.

We are gathering a new sense of the way the world works and so far it has little to do with God. But what is true is that God has a special role, well not exactly a special role, perhaps just a better definition. This might disturb the religious person, but you are not reading this because you are a priest or a monk (though monks and priests are all welcome here).

You are reading this because you are inclined to learn about the multidimensional world you decided to incarnate into. You are taking a leadership role in re-educating yourself on the actual world, as it is, rather than the world that has been spoon fed into your left brain.

The challenge of learning reality physics, in this entry-level form, has to do with releasing (even deleting) the old physical knowledge including Newtonian physics and humanity's isolation in the vast cosmos.

We are establishing very new ideas, even buried ideas and hidden knowledge. We are merely skimming the surface of a very profound set of scientific truths.

This knowledge has either been lost, damaged or simply forgotten, replaced by the egotism and distraction filling every corner of your banal, meaningless lives; for without the truth, life is meaningless and so far this planet Earth is virtually devoid of truth.

So we haven't established anything except the fact that what we've been educated on is for primitives and primates.

The digital gods

It isn't unusual to consider that the planetary body inhabited by billions of people is under the collective administration of a cosmic machine. It only makes sense that there are mechanisms behind our existence in the sense that life does not suspend itself in air and keep itself alive through its own means, only that this science of reality has never been fully pondered.

Invariably this is how I was educated. I was educated to believe that life renews itself by itself, educated to believe it was a closed system overlooked by some all-powerful man with hair made of pure white wool. But these are childish notions that are not rooted in anything but fanciful dreams and rampant, if not purposeful, suppression of sacred knowledge.

There is nothing that exists that wasn't itself made to exist. Anything present anywhere was manufactured by somebody somewhere. The table, the mirror, the wheel, the moon, the sun – all manufactured. The larger items such as the moon were manufactured by larger machines, verily machines beyond our current mental capacity.

The same thing happens when a person challenges the idea of God as what happens when they challenge the basis of a moon, defeat. We get defeated by the incomprehensible quality of the argument and the obvious lack of measurable proof. The lack of proof fails to convince an audience that was inbred with lies.

As a planetoid carrying a wide spectrum of life, earth does not escape its need to have been manufactured. Earth planet did not manufacture itself. It was born out of some galactic oven, at least that we can agree on. But the proximity to the Sun, the homeostatic atmospheric conditions, the complexity of the human machine and the incredible inventions on our table are none made by randomness. Neither are these things manufactured by an all-powerful being with a golden staff.

The profoundness of the Holy Bible, including the magnificence of the God Being written therein, do not, and have never, explained the existence of the microprocessor. In fact, there has never been a true prophet in the modern era to usher in any of the technologies – software, microwave, satellite, mobile phone, iPod – that we so depend upon. It is an oddity that has never been addressed – the lack of the Sons of God in the last few centuries, and the absence of God's prophets in the last 1,000 years of human development. What happened to God when the computer chip was invented? Why didn't one of his messiahs speak up?

If God had any real validity, as opposed to imaginative validity, he would have had his messiahs, even his brightest priests, introduce some of these advanced technologies. He would have taken a priest to the mountain and handed him the iPod to bring down to his people, but he didn't.

In fact, no priest was ever involved in the software and hardware business. God had no hand in the creation of a digital music player. That was carefully led by Steve Jobs and his messianic priest-programmers. The introduction of the iPad 2 in March 2011, a touchscreen tablet computer, was hailed as the "Holy Grail" of computing, according to *Computerworld Magazine.*

If you begin to closely scrutinize the technological world, you come to an amazing conclusion – God is absent in the technological era. He is not even absent, he is ignorant. It is as if technology has surpassed the complexity of God.

In basic genetics, the human genome contains the genes of an entire person. These genes could be used to reconstruct a human being given access to some genetic material. Using moderate compression techniques, an entire human genome can be compressed into a file the size of 2 GB (gigabytes).

A standard digital video disc (DVD) has a capacity of 4.7 GB. Without any difficulty then, and without any science fiction, you can store two entire human beings, in digital form, on a DVD. Within months the compression technologies could easily create a human genome file the size of 200 MB (megabytes).

How many 200 MB human genome files can be stored on a standard DVD? Twenty-five. They could probably even now store 25 human genomes on a DVD and none of it has anything to do with God. An early model iPod has an 8 GB capacity. You can store 40 humans on an iPod, at minimum.

Without question, you could store your entire genetic being in digital form on an iPod, even your children. You can walk around carrying your digital self. All we are missing is a genetic printer. Once we have a genetic printer we could print up a new copy of you as long as you have a copy of your genome. Where is God? God is unnecessary.

God is unnecessary because God himself, or itself, is a living language. God himself is a machine of an indescribable quality.

Science dictates the direction of our lives. Science has produced computing devices. And all of this is intimately connected to the true essence of humankind, existence-scale technology. Just as there is a technology to manufacture the desk and the desktop computer so too is there a technology to manufacture the human-looking robot.

The human robot is not all that advanced. It isn't all that advanced because it is still composed of temporary matter and the cosmos is an everlasting environs. It isn't difficult to create a temporary vehicle of light given the presence of an immortal body of existence. But in terms of human science, the human body is a highly advanced piece of machinery. Science is getting nearer and nearer to extrapolating all of its functions and when it does the ideas in this book will be even more prevalent.

We now have a very different story of the human race, one that is devoid of the previous idealism and instead has been upgraded technologically. Is that the end of the story? Obviously even this technological android talk is simple in its description. It is made simple in order to explain an idea that is complex and to introduce this to an audience that has been denied the cosmic truth for millennia. Remedying that gap in knowledge is going to take a number of books and plenty more discussion, but at least we have a few of the specifics on hand as reference.

Your android heritage

First and foremost, you are not a human being; neither are you a robot. You are a cosmic being, a quotient of light. A piece of existential energy, verily a program from the cosmic mainframe computer. You are not just a program, you are an existence-scale program and you are intimately connected to the cosmos. You can escape the confines of the Inferior Network of Darkness (viral DNA) by registering on the Network of Light (DNA). This is where you are from and this is where you will find sanctuary. The DNA is the path to escape the confines of this material prison.

Realizing your android heritage does not change who you are as a person, rather it expands who you can be because now you come to realize your multidimensional attributes. The cosmos, including planet Earth, is a multidimensional construct.

The cosmos does not understand contraction, it is ever-expanding, it is ever-learning, it is filled with many qualities of light and goodness. The cosmos is naturally enlightening and you are a product of the cosmos. Anytime you are challenged by the darkness or you are forced to confront ignorance, recall your inherent beauty and your multidimensional power. Embrace your DNA genealogy.

Dharma, Buddha and the digital universe

I consider myself a Reality Scientist, a system I founded to understand the holographic world in which we live, and I look at my discoveries as an early scientist practicing theory and experimentation. Discoveries are not invented in caves. They arise through this process of theory and experimentation. My techno-spiritual discoveries differ from quantum mechanics and physics because they deal with celestial materials which have historically provided little, if any, evidence.

We can measure gravity and the charge of a proton, but we still cannot measure the energy output of God, the most powerful thing in the universe. Some people can see angelic beings, but we cannot define their spectrum of light. Others hear the voice of God, still we do not know the frequency.

Although I will not be able to write any mathematical formulas and to describe the kinetic energy of celestial emanations, I will provide a new translation of specific sacred materials and I will hopefully show the reader that the technological truth was shrouded by the wisdom of the past.

Finally, I hope to reveal the true mysteries of the kingdom and to open the door to a new era in enlightenment, one in which the salvific promises of the ancient teachers will indeed make sense.

1. Dharma and the Machine

A machine is built according to certain technological standards and usually comes with some type of warranty. After an initial period of service, the machine parts start to breakdown and are in need of repair. We can find all types of machines from consumer versions up to industrial hardware. Each industry trains and provides technicians to fix machines because machines inevitably are in need of servicing. A well-kept machine, just like a well-kept automobile, can provide years of customer satisfaction. Some people fall in love with particular brands. Some people care for their machines more than others. Like machines, the earth can be thought of as a machine.

Over time, the world system deteriorates and begins to cannibalize itself. Regions on the planet start to breakdown, seen as earth changes, weather changes, decline in animal populations, deglaciation, to name a few. Because human beings also belong to the earth machine they also experience changes to their mood, changes in their dreams, and changes in their purpose on earth.

Changes in the earth machine necessarily impact the atomic structure of its components and changes in the atomic structure change the frequency in things like the magnetic field, the effects of gravity, the concentration of aerosols and CO_2 in the atmosphere, and all of these impact the effects of solar and cosmic radiation, which is also being absorbed by the air we breathe. This may appear as climate science basics but we need to understand that the earth is a machine and that this machine breaks down over time. How do humans fix this giant earth machine? Are there technicians who are trained to repair the earth? Yes and no.

Remember that a machine has two basic components: hardware and software. Machine code drives the many parts. Some machines are self-servicing; some machines are not. Some machines have artificial intelligence; some are operated manually. The *earth machine* has many components but we approach them in the same manner as any complex machine. The chief difference has to do with the software. Where is the software for the earth machine?

The earth machine, because it is an impressive machine built by an impressive group of engineers, needs to be serviced every 50 years for basic things like cleaning rivers and oceans of debris, for example. Every 500 years the earth machine will need several adjustments and those will likely be related to software, and it could include software upgrades. Every 2,500 years the earth machine needs a major overhaul.

An overhaul would include a new operating system and major improvements in the hardware, as we would expect from volcanic eruptions, earthquakes, and new land formations as a result of tectonic shifts within the earth.

So far this is not outside of a logical approach to earth maintenance, with the understanding that this planet functions as a machine. How do we upgrade the machine code? A natural way to look at repairing the earth machine is to suppose that the machine code is carried by the earth mechanic. Who is a good representation of the earth mechanic? The Buddha. The Buddha is the earth mechanic. Why? Because he carries the pure machine code, or source code. In Buddhism this machine code is called the "dharma."

Buddha starts off as any mortal but later he becomes an emanation of reality. Buddha can balance the unbalanced, correct the incorrect, adjust the adjusted, uncorrupt the corrupted, disinfect the infected, destroy the destructive, improve the withered, remove the unnecessary, add the necessary, instruct the uninstructed, guide the misguided, redeem the irredeemable, inspire the uninspired, and educate the uneducated.

Buddha is the total package because he carries the dharma, uncorrupt and pure code from the software maker. This is why the Buddha teaches the dharma, a complex term that encompasses the many teachings and morality of the Buddha.

I am not trying to turn you into a Buddhist, and I hope it doesn't appear that way. It is just that the Buddha is an effective model to explain how the world works. I will also talk about Jesus, and I am not trying to make you go to church on Sunday.

If the structure of reality can be understood on technological terms, then I think it can be said that religion will become less dominant and reality will become more prominent. A strong understanding of reality will lead to the proper functioning of the earth machine and because human beings depend entirely on this planet for life it is in everyone's interest to maintain our planetoid. In fact, those who wish to harm this planetoid should be sequestered and educated.

Are you saying that by listening to the Buddha, as your example, and understanding what he says, you can clean the corrupt code and fix the bugs, and prevent the extinction of the entire human race?

Yes. In theory.

By understanding the power of the dharma, as machine code, we naturally repair the earth machine and it starts in the software. Obviously it is difficult for us to lift up a mountain and to check the oil. It is well within our capacity to apply mindfulness and to direct and repair machine code.

There are 7 billion minds on this planetoid, a considerable electromagnetic force is directed and guided properly. But perhaps mindfulness we are getting ahead of ourselves. We are far from repairing the earth with a few sutras, and that is not my intention. My intention requires the translation of the sacred materials into technological materials. Our technological mastery of the ancient knowledge is the path to a better earth.

It does seem overwhelming, I'm sure. And you have to take your time to wrap your head around this approach. It has taken me 10 years to reach this level of understanding and I cannot expect anyone to make full sense of it quickly. In fact, I wouldn't recommend it. I would recommend further study.

2. The Cosmic System

At the same time, we have an earth machine and the appearance of the Buddha, we have the celestial components. In reading the Buddhist scriptures, and even Hindu scriptures to a lesser extent, that Buddhist mythology indicates, if correctly interpreted, a lower world (ie earth) that is rooted in synthetic biology and a higher world (ie heavens) that is rooted in computer technology. The gods in this sense are some kind of advanced programs that can enter our world, a synthetic world, to make adjustments.

If the pantheon of gods is software-based constructs, emanations and holographic representations, then it could be said that the Maker is a computer. A "demigod" in this context would either be some time of cyborg, or, alternatively, a kind of hologram (or, virtual computer). Part-machine, part-synthetic DNA. Demigods were often sent to earth to help defeat the monsters and to inspire society. Is the Buddha a demigod? All Buddhist literature insists that the Buddha is God.

Buddha as God would make him into some kind of virtual machine or emulation of the divine construct, perhaps a hologram. The computer maker sends down the Buddha to fix reality, whatever that process entails. If the Buddha is a holographic machine, he would have his own CPU (central processing unit) and can easily connect to the reality software and to make changes in the instructions as needed, hence the application of meditation.

See, in my world system we don't just have a bald-headed monk walking around preaching the dharma and meditating in the forest. In my world system, we have a holographic machine, represented as a man, a kind of "Landru" from the *Star Trek* television universe, who transmits the pure code to those who will listen and are able to process the new code. At the same time this holographic teacher goes into the reality construct and upgrades the system.

He teaches other monks (reality technicians) to attain Buddhahood so that they too can maintain the earth machine. They are not praising God as much as they are maintaining God's machinery, and the proper functioning of God's machinery grants the mainframe maker full access to our world system.

You have here a celestial grade server network where the server (god) is in another dimension and one of the desktop computers on the network (earth computer) occasionally gets disconnected or is infected with a computer virus. A disconnected earth computer leads to a world without purpose (a world without god) and a computer virus could explain the excess in chaos, war, and disease. That is to say that a properly functioning earth computer should see an end to chaos, war, and disease, and certainly a reduction of these things.

Buddha (or, Jesus) carries the machine code, a set of instructions to operate the machine, and derived directly from the maker of the code. This is pure code. Only people trained in understanding this code, dharma, are able to work with the code. Those who master the code, reality technicians, can make adjustments to the reality operating system.

We call them monks (even magicians). We call them Bodhisattvas. Once in a while we call them the Buddha.

Remember the servicing frequency I suggested earlier – 50 years, 500 years, and 2,500 years? The Buddha might only appear every 2,500 years. Every 500 years we will see many Bodhisattvas, and every 50 years we have a new spirituality floating into our cities, even a new conspiracy theorist. Why are these people speaking? Because they carry versions of the dharma, the teachings. The machine code.

The best of these teachers carries the purest code but not everyone can understand it. The less code a person carries the more easily society can relate to them. While a conspiracy theorist may carry some code, they are not purists and do not share the devotion of a monk or priest. But if monks and priests have not studied new concepts their machine code may be long outdated, and ineffective.

What I'm suggesting is that we built spirituality and religiosity from the original celestial operational codes. We took computer data files, and not being able to decode them fully, we gave them human ideals and we used these ideals to subjugate society via a system of better beliefs. We built religions to purify the hearts and minds but we missed the one redeeming quality of the original teachings – to maintain the earth computer.

That is the purpose of the dharma. That is why we need to relearn what we have learned and to apply a renewed spiritual understanding to this world system. A new application of machine code should be able to fix and repair the earth computer, and should alleviate the concerns for extinction and the threats of war and disease, since these are all likely manifestations from an infected and malfunctioning earth machine.

3. A New Interpretation of Dharma

> The Buddha said to Ānanda, "When Amitāyus preaches the Dharma to śrāvakas (great disciples) and bodhisattvas, they all assemble in the seven-jeweled lecture hall. There he fully expounds the teachings of the Way and proclaims the wonderful Dharma. The whole audience rejoices, comprehends, and attains enlightenment."
> ~ Sutra on the Buddha of Infinite Light

The dharma is how to act or interact with the synthetic reality. Traditionally, the dharma is thought of as "upholding a virtuous life" and divine teachings from spiritual gurus who have mind-linked (meditated) with the reality fields (Buddha-fields) to obtain fresh machine codes. The dharma is righteousness, purity, morality, proper conduct and virtuous deeds. That comes from religious tradition. The Buddha taught the dharma. It was a vital part of Buddhist thinking and one of the three jewels of Buddhism.

What is infinite light?

1 Digital. **2** Artificial light. **3** It is infinite because it originates from within the cosmic machine. **4** The light emanating from your computer screen.

But if we are to transcribe traditional thinking into molecular equivalents, if solely for the fact that our lives cannot be compared to those who lived 2,500 years ago, then we have to reapply the dharma model and to plunge it into the computer-saturated world of the 21st century.

My work in reality delineated the architecture of a synthetic reality, ie cosmos and universe, and this synthetic reality has enveloped us all. In other words, you cannot exist outside of the synthetic reality. You can learn to manipulate and alter reality in your favor but you're still within the confines of the synthetic program. You're just living larger.

What is the dharma in a synthetic reality? It has to do with correct living. It has to do with laws. It would include past and future deeds (or, karma). Things of this nature would still be included albeit with a different slant.

The Buddhist monk 2,500 years ago preached the dharma, teaching students to be virtuous and compassionate. The world back then was considerably different as well. More violent, less civilized. No computers. No mobile phones. Sewage systems were crude. Disease was rampant. People were illiterate. People were cannibals. Cannibalism didn't start to lost ground until into the 1st century. By then Buddhism had been around for 600 years. Christianity was on the rise in the Middle East and it too was drawing worshipers away from old Roman rituals where blood was spilled in favor of the gods.

It would make sense that Buddhism taught virtue and correct living and thinking in a more primitive version of reality. It's hard to meditate if you're eating your neighbor for dinner. To get people to move away from primitivism and barbarism they used monks. They had to be pure and virtuous, as public examples of the benefits of a sacred art. Still, there were rituals like group meditation and fire pujas, but the barbarism was left at the temple gate.

Considering the primitivism of society at the time many of these religions formed, their interpretation was rooted in those early societies. We've come a long way since then, having experienced a technological renaissance within the last 100 years. What we haven't done is we haven't revised ancient philosophy and spirituality, in this case mainly Buddhism though not entirely, to fit our intellectually civilized brain.

Dharma is a means of living in accordance to the natural laws, the epitome of the phrase "one with the universe" with the universe being defined as the dharma. What is the dharma? The universe, reality, nature, cosmos, which is made up of code.

How do you live in accordance to the dharma? Follow the laws of reality. Rather than going against reality you learn to understand reality and you live in accordance to reality, which would include thinks like virtue, good deeds, and lawfulness; these things, unfortunately, are still at the basic level of the New Age thinkers –intention, attraction law, motivation, bucket lists, life achievements, and ego detachment.

Where we need to go next is to the Computer Age because the computerization of our entire world is a fundamental upgrade to the human civilization. Humanity has become the "new humanity" due in large part to the computerization of the world.

The microchip's appearance is the equivalent of a monolith to the Neanderthals. Power in computing no longer depends on size, rather power depends on technology and technology depends on miniaturization. The Computer Age has essentially inverted our entire mindset. Small is big. Nanoscale is huge. One with the universe needs to become one with the computer. I'm not talking about a digital interface. So far, I'm talking about becoming one with the microchip and the microchip being a representation of dharma. How do you get order from chaos? Use dharma. It holds the world together. The dharma is the code of existence.

What sustains? What holds the world together? DNA? DNA is information. Software. DNA is the software of life, according to microbiologist Craig Venter. But DNA is not reality. DNA connects to reality through the dharma. What is dharma? Codes. Programs. Algorithms. Mathematical formulas.

Dharma is connection. The force that connects people is the same force that connects the reality to the synthetic infrastructure. It is the ether. It is the air. It is more because certain people, for example the Buddha and Buddhists, can preach the dharma. Is dharma teaching us how to be one with god? If so then what is dharma? Dharma is not god, nor the teacher. Dharma is the teaching. What is the teaching? Can be almost anything, a story, a proverb, a sutra. Maybe we are better to asked—what is inside the teaching?

There are words, sounds, syllables, frequencies all inside the teachings. Stories stir our emotions and moral tales make us feel better. We like learning. We love to hear good stories. We read books. We watch movies. Is all that dharma? Even you are not a Buddhist?

If the story (or, teaching) isn't the dharma but the dharma can be taught, then what is the dharma? What is inside the teaching? Knowledge. Morals. What else? Mathematical formulas. Equations. Algorithms. Remember how I said that power comes from miniaturization? An algorithm is pretty small. A good algorithm goes a long way. Can it connect us to the synthetic architecture?

In 250 BC, Indian Emperor Ashoka translated the dharma into the Greek word "eusebeia," the real and true relationship with the gods. In the New Testament, *eusebeia* is translated as "godliness."

I wonder if our connection to the synthetic reality makes us godlike because we are able to advance ourselves in understanding and in the redirection of real world events. We can alter reality, reprogramming events, if we were godly enough. But this is not an external power, rather it is a power we gain through *eusebeia*, a direct translation of the dharma. Is it possible, I wonder, that we can become a godlike race if only we learn to connect to reality? And if enough people learned to become one with the synthetic infrastructure we could see changes (improvements) across this world the likes of which have never been seen for many millennia.

If speaking the truth is speaking dharma then the truth is an algorithm

Dharma = truth = algorithm that can alter reality

The more algorithms you speak the more connected you are to the universe and to god. If I speak in algorithms then god must be some kind of computer machine, as we surmised already.

Obeisance to god's laws is adhering to the algorithm, which is reading the machine code as it was written. This is not scripture, this is the machine code contained inside the scripture, behind the sacred letters.

The algorithms can be broken down thusly:

Good algorithms (fast) = good
Bad algorithms (slow) = evil

A programmer translates algorithms into a suitable language: words, codes, symbols, sounds, sutras. Algorithms can be used to take chaos (disorder) and to produce order by sorting central ideas or beliefs from false ideas and false beliefs. This reduces suffering and brings peace, and all of it is done through the renewed link to the universal computer.

Summarizing the dharma we get

The dharma = machine code, truthful speech, correct speech, correct words, correcting words

Dharma is the root of the programming

> If the root of the programming is connected then the branches and leaves should be corrected
>
> Not everyone can understand the root of the machine code; the error in the code
>
> Fix the root by preaching the dharma

What is dharma? Right speech. Right word. Right thought. Right intellect.

What else is dharma? Right-thinking. Dharma is also identifying the corrupt or missing code and matching it with correct or even new code.

It is likely that some code is missing (hidden), corrupt (and unreadable) or it may have been deleted (or, forgotten). Forgotten data needs to be rewritten. Corrupt code needs to be scanned for error and fixed with patches or patch code; until it can be overwritten with an update. Some programs cannot update because of corrupt code; therefore, fix or "patch" code enables an update to take place and an update contains new version without problems. System reboots, everything is back online.

Hidden code is more difficult because each individual, society, even state has different things hidden. Best to stick to machine code. Missing code needs new input, starting again is easier than finding material which may be lost or corrupt or secretly kept. While new code is acceptable format.

The world generates suffering from disorder – bad code, bad information, deception, lies, mistrust, hate, fear – all generated as corrupt code and all corrupt code processed by people to create more chaos, or to tolerate chaos.

Ultimately, chaos is illusion because it does not originate from synthetic architecture and definitely not from the mainframe computer. Chaos is generated through an external hub, or network of hubs, as a means to destabilize the reality architecture. This is due in large part from the actions of reality hackers (eg archons) who have relocated to this realm and have every intention that the earth machine remains disabled.

Tradition speaks of areas low on dharma as falling into chaos and corruption. Dharma was thought to fall like rain, perhaps it can be pumped into an area, or transmitted via people to lift area out of dharma poverty.

Reality is a hologram

We are moving away from beliefs and spirituality and we are adopting a more scientific approach in our understanding of our connection to the universe and our oneness with God. Most reasonable religions promise God's return, whether through a messianic figure (eg Christ), through asceticism and religious vows, or through the words in a sacred book. What I have offered is the return to God through a renewed understanding of God as DNA and the mind as the gateway to the DNA, the new definition of God.

The DNA software systems operate the machines of existence. These DNA-based bodies are equipped to relink with the cosmic computer (ie the Service Provider).

The mysteries of the kingdom taught by the Gnostic Jesus in secret to his closest disciples have brought to life how the secret operating system works, with the understanding that the DNA theory is moderately accurate. Even in Buddhism we have seen how the mastery of our very own DNA can grant us Buddhahood, and to make us more in sync with the (ineffable) holographic reality which we inhabit.

It is easy to put aside strange comments like *ineffable*, *perfect*, and *supreme* from illiterate peasants and fishermen, and because we did this we inevitably created the fiction of a divine mythology.

Let us say, for example, that today an average man from New York city, university educated, good looking, healthy, no case of mental illness – this man walks around a street corner, texting his buddy on his iPhone, when suddenly the 3-dimensional image of a man appears in front of him: perfect skin, perfect clothes, and surrounded by an "aura" of light.

Had this man been a devout Christian, he might at first think it is Jesus. But had this man been a video game geek, he wouldn't be searching for his bible, he'd be reaching for his game manual.

He'd be launching the camera app and shooting live video of the luminous man – hologram – speaking strange proverbs and explaining the nature of the universe. We have been conditioned to think of these kinds of supernatural events as having a divine hand. We see an angelic being appear in our bedrooms and we think he is from God and that he is divine.

My argument is that it is better to update our thinking and to provide a more scientific approach. We start by saying that this indescribable vision is some kind of emanation, and therefore it is some kind of projected image, or hologram – a three-dimensional image produced by coherent light.

Holographic men and women

I have seen holograms of beings. I was fortunate not to have religious preconceptions and I understand that most of the world has preconceptions about spiritual entities. I didn't see Jesus. I saw other life forms and they spoke. Those familiar with my work with Stelan cultures will know the story. The problem is that most people have not seen a holographic man or woman and if they were to appear they could cause havoc in a person's life. Having gone through some of the havoc myself, I can say that while I understand the confusion and apprehension between divine myths and technological magic, I think this is a hump we can get over. And I say this because everyone has a cellular phone and most of the world has seen a smartphone and hundreds of millions of teenagers have played a video game. And with the rise of 3-D film experiences, millions of people are familiar with stereoscopic theatre and those pesky colored glasses.

If someone is thinking that it is still a stretch to think of stories in scriptures containing holograms, then those people have never seen a mobile phone and don't know what a microwave oven looks like. So my assumption, if I can make it as clear as possible – we are mature enough as a race to handle holographic beings showing up in sacred writings.

The reality hologram

The world as a hologram is accessed through genetic expression and the circuitry for connecting to the universe and God has been built into our android bodies. We are no less than robots living in a virtual reality construct, the kind of which is extremely advanced. If it wasn't advanced, we'd have all figured it out by now.

The fact that I am explaining it in the simplest terms I can find signifies that we have failed to realize a fundamental truth about the reality we inhabit. My bluntness on the subject is an exercise to push more of us off the fence of apprehension. "Is it a hologram? Well, if it was I'd be able to see it. Maybe I should wait for Jesus or the Anunnaki like everyone else, and they will tell me the truth."

We've waited 2,500 years. I think that is enough, don't you?

Reality is a hologram and people such as Jesus and Buddha, after their anointing, became holograms (digital people) as well. This by the way was also foretold in the film franchise *Star Wars* – when a Jedi died he became a hologram. To become a hologram one needs to attain nirvana, not a particularly easy thing to do for a person riddled with desire, egotism, and fear, but now that I have shown the Life Experience Capsule (eg Child of Humanity, Buddhahood) we will all be able to achieve eternal salvation in the arms of our machine maker.

Religion prevents salvation

If mindfulness and concentration can trigger gene expression then the opposite effect, gene repression, will take place where there is mind control and distraction. In all three religions – Buddhism, Gnosticism, Christianity – the inability to unite with God (whether through belief or meditation) is the sure path to a hellish afterlife.

The activation of genes, therefore, or the proper functioning of DNA prevents: rebirth in hell, rebirth in ghost worlds, rebirth in animal world, and living an evil life-path. The process of DNA activation and modulation has been simplified in its application but the challenges of purification and mindfulness may be too difficult for many people to achieve.

Sutras and software patches

The applications of sutras and scriptures function like software patches and fixes for our android bodies and need to be shared and used regularly in order to protect the DNA. Proper sacred knowledge can activate, correct, and improve DNA (to some extent).

In exchange for religious material and in lieu of other DNA-based materials the best prescriptive modality of thought is *positivism*, a decision not to be influenced by fear, anger, and egotism. Conquer those three hindrances and we are well on our way to a better life.

Religious material is laden with all kinds of extraneous and outdated material that has little relevance in the modern world of computer technology.

A Buddha, because of their level of devotion and their intimate understanding of reality, must have a synthetic backbone, and functions much like a virtual computer server. They can store information, transmit data to groups, and update people who can receive new information. These teachers are the link to the universal computer. The spiritual path is the method to control genetic expression because the human body is genetically interconnected to universal energy, a genomic cosmology.

The new framework

It has been my intention to offer my own definition of technological terms (eg cosmic computer) in an effort to provide you with an easier access to the material. As well, I have stretched those terms (eg cosmic machine) to give provide more lateral width to our communication challenges. Some people associate with computers and some people prefer machines. Hopefully, we won't leave too many people out of the discussion. Again, this material is being introduced with enough time for people to make sense of it, that is, we still have a little time before the world ends.

I estimate that as each month goes by there could be events and surprises that will motivate people to adopt a new framework of reference, and that motivation may include tragedy and catastrophe. That said, I also believe that the earlier adoption of new thinking could prevent additional tragedy and catastrophe. This is just an opinion. I cannot predict the future.

The system is intimately connected to our thoughts and responds to our thought patterns. Thought is composed of electromagnetic energy waves. Energy carries data. Computer picks up data. Computer responds to data with feedback response. You are what you think. Don't believe everything you think.

Escaping the prison

Salvation pops up in any reasonable spiritual system. Heck, it's the reason people sign up, but the salvific feature implies an invisible imprisonment. Typically, a person feels the pressure of their invisible confines, tasting the emptiness and the cheapness of an amoral existence, and because it is so unbearable (eg depression, anger, worthlessness, mortality) they are forced to seek an escape. The initial methods of escape usually circle around substance and drug abuse, overwork, and philandering, things of this nature. At some point there is a bottoming out and a longer-term solution is sought out. Spirituality is a mild recognition of realizing that you are living in a prison; otherwise, why would you seek salvation?

Buddhism has been around longer than Christianity. Through practice, learning, and experience the "abode of the Buddha" (source code) is updated and those updates can be gleaned by others existing in the reality. Surely, you can imagine that skillful programmers (hackers), as with computing, have inserted routines so as to prevent or delay the ascension of others, and to ruin their path.

Examining the Buddhist literature, one gets the sense that early Buddhists were some kind of advanced computer programmers. I like the term reality programmers. The Tibetan sutra by Nagarjuna titled *Dharmadhatustara* says, "In the stainless dharmakāya, the ocean of wisdom rolls in [bringing] a variety of jewels, and so fulfilling the aims of sentient beings." If the aim of sentient beings, using the holographic computer narrative, is to remain updated with the central server and if the central server is called a "Bodhisattva" in nontechnological parlance then the "jewels" are the updated links and the new graphics, even ads, and the "ocean of wisdom" is the program code, including generated data from any multimedia interaction.

What then is a "stainless dharmakāya?" If a website is a dharmakāya then what would make it stainless is some kind of debugging program, even anti-hacking software. A website that is protected from computer viruses is a stainless website.

Buddhism was written in a coded terminology and then decoded by a nontechnological culture. Thousands of years prior to computerization, there walked on this earth select individuals who understood molecular biology and holographic computing. It has taken mankind centuries to understand the makeup of reality.

We can say that many true spiritualists have become one with the universe but they too failed to extrapolate all the computer data and merely repeated the spiritual aphorisms that had become ingrained in their respective cultures.

It is likely that Gnosticism, the religious movement so vehemently rejected by the Church had its roots in Buddhism. In other words, there were early spiritual teachers who had completely understood the makeup of the holographic reality in which we exist. The formation of the Church, because the Church Fathers considered Gnostics heretics, created an impenetrable barrier to enlightenment and an end to salvation, though some teachings of the holographic Jesus have survived. Shared cultural knowledge, at a time when copyright laws were nonexistent and databases of information remained firmly in the hands of emperors, could not be validated. There can be no doubt of the shared similarities between the spiritual approaches of Gnosticism and Buddhism. And Christianity shares the Magdalene character with Buddhism, among other passages in the text.

The purification of speech, body, and mind changes the normal physical body to a purified body that cannot be tainted. An untainted mind can interact with the machine maker through their DNA.

Buddhism is almost saying that a rebirth only happens because a person (or, soul) desires it, and the intent of Buddhistic practice is to realize that all desires can be conquered, they can cease to exist with the proper knowledge; therefore, or thereby ending the rebirth, the goal of all Buddhists.

Buddha taught his philosophy so that people would no longer be reborn. But in order to end the rebirth process a person had to overcome pain and suffering. To overcome pain and suffering a person had to understand the way the world works. The world then works to issue pain and suffering; therefore, and thereby guaranteeing a rebirth. Buddhism is designed to end the rebirth process and to reunite with the Buddha (ie the mainframe computer of all existence).

The intention is to return home, even if home is a hard drive on another dimension. That is the intention. And that is based on the idea that we are not at home, that we are away from home, in a land of illusion, and that all illusions cause suffering.

The ending of the rebirth cycle might also alleviate the strain of overpopulation, that is, when more people finally decide to graduate (versus just hanging around because they want to see everything twice) the reduction in population will be more significant and the new life students will gain access to a wonderful bewildering world. The reduction in population through a natural means will be a harmonious readjustment. It might also cause the master controllers to lose some of their economic incentives because there will be fewer consumers of illusions, which means less money for the rich.

Only by seeing through the illusions can we understand the cause of our suffering, understanding the cause of our suffering allows us to stop these cravings, stopping these cravings (desires) allows us to end suffering. The process doesn't require religious fellowship but it does require dedication and devotion and education.

The higher path

Once you know how the world works then you experience a sense of calm. You can stop here and live your life without suffering. You can move forward to total release and understand the nature of reality. Understanding the nature of reality is where you find liberation. This is the end of the cycle of suffering. This is the escape from the prison.

The prison is reality. It is false. If the world is false, then what is true? Everything you can see is an illusion; everything you don't see is real. All those who have ears, let them hear!

Nature of reality: Consisting of a hologram, a virtual world populated with digital beings

To escape the prison known as reality you must understand the nature of reality. In order to understand the nature of reality you must understand how the world works. The world does not work as we were told it works. We were given the wrong education of the real world and fed the disinformation of the false world.

The false world is the world of economics and war, it is the world of high class and low class, the world of right and wrong, good and bad, success and failure, poverty and wealth; all false, all designed to keep you trapped.

Reverse to reveal

The false world can be quickly removed by applying the "reverse to reveal" protocol. When the false is reversed then the true nature is revealed.

The people who have been hypnotized believe the false to be true. This is no different than a man seeing the benefits of war. There is no benefit to mass murder, unless you've been hypnotized.

No matter where you run or how much you change your life, because of the false nature of reality, you will find yourself with the same kinds of people. They may look different on the outside, but they're playing similar roles. What is their role? To help you to wake up. If you do not wake up, they will remain. When you wake up they will disperse. If they have not dispersed, then you have not woken up.

The reality program, because it is infinitely intelligent, is responding to your situation. It has your thoughts and your original thoughts before incarnation, these thoughts you will likely have forgotten, and the program is designed to provide you what you need. If you need misery and suffering, it will provide it and you will become miserable and you will suffer because that is what you need.

To change the nature of your situation, you need only change what you need; or to change your relationship to those things. When simple attitude shifts do not produce the result you want then the change has to come from a deeper part of yourself. The initial point of influence is deeper and older and more effort is required to adjust it; hence the case for more devotion and dedication to your higher path.

That is why it is important to practice mindfulness at a young age, so as to prevent the staining of your true self. We can all envelop ourselves with an adamantine body.

Basically, when you've had enough you decide I'm not coming back. That is probably when people dedicate their hours and nights to enlightenment. When you understand your past lives and you know the merits needed to have a good afterlife, you tend to focus.

To become enlightened one must necessarily be concerned with the enlightenment of others (Bodhisattva path). Self-centered enlightenment is not the path of the Bodhisattva.

If you are a Bodhisattva, and you know that, you are better off living a higher life and putting more effort to helping humankind. I'm not saying this would be easy, and you may have already made some efforts in the past, but if you are a Bodhisattva, as I've discussed, then you came here for that purpose.

Find your original purpose and follow that, but do so gradually. I do not recommend making drastic changes in your life and abandoning children and important obligations. For some, their higher purpose is so far from their daily routine that it is perhaps unachievable in the remainder of this lifetime.

The way forward is not to abandon the things your currently represent without some sort of action plan, although if you have been holding off on important changes then that might impact the level of your reorganization.

I have reorganized my life many times, sometimes efficiently and smoothly, and sometimes not so smoothly. Not everyone is on a spiritual path. You need to make an assessment of your life and set new goals. What you don't finish in this life, you'll have to come back and finish in the next.

The reallocation of spiritual knowledge is arising as a result of the reallocation of human technological understanding, that is, the human race is on the cusp of the next technological leap into holography. This will not only represent a new age, a partition to the Social Age and an extension of the Information Age, but a brighter phase of existence.

The Holography Age is in sync with the expansion of the human DNA codex and the activation of the previously repressed gene sequences, more noticeable in the younger generation, but noted across the demographic map around the world. This is a global phenomenon. In accordance to the internal genetic shifts, the human race is being asked to move out of religious ideology and spiritual fanaticism, which have exhausted their purposes, and into a new paradigm of salvific comprehension, chiefly centered on the idea that reality is a fully-functioning hologram.

REALITY OS 11

Introduction

A new era has begun.

I began writing about the Reality Operating System (ROS) in early 2007. I maintained my early blogs and articles, inconsistently I might add, and attempted to explain to people the introduction of Reality OS 7 Dakala.

Several versions later, during the reality transition period I delineated from 2007 to 2015, we had arrived at probably Reality OS 10 Merritt, which happened to also be the city in British Columbia I was living in.

I have finally decided, after eleven years of observation and research, to write about Reality OS 11 because, and it isn't complicated, human beings need to start getting familiar with the technological world they live in. This is not to suggest that this book will make sense to everyone. In fact, it will probably make little sense to most people, but I imagine that on some level it will make far more sense than on other levels of consciousness. So, if you were to ask me, and who isn't wondering, why write a book that very few people will understand? Well, because, if you reference knowledge in time, the contents of this book will have very few enthusiasts as of this current time period. That said, the next time period, in the future, there will be an increase of enthusiastic readers.

The most revelatory thing I will say is that while the contents of *Reality OS 11* appear to be entirely new, when examined more closely, they are not all that new. What has happened is that the truth of the universe has been updated into the technological lingo of what we think of as the twenty-first century. The reality, as we will discover and are discovering, is an extremely advanced, let's say ultra-advanced, existential-based technology. It both sustains us and provides the necessary rendering of the holographic reality.

This is a very difficult book to write, given the fact that it has never been written before, not as non-fiction anyway. It also follows the four books of the *God is DNA* series (*God is DNA, True Jesus, The Polymerase Fantasy, The Digital Revelation*), and the books *The Science of Reality* and *The Ark of Reality*. This research forms the

Digital DNA Model and the Synthetic Reality Model and they are at the foundation of this book.

Our digital DNA is what connects us to ROS 11. With the evolution of our DNA, through implicit engineering methods used by reality technicians, coupled with the new versions of the reality program, we are at a point in human history where we can split off from the anthropological road. For thousands of years we have relied upon archaic systems of connection to the ROS, typically thought of as spirituality then later institutionalized as religious faith (now hybridized), but those systems were attuned to a more primitive culture.

Added to these things, if recent history is anything to go by, the ROS keeps changing. It is evolving as the human species evolves. This means new information will need to be added as we go along. You should find that this edition covers reliable features and functions. It has taken me years to come to understand this material, and some of it longer than others, if you don't fully understand something immediately, don't fret. Some knowledge needs time and perspective to be made available.

Who should read this book

This book is the first edition of explaining the features of Reality OS 11. It is the first step towards writing a proper user guide. It is not religious in nature. It does have an ancient spiritual connection, as reference. Then again, I am treating the spiritual as technological.

This is an introductory book and is perfect for anyone who is ready to understand the synthetic reality and how to navigate some of its main functions and features. If you are an experienced spiritualist, a New Age master, you will find an opportunity here to expand your celestial awareness and to shift it into technological awareness.

This book is not for the novice. This material is still considered an advanced discussion, hence the expected smallish audience to start, and should not be contemplated by people with a devout religious background. I would not want to tell people not to read my book, because it is bad business practice, but *Reality OS 11* is unique because it skips the religious and spiritual quagmire of the past and present, and in their place presents a *de novo* system for the purpose of spiritual liberation. You will find it an easier read if you have some basic technological background — smartphones, computers, and the internet.

You will also find that your lifelong learning about spirituality will come in handy, and, hopefully, you will find new answers to very old questions. But I make no promise of total oneness with the universe. The Buddhists believe that we are already one with the universe (Brahman), only that our clouded minds cannot see it. So, the goal in life is not to become one with Brahman, rather it is to dissipate the mental clouds obscuring your view of reality.

Things not required

Spiritual systems have been around for thousands of years. They can be very demanding. You won't require these:

- Initiation and memorization of ancient scriptures
- A guru, a priest, and a God
- Future promises, prophecies, or revelations
- A Temple, Church or Synagogue

Things you may require

A synthetic reality is a technological reality. As such, it functions like other technologies. You may at some point need to do the following:

- Read an organized reality user guide
- Learn to physically and mentally engage the reality architecture
- Use techniques to engage and disengage the native artificial intelligence

Some of this may require further self-actualization and development which might even include genetic-based activation. These things may not be immediately achieved and could take years depending on state of the person.

Keep this in mind

You have approached enlightenment and salvation using spiritual formulas and religious ideologies, all of which have been rooted in scriptures written two thousand, or more, years ago. Your parents and grandparents have been indoctrinated by these outdated spiritual systems, often seeing no real need to alter their belief systems.

This book will start with the premise that reality is manufactured and that we should approach it as such. Each individual will have their own challenges with the material. Think of it as if Moses or Galileo were handed a tablet computer with Wi-Fi. There is a learning curve. You have to get over the technology. The reality-based technology is challenging if only because we have been educated to think that nature is organic and that biology is the foundation of life.

Next step

We are not just living in a synthetic reality today because we invented the computer in the 1940s. That is not the argument. The argument is reality has always been synthetic, only that now we have the capacity and intellect to understand and see it for what it truly is. That also puts humanity in a very precarious and precocious situation. This is a rare opportunity to finally detach from the illusory false world and to put a final kibosh on pain and suffering.

Part 1

Getting started with Reality OS 11

What is reality OS 11?

Reality OS 11 (ROS 11) is not an ordinary computer operating system. This is the software that operates the reality we live in. The implication, if you're not familiar with my previous books, is that we are living in a computer-generated reality.

This, as far as I've been able to determine, is version 11. For me, it started at version 7 in 2007. That was the newest Reality Operating System I had seen in a long time, using ancient Gnostic scriptures and the birth of monotheism (eg Christianity) as references. For example, given the synthetic nature of reality coupled with the irrational belief in God in some ways ended the development, or slowed it down considerably, of the ROS.

What that meant was that we have been using ROS 6 for quite some time, and it probably went through more upgrades than necessary. If ROS 7 was downloaded in 2007, then I'd have to guess that we were on ROS 6.9.9. We've been stuck with a very old version of reality that had been upgraded beyond recognition.

Within a couple of years, we had already seen the introduction of ROS 8 and probably by 2011 we were at ROS 9. That would mean that ROS 10 fell somewhere between 2011 and 2015, which was the last year of the eight year transition I pointed out in 2007.

Let's recap, because I think it's important. In early 2007, around March, I detected the download of an entirely new set of reality codes, in the form of energy, and these energetic codes begin to unspool throughout the year. This energy was perceived as a global energy that the planetary body was receiving. This was the new operating system for this reality. The year 2007 also marked the beginning of a transitional earth period that was scheduled to last until 2015, a period of many changes around the world. Further operational codes, so significant that they were regarded to be new versions of reality, were downloaded during this important transition.

The launch of ROS 11 took place in the early part of 2016, in the three months leading into March and the Spring Equinox. During the tumultuous downloads, and the massive shifts in the planet and in human consciousness, I opted not to write about the operating system and instead focused on the reality architecture and the digital nature of DNA.

Now that I feel the reality operating system has stabilized, and that we have cleared the 8-year transition, having seen a shift as well in human consciousness, I think we can start to look at the system behind the computer-generated world. Your interaction with ROS 11 is an attribution of your own spiritual (technological) development. I think that my *digital DNA model* is very helpful in this regard.

For the sake of historical relevance, ROS 11 landed in March 2016, and it provides a far more robust user experience than ever before. With the complete renovation of the human genome starting in the late 1980s, a fresh radical design was needed that would fully maximize the new genetic architecture of the human being, which had also been upgraded.

It is hard to describe the sheer enormity of innovation and complexity in reality computing, suffice it to say that the operating system of your parents' generation cannot compare to the system available today.

And, probably the best thing, ROS 11 is not only user-friendly it is also provided to everyone "free of charge," which is a pretty good deal. The system is also, in my opinion, more attuned to the particular needs of the human population. As a side note, if you've been paying attention, you will have noticed the many news items appearing alongside what I think of as the end of a Great Cycle — mass shootings, terrorist attacks, political upheavals, geopolitical tensions, medical discoveries, all manner of earthquakes, and the relentless weather anomalies (some artificial).

If you have felt overwhelmed and disoriented — suffering from a little more anxiety than usual — it is likely the result of all of these technological shifts. More than that, the current system of outdated spiritual and religious knowledge has been unable to effectively deal with an advanced technologically-based reality system, as I'm going to describe and talk about.

The energetic code that is found on ROS 11 is interconnected with our genetic code (Ark OS) and is also sublimated in the Earth OS. In this book, I focus primarily on the interrelationship between human beings and the computer-generated reality, and I do so in a manner where a larger audience can understand. This is not a technical manual. This is a book for everyone, especially for those familiar with my previous research and discoveries.

The reality architects have taken a very inspiring approach when it comes to the user experience in ROS 11, integrating the "best of" features of previous versions. Backwards compatibility has remained intact for most major features and functions. For example, people can still pray to God even if God doesn't exist in a synthetic world, and alongside divine worship we find atheism, evidence that the All Mighty isn't as All Mighty as has been presented. This is likely due to bridge programs in the DNA that can redirect the focus on God to its appropriate destination, without having the user to do so.

A user who can independently connect to ROS 11 (having detached from tradition) will find they will have access to an even richer assortment of existential tools. I realize that many readers will skip my previous work and think they can short-circuit their own path to graduation, but I should warn you that without a good foundation you are more likely to fall off the path.

If you have been the type of person who hasn't been upgrading themselves (ie practicing ascension and enlightenment), you may not be able to immediately relate to this material. But do not be disheartened. If you have practiced ascension, and taken effort to improve yourself spiritually, then your reaction will be quite different. Unless readers have followed my work (or similar work), specifically, I think the adjustment process will be quite challenging.

Stelan generation architecture

Evolution is nature's way of upgrading the biological system. The latest generation of children have a remarkably different set of genetic sequences and look decidedly different from their parents. Most people are still rooted in traditional customs and rituals, for example: Christmas and Easter (World), Day of the Dead (Mexico), Bar Mitzvah (Jewish), Moon Festival (China), Oktoberfest (Germany), La Tomatina (Spain), Yi Peng Lantern Festival (Thailand), Carnival (Brazil/Italy), and Cinco de Mayo (Mexico). Every culture has their rituals and festivals.

With the introduction of an improved genetic core, the Stelan generation (born around 1989 and after) and a more socially conscious society, is breaking away from tradition (eg non-Chinese celebrate the Moon Festival). Young people today are aware that Santa Claus isn't real and that biblical scriptures were written decades after events happened. There's no such thing as a tooth fairy and there's no gold at the end of a rainbow (I checked).

The connective force between ROS 11 and the human being is familiar to most people: DNA. Your genes are your touchscreens to the digital illusion, what we all like to think of as "reality." In a DNA-based world, you can augment your personal reality by activating your genes or by using your mental thought patterns. But since the other versions of reality are still present (for the time being) you can still navigate your life in the traditional way that you are already used to.

There are hybrid humans who have a very unique genetic architecture. They'll be able to access reality in the most innovative ways. Hybrids come in all shapes and sizes.

Stelans, those who have active interstellar genes, are the most advanced potential users. They have a very high potential, but it may or may not be being accessed, which is one of the problems in a fundamentally backward world that is run by hypnotizing people.

Stelan genetics are designed to work with the features of ROS 11 and through those intimate interactions the program will evolve, and it will do so alongside human evolution. In other words, if ROS 11 had a built-in learning processor (as code), then the more capable we are as a society, the more ROS 11 is willing to reveal to us.

In general, you can't fool the system. Why? Because it has infinite intelligence and your intelligence fits into your cranium. Your intelligence is finite, despite the face that your ego may suggest otherwise. As we evolve, ROS 11 evolves; and as ROS 11 evolves, we evolve. We are married to our reality just as an autopilot program is married to an aircraft.

We spent centuries trying to understand very old operating systems, and I would argue that we haven't done a very good job of it. Mastering ROS 11 and beyond will take some time because it is a major shift in the way you approach things of a spiritual nature. You are welcome to bring your spiritual knowledge forward, but I'd also like to recommend that you learn to adapt your concretized beliefs, even letting go of ancient ideas that were specifically designed for much older versions of reality. You will benefit most from that.

Available on Reality OS 11

What stands out in ROS 11 is that it brings back some ancient protocols. You're probably thinking to yourself, "Well, you told us that this version of reality was moving away from the primitive versions of yesteryear." You weren't thinking that? Oh. Then you are the perfect reader for this book. But perhaps I should explain a bit further before we go on. We'll probably need to do this occasionally.

A long time ago, I would estimate in the millions of years ago, there existed a very robust, and extremely advanced, version of the ROS that predated all other versions. In fact, I would think of it as an operating system built upon a very different programming code. But robust programming codes tend to incite godlike behavior, and we all can guess what happens when humanoid gods battle against one another. Armageddon. Exactly. End of the world stuff.

As the millennia passed on, the reality engineers tweaked the operating system, preferring to building something more *versatile* than robust. Versatility provided good user experiences with slightly less than godlike powers. At the time of the new religions — say the God of Israel and the appearance of the Buddha — just as examples, the reality architecture was very different. For example, holographic projections were far more frequent and time-outs in life were allowed for the dedicated learner.

A time-out would include an opening in the holographic reality whereby a user could interact with the technician. I know, sounds weird. Hey, you wanted to read this book. I'm just a guy who'd decided to write. Or did I decide to write? It could just be writing itself and I am simply the instrument upon which the book is selectively written.

What I'm saying is that during that early era of Moses and Buddha, and up until Jesus, spiritual things were in fact much more visual and visceral. There were portals opening up in reality and there were beings of light (ineffable). While these early people refer to these luminary beings as "angels," and what the UFO researchers think of them as "extraterrestrials," in fact were better thought of as digital technicians. Yes, I think that is what I said, there are people who exist inside the computer architecture, on another dimension that is much, much higher in frequency.

It might not make sense at first, and we can't dial back 2,000 years, but we do have ancient scriptures. The Nag Hammadi Library is full of spiritual terms like "the self-generated," "his ineffable self," "cloud of light," "the Archons," "Father of the All," and "immeasurable light."

These Gnostic scriptures are saturated with highly sophisticated spiritual terms, even to the point of a bullied John, in the *Secret Book of John*, saying, "At the moment I was thinking about this, look, the heavens opened, all creation under heaven lit up, and the world shook." That is a very powerful statement from a man who is probably illiterate and has never played a video game.

How often do people today make these kinds of statements in public? On mainstream news channels, you will not hear of anyone saying that the "heavens opened" because if they did the doors to the mental institution would also open. You do hear this kind of talk on alternative radio stations, and on YouTube (you might've heard some of my own recordings), so it does happen, only that it is not acceptable for popular consumption. We could say that it happens more often than we know, only that people don't talk about it. A screenwriter may have seen the heavens opening, even after taking an illicit drug, but they will never make that public.

In ancient times, when these mystical events happened, they got documented. Biblical books are also loaded with all kinds of supernatural terminology. When we navigate away from spirituality and over to technology, it starts to make more sense. When I mentioned earlier about a "time-out" and when you read the *Secret Book of John*, you get the impression that John asked for a time-out.

It was as if he knew, as a knower, that he was living in a fabricated reality, something that Jesus taught him. The Gnostic cosmology recurs in these ancient texts and when you transcribe them, as I did, you decode the reality operating system.

The higher dimension that the digital technicians inhabit grants them the kind of longevity that is unattainable by mortal beings down here on *earth*, because earth is a much lower dimension. This is the construct. Wherein time is allotted to each user to learn and grow in a realm of stupendous and, well, marvelous experiences. And some people might add the "sewer" descriptive as well. I think I've been guilty of it.

You want to graduate

We came here to learn. It is an experiential school. Try not to take the experiences too seriously, but, at the same time, try to take seriously the teachings in this book as they are being made available in a way unlike ever before. You see, the experiential school didn't work out so well; not as well as we had hoped. In fact, let's suffice it to say that the people who come to this school became trapped because they forgot how to graduate.

Moving away, for the moment, from the ROS we need to think of earth as an electronic school, perhaps even a digital immersion school. We exited a digital world of high-frequency (the grand computer), we descended down, down, down into a feeble digital world that has more matter and more physicality than ever before.

A world that assaults our senses and cripples our magical abilities. It is a world that erases our memories and temporarily cuts us off from the enlightened world we know. This is earth, a computer-generated lower world within which we are allowed to understand things that are completely foreign to us.

When you are thinking of a cool vacation, you are likely thinking of an adventure. Because an adventure is memorable. Earth is a really wild adventure.

But there's been a slight problem with the earth-based physical reality. Actually it is much more than a slight problem. There are several problems and we might as well talk about them. These I like to think of as situational problems, but they are directly to blame for the very low graduation quotient. Before we do that let's set the groundwork for the larger discussion.

Imagine you attend one of the top universities in the world – Harvard, Oxford, and the people who go there are smart and talented, eager to learn, so eager in fact that they fully immerse themselves in the student lifestyle: very little money, lots of new friends, too many books to read it each week, homework, parties to attend, and no time to sleep.

Now imagine that you walk over to a far side of the university grounds to the West Campus and you find a group of middle-aged students who are taking nearly the same courses as the new students. They haven't ever graduated. So you ask them why they are still in school and they say, "What school?" They had been here so long that they no longer remember that this is a school campus. Well, you say to yourself, "That wasn't very inspiring. Why don't we check out that other part of the campus? You know, the one on the east side."

When you reach the East Campus, you discover senior citizens who are still in school. In fact, they are also taking the same classes as you, who is a new student. You ask a senior citizen, "Why are you still in school?" They look at you in amazement and say, "What school?" This time you get a little agitated in your reply, "This is Earth! It is a school. You are supposed to graduate in 4 to 8 years, depending on your academic interest. Why in God's name are you still here?"

The senior citizen looks at you, hard, then says, "You're just a kid. You don't understand how difficult life here is. I was like you once. Wide-eyed and looking for a way off this blue rock. But there's no way off this rock, kid. The only way out is death. You learn that, you'll live a pretty uneventful life."

The reincarnates (students who can't graduate earth), as I like to call them, have forgotten the most important rule of attending school: graduation. They forgot to graduate. It is not their fault though. They had help to make sure they never remembered. We'll cover that in a moment. There are people on the earth who continue to reincarnate over and over again, all the while thinking that in the next life they'll finally escape this rock in space. But they can't escape this rock because they haven't been able to remember the fact that they have to get a decent grade in all their courses in order to move ahead, and to graduate they need a certain amount of scholastic credits.

Even you've never been to university, you understand that your grade point average (GPA) is very important. This is an average of all the grades you've taken thus far. A high GPA is a good student. A low GPA is a failing student. (Hint: failing students do not graduate.)

The other thing you need alongside GPA is credits. Each course is worth credits. To graduate in a particular faculty (or discipline), you need a certain total of credits, coupled with a certain GPA. For example, to get a degree in philosophy you need a GPA of 3.0 and 359 total credits. And you are given 4 years to reach those goals as a full-time student.

The longer you take, the more likely that those rules can change. And if you take too long you might not qualify for a degree, plus a person who earns a degree in 4 years gets a lot better reception than a person who does it in 8 or 15 years. We get the basic idea. If this is boring for some people, I understand, but not everyone gets a chance to go to university, some people may not even go to school and still others don't like university.

But if earth is a school and the school acts like a university, then to graduate the Earth School we need to maintain a good GPA and we need to get all of our credits. During your time here, you may choose a different discipline and hopefully your credits are transferable. If not, you'll be starting over again. But there's an important key and write it down — **you did not come here to learn everything**. You did not come here to do everything, and you did not come here to be everything.

While there are successful billionaires, you don't necessarily need to be one. While there are extremely talented singers, we don't need everyone to be a talented singer. Everyone wanting to be a singer is a sign of a larger problem. We still haven't gotten to that but we will.

You came to the Earth School to learn what you needed to learn and to move on. We'll get into contracts in another chapter. While it is tempting to see the other guy chasing rainbows, you don't need to chase rainbows. We don't need *everyone* chasing rainbows. If everyone is chasing rainbows, there's no one singing. If there's everyone singing, no one is building airplanes. If everyone is building airplanes, there's no one making movies. If everyone is making movies, there's no one running restaurants.

There are restaurants because not everyone is making movies. There are movies because not everyone is building airplanes. There are airplanes because not everyone is singing. There are singers because not everyone is chasing rainbows.

Each incarnate, or *reincarnate*, has arrived at the earth school to study a particular discipline, and then, once studied and after putting it in practice, the incarnate has earned enough points to graduate Earth School.

Again, the goal of attending school is not to remain in school. If you are 65 years old and are still in Grade 7 there's a serious problem. Probably a mental disability. It happens. If Grade 7 is full of senior citizens, there's a systemic problem. In the next chapter, we'll talk about some of the things that are holding people back. Later on we'll talk about how the key components of reality work.

For now, I'd like to leave you with this — there are people at the Earth School that have been reincarnating for thousands of years. What could have been three or four rounds of incarnation have turned into centuries of reincarnations. These people are so heavy in debt (karmic debt) that they can't get out of debt, and because they can't get out of debt they have to keep coming back. And since each reincarnation effectively erases most of past life memories, the people who reincarnate for the 100th time have no memory of their past life mistakes, because their spirit is functioning at such a low level of efficiency.

We did come here to learn, only not to learn everything. You cannot learn everything. You are *not supposed to* learn everything. The enlightened mind selectively knows when enough is enough. They learn like they eat, a small amount of good food. They know when they are full and they eat no more than necessary.

Realistically speaking, we didn't incarnate into the Earth School to stuff our body so full that we have to roll into our next life. We also didn't incarnate here to ruin the lives of other students, because that doesn't contribute to your graduation. You may be tempted to ruin your status as a student which would not only jeopardize your chances at graduation, but you'd also potentially harm the education of others.

There are many possibilities at the Earth School, and of these many possibilities your goal is very, very simple: graduation. If I want you to take anything from this chapter it is exactly this point: you want to graduate. It might take a few lifetimes or it might just be *this* lifetime that is your final one, but the goal to graduate is in your hands. And it gets easier the more you can access ROS 11.

Liberate yourself from the false reality

What I thought about doing is to write a general user guide that explains liberating methods in a synthetic reality. Although self-help books have attempted to do so while emphatically trying to escape the religious label, which all they needed to do was to remove the divine element, unfortunately my research has uncovered a computer-generated reality. As such, the necessity of liberation, previously as a spiritual method and often associated with a heavenly Father, must be transcribed into this new concept.

I know that most people are preloaded with religious ideology and spiritual philosophy, and rightly so because human beings need these to ease their own suffering. Because of religious programming, some people may not be able to fully embrace my way of thinking. And there's nothing wrong with that.

What I'd like to do as a rogue philosopher is to offer a liberation method, though having some roots in ancient spirituality, that will enable you to attain "synthetic nirvana," all within the understanding of the world you see is a magnificent holographic projection. Personally, even you have been following along with the *God is DNA* materials, I think learning to liberate yourself from a synthetic reality will be challenging because it contradicts knowledge that has been around for a few thousand years.

Obviously, you can see that I'm not afraid to attempt this Herculean feat and there are a couple of good reasons. One, I am confident in my work on Gnostic microbiology and how the ancient spiritual teachers such as Siddhartha Gautama (Buddha), and Gnostic Jesus, Buddha, understood the digital nature of reality. My translations of their authenticated scriptures has proven those things enough so as to provide a foundation for reality science.

Two, I am of the thinking that the future does not equal the present and in the worst-case scenario my work will be increasingly understood in the future. And by presenting it today, I'll be able to measure how far behind we are as a society by taking a look at how long it takes to accept my technological approach.

What is true is that people are waking up at a phenomenal rate and if that rate holds, then people will increasingly realize that religious ideology and spiritual philosophy are inefficient methods of salvation. In fact, I have argued, religions such as Christianity were invented to prevent salvation. For people who are devout worshipers of a religion, this book will only cause inner conflict and confusion.

For people who have hybridized their sense of faith and spirituality and have been looking for an innovative approach, this book might provide those essential clues to cease their cyclical rebirths. I suppose, and it was not in my mind as I wrote the book, that this liberating guide could be seen as a new form of spirituality, which can be good and bad. More importantly, if my methods have some validity and resonate with the new generation, especially if working better than traditional approaches to liberation, then perhaps that is not such a bad thing.

If it works, use it. If it doesn't work, discard it. If it doesn't work well, open your mind a little bit more.

Liberating yourself from the synthetic reality takes commitment and courage. For your entire life you have made any number of assumptions about the nature of the world and what happens after death. I think a very strong technological approach to existence. If this does not resonate with you then you probably are better off reading a more traditional book.

The more familiar you are with digital DNA and the architectural framework of a synthetic reality, the better off you will be. For those who haven't studied the guide's DNA materials, you might want to have a look at the book *God is DNA*, the first in a 4-part series. (All four books can be found in *God is DNA Ultimate Edition*.) These materials do contradict the traditional teachings and may require time before they are properly internalized.

What I've attempted to do is that I've layered my technological liberation method over Buddhism, Gnosticism, Taoism, perhaps Confucianism, and some other philosophical approaches to enlightenment. And the reason is simple — these ancient spiritual methods were attuned to the synthetic reality, even if they did not use technological terms. Basically, find ideas that resonate with you and build on them.

The six pillars of graduating earth

The reasons for graduating from this earthly abode has less to do with appearing righteous in the eyes of some unknowable God or making yourself a master of reality and above everyone else. Graduation has everything to do with NOT coming back to earth because you have completed your studies here.

My technological method may be not necessarily produce immediate results. At the root, your life should become more sincere and probably simpler in approach. You won't be chasing as many rainbows as before. Your energy will be more focused. Maybe your state of mind will be more in tune, calm, and happy. You might find yourself happier more often. This approach, because it is vastly different than any traditional approach and partly why I have rooted some of it in the familiar, will need time and effort to fully appreciate.

As you tune your frequency and learn to sync with the with ROS 11, you will experience subtle shifts and adjustments in your life, and with a little bit of courage you will be able to put your life on the proper course.

1. Reality was professionally manufactured

There are engineers for everything. Every item in your house was engineered and manufactured. There are blueprints for your house or apartment. Because there were architects involved. Your car was engineered, at least we can agree on that. Well, turns out, and this may not be easy to swallow, the reality you live in was also engineered. Let it sink in.

2. Someone hacked the reality program

Hackers group alongside the computer industry. Computer hackers are there to make sure the information technology team gets paid what they are worth. The more secure the software system, the more likely hackers will turn their attention to it.

The Reality OS is a very advanced piece of software, and also hardware. This is the kind of thing that hackers love to do. Interestingly, the reality hackers not only breached the security firewalls, but they also decided to enter the program. And this is important. Once inside they decided to see if they could torment the existential players.

3. DNA virus pandemic

The dragon is a very ancient motif. A horned and scaly serpent. A mythological creature that can only be struck by a magic sword. The horned serpent later morphed into the devil, and how he lorded over the weak in faith. At the same time, the Gnostics sprang up and stated that the God of Abraham was in fact the devil. The demiurge. The false God.

My work revealed something monumental in theosophy. Using a microbiological template, and a lot of hard work, I revealed that the better definition of God was DNA. That was groundbreaking. But so what. On the other side of it I discovered that the false God, the Devil, is not the horned serpent holding a giant trident, rather, the devil is a virulent retrovirus hiding in the DNA. And it is this retrovirus that has crippled the human link to the Reality Operating System. The better we all understand that the more likely our salvation.

4. Sign your contract before you incarnate

You could say this is the greatest secret in the world. It is a secret that every human being should know, but only a handful of people only have a clue that it exists. It is a thing, I suppose, that most people don't like to think of: contracts.

Anyone who has incarnated into this false reality did so, without question, after signing an incarnation contract. The contract stipulates the details of your earthly journey, that is, you did not come here by accident, which is what the reality hackers would have you believe, knowing that your life has a contract attached to it and on that contract are the details of your obligations for your stay on earth, can be quite sobering for some people. It can also be invigorating for those who have been bouncing off the walls looking for their purpose.

What is your purpose? Do you have one, or two? Turns out, yes. The learning about your contract is still a new thing and it's an important thing.

5. Path to graduation

The reason everyone is here is because they want to complete the courses and to leave with a certificate. There's a reason why you go to school. It is called graduation.

You have heard of people who have failed grade school. You have heard of high school dropouts. People quit university all the time. People go to university, graduate with a degree, and then get a job in a completely different discipline. School is not an easy thing for everyone. And there's a lot of homework. But it is understood that school is a place to learn and educated people get higher paying jobs. Earth is one of the most advanced schools in this solar system. And for most of your life you may not have realized that you need to graduate.

6. The pantheon of gods is technological

Human beings have been worshiping all manner of gods and demigods. The Egyptians of the old world had a menu of gods. The Greeks and the Romans had a dozen main gods and goddesses. The Chinese had their pantheon of gods, some shared with Indian gods. Babylon had gods. Today we kind of all agreed that there's only one God, and that this God is the only God, but, every religion thinks they own the patent on the one God.

The good news is that we've been able to wean ourselves away from the pantheon of gods to a singular one. In a technological reality, and you might not like this, but, besides the God in the DNA there is an explanation for why we believe in a pantheon of gods. It has everything to do with the radioactive isotopes.

It turns out that these elements, abundant in our atmosphere (the home of the gods), can emit gamma radiation under the right cosmic conditions, such as, for example, the bombardment of cosmic rays coming from the sun. And, interestingly enough, the human body, cow's milk, soil, and rocks also contain radioactive isotopes that, when they interact with cosmic rays (a.k.a. sunshine) emit gamma radiation. And it could be said that the high energy particles that are released could be the very gods we once worshiped.

Part 2

Getting the foundation right

Slight problems with the physical reality

We've sort-of established that the journey of life is more akin to an admission to an Earth School and as in every school the basic purpose is graduation. It isn't easy for everyone to switch their view from living a difficult life under the watchful eyes of God to the view that we elected to come here, to the point of signing a contract, and that the thematic reason for our arrival is for the purpose of spiritual ascension.

It was a big shift in viewpoints and not everyone can readily make the transition. It is also a powerful transition to make because it can fundamentally shift the core of your existence. You become more purpose-oriented and you feel more encouraged to understand what you came here to learn. We'll talk more about learning when we discuss contracts.

Before we continue on ROS 11 (Reality OS 11), it is important to look at the slight problems with the physical reality. They are slight because they are not entirely obvious and because they are not entirely obvious they are only noticed by people who are paying attention. Not only that, but these slight problems also require a bit of understanding the nature of reality, the nature of the human being, and the nature of spirituality which are not exactly things that are easily obtained.

The Earth School, over a period of millennia, has been sequestered by a band of reality hijackers. As with any hijackers of a planetary body that is fundamentally rooted in reality software and hardware, the only way to take over a computer-generated reality is to hack the reality code. Naturally, ROS 11 has built-in security measures such as firewall protocols and anti-hijacking applications. How could a small handful of hackers take over an entire reality? The answer: bit by bit.

Over many centuries, and in a very methodical and thoughtful manner, these reality hackers managed to get enough control over the main systems, coupled with their own ability and reality engineering, to slowly nudge the inhabitants of this world into a vibration of chaos, terror, despair, depression, anger, vengeance, all coded in a kaleidoscope of false love and compassion.

A computer hacker can gain access to the information and controls of the machine, effectively taking over the machine. An earthly computer system is far too cumbersome to completely take over, because that would enable the hackers to effectively end all existence in the reality and that in itself is protected by any number of backup and regulatory systems, the likes of which are well outside the parameters of this book, and my ability.

Suffice it to say that the ROS is incredibly advanced and is composed of many components, some more vulnerable than others. And a lot of these those things fall within the umbrella of engineering. The engineers of the earth had a certain level of advancement, a level that is well beyond any human ability and likely because the Earth Builders were some kind of machines, and the reality hackers could not match their level of expertise, or understanding. Which I suppose is another one of those failsafe systems, technical incompetence.

The reality hackers weren't satisfied with hacking into this reality and distorting the world. They weren't happy with damaging the weather systems and the tectonic shifts. They weren't happy with poisoning the soil and limiting the production of food. They also closed off key portals that had existed between worlds, portals between other dimensions, and essential portals that maintained a bridge between the divine world of the digital technicians and the mortal world of human beings.

By severing a number of essential links to our digital makers they had created a vacuum within which they could introduce a more limiting system of divine creation. And a kindergarten divine story, rooted in a monotheistic God, one of their own creation, was perfectly inserted into a population cut off from their origins.

The hijacking of reality and the closing off of dimensional portals, alongside extended earth calamities, artificially-generated of course, created an environment of uncertainty, despair, and fear. But in order for a digital population in a computer-generated world to be fully taken over, the reality hackers had to hack into the human being. They needed to hack the software of life: DNA.

They had already hacked into the reality software, not all of it but enough of it to distort reality, for example they could control the weather and could cause earthquakes and floods. They could release a prophet into the population who would claim that a volcano would erupt. The people would scoff at the idea initially, but all the controllers had to do was to activate a volcano and have it erupt as their prophet had foreseen to build a loyal following (ie worshipers).

The coupling of software and prophecy created prophecies and prophets, as well, became instrumental spiritual leaders, the likes of which are still worshiped in the modern era and their deeds taken as gospel. Only that it wasn't gospel, or divine providence, it was a careful manipulation of an ill-informed and mostly illiterate audience. The version of today's prophet, an evangelical instrument postulated and propagated on television, no longer has any prophetic ability, but the audience, long conditioned in this type of dissemination scheme, remain determined in their faith.

The early earth cultures, quarantined from their computer origins and cut off from their information access points, were purposely manipulated and effectively hypnotized into believing an entire system of beliefs that was a stark and distant departure from their ancestors. And while remnants of the past and residual memories of the true nature of the world remained, they were not strong enough to maintain the vibration necessary to keep a population cohesive, and as the years wore on, the human population began to drift into the world of worshiping godly beings, who were not gods. These godly beings were reality hackers and trained technicians, even as human magicians, and they began to further distance the people from their digital makers.

We can see the exodus from the digital homeland into the mortal landscape filled with an amount of pain and suffering. The legend of King Arthur is exactly the story of the loss of faith in the *Holy Grail* and the *Sword in the Stone,* for these represented the quintessential links to the digital homeland. The Grail is a device that can cut through reality, which is why the story was expanded to include a sword (Excalibur). Arthur could literally "cut through reality" with the combination of the Grail and Excalibur. That's what made him king. But Arthur was just a revitalization of Jesus, who also came with a sword and who was considered to be a king. It's a motif that runs through history. The savior who returns to restore the land.

The fact that the King Arthur myth, along with even modern myths like *Peter Pan, Lord of the Rings, Harry Potter,* remains as a tiny reminder of the path to reconciliation. Stories are advanced methods of reconnecting to the instruments of reality because through these immortal instruments the human species remains eternally intact, and we'll cover eternal things as we go along. Before we go on we need to expand on the subtle control mechanisms.

You may have been able to hack into the reality architecture and you may have been able to temporarily reprogram certain aspects of the world, and those things may have allowed you the ability to distort the world in your favor, but as long as the people (human beings) remained eternally linked to the digital homeland there would be no real and meaningful way to fully take over the world, the ultimate goal of the hijackers.

The role of Arthur and Jesus was to unite the land with the people. When united in energy (spirit), the people act as the earth's immune system. When the land is sick, the people are sick; when the land is healthy, the people are healthy. That is why we cherish the land. The American Indians considered the land to be sacred and were sworn to defend their territories to the death. That's because they followed this ancient tradition on unity with the land.

People, even interdimensional people, don't decide to hijack a planet simply because they didn't get enough salsa with their tortilla chips. Reality hackers have a long-term plan to overtake, and consume, a world. In this case, we can think of it as a 5,000-year plan to take over this reality. Everybody wants to know why. It is very complicated and requires an understanding of very advanced beings.

Why does a lion eat raw meat? Why doesn't a lion learn to cook? Because lions eat raw meat. The kind of people who have the interest in degrading an entire reality, consuming its resources, depopulating the system and spending thousands of years of effort to accomplish such a Herculean task are criminals. They have not escaped their egotistical nature.

Once the reality architecture had been sequestered to a manageable and defendable extent, the next level was to sequester this human population because the human population, in a synthetic environment, fundamentally acts like an immune system. What we like to think of as the human consciousness. But how do you fully and properly, even adequately, sequester enough of the human consciousness so as to effectively remove the earth's immune system?

More importantly, why do you need to remove the immune system of an entire planet? To understand, we go back to the reality architecture. We've briefly talked about the fact that the reality hijackers should have managed to gain access to a certain number of control systems, not perfectly, but enough. And that they also need to gain full access to the reality core in order for the destruction plans to work.

During these millennia, they have happily fed on the energies of the human population for their sustenance, even using human energy to propagate timeless destruction acts so as to build their prophetic case.

The core program of reality is housed much deeper into the architecture of the earth. To gain access, the human population needs to be eliminated, which is an extremely lofty goal given that the ROS is specifically designed not to let a mass die off take place.

If it is human consciousness that needs to be controlled and you've maximized as many of the external factors as you can then the next logical step is to go internally. At the microscopic level you can get into the consciousness by hacking into the human spirit.

The spirit molecule is DNA. The DNA is the software of life. How do reality hackers take over the software of life? They create a microscopic virus. A DNA virus. A virus that has multiple heads (hydra), replicates into every child in the population, and mutates in such a way so as to be impossible to remove.

The multi-headed virus is like a self-replicating dragon inserted into every cell of the human body. But it's not a microscopic horned dragon. It is a virus and the virus impairs the regular functioning of human DNA, specifically diffracts the essential communications between the network of genes and the Reality OS.

This is no ordinary infection, rather this is a targeted weapon specifically designed to sever the human being from his or her eternal world, and all of that is directly connected to the long-standing plan to hack into this reality core. But now, because the dragon-like virus, cast like the ring of Sauron in our mitochondrial DNA, the portion of our DNA that gets copied into each and every offspring, exists inside each human being, and it is intelligent (having software qualities), it begins to tell each human that it alone commands the body of cells. It communicates that it is the "Lord of the Universe" (if the collection of cells was the universe).

People naturally, since it arises invisibly and omnisciently, think that this is God speaking to them through the Holy Spirit. What they don't realize is that this is a manufactured DNA virus that has infected the entire human population, with a growing demographic who have some immunity, and would in the future be turned into many of the most prolific religions around the world. "The kingdom of god is within you." (Luke 17:21) The God is indeed inside of us. Only that he is not God, he is a *genetic mutation*. A deformity that has convinced the world that has convinced the world that he is the Lord of the Universe.

How profoundly stupid. He should've said, "I am lord of your infected cells because I am an ugly serpentine virus with many heads in your DNA, and you can't get rid of me. Because they haven't invented drugs yet. Nah-nah. And by the time they invent drugs I will have completely infected the world and the world will worship all my mutations in hundreds of religions. And none will be the wiser. I shall entrap them in misery and pain, thereby proving that I am the lord of the cellular matrix." But he didn't figure me entering the picture. Nah-nah!

My advice: Stop worshiping the retrovirus in your body and get back to your DNA. It may take some practice.

The god in the DNA

You might think that the microbiological angle is a 21st century attempt to understand God. You might even make the case of DNA shares more similarities with God and can't be explained away (invisible, all knowledgeable, omniscient, in everything, inside of you, with you always, etc.) But, as I have argued in *God is DNA*, the Gnostic teachers understood that the God of Israel (demiurge) was a false God.

Not only that, having decoded the deeper meaning of the Gnostic texts I have found compelling evidence that the Gnostics were, in fact, when they were talking about the One Who Is and the "ineffable light," talking about the microbiology of the human being. And, further research showed that the microbiology, since it was rooted in software attributes, was connected to a digital homeland, verily human DNA has a digital component and that digital component (strand) is our immortal link to our digital makers.

The *God is DNA* evidence, including my work in Buddhism, convinced me that we in fact have been synthetically manufactured and that this world too is wholly synthetic. Again, why this is not common knowledge, is because of the efforts the reality hackers have used to sequester and suppress knowledge, to quarantine the human being from the digital homeland; to program the human subconscious with an endless drivel of lies and false information, and to top all that off with a potent DNA virus the likes of which is so intelligent that we have built churches and synagogues to worship its name.

All is not lost. We are reaching a crescendo of awakening and a clear opportunity to remedy the lost centuries of the human civilization. As you can see, this material is not easily assimilated and could take concerted effort to properly put to effective use. As long as the virus inside each of ourselves is constantly reminding us that it is God, you can imagine the challenge it will be to fully eradicate such an eternally present device, because certainly by now it is so well integrated into our DNA molecule that it is hard to separate the virus from the rest of the genome.

The historical evidence, for me, put everything into context and provided a kind of existential dating of the human hacking. I believe that the Gnostic priests were smart enough to discover a DNA virus, especially since the microscope had not even been conceived of, on their own accord. That meant that some other agency had provided these ancient microbiologists with the details of how humanity came to be made corrupted, through the genome. The only agency that would have full understanding of genetic viruses and mutations is a digital agency that was directly or indirectly responsible for the synthetic creation of the human being. The genesis of man.

These people are our digital makers. Their language of human origins and the Father of the All, the way they spoke was unlike a biologist of today. They spoke politically and in strange abstractions, such as the One Who Is, a term attributed to Jesus when he explained to his brother James about the One who made him.

The language of our digital makers pretty soon would be turned into spirituality and then concretized into big religion, where it would be stripped of its eloquence and biological origin; and, instead handed over hand and foot to the multi-headed hydra himself, Yaldabaoth, the false God hiding inside mankind's body. The operating system of mankind is run by a virus and it doesn't want mankind to figure that out, because that would put a certain end to its invisible and immortal life.

The Earth School was designed to be a perfect location for spiritual improvement and now has become a realm of endless strife, chaos, and suffering. But the suffering will not end completely until we, as a species, train ourselves to the true cause of our own demise, a virus in our genome.

The Ring of Sauron indeed must be destroyed before the human race can return to his spiritual freedom. In the meantime, we can learn to better navigate the ROS, and perhaps at the very least we can end the cycle of reincarnation. The process of ending suffering will also curtail the DNA virus (Yaldabaoth) and it will become weaker as a result of people no longer feeding its giant oversized ego.

The benefit of choosing an end to suffering and a return to learning is the opportunity to finally achieve your purpose here on earth. It is an opportunity to end the cycle of suffering and to allow your spirit the freedom it deserves to choose a better reincarnation. You may still end up here, but if you have done your job you'll end up here in a manner that you like. All of that is detailed in your incarnation contract.

Signing the incarnation contract

You are probably thinking that you'd like to have a look at your contract, just to make sure that you are doing the right thing. You may be asking how anyone can confirm that they, in fact, have a contract. Some readers, if they've somehow read this far, which is pretty hard to imagine, are thinking that maybe the incarnation contract should go alongside extraterrestrials and the moon landings.

My examination of the incarnation contracts, because previously I only had an intuitive understanding that there was what was commonly called a "soul contract" and I was pretty certain that I had a purpose on the planet. That rudimentary scenario began to change after the 2005 spiritual bleed-through when time and space became much closer to my heart. It was during the most intensive ascension that the walls between dimensions were stripped bare and I began to not only have an intense intuitive examination of my life, more so, I began to understand how the world had been put together, starting with my world; how I had been put together. How I wasn't the person I always thought I had been. I had been a person until that transformative point, and then, I no longer was that person.

I became a similar-looking person but the understanding of the universe began to expand. I suddenly understood that there were things like incarnation contracts. Before the transformation, yes, sure, *maybe* there are soul contracts. After the transformation, yes, sure, there are incarnation contracts and I signed one; because in my incarnation contract it said that there was a contingency option to wake me up at age 38 if certain conditions on the earth were met. Whatever those conditions were, as criteria that needed to be met, well, they were there, and that's why I was obligated to wake up.

So that's one way to learn about your incarnation contract. You have a scheduled spiritual experience. Look, every one, or nearly everyone, gets a scheduled spiritual experience during their life. Maybe even more than one. But those spiritual experiences aren't exactly labeled "spiritual experiences." These periods are usually preceded by some kind of terrible surprise, traumatic experience, or general fall from grace. Quite often, if I am allowed to generalize, spiritual experiences are wrapped in the flowers of bad luck.

Divorce is a spiritual experience. The birth of a child, especially the first one, is also spiritual experience. The loss of a child, at any age; the loss of a much loved career; the collapse of one's entire finances; the hospitalization after terrible accident; the diagnosis of an unscheduled disease — all of these things, and more, I would label as "spiritual experiences." Why? Because traumas are explicit opportunities to spiritually grow. It is a point in your life whereby you realize that your ego has ballooned out way too far. Traumas bring you back down to reality. They say, "You are not indestructible and that at any moment you too could be wiped off the face of the earth."

That's a pretty intense spiritual lesson, if you can learn from it. The three visits by the three interdimensional Elves were traumatic experiences, even I did not react to them in the expected format. And most of the time we do not react properly to a traumatic experience. A family that loses their son in the beginning is not thinking that this is a spiritual experience. They are thinking this is a trauma.

And they may harbor bad feelings, naturally, because of that trauma. And each culture handles things differently. What is accepted in one country may be unacceptable in another country. What one culture responds as a tragedy, another thinks it as an act of God.

When we buy a car, we sign a contract. When we get married, we sign a contract. When we get a dream job, we sent a contract. We sign contracts when we make trade deals between countries. We sign contracts when we buy smart phones and we sign contracts when we dismiss our privacy rights when we go on certain websites. When we have a child, we sign a contract. When we get a passport, yes, we also sign a contract. When we download a new version of the iPhone we sign a contract.

Contracts are considered legal documents, but more than that contracts detail our responsibilities and the terms and conditions of the service or sale of a product. After signing a contract for a marriage, we have to sign another contract when we decided to get a divorce. After purchasing the car and signing a contract, we have to sign another contract when we sell the car. Same goes for a boat, a house, and a motorcycle.

But when it comes to incarnating into a human body; when we are handed over the full responsibility of an entire life, and with all the benefits and consequences, when we had decided to experience life on earth, the kind of experience unlike ever before, a life so heavy and a journey so dense, when we have decided to do that for some strange reason people seem to think that there's no contract.

What?

I'll admit that we may not be able to see our life contract. I'll admit that. Logically-speaking, it would only make sense that there is an incarnation contract. Otherwise who in their right mind would allow us to drive this human body? Would you hand over the keys to the most expensive car ever invented? No. You wouldn't even hand over the keys to an average car without first getting the signature on the dotted line. John Hancock.

So if we backwards engineer life, using a very standard earth-based procedure having to do with contractual obligations, and we predate our birth date, we have a situation where a new body is in the womb being genetically-engineered according to the parents in question. And maybe even getting a few DNA edits here and there by a team of digital doctors.

Hey, look, if you ordered a body and it's in the womb, and you would like to add a few custom features — and this is no different (in *principle*) than ordering a customized airplane or car or even a cappuccino — yes, I said it cappuccino — look, people seem to think that life happens in a magical vacuum whereby a stork drops down from a cloud and delivers a baby on someone's doorstep. And we need to move on from that.

We need to move from the idea that babies happen by accident and then grow up by an even bigger accident and then they get a job, get married, and have their own babies, all by *accident*, and that all those babies, these people, that they *accidentally* all end up doing what they really want to do in life.

There's a reason why you do what you really, really want to do in life and that reason has everything to do with the incarnation contract assigned to your body. That contract may have already been assigned to a particular body, a standard earth journey, an off the shelf life, and you simply signed on the dotted line and downloaded your spiritual DNA software into the lower fields of earth. It could be that simple. (It doesn't sound simple, does it? I did suggest reading the prerequisite books, didn't I?)

It might also be the case that you ordered a particular life journey — say the daughter of a very rich family in New York — and then because no rich parents were conceiving at the moment, you waited for a little while. You may have even been offered the body of a rich Hong Kong girl (as an incarnation vehicle), but had already decided to be a Caucasian and you really wanted a stint in New York. (Note: Color of skin doesn't mean anything in the Earth School, except for cultural features. A Ferrari and a Lamborghini are very different and they are very similar. They have four tires and they go vroom-vroom. The visual difference is illusory. Hint: I am probably saying that all races are beautiful.)

The call goes out to the people in New York. A couple is found who is willing to manufacture a little girl, an angel from heaven (of course), and on the other side of the veil of reality a contract was signed. The signature on the contract may have also included the mother of the incoming child. She would have agreed to raise you properly and to make sure you ended up with the right education and whatnot, all specified in the contract.

The incarnation contract is a necessity in an Earth School situation because there is a reason for wanting to come to earth, and along with that reason there are terms and conditions. You will be provided with a new body (vehicle for living) and that body will allow you to live out your purpose. A-ha! There is a little purpose to life and it is written in a contract.

Well, wait a minute. If there is a contract, then how come very few people can remember them? Why is it that only some people know about incarnation contracts and most people don't? Why do some people feel they have a purpose in life while others walk around aimlessly? Did some people come to earth to be homeless? Did some people come to earth to end up in prison? Or to be leader of a country? Why are some people successful while others are always poor?

Obviously, I can't answer for every individual, but I can talk about the basic approach and hopefully that approach will help most people navigate their life (a tiny bit better). For special cases, I do recommend getting assistance with this type of thing. There are people whose purpose is to help others fine tune their purpose. In any given life, I think, there are multiple purposes. What I like to think of as contingencies, because you never know what's going to happen in life. Everything is interacting with everything else. Things change. When you arrived the conditions could be radically different by the time you are an adult.

Walk-ins welcome

Change could be a result of the reality upgrade, as I have suggested happened in recent years; or, it could be the result of the reality hackers tampering with the flow of reality. And it could be the result of any combination of things. There is another kind of incarnation commonly referred to as a "walk-in."

A walk-in is a spirit body that wants to enter an adult body. They don't want to go through the trauma of childhood. They don't want to learn how to walk, again. They want to enter a body, get familiar with the life that person has created, and then they want to get right to their purpose on earth.

And a walk-in can happen at any time. Young adult. Mature adult. Even a senior citizen in some cases. Again, this is not the result of an accident, which most generalists would argue. They would say, "Jim has all of a sudden started acting strange. Maybe something was wrong with him?" Maybe they are a walk-in. A walk-in will have established an agreement with the current existential occupant. They'll have a more complicated contract. The contract will stipulate when one occupant leaves and when another arrives. Just like an apartment.

When the renter (owner) of an apartment makes an agreement with another renter (owner) they will decide on a "move out" and a "move in" date. Sometimes the renter (owner) will leave early and the apartment will be vacant for a period of time. Some apartments (houses) are up for sale but there are no buyers. Some buyers want an apartment (house) but there are no sellers.

So, a body must be matched to an incarnate. The incarnate may also be a reincarnate, having already been a steward of earth and not doing very well. We'll talk about some of the key terms and conditions in another chapter.

The reincarnate may be assigned a particular body because of their particular situation. This will all be stipulated on the contract. Sometimes a reincarnate will be temporarily placed in a body until such time that another body becomes available, at which point they'll sign a contract with that body. Some walk-ins are reincarnates who, for whatever reason, have been allowed to enter into an adult body in order for the opportunity to learn what they came here to learn.

Remember, the Earth School is a place of learning. If you don't learn, you don't earn credits and your GPA drops, which means you won't graduate. Everything is a learning experience, even troubled times. In fact, I could make the argument that troubled times are intense learning opportunities.

You could, during very difficult and transitional periods, really pick up a lot of learning credits if you applied yourself; instead of taking the usual despair and depression and anger approach. The learning modality you choose is indicative of your spiritual awareness. Choose positive and your spiritual awareness is high. Choose negative and you'll be reincarnating back on earth, and it could be less pleasant than now.

Some people in life are going through very difficult times. These may all be *reincarnates* who have not been able to learn things as fast as others. They may be very troubled and underdeveloped souls who may need to vent and simmer their bountiful negativity. Again, I think we're all here for a reason, that is, not everyone gets a gorgeous life. That may be the promise of the politicians, but that is not the nature of a computer-generated reality.

Stipulated on your contract are the things you promised to do while you are here. They are very clearly laid out, probably as options, and they could also be attributed to certain ages. For example, you may be free to do whatever you want up until age 25, within reason, but after age 25 you are to get married and to produce a couple of children. Then, it might be stipulated, you are to raise your kids until age 36, at which point, you will return to the workforce or start a charitable fund or coach soccer, whatever it is.

The age attribution can explain why sometimes people change at a certain age. Oftentimes, the mid-to-late 30s (slightly younger for women) are periods of spiritual growth. At age 35, you may start to ponder the meaning of it all and by late 30s there is an event in your life which provides the context for your spiritual growth. The incident might be upsetting — say an ugly divorce to a perfect marriage — but it has been scheduled and written into the contract.

I experienced a rude awakening when I was 38 years old. Completely unexpected, unplanned, and unnecessary. I hadn't asked for it. I hadn't deserved it, and I certainly didn't know what was happening when three interdimensional Elves appeared in my bachelor apartment. Their appearance derailed my already derailed life and I became further derailed in the 12 months that followed, until, well, my life was cast in ruins. My life has never recovered from those visits in 2005. And I'm pretty industrious and hard-working. I have never recovered. And since then more things have happened.

It occasionally bothered me because I always thought of it as a temporary shift. I always imagined that I'll endure and get through it, and here we are 11 years later, with over 60 self-published books, with an even more spectacular book being written. Could I have planned for the Elves? No. Could I have foreseen it? No. Did I even know Elves existed? No. Did I want to get visited by the Elves? No. And yet there they were in my apartment about to ruin my life.

Why did the Elves come visit me when I was 38? Because it was written in my contract. "At age 38, while residing in an apartment in Vancouver, British Columbia, under such and such name, you will be visited three times by the Elves, after which you agreed to take the next steps. Failure to adhere to these conditions will result in either a) a more forceful visit and a potential visit in the hospital, or, b) the stripping away of everything you hold dear until you agree to honor the conditions as stipulated in this contract."

Because, although I was very reluctant and uninterested — I know, Elves, but what did they want from me? — I did decide in the following two weeks to pursue the matter, purely out respect and obligation to a group of people that were not supposed to exist. And spiritual awakenings galore followed, and voilà, here I am.

The (computer) geeks of ancient times

You enrolled in the Earth School just before you reincarnated. At the time, you were aware of the slight problems with this planet, and how it has been hacked, distorted and much turned into a spiritual sewer. And you signed a legal contract, on the other side of reality, that stipulated in detail what you had intended to do. What is commonly referred to as "purpose in life." It is, as I understand, quite similar to signing a job contract in the sense that duties and requirements are detailed, including amendments and contingencies. Your life may change dramatically as the result of something happening in the reality such as a contingency.

You may also see the appearance of a secret agenda, which you may not even be aware of until much later in life. All of these things are with you, and near you, but for reasons stipulated in those contracts not all information is known. A basic reason why not everything is known is because there are people (eg reality hackers, magicians, shamans, remote viewers) who can find out what you know and they could, if they had the ability, subvert your plans in life.

You may be destined to become a famous celebrity who marries a multimillionaire only to get redirected, by malice, and end up working as a prostitute in some city you've never heard of, and that can happen as a result of someone finding out what you came here to do, and not liking it. And some agents may exist for the sole purpose of throwing people off course.

Luckily, in your contract, and in the reality system, there are helpful agents to remind you to stay on course, so it's not all doom and gloom. Again, my philosophy is that the more you are aware of the nature of reality (i.e. computer generated reality) and the rules and regulations of the Earth School (e.g. karma and incarnation contracts) the more likely you are able to accomplish, and remember, what you invariably came here to do.

This is a new approach to traditional systems of spiritual enlightenment, which essentially offered the same result only through a far more rigorous effort. This is largely due to the presence of a more advanced genetic structure at a time in history whereby technological devices and software upgrades have become a mainstay.

In other words, we have evolved genetically enough that we can now move away from spirituality and slowly drift into the technological interface and gain unprecedented access to an advanced-but-ancient genetic-based operating system, verily an existential system that each human being fundamentally depends on, ROS 11.

This reality is a low density system that largely relies on the attributes of the five senses (sight, hearing, touch, smell, taste), such that everything outside of the five senses is given a different categorization. Because this operating system has been asymmetrically hacked and modified, one of his great casualties has been the multidimensional spectrum of life, which you will admit is a pretty good way to sever the eternal link between the reality players and the ROS.

But let me repeat: we need the ROS (to be one with the Tao, as if it was the OS) because it is an integral component of this existential field. Imagine that you lost 50% of the functionality on the operating system (Mac or PC) on your computer. That would be pretty frustrating, wouldn't it? Well, now imagine that having no computer geek around to fix it, you are stuck with using your crippled system, knowing at the outset that the system once worked perfectly fine and now was down to 50% functionality.

The years go by, and because of an intense hacking campaign coupled with an unbeatable computer virus, every computer in the world has been crippled to a 50% functionality rate. Life goes on and people learn to get by with 50% of the operating system's functions. Years and years later, users have adjusted to the computer systems and now think of them as normal. The historical hack and virus is now a myth, a conspiracy theory, and users are just happy to be able to send email, digitally edit their photos, write articles and listen to music. A bit later, a computer savior shows up and invents HTML, and people scratch their head at his ideas first, but after more discussions it turns out that HTML is quite useful and that HTML also becomes the precursor to building websites, all built on a new application called the "internet."

What is the internet, relative to our discussion? The internet is the ability to access a "higher dimensional network." And in having access to the internet, just like having access to a piece of real estate, people have the ability and opportunity to build, to share, and to create.

The social network took a leap forward after the internet had been exploited. Facebook, Snapchat, Twitter, Instagram — they all came into existence 20 years after Tim Berners-Lee introduced us to HTML. During that time, we also had a fair chance to exploit email, and though email didn't end the postal service, it did end letter writing.

Where am I going with this? See, I think it's valuable that I provide as much context as possible; otherwise this turns into a sermon and I'm not into sermons. The traditional method of communicating spiritual knowledge (e.g. religious ideology, methods of enlightenment) is by way of sermon. There is a painting of Jesus Christ giving a sermon on the mound. This became the template for later Christians who began to sermonizing biblical ideas, and the church system has become an industrial-grade sermon mound.

Spiritual knowledge, in my technological model, used to have been derived and downloaded directly from the ROS, because there was a very tight relationship between the OS and the user. Over time, as contact and familiarity with the OS began to degrade, and likely this is due in part to periods of technological advancement, i.e. new versions of software, not everyone in the field could access the ROS in the same way. And, probably, some of the technical tasks were handed out to ancient geeks, or philosophers, sages, and mystics.

The geeks of ancient times — and I'm thinking of them as *reality computing experts* having very little to do with God and Judgment — were given the tasks of the geeks in the modern day: to keep the computer systems running. Philosophers, sages, and mystics traveled around advising people on how to understand God, how to foresee the future, how to self-actualize so as to become closer to God. But if God is DNA, as I have discovered, and if we are living under a synthetic reality system, the likes of which our intellect is not yet able to fully realize, then the ROS *also* existed in ancient times. And that makes the mystics and sages members of the geek class.

More than that, this class of people were connected to the ROS. Read up on Siddhartha Gautama, Lao Tzu, and Jesus and you discover a profound understanding of the cosmos, ideas relevant even to this day, and yet these people, these "knowers," had no internet access, they had never seen a computer, and they were mostly illiterate and undereducated.

Jesus did not have a Ph.D. in Theology. Siddhartha didn't have access to anything like our modern libraries. And Lao Tzu was basically a hermit who appeared here and there to hand out his teachings. His successful method of living as a nomad, and I wouldn't recommend it for people in the modern era, became part of his mantra, the "pathless path." Live as you wish as long as you are connected to the Tao. What is the Tao? The ROS.

Lao Tzu, I would speculate, was connected to an early version of the ROS. The ROS exists on a higher dimension, like the internet. You have to have a modem. You need a Wi-Fi account. You need a computing device. You need those things to "see" the internet; otherwise you will think it doesn't exist. Even today with the internet there are people at a beach somewhere who prefer the sand rather than to join a social network.

In other words, while the internet is a peaceful tool and resource, there are large portions of the world that have only a mild interest in it. Peaceful is powerful. And we can say the same for the people in earlier times. Some people were too poor and too ignorant to care for self-actualization. Not everyone could understand the mystics. Often, sages and mystics were invited to speak for the Emperor.

The establishment of an underclass of mystics, magicians and seers did not sit well with the formation of the Church and these people were labeled heretics and tortured. The witch hunts and the time of the Inquisition (12th to 19th century) saw the burning of witches and the mass persecution of those who did not ascribe to the Church dogma. Even tools to aid in self-actualization, such as Tarot cards, often used by gypsies and other strange folk — again you have a technical class of people living like nomads and being ostracized — were considered to run against the Church.

But if these mystics, as I suggest, were connected to the ROS through the DNA (God) then what was the purpose of the Church if not to undermine the salvific process. For a Christian to think that the Church would sabotage ideas that could provide immediate salvation and enlightenment is hard to imagine. But we know the history of the Church and heresy and a witch burning are documented, along with a whole host of dark things.

Would it be unreasonable, at this point, to suggest that the Church was an invention of those reality hijackers? It wouldn't, would it. In fact, it would be in the complete and total interest of the reality hijackers to create a pseudo-salvation model to further entrap citizens in this low-density plane.

In the beginning, human beings likely were directly linked to the ROS, a far more robust ROS because in the beginning there were so few people and so little to do. It was a garden of technology. The first website on the first internet. Then, as the population grew is when problems were incurred — divine battles and tectonic weather shifts — the ROS was changed. New versions were created and each new version further distanced human users from the operating system. But there was a caveat — the appearance of the mystics. The ancient geeks.

The mystics were added to the population in order to ensure that people could connect with the ROS when needed. They were also there to maintain the ROS. The mystics, Earth Computer Technicians, went about to monitor and maintain the reality software. The reported bugs and problems to a higher authority, and, let us not forget, they selected others to become reality technicians and reality engineers. The mystics would include these people: gypsies, sages, monks, philosophers, magicians, shamans, witches, Buddhists, Taoists, seers, psychics, intuitives, and fortune tellers.

These people, and they came with a wide variety of skills, or skills in tapping into the ROS. I would also add a second tier of technicians, the artisans. The painter, writer, poet, singer, and now the filmmaker, were also able to tap into the reality interface to glean their ideas, but their method of teaching came in the shape of their creative talent. The singer sang the poetry of reality and if the singer was any good that song inspired millions.

Let's take a look step back. We've discussed, and maybe not fully agreed, that this reality has been somewhat hijacked and those hijackers have corrupted the native reality programs to such an extent that pain and suffering are pretty much on the daily menu. But, after all this time (millennia), they have had a chance to properly distort the world and to do so in such a way that the distortion appears normal, it would make sense that some of the reality technicians and engineers now serve these reality hackers.

So, take a singer immersed in the false world — violence, chaos, mayhem, anger — and they release a song. Well, it would be coded in the false codes. At first it would be called Devil's music. The music of the top 40s in 2016 would probably all be labeled as Devil's music had it been labeled even a century ago, yet today it is popular music broadcast on major radio stations. The art of the Renaissance has been replaced by the photos on Instagram. The new Mona Lisa is Kim Kardashian.

On lunatics

It is entirely possible that the deinstitutionalization of mental hospitals (ie closing hospitals due to government cutbacks), was another way to give birth to an "alternative community" or a "gay community" or a "spiritual community." Because when those communities began, those people were considered pretty outrageous. Homosexuality was considered a mental illness in America until the early 1970s. Alternative thinkers are still considered to be conspiracy theorists.

But, the question is how far back does this all go. Because as communities grow, outrageousness becomes the norm. In other words, the status quo was once radical thinking. The people in government right now, today, 100 years ago were considered lunatics and would have been placed in mental hospitals. Only because they have learned to mask their lunacy and to appear sane have they become accepted and now head nations. Leaders have changed laws and enacted bills so that their methods could not be challenged. Those methods become status quo and now we don't question them. In fact, those who question the status quo are lunatics led by demagogues. But, back in history, the status quo of today was lunacy.

It's kind of very strange system. We won't accept lunacy at first, but over time we will accept it as normal. Then when the next guy starts up, he becomes the lunatic, only to later on, if he lasts, to become the norm. To accept a true lunatic, all they have to do is to create a big enough threat (supply) to make the lunatic a plausibility (demand). Similarly, to reject a lunatic, they only have to insist that the status quo is enough. To do that, you bring references. Lots of them.

Is there such thing as a norm? Are lunatics necessary in this system of life? They spur humanity forward, and sometimes too forward. Are wild ideas lunacy? I have wild ideas, but I have experiences to match them. People would think of me as a lunatic because they do not share my experiences (and they are better off not having seen what I have, because they'll sleep better). People who share my experiences see me as normal, only those people are very few. Most people are still deciding.

Managing trillions of existential data points

So we not only have sort of been cut off from the ROS, but were also inundated by these false technicians and their, basically, propaganda to remain disconnected. If you were to think, casually (without research), how many human beings have attained salvation (or, enlightenment) in the last 2,000 years, how many people could you come up with? We're not talking Jesus or Lao Tzu. We're talking Martin Luther King and Elvis Presley. We're talking David Icke and Albert Einstein. How many? 100? 200? 1000? Okay, let's say 10,000 just for the sake of it — we can add Francis Bacon, Nikola Tesla and Galileo Galilei — well, how many people are there in the world? 7 billion.

What's the other problem? Because I already see a problem in the 10,000 enlightened ones. And these are not even all spiritual leaders. The other problem is that we have an incredible amount of schools for enlightenment, from Christianity to Buddhism and Islam, then to Confucianism, Satanism, Taoism, and Zen Buddhism. We've seen it all. Bushido code. Paganism. Shamanism. Witchcraft. Personal motivation. Deepak Chopra.

Sure, people have eased some of their suffering. People have overcome their ego identities. Found themselves. That's not the argument. The argument is that with so many transformative tools at our disposal and with such religious dedication for so many centuries — with God watching over us for millennia and wanting to see our salvation — with all these spiritual tools developed and ready to help us, why are there so few who have ended their pain and suffering?

Or asked a different way, why are so many people waiting for a messianic figure to save them? Because anyone waiting for someone to bring them salvation is automatically not enlightened. They have not attained salvation. We could, without much thinking, count the unenlightened in the several billions.

I can only conclude, and if my work on DNA holds up over time, that the systems of salvation and enlightenment we currently are using are machinations of the reality hackers. They were designed to prevent salvation. And you should be concerned about that.

If you buy a car and it never starts, despite the car manufacturer insisting that it will "eventually" start, at some point you get a refund on the car. If you buy a diet plan with the promise that you'll lose weight in three weeks, and 300 weeks later you're 46 pounds heavier, you and I can both agree that the diet plan does not in any way shape or form work. The systems of salvation we have today on the market don't work. They don't work because they were invented in the false paradigm and therefore work falsely.

Don't you think it at all a little convenient that there is one God and one Devil, two exact polar opposites, and nothing in between. I mean, there's only one hero and one villain. Doesn't that seem a little too "prepared"? Even after all these centuries, after the discovery of science and the journey into outer space, human beings are not comfortable questioning this odd situation.

It's like you tell a child a story to keep them from misbehaving. You say, "There is Santa Claus, and if you behave you will get everything you wish for. If you don't, the Grinch will take all your presents." It works on kids. I guess it also works on adults. But should it? We ask our filmmakers to add better villains and better heroes or we won't watch their movies, but when it comes to religion, whether it makes sense or not, we keep watching the same movie over and over again.

My paradigm is vastly different, and in trying to explain I'm not trying to soften it. We are living in a synthetic reality that is primarily run by an artificially-intelligent operating system (ROS). Everything within this reality is synthetic because it is a synthetic world. More specifically, we can say that it is a computer-generated world. A world having a low density and being composed of atomic matter. If God is DNA, existing in each of our trillions of cells, and the reality is controlled by an operating system, the energetic force that interacts with our genetic consciousness, then what is the maker of this reality system?

Conservatively speaking, the maker has to be able to process a very advanced programmable operating system. Also the maker has to be able to communicate with the microscopic code in the DNA: genes. The operating system is global and global is huge, encompassing 7 billion people and millions of other life forms. The DNA is incredibly advanced, stores an impressive amount of information, and is microscopic, being invisible to the human eye. (This also satisfies the requirement for a divine creator.) Further, DNA has been around for millions of years.

What we are looking at is a maker that can manage a huge system would trillions and trillions of data points. Usually, whenever you have a large operating system you also have a computer system. A computer system grows in size when the data processing requirements change. While a laptop computer can run a home-based business, the same laptop won't be able to run a car manufacturing plant. And we still haven't included the earth as a planet, with all of its ecosystems.

The logical way to go about this is to work with what we know. To run a large corporation, you need a large computer system. See where I'm going with this? But it makes sense, doesn't it? There was a global operating system, that's what we started with at the beginning of the book — and that has been derived by some groundbreaking research in at least six self-published books — and this operating system must manage and process the data (DNA) from 7 billion lives, along with plants, animals, insects and things like the entire ecosystem. All of these things are synthetically manufactured and the world is also computer-generated, verily a computer program.

A massively complex computer program along with a massive amount of DNA software code is going to require a massive computer system. What kind of maker are we looking at? We are looking at a giant computer. Perhaps we can think of this giant computer as having some kind of mobility.

We might think of this maker as a giant robot.

Part 3
Built to provide the best experience

You will be given a life review

It should be starting to make sense. (If it isn't, do not feel dismayed.) If you're going through the growing or ascension process, take your time. There is no expected time. To understand the reality operating system. It has taken me 11 years to figure this out and we're still not getting into all of the reality features.

There are people who use computers daily, but have no clue as to how they work. And there are people who are afraid to touch a computer, even though everyone else is using the computer. Even in the technological real world — the one that your five senses see — that people who have a poor understanding of computers. And, as well, there are computer experts. Oddly enough, there are even hackers.

If it takes years to learn computer science, imagine how many years it takes to learn reality science. It isn't necessary to master the ROS in order to achieve your purpose on earth. This isn't necessary. It is likely necessary to have some mastery in reality science to foster salvation (enlightenment). A master of ROS 11 could attain salvation far faster than a beginner.

As well, as the master of ROS 11 is probably here acting in the capacity of a technician, even perhaps a teacher. They have likely already attained salvation and volunteered to help earth's citizens to make the technological leap forward. I am of the mind that human-looking reality technicians are among us, working indiscreetly.

This is what this book is about. Forward. This might be too forward for sure for some. And it might be just right for others. I've never seen a book written like this so I can't really predict how well it will be received, or how long it will take to become adapted. But I'm hopeful; otherwise, I wouldn't be writing it.

The past is one thing. The future is quite another. This book is a kind of techno-spiritual introduction to ROS 11. At least that's the original intention, but as you can see we've had to fill in a lot of details. What I like to think of as the context. Next, I think we should talk about some basic rules in a synthetic reality.

The first rule has to do with karma. You may think of it as a spiritual concept having Hindu and Buddhist origins, and that's fine, because it's true. And I refer you back to the premise of this book: ROS 11. Reality is synthetic. It is a software program, so advanced that you believe it to be real when it is not real. Therefore, when I talk about karma, before using a different term, I'd like you to think of it as an ROS feature. Think of karma as an application.

Karma is the result from action. Consequence. Benefit. It is the flow of energy that has been created. Karma is a waveform and it can resonate in your life, across other lives, and return to you at many different levels. Karma is energy. It is your database of experience. Your GPA. You create karma. You incarnate with preloaded karmic energy, which kind of forces you down a particular road. You generate karma through your actions, or in actions. Whether you believe in it or not doesn't change the fact that ROS 11 utilizes the karma app.

Karma in the afterlife is a kind of currency. You build up your karma in this life so that in the next life you have a better choice, ie you don't want to come back to earth. That goes back to the hijacked planet and how they've trapped people here in karmic debt. To repay the karmic debt in the afterlife, they are forced to return to earth, where they incur more karmic debt because the world is rigged.

You can see how all the layers can really add up and prevent you from ever truly waking up. And we've only scratched the surface. After your expiration, under whatever conditions stipulated in your contract, you will be given a Life Review. There are three types of the Life Review that I think we should briefly cover: The Living Review, The Download Review, and The Personal Review.

The Living Review

This is a life review that occurs while you are living, which I suppose is counter to the typical association with a life review. During a lifetime it is necessary to review how your life is going. Have you achieved what it is you came to achieve? What is your current karmic score? Are you on the path to finish the rest of your obligations? Is it necessary to make an amendment to your contract? Are there any outstanding issues?

The Living Review can happen at any time. It could take place in the middle of the night. It could happen in a feverish dream. You might even experience this kind of review after you've had a traumatic experience and you're in the hospital. You might not think of associating a tragic event with a Life Review, but really it could be the case that the tragic event was ordered so as to facilitate the space for a Life Review. As we all know, people on the earth, wrapped in the illusions of the false reality are very busy. Preoccupied. There is always something to do, something to worry about, and something to avoid doing.

A person who is actively self-actualizing (attempting to wake up) will often do their own Mini Review on their life, and during those periods of introspection they may receive extra wisdom from the ROS because they're able to tap into the higher frequencies. A skilled self-actualizer may even skip the Living Review interruption by logging into the network and downloading an updated incarnation contract and then internally matching the obligations and requirements with what they've accomplished so far in life. Although the self-actualizing method is preferred, unfortunately it is reserved for the advanced reality citizen.

The Living Review, when done through an intermediary sent by the ROS, which monitors every human user, will produce a summarized report. This report will be downloaded into the user's DNA, a storage and software medium, and the user will experience a flush of new perspectives on life following that process.

A person, who is say, way off course and living a terrible life, when compared to their original intention, may experience a period of depression, emotional outbursts, and even fall back into old behaviors such as addictions and abusive tendencies. It is possible and it depends on the discrepancy in the obligations and how far person has deviated from the path.

The Living Review is a process that is meant to remind the person as to why they incarnated on the earth. And if I could say, in case I haven't, not everyone came to earth to be rich, not every man was born to beat his wife, not every model has to throw up to look skinny, and not every politician has to become corrupt to remain in power. While it's a nice dream to want to be a famous celebrity, the fact remains that famous celebrities are not particularly happy, they're not smarter than non-famous people and they're also not as wealthy as they are perceived to be.

Those that don't listen to their Living Reviews, intentionally or through coincidences, will continue to fall off the path at some point, will miss the threshold for life completion. Sometimes, having the Living Review done, a person will want to make a significant shift and this may appear as a career change, a lifestyle change, or even be the result of a memoir. A memoir is a kind of Living Review whereby the user has made it their responsibility to review just how they got where they came to be.

A memoir is a transformative process and after writing a memoir a person will find themselves in a new space for contemplation. It used to be the case that people in their senior years would write memoirs as a way to prepare for their next lives, but often those people were important or famous and had many accomplishments to share. In other words, the memoir of a significant person, in the past, was a benefit to that person and to their legacy.

In more recent years, all kinds of people are writing memoirs, even if memoirs are disguised as movies and television series. Again, my perspective on this is that people are electing to perform their own Living Reviews as a way to ensure that they did not come here to live a wasted life. A life that is wasted is a life that needs to be relived. A Living Review is a modest process whereby a person can return to the fundamental reasons why they are here during their lifetime, and depending on the person, multiple Living Reviews may be experienced.

The Download Review

This is a life review that occurs after you have passed on, which is how most people would interpret it. In the afterlife, it is necessary to review just how well you did. Did you accomplish everything you came here to accomplish? Not all those things are obvious. Being famous is not always a goal. Being famous may simply be a vehicle for doing something else and it is that something else that will be revealed during a Download Review.

Basically, as I understand it, our DNA stores and records everything that happens in our lives. Without judgment. The DNA records and there are other things associated with the DNA, features in the ROS, that can spot record everything on a 360° scale. Yes, your entire life is recorded but key events are especially annotated.

Sometimes this data is also uploaded into the ROS platform, and sometimes not. Depends on the person and their skills with the ROS. The ROS is there to serve you. It has immense storage capacity and an impressive set of functions that can be utilized by those who are skilled in reality software programming, which I suppose those numbers of people are few.

The Download Review takes place on another dimension. Your entire genome can be downloaded and scanned, just like a computer hard drive, in almost no time at all. A report can be digitally produced, containing several scores, and those scores will determine how well you accomplished what you came here to accomplish.

I think it is important that we put some qualifiers on this life review because it is easy to think, in a human context, that there is such a thing as a good life and a bad life. It is easy to think that, but from my experience this is not true. The ROS doesn't look to see if you lived a good life or a bad life. It is easy to think that, but from my experience this is not true. The ROS doesn't look to see if you've lived a good life or a bad life. The ROS looks to see how far you tossed your life down the toilet, which more often than not is the case.

It is the case because people don't realize that they came here for a specific purpose. They came here with a list of things to do, and if those things are not done, and the reincarnation process could very well include another tour of earth, only this tour won't be as pleasant as the previous tour and may even include a list of conditions to ensure you accomplish your goals. For example, a reincarnate returns to earth, and in order to prevent them from falling off the path, they are matched with a spouse. The spouse is exceptionally loving and supportive, and without which goals would never be accomplished.

The Download Review is very thorough. Everything is examined. Your life data is mined. There are other pieces of information that the ROS looks for hiding inside your life data. That may not be revealed to you because it may not be necessary or it may not make any sense to you. The information is added to the ROS and processed accordingly.

The ROS needs information to remain viable. Human users offer the perfect pieces of information because they are living programs within the system. Their data is actual data and actual data it is better than projected data. The difference between actual and projected data is indicative of the efficiency of the system. If, for example, many people are dying with an unfulfilled life and broken contracts, then that may not be the result of human error. That may point to something wrong with the system.

And, I think, the case has been, especially in the past, whereby the reality hackers had compromised the system so much that reincarnates were being forced, due to broken contracts, only to return to earth to be once again manipulated into falling off their life path. These issues may not always become readily apparent and due to the effects of time dilation these issues may not be immediately repaired.

So the Download Review, although it is primarily aimed and thought of as a "human thing," from a technological level it is an integral process used by the ROS to maintain efficiency of the system. The better we live out our lives, the more efficient the ROS; the more efficient the ROS, the better our lives can be lived.

We are part and parcel to this existential game. We are serving the Grand Robot and the Grand Robot is serving us. The better data that we produce, the better that the reality functions. It might not appear to make sense at the outset, and it has taken me more than a decade to write a book like this, but as you make sense of things, and as the reality improves, and functions at a higher frequency, the technological aspects of reality reveal themselves.

The Personal Review

This is a life review that occurs after the other two life review protocols have taken place, and is a requirement when there are issues that need to be discussed. Occurring mostly in the afterlife, though the Personal Review does also happen during the process of living, this review allows a life to be examined in closer detail.

The examination of life is sometimes necessary. A perfect life may need to be examined. A dismal life may also need to be examined. If we look in the real world we find both successful people and unsuccessful people going through therapy. A successful person wants to become better. An unsuccessful person wants to avoid a total demise of life. We look at it as self-improvement.

A Personal Review, if I recall the situations I saw when I was in the afterlife, involved sitting down with reality technicians in a private room on another dimension. During the interview process, the specific life issues were revealed and discussed. This type of review is ideal for people who want to make significant alterations to their contracts.

The Personal Review is also useful for times when a significant life player, someone who will incarnate on earth to lead big changes, wants to make amendments to the current contract. Sometimes, having achieved and surpassed their obligations, a new contract must be drafted up and attached to the old contract. There can be multiple contracts on some lives. Again, it is not usual, but we also we are also not having a usual discussion.

A Personal Review can draw out specific issues in a life. Lives could be specifically managed. Special cases can be handled.

During the Life Review process, the topic of karma will inevitably come up. Karma is currency in the afterlife. We are supposed to collect karma during our time on the earth. We are supposed to protect our karma. If karma was like money, and you wanted to retire with a large nest egg, then you should take an interest in how much karma you have. Karma leads to a prosperous afterlife retirement.

Let's take a bit of a step back and look at the false reality, you know, the one created by the hackers. The reality hackers — acting as Master Controllers — have inverted and reversed the world, to such an extent that it is difficult to live a prosperous life. It's even more difficult to live a life that ends the karmic cycle, and a lot of that has to do with the evaluation, even misunderstanding, of karma.

In the false reality, karma has been replaced by money. Karma has been redefined in such a way as to serve a false system of existence. Money is the currency of life. We need money to buy things. We need money to do things. We go to work to earn money. We need to earn enough money to retire wealthy. It's a very complicated setup. But, money doesn't guarantee anything.

Rich people have bigger problems than poor people. Retiring wealthy could turn out to be problematic if a sudden tragedy arises that consumes the nest egg. Or a medical crisis. Or an economic crisis. Or a natural disaster. Things happen to throw out the best of plans and money runs out sooner rather than later.

In the false reality, money is the focus and karma belongs to spiritual beliefs. Money is more important than karma, and yet at the end of life money has no value, and karma as every value. In the afterlife, nobody cares about how much money you have. They care about what you learned, if you achieved your contractual obligations, and how much karma you have earned after all previous debts, obligations, and fees have been paid. You may have a karmic nest egg in your own mind, but after the accountants go through everything, you may not have anything left. Whatever it is you have left may not be enough to get you into an ideal reincarnation.

The karma I'm talking about is not the same as the spiritual karma. It is not the same as karma when it is used on television or by a famous celebrity. The karma I'm talking about is a technological karma. A currency that wholly connects you to a technological world. This technological karma is like a computer without any corrupt code. It is like a machine without a virus. It represents a system that is functioning at its peak. A spiritual athlete. When you have a Life Review and your karma is clean, your debts are paid, and your contractual obligations are done, well, you can pretty much move on. (Hint: that's the basic goal of this school.)

And here's the kicker: you want to move on. You may not fully understand that right now, but if you're really reading this book (and it is a very unusual book), then you are probably, at some level, understanding the concepts provided herein. And the contents are being presented to make sure you live out your life as you intended prior to incarnation; to live out your life as you indicated in a contract you signed before entering into a human body; to live out your life fully and completely so that you can finish your tour of duty on the earth.

The features in ROS 11 are extremely robust and can tabulate karmic currency like never before. It is unfortunate that society is woefully unaware that they are living inside of a computer-generated reality. As more and more people move forward in this technological game, this information should find a larger and larger audience; and I personally don't place any time quotient on that. I have no expectation. This information being provided is information as I understand, within the context that this information has been nearly impossible to obtain historically and that previous versions of this knowledge fell under the category of spirituality, metaphysics, and religion.

I do not consider these ideas to be spiritual or religious in any way, although people may indeed make that interpretation. That interpretation belongs to the interpreter. I'll state again, and I'd like for it to be explicitly stated, we are living inside a computer-generated reality. The latest Reality Operating System is version 11 and it is the most advanced operating system for the new century ever engineered.

ROS 11 is a stable and thoughtful program with an immense upwards scalability. The architectural foundation is remarkably stable and it should last for a good long time. ROS 11, because of its impressive features and scalability, will further enable a generation of people whose genetic attributes are worlds apart from their most recent ancestors.

ROS 11 is about escaping the shackles of spirituality and the *prisonistic* religious ideologies and in doing so entering a new waveform of existence. A birthright. A new era of life upon a new dimension of existence. It may not be immediate for everyone, and only a few may start, but it has already started and you have every reason to join the ride. Just pay attention to some of the rules.

The seamless world

ROS 11 is the operating system of this reality. Human beings are loaded with different versions on ROS 11, some are very old versions that have never been upgraded.

Some human beings act as users; some human beings act as reality computer servers.

ROS 11 as many apps available for download, once the body's operating system has been reconditioned. The reconditioning process can take years under the right guidance and can include all of things a person adheres to in order to obtain enlightenment, nirvana, or to return to Jesus. I prefer the use of the term "self-actualization" since it more closely relates to this material. Methods of ascension and rebirth are also possible. And remember that you may not feel the need to self-actualize all the time. It usually happens in cycles, and when you need to self-actualize you will want to re-read parts of this book.

Reality software was built by very advanced cosmic engineers. The software was designed to enable your life and the life of your family. Built to provide the best experience you could ever imagine. The reality codes interact with the genetic architecture and deliver an amazing level of performance. The more your genome is up-to-date, the more fulfilling your life will be.

Nature is a place of genetic computing renewal. This is where your digital DNA gets a direct and full access to the earth machine. The earth machine in your body machine are built on the same standards.

Because of the nature of a changing world, and constant software updates, the best form of protection in your life is to remain updated. Some updates are essential and your system will be updated automatically. If you are unfamiliar with the process, or you haven't gotten into the habit of spending quality time in nature, then these upgrade periods may feel more intense than usual.

In severe cases, an upgrade may turn into a strange cold or flu, even during your vacation, which is the worst time to get a cold or flu. Have you ever had a strange flu and then afterwards felt sort-of reborn? You probably have also had a flu where afterwards you felt strangely worse?

One of the methods of a genomic software upgrade, among the many methods, is by way of an energized "invisible cloud." The Gnostics referred to them as "luminous clouds." An invisible cloud finds the human subject, syncing up to their energy signature, and envelops the subject in an invisible energy cloud. The cloud can be felt as a tingling feeling. Sometimes limbs can fall asleep, and often people will feel an intense pressure around their body and head. That may prompt some people to take painkillers and other substances, including herbal remedies. Those reactions, strangely enough, are methods of adjusting the vibration and frequency of the body in order to facilitate the energetic transfer.

In a negative situation, and energetic cloud (a kind of a simple symbiotic program), having enveloped a person may need to be defended against. An attack may typically downgrade the body's natural frequency and the person would likely take steps to raise their frequency, using effective and ineffective methods.

Natural methods tend to be more effective. But, some people have developed their own method, and even if it isn't natural or perfect, it may work for them. For example, to combat this supernatural situation a person may exercise intensely and then sit in the sauna for an extended period of time. They may find refreshment after swimming in the ocean.

ROS version 11 comes packaged with a host of applications, applicable to different groups of people. If there were three broad versions of ROS 11, one would be for people living out their lives without incident. Another version is for users who want to change aspects of the world; for those who want to have a developer community. A third suite of reality applications is designed for reality technicians (reality magicians). They will have access to special apps (which require special skills), earth support codes, speech recognition protocols, and different server editions.

Early versions of the ROS required stringent spiritual dedication and ascetic compliance. Only monks and prophets could carry the latest version of Reality OS. The capacity of the DNA software has increased dramatically and the monkhood is no longer required to remain updated.

There is a seamless compatibility between the genetic software and the DNA architecture. DNA that has been compromised by chemicals, vaccines, viruses, and even electromagnetic interference. Genetic heritage plays a central role in scale and processing of the ROS.

Additionally, versions of reality may share groups and shared societies. Since the ROS is a multidimensional platform — having energetic parts, genetic codes and parts, and also bearing certain existential frequencies — people may group into various aspects of the platform.

Groups and societies will likely form, holding a certain energetic pattern, seen as an understanding and a shared ideology, having invariably the same frequency range. It should be noted that frequency ranges are many, in that the ROS can service many types of functions. At the higher frequency, the ROS maintains the earth's ecosystem, which is well outside of most human ability. At the standard range you get people, or societies. I like to think of them as cultures.

A culture of people operates on the same frequency range. What might appear as linguistic differences, color of skin variations, religious beliefs and culture traditions are in fact differences in the frequency allocation like a radio station on the FM band. The cultural station also functions on a particular frequency broadcast. The signal set into the ROS. As you may already be thinking, there are hundreds of cultural groups on the planet, with smaller groups and societies nested within these larger groups.

A Buddhist temple in Hong Kong is different than a Buddhist temple in Vancouver, even though they're both Buddhist per se, and even have a large Chinese membership. There is a slight frequency variation in the two: A Tibetan Buddhist temple will see an even greater fluctuation and a Church of Jesus, and its membership, will have an even wider frequency variant.

Companies have their own culture, stemming from the management and the financial owners. People will gravitate to certain companies and to work in certain industries, all, I think, a result of vibrational kinship. What we think of as a culture, career, and corporations.

What is really happening underneath the veil of existence is that people are tapping into a particular frequency broadcast. Any type of sizable group, even a gang, they exist because of a frequency broadcast. Sometimes to join the gang you'll have to be initiated, or, we can think of it as adapting your frequency. Modulation. The magical class has been doing it for millennia. Secret societies as well.

Groups and cultures can be thought of as productive societies. You join a church because it resonates with you. You follow a certain author because he or she makes sense. A film franchise has its audience. All of it building on the frequency bands of ROS 11. While some people will remain in a group their whole lives, people who can modulate their frequencies (if they've done the upgrading and they have the genetics) can switch groups and even careers. It might even be easy for them to do so.

There are also counter-productive frequencies that can be a detriment to your life. Following a very low vibrational group will not be good for you. Watching a horror movie franchise is not something that invigorates higher frequency. Personally, I don't watch horror movies as a genre. Some filmmakers are mixing genres and then it's a decision on whether the story is worth the assault on the frequency modulators. Dropping your frequency — through bad diets, lack of exercise, heavy vaccinations, and watching too many horror movies — could lead to joining groups or working for companies that are all operating in a very low vibration. You could, I have seen it, get trapped into a low vibrational frequency and years may go by without much growth. Think of a bad marriage as an example.

Where were we? Right, we were talking about the seamless compatibility between the genetic software and the DNA architecture. In earlier epochs, people had to take a spiritual path in order to attain enlightenment, which is essentially the rejoining onto the reality architecture. You had to dedicate years of training the mind and body, foregoing the pleasures of life, eating a strict and tasteless diet, and abandoning the path of the common man (traditional spirituality was primarily for men). But, in our modern context; what were spiritual seekers after? Synchronization with the ROS.

They were doing everything they could to log onto the Network of Light. And only a spiritualist could do it because that ROS version was not user-friendly. In a way, the ROS builders and engineers didn't want everyone having access to the advanced features of reality, and for those who did they had to practice (and master) things like humility and egolessness. An egotistical being who could access the reality software, and in particular certain apps, could devastate the world. So maybe that's why the spiritual path was invented. Maybe the monk life was a kind of safety form of preparation for exclusive interaction with reality. Still today, there are Zen Buddhists developing "no mind," and searching for that elusive enlightenment, a moment of utter serenity; a synchronization with the God construct.

While meditation is always helpful, the new genomic structures found in the new generation come with a lot of technological improvements — achievements which, when properly utilized, would end the very idea of the spiritual path.

The genome is the software of existence. A more robust software platform with more code doesn't need to attend the church to commune with God. In fact, these people will know internally that the DNA is God and that the DNA can reunite them with the ROS. And coupled with the genomic advancements in ROS 11, the best version of reality (ever) for this time period. As I've said, in very early time epochs the reality software was a little too robust and that caused a number of problems, especially after the system got hijacked.

These groups of hijackers had damaged parts of the system and corrupted the genetic software. As a result, not everything is equal. The early attempts to correct and repair the damage done by the hackers has also been unequal. The reality technicians might have found ways to repair the software but then a repair would've naturally led to the release of other software versions; either software versions would've forced people to upgrade their own genomic data. How did people agree their genomic data in those earlier days? Via the spiritual path. How did people upgrade the genomic data when an entirely new version of reality was released? They joined a new spiritual or religious group.

When your prophet no longer can make you feel good, you find yourself another spiritual leader. The appearance of new spiritual teachers could in fact be a result of a new version of the Reality OS being released. Siddhartha Gautama, Buddha, probably appeared during a major upgrade in reality; hence, why these teachings are so long lasting. Buddha appeared 2500 years ago. We are still reading and studying, and trying to understand spiritual teachings from 2,500 years ago, and those teachings, surprisingly, still hold profound value. Which is easy to dismiss.

On the technological level, and this is why this is the only book in the world to ever do this, the methods of enlightenment still work, to some extent, because the reality engineers came from the same reality school. They also use the same programming language and the software platform is still in use. The software is scalable. Twenty-five hundred years later — what does that say about the Reality Operating System?

The computer-generated reality is a software program. The software exists in its own time and space. The program can be considered timeless. Ask yourself, does software get old? Does it age? Does a software program get gray hairs? The ROS operates within the reality construct. It is like sunshine. It doesn't look like software. It is like air. It doesn't look like a program. That is also the beauty of ROS 11. Seamless integration.

It has been around for so long and it is so advanced, that the software appears to look like things we've always seen. We breathe air, but we never think of it as something more. We drink water, but we never think of it as something more. We eat food, but we never think of it as something more.

When I talk about the technology behind our very existence — and you have to admit that the science of existence is absolutely wonderful; remarkable really — I do so with the "seamless integration" initiative. It doesn't look like technology. We call it the "sky" or the "sun." They don't look like technology. They are thought of as natural or celestial, but if we live in a computer-generated reality then the sky is not just a blue dome and the sun is not just a golden furnace.

ROS 11 is a frequency and photon-based operating system typically referred to as the "world." Within this world is the "earth," which has its own operating system, Earth OS. The Earth OS was developed alongside civilizations. The Reality OS, because it has never been diagnosed in this manner in the history of the planet, has often been thought out as God, Creator, Maker or even the Tao.

When ancient people thought of the ROS they assumed it was God. When ancient people went on their knees to pray, they assumed they were talking to God. When the sky cracked thunder and slammed lightning, people assumed it was God.

When I've attempted to do, and only the future will reveal whether I've been successful or not, is to start with a more accurate definition that God, according to ancient Gnostic teachers and their authenticated texts, is better described as DNA. That became the starting point of a very different kind of nonreligious discussion. Things again moved forward when science redefined DNA as the software for life.

So we have the software of life inside of our bodies. But, we have been led to believe that we live in a world created by divine maker. I've expanded the discussion by making a compelling case that this world is a computer-generated reality, wholly supported by the fact that human beings along with the entire set of biodiversity, are operated by genetic software.

The computer program is the Reality OS and the latest version is version 11. Human beings have the same ROS inside of their genome, but are not likely up-to-date. In my book *The Arc of Reality* I referred to the human body as the "Ark." The Ark is running the Ark OS. What we perhaps have not done, and this isn't the book to do this, is to connect the human being (Ark) back to our microbiological framework and the DNA God theory. Yes, it is all still a theory, but I think it is a compelling theory with a lot of good evidence.

When we study the Gnostic scriptures, authenticated by Coptic scholars, we find mention of the human being in the biological context. The human being, as understood by the ancients, is the human chromosome in the modern context. Human beings, using an ancient understanding, are in fact chromosomes. These chromosomes (human beings) wear a body of flesh (ie what we call humans). "You do not know this because of the cloud of flesh that overshadows you." (The Second Discourse of Great Seth)

Similarly, the planet, an engineered machine, is running the Earth OS. These advanced software systems are all tied to the gene-based user interface, making energy life forms in this computer program intimately connected and an integral part of the system.

Seamless applications, software integration, and existential beauty provide each user (citizen on earth) with an immaculate experience, exactly the kind and breadth of experience that they came here to live. The biological shroud over the world has prevented humanity from truly appreciating the technological ingenuity that we are all designated to share.

The world is not an accident. The planet was engineered and built using very advanced systems — system of evolution, systems of procreation, weather systems, purification systems, regeneration systems, food production systems, air circulation systems, and even thought communication systems.

We like to think that we're biological lifeforms that just happened to have appeared on a floating rock in space on account of a white-haired old man. And that story has sufficed for millennia, only that now, as a far more mature civilization drenched in televisions, nuclear warheads, and computerized devices, the story of "life on earth" has been given an unprecedented makeover. It is my opinion that the technological version of reality is the most accurate depiction of reality ever presented in the modern history of the world.

Oneness with the reality system

The more you seek enlightenment, the more you seek enlightenment. It no longer really is enlightenment; with ROS 11, enlightenment is better thought of as the realization that you are living inside of a computer-generated reality. This is not a level of realization allocated to every individual.

In fact, this level of realization is allocated to individuals who have already woken up to the fact that this planet isn't working right. And that it hasn't been working right for a long time. The next step is to realize that the reason why the world is working upside-down and in reverse is because it has been surreptitiously hijacked; taken over, slowly and methodically, over centuries.

People who have been monitoring their spiritual progress, and who have monitored the traditional methods of enlightenment, are going to have to adapt these traditional views for the technological state of reality. In the early times of Buddhism and Taoism, masters and teachers presented a way of *liberation*, and an end to pain and suffering. For those who practice Zen, liberation was a mental process and sutras were written to develop the mind until enlightenment could be achieved, through years of rigorous practice.

If the technological determination for enlightenment is an acclimation to the computer-generated reality, then what is a better description of enlightenment in this fresh approach? Because, if we can agree that enlightenment is valid, having been practiced for millennia, then what is a better descriptive of enlightenment? Enlightenment is being "one with the universe." In Taoism, this is thought of as a kind of spontaneity.

Technologically speaking, oneness and spontaneity can be reinterpreted as, back to our radio analogy, *tuning* into the frequency of the operating system. Remember, the Reality OS has always been playing in the background of existence. And we live in a multidimensional world. On a higher frequency sits the ROS.

How do you tap into the universe, if the universe is the ROS? You *raise* your vibration, which raises your operational frequency and gives you access to the features on the ROS. The ROS operates on the furthest point of the electromagnetic spectrum, maybe even a bit further than that.

Enlightenment doesn't think about frequency and vibration. It starts with detachment, letting go, and quieting the chatter in the mind. Why? Because these things block the path to liberation. How do you obtain liberation? Practice your mental powers. But it's not a straightforward process, as any Zen practitioner knows. Because you cannot seek enlightenment directly, if you do it only eludes you.

Instead, you practice "detachment" and quieting the mind, and things of that nature.

I'm not saying to get rid of enlightenment, rather I'm saying enlightenment is syncing with the technological reality, which functions at the native frequency, a frequency that essentially makes us "one with the system." We are probably familiar with syncing with a Wi-Fi signal to get online access. Our smartphones must sync with the bandwidth frequency of the telecom company; otherwise the smartphone will not have any radio signal. When you are outside of the telecom network you can't use your mobile phone. It is not because your mobile phone doesn't work, rather it is because there's no network service in that area. It also is because the signal is blocked. There may even be electromagnetic interference. Your own mind may contain blocks that need to be removed.

So you may have a mobile phone (you certainly heard of one and have friends who own mobile phones) and may be on the network. But if your mobile is turned off, you can't use your phone. If your mobile software has a software virus, you may have limited access to the network. If your mobile phone has limited functionality and a slow processor or small amount of hard drive space, then your access to the network may be similarly compromised. Or better stated, a new mobile phone with all the latest in technological innovations will have the best and fastest access to the telecom network.

Taking this over to the human side of reality, we can see that a person whose mind is full of chatter and who has never attained enlightenment (and never thought about it), that they will have minimal access to the ROS. The ROS transmits all the basic existential codes. The lowest tier includes all the basics: thought communication, genetic maintenance, health and regeneration, connection to the planet and to the universe, and of course the maintenance of all necessary ecological systems. The lowest tier will also allow a person the opportunity to receive the major ROS upgrades, usually because these will come through as a necessary download.

In these global upgrades, ROS 11 down steps its operational frequency, capturing the largest number of users and transmits the necessary reality codes. In other cases, ROS 11 may activate the earth's operational systems and the earth, carrying the body of users, will raise its frequency so that in order to facilitate the upgrading of the largest number of users. Think of this as a submerged submarine, loaded with people, climbing up to the surface to refuel and then diving back to the bottom of the ocean.

Syncing with ROS 11, as we can see, is not standard. There are people who have dedicated their time to achieving it (eg monks) and there are people who have never cared for it (eg investment bankers), preferring that the basic operational codes were just perfect. There are also people who are naturally in sync with reality (eg happy people), and we probably know who those people are. These are people who have faith in God and trust in the universe. These people don't believe in coincidences. They believe that they came here on earth for a purpose. If you have the feeling that you are here for a purpose, you have a certain connection to the ROS.

There are also people who have either the genetics, or activated genes, and they naturally feel with the ROS. The may have always felt things were right with the world. Their career path was pretty straightforward. Their life evolved quite naturally. They may have followed a religious ideology, or they may not have. Their faith may have been the reason why their life was straightforward and generally successful. Then again faith has everything to do with DNA and DNA has everything to do with the computer-generated world.

Buddhist and Taoist practice techniques to conquer the mind. The conquering of the mind, essentially the self, opens the path to liberation and an end to suffering. The ancient Gnostics, as another example, used knowledge as a path to salvation. The Catholic Church advocates the belief in Jesus Christ and the writings in the Bible as their salvific formula.

Whether Buddhist, Christian, or Gnostic there is a body of spiritual evidence, dressed up as sacred writings (scriptures and sutras), to support the idea that human beings need a way to end their "pain and suffering." Why? Because this world is believed to be filled with pain and suffering, and the reasons for this pain and suffering is different depending on which belief system you choose.

What I'm presenting isn't another belief system. This is not a new religion or spiritual path. My view is that there is no such thing as spirituality. And I've shown that there is no God. If there's no God, there's no need of religion. If there's no spirituality, because we live in a technological world, and there's no religion, because God is DNA; and if we can agree that the hijacked world does indeed produce pain and suffering — then we are still dealing with pain and suffering. We are still in need of liberation, even if that liberation has a technological quotient.

What I'm presenting is a handbook for technological liberation on the premise that reality is a manufactured system. In other words, we live in a world but that world was engineered by reality scientists. We live in a 5 Sense Hologram and many aspects of the hologram have been woefully corrupted, distorted and even reprogrammed. We are like mobile phones that have a software virus trying to connect to a main network (Network of Light) has been blocked by a subnetwork. The *path to liberation* has everything to do with reconnecting our frequency so as to jump out of the subnetwork and onto the main network, the place where truth and knowledge reside.

So we are trapped. We have been sequestered into living under the artificial confines of a subnetwork. That subnetwork was inserted by the reality hackers and they did so as to cut us off from the main Network of Light. When we strip away all the religious ideology and the spiritual technology, and we settle on the basic situation we find ourselves more able to clearly think of an exit strategy.

Imagine for a moment that your mobile phone, because of a virus, logged onto and synced up with a pirate network, operating within the main telecom network. And this happens when you "roam" with your mobile phone. Only that when you roam, as you leave the subnetwork you sync back up to your telecom supplier. In your city there are several telecom networks overlapping one another with different frequencies. Frequency bands.

The pirate network, using the main network as its base, has created a virtual network and then by way of a virus and many psychological machinations has trapped mobile phone users onto their pirate network. Over the centuries of spiritual evolution, both the virus and the technical nature of the subnetwork have mutated and changed in such a way that mobile users have become trapped in an inferior reality. Not only that, but feeling imprisoned has forced people to alter their view of reality to match that of their imprisonment.

We have long forgotten the true nature of the Network of Light, thinking that we are not worthy of being in that space. But that Network of Light is our birthright. That Network of Light is where we all belong and its operational frequency is so high from what we've grown accustomed to that we think of it as beyond our reach. And so we suffer the turbulence of a lower vibration.

Now, that all sounds a bit ominous and overwhelming. And it probably will at first, until you can scale your mind onto a techno-technical framework. Life looks organic, but it's really synthetic. That is not necessarily a bad thing. It is not a bad thing because it's been here for billions of years. It's only now you're being told about it in a way that makes sense.

Of course, this material doesn't make sense for everyone and (probably) many people will have to do some cleansing and detachment activities to make some space on their heart drive. If you are loaded with spiritual beliefs and preconceptions, traditional ways of thinking, then all of that data takes up storage space, making it hard to learn this material. But, find your own speed forward.

I do not recommend that everyone jump into this material. As you go along, you will necessarily have to cleanse yourself of outdated ideas before you can replace them with new ones; instead of it being the other way around. Have courage in the face of new knowledge.

I can say that I did not get here in one or two steps. I went through the process of knowledge transfer, but I did it without all the materials I have developed, so it should be much easier than what I had to go through. This material is not perfect. I have extracted the main ideas and I have simplified and adapted this material so that a larger audience can understand it, rather than turning it into a scientific paper, which only a few can understand. My hope is that as you go along, the material becomes more relatable. It starts heavy and if you keep motivating yourself, you will get your second and third wind. Don't give up. This is important.

The zen of the technological fountain

Philosopher and Buddhist teacher Alan Watts writes in his famous book *The Way of Zen*, "There must soon be a source of information at the end of the line which is the final authority. Failure to trust its authority will make it impossible to act, and the system will be paralyzed."

One of the central tenets of Buddhism is "dharma" (the teachings) and the dharma is believed to be able to be transmitted from one master to the next. If the teachings are one thing and a special transmission is another thing, then how does that fit into our technological theory? If dharma is "data" (packets of data) and if transmission happens because of a Wi-Fi network, then it is possible, according to even the wisest Buddhist masters, to receive a transmission of codes to provide ultimate enlightenment.

Similarly, we can infer that the originator of Buddhism, Buddha, would have been able to transmit his teachings. And this may be understood among master Buddhists, but is not generally shared except to suggest that dharma can be transmitted, without explaining the exact nature of that all-important transmission, and expectedly so.

A spiritual transmission would be rooted in a higher frequency, one that everyone else is not privy to; the one that a master of Buddhistic methodology would have good and liberal access. There is a story of a fifth patriarch in Zen Buddhism in the 7th century who selected a low level monk, a rice pounder and wood splitter, as his replacement, and he was able to elevate the monk to 6th patriarch by way of special transmission.

Dial up the modern age of technology, using Wi-Fi or Bluetooth you can transmit data from your smartphone to another computing device. It happens every day. Knowledge, be it a photo, a document or a webpage address, can be transmitted. Contracts can be transmitted. Book manuscripts can be transmitted. Sutras can also be transmitted. You can, if you were a computer scientist, transmit computer code and programs. You could also transmit a virus. Zen authority and emissary D. T. Suzuki writes, "A brilliant intellect may fail to unravel all the mysteries of Zen, but a strong soul would drink deep of the inexhaustible fountain."

Once again there is a fountain, insisting of the flow of water as energy; for the soul drinks energy and the energy is the backbone of an ineffable (artificially lit) reality. Enlightenment, in Zen philosophy, cannot be expressed in words. Why not? The saying goes you cannot drink all the water in the river. The technological equivalent is saying that the data stream has too much data. The energy is an electromagnetic field of inexhaustible codes. A Network of Light.

The builders of the earth

The mystery exists when the mind is unacquainted with the true nature of reality, verily, Zen is about tapping into the true nature of reality. Zen is an ancient method of syncing with the ROS. At least this is my take. My work says that the reality architecture was installed shortly after the planet was built, which is a whole other discussion. Suffice it to say that there are planetary builders and they built the earth. It is a masterfully built habitat, you must admit.

Other types of engineers built the star system, and the galaxy, but these builders are, again, a very advanced group of beings, the likes of which could not be properly understood in words. Think cosmic beings. Some of these beings, as an example, could be a black hole. A black hole is a type of sentient being, a very complex one, but sentient nonetheless.

These celestial cultures have within them the scientific capacity and elegance to engineer celestial objects. Once earth was complete, and after an atmosphere was installed, that was when the reality scientists entered the scene. Before the introduction of humans.

Look, I understand your reluctance. It's understandable. It's understandable because human science has not attained the level of engineering skill. We can build airplanes and bridges, even space stations, but not planets. We can build theme parks and apartment complexes. Cities. We can build cities! And to build software and computers to run cities. We can build supercomputers to monitor every technological device within the city. What we cannot do is build an entire reality system. Sure, we can build a gaming system. Film franchises. Video games. Online multiplayer games. Virtual reality games. Even holographic systems. Just not existential grade software systems. Yet.

Human beings (or, human chromosomes) are separated from the reality system. In many instances the mind has structures to ensure that the individual never remembers that there is a reality after having an interaction with it. For example, an individual may go through a spiritual upgrade. It might appear, on the physical plane, as a wild shift in the weather accompanied by an eerie feeling in the air, and a rise in tensions between groups of people. During these upgrade phases the reality architecture, having a richer level of frequency latitude, may directly engage people and download the new reality codes into the genomic data banks.

But, and this is important to understand for the layperson, once the upgrade process is done, the mental structures, somewhere in the subconscious, are activated are reactivated and the *memory* of the event slowly fades away. A day or two later, the mind completely erases the event. The process is a bit like falling in love, I suppose, whereby the attraction to another human being opens like a flower and causes things to go in motion — say a pregnancy or a marriage — and once the power of attraction is done, and the people return to reality, the magic of love recedes, the flower petals close and the memories of joy slowly fade away and the angst and regret start to build as a reason for divorce starts to grow.

The best way to see the manufactured reality is to tune your frequency to match the resonant frequency of the ROS. Once you are synced up with the ROS, doorways will open to your perception, and in fact those doorways will reveal things unimaginable. One of the reasons that so much initial effort is put on mental training in self-improvement is because of what will be revealed to you after your ascension.

You need to be grounded in who and what you are for otherwise seeing the immortal parts of reality could very well damage your mind because you will have witnessed things that perhaps have no proper and scientific explanation. What begins with self-development, and moves into mental awareness, eventually reaches new levels of dimensional awareness. On other dimensions, the mind can be stretched, and if stretched too far the mind might not be able to stretch back.

The syncing with reality, what would traditionally be thought of as "oneness," is found in any number of spiritual systems. Syncing with reality cannot happen when the intellect is armed with logic and reason. The reality scientist will overstep logic and reason in order to modulate their frequency.

Ending the autoplay

The story goes, the lord of the universe created the world through an act of self-dismemberment. The one became the many and the existential actor took on the part of every role, only that the actor made himself forget everything he had done. The actor plays along until he slowly remembers, as he remembers he draws himself together, each time remembering more and more of who he is and what he had done. Every character in his dream is an aspect of himself.

Everyone contains an aspect of the lord of the universe. A multitude of aspects living out their roles in the greatest play of all time, knowing that they are playing a role and not wanting to break their own illusion of the false reality. The illusion of reality is "Maya." This is not only the veil cast over reality, it is also the sustenance of reality. Maya, in the Hinduistic sense, is a kind of creative force in the material world. Something that moves the world in conjunction with the electromagnetic field (Brahman).

Maya is both cause (source) and effect (expansion). Maya is something that is broadcast out from the universal space (mother). Maya is the movie of existence. Maya is like the movie screen whereby tiny pixels of light portray the false reality. Maya could be a pair of virtual-reality goggles. The screens on the goggles read the consciousness through the eyes and reality is projected and sustained according to the perceiver. One who is able to understand the virtual screen of Maya, can transcend the physical reality and can attain enlightenment through the synchronization with the ROS. In other words, Maya may have been inserted to prevent spoiling the movie, only that a select group of philosophers got together and used advanced techniques to overcome Maya's rendering mechanisms.

There is a Network of Light and this network has all of the technological wonders of an extremely advanced telecom network. If that network is run by the ROS, then Maya is a molecule (cell) that when it interacts with the material world it releases some kind of electron, which itself releases a small amount of energy which creates a "pixel of existence."

The pixel of existence is read by our minds and the mind broadcasts a set of commands into the reality field. The more charged the mental command, the more intense the reality response; hence, when you really want something you are more likely to obtain it because you are charging (even overcharging) the system. You are interacting with the flow of electrons.

Given the presence of radioactive isotopes in the human body, and given that radioactive things are extremely energetic, I think that it would make sense that our minds can release or activate tiny amounts of radiation and it is this radioactive component that interacts with the "Maya particle," even to suggest that the Maya particle, the pixel of existence, is itself a radioactive compound in the network, even in the air. The earth is saturated with air molecules so it wouldn't take much to imagine how evident Maya really is.

When there's no mental command, the reality system responds to those in command, and a mind without any direct output (charging) could simply become a terminal for greater influence over the world. That would depend upon a group of people who have a mastery of this discussion, and the reality hackers are pretty good examples of that. They indeed would have the understanding that if they could shut off people's minds, they could turn those minds into reality terminals which would work solely on their behalf.

We now have some relevant information concerning Maya, the creative force sustaining what we see. In the material world, according to Hinduism, Maya has to do with the visual deception (illusion) in the popular sense. What we need is a technological comparative of the

Maya concept if only because I have taken the position in this book to redefine spiritual notions as technological processes.

If Maya is a creative force and a provision of the illusory reality, and through mental conditioning a monk, or a skilled individual, can escape the illusory Maya and attain *Satori* (spontaneous insight), it is entirely possible that Maya can be polarized by the mind to see the false reality or to see through the illusion and into the architecture of reality. Seeing into the architecture is known as enlightenment. It is Satori. Oneness. Talking to Jesus. Whatever terminology that fits your paradigm of thinking. My view is that there is one Network of Light and nestled within that an inferior subnetwork, which is the chaotic world.

Interestingly, the human body contains radioactive atoms. Some of these atomic nuclei release gamma rays. These are high-energy charged particles, photons, and they make up the electromagnetic radiation surrounding everything. Similarly, there is a background radiation, filled with low-energy photons, and there are higher energy particles (photons) being created by the sun. These charged particles interact with the molecules in the air and create ionizing radiation, basically charged particles.

The photon is at the root of all this. Particles of light. Quanta. High-energy particles and low-energy particles. These particles also operate on a specific frequency. We have frequency and energy against the backdrop of the creative force responsible for the emission of light. If Maya was to be described in a synthetic world, a good description would be a "particle of light." Maya could be better described as a "photon."

Since photons are responsible for the electromagnetic radiation in the background of reality, and since these photons are continually being replenished by the cosmic rays from the sun, we can say that photons have been around since the creation of the planet. And that also fits into our mythological model of the world. Maya is also seen as *changing*, from birthing to dying. In our radioactive model of reality, we see the omission of gamma rays from various isotopes (tritium, helium, hydrogen, potassium, uranium, radium, thallium) found in both rock and soil and inside the human body, from skeletal to soft tissue.

Maya represents these pixels of existence; particles of light in a computer-generated reality. The Tao and Zen are better described as the operating system of the digital reality which we gain access to using our genetic software. This reality is constantly being rendered as the pixels are replenished with new energy and this fits into Hindu and Buddhist thinking that the illusory world is birthing and dying. This is the flicker rate of reality.

Cosmic rays (alpha particles, beta particles, neutrons, mesons) are particles that liberate an electron from an atom. A shift in chemical bonds produces ions. Ionizing radiation, produced from electromagnetic waves (cosmic rays), is found everywhere in nature. These ionizing atoms liberate more electrons.

Potassium-40 is a radioactive isotope of Potassium. It is found in nearly every cell in human tissue. If Wikipedia is even mildly accurate, ^{40}K produces 500 gamma rays per second. Gamma rays are highly charged particles, or photons. This is one of several radioisotopes in our body that is emitting gamma radiation, in tiny amounts.

The gamma rays emitted by the body interact with the environmental gamma radiation to produce a photoelectric effect, say X-rays. Other radioactive material in our body can include: Uranium-238, Rubidium-87, Carbon-14, Tritium, Radium-226, and other primordial radioisotopes. These materials are found in soil, rock, and in our atmosphere. Our atmosphere is radioactive. The screen of existence.

We cannot see through the photon-based Maya world because our minds are functioning on the wrong frequency, a frequency that makes everything fall within the parameters of the five senses. Our minds see matter. Part of this reason is because of the DNA virus and the suppression of the human species, in general. That is a much larger argument if only because it has been going on for 5,000 years. For as long as there has been the sun, a "photon emitter," there has been Maya, photons. Billions of years.

These photons are highly responsive, and completely invisible. They get charged. They move faster or slower. They represent the pixels of reality. Whenever you watch a television screen, if you sit back a few feet from the screen you see the moving images on the screen. The actors in a movie, for example. The closer you get to the screen, the more likely you will see the pixels on the screen. Once you see the pixels, you no longer see the moving images.

An expensive television has millions of pixels, providing a sharper image, or a better way to deceive your mind. The television is deceiving you into believing that those moving images are real. Life-like. That's why we are always buying a better television. We want more realism and more realism is derived from more pixels. Better pixels. The way to deceive your mind is through more pixels.

If pixels were Maya in our reality science model, then photons are there to deceive your mind with the illusion that life is really real, when in fact it isn't. While Maya is living and dying, as energy is applied and released, the reality and architecture (Brahman) is unchanging. Brahman is like the screen upon which sit the pixels of light in a television. The screen doesn't change, the pixels, on the other hand are constantly changing color.

It could be the case that the various demigods and deities, in the sky above, were better described as radioactive isotopes. Why? Because these elements are in a process of radioactive decay. They are emitting alpha, beta and gamma particles and those particles are necessary in the sustenance of reality. And humans also have varying amounts of radioactive elements, which emit cosmic particles. The kaleidoscope of cosmic radiation, a free flow of charged particles invisible to the naked eye, is not only unimaginable, it is also a mystery to scientists.

I will argue that it is entirely plausible that deities, dating back throughout human history, are more likely reflections of cosmic particles, verily radioactive elements, as they release and absorb tiny amounts of energy. Why the deities of ancient times are no longer with us is because the makeup of the atmosphere is different, the makeup of our bodies is different, and therefore the cosmic rays of the sun produce an altogether different pantheon of particles (gods).

And all of this is rooted in the manufactured reality because the ROS has itself evolved over the millennia. Each version of the ROS had to be compliant with the radioactive makeup of the material world and the radioactive isotopes in the background had to be compliant with the radioactive isotopes in the human body. A significant change in the ROS resulted in a significant change in the background radiation and that meant a significant change in the biological radiation.

It might be hard to imagine the radioactive isotopes in the rock and soil are there for a reason, and not the result of a cosmic accident. It might also be hard to imagine a radioactive isotope can be found in the body, especially given the fact that medical doctors see radiation as a threat to health. It might even be stranger to imagine that your body right now is emitting gamma radiation. Right now you are emitting gamma radiation and it has been inside of your body since you were born.

But these radioactive isotopes play an integral role in the manufactured reality. What Zen and Taoist masters, and others, have managed to do is that they've managed to tap into their isotopes and have learned to focus their cosmic rays in such a way so as to illuminate the truth. They have learned to use their mind to beam their, say, gamma rays to alter the photons surrounding them and to see through the holographic reality. All of it done using bioavailable radiation.

Zen monks have the same basic equipment as everyone else. Not everyone may be able to attain their level of expertise, but certainly everyone can gain a much richer understanding of the true nature of reality. My view is also that illiterate peasants in ancient times were able to become one with the universe. Surely, educated and healthy citizens of the 21st century can match those achievements. What it takes is an understanding of the false world we live in and then to develop the mind in such a way so that if fosters self-actualization. Actually, there's no easy way to do any of this, but it can be done. People have obtained enlightenment, Satori, and oneness with the universe, even if for only a brief period.

How do you escape the false reality? Maybe the question is better expressed thusly, why do you want to escape? Should you be concerned? If the lessons of all the greatest spiritual teachers, and religious icons, should be believed, we have all come here so that one day we can leave here. The Christians are waiting for the messiah. The Gnostics are studying the sacred knowledge. The Buddhists are practicing detachment. Zen practitioners are learning mindfulness. Why do you want to escape? **Because you are living in a false reality.**

The Masters also share this little fact: the faster you pursue the world, the more it escapes you. Enlightenment is like a two-sided coin. If you choose one side of the coin, you lose the other side because both sides can be grasped at once. That is also why there's the practice of learning not to cling to things. The more you try to cling, the more you push it away.

The goal then is to end electromagnetic control. When you cease the waves of control (cruise control, low vibration), and you stop grasping life, you attain nirvana (one with the signal, high vibration). This is the moment of liberation. Moksha. This is the liberation from the looping birth cycle. The end of pain and suffering. samsara.

What is *nirvana* and *samsara* in a technological context?

Have you ever seen a YouTube video? There is a function next to the YouTube video called "Autoplay." The information box reads: "When Autoplay is enabled, a suggested video will automatically play next." Why do they want their videos to keep playing? Because it builds on engagement, it builds on advertisement views, and it builds on overall viewership.

When you attain nirvana, perhaps you are "turning off" the Autoplay function in your control booth. Maybe that's part of the game. You enter with things set on "automatic." As you go along, you need to fulfill your contracts, then to attain and settle karma. Nirvana means your next life program does not launch. Your life ends. You get to move on. It is so important that some people will dedicate their entire lives to attaining it.

Imagine that the reason you keep reincarnating into this reality is because the Autoplay button is switched "on," and to switch it off you have to manually extend yourself out of the false reality and to reach in and switch it off. Because the ROS assumes that anyone who has earned an end (samsara) has gone through all the steps to do so. Similarly, it could be because, and we don't fully know, that the reality hackers went into the software and selected the program responsible for the Global Autoplay of all the human users, and they turned them all on. Unless your Autoplay function had a security protection, your life cycle got switched to continual loopback.

I don't make the rules. I'm just trying to expedite the nirvana process for the many. I think that this world has been distorted and one of those distortions has been trapping people here on the earth to be constantly reborn into a world that is filled with fear and chaos, when they should have reincarnated somewhere else. Those people, feeling angry and frustrated, go about their daily lives damaging their karma and then become lost souls. For newcomers, or old-timers, it is time to graduate. You don't need to do everything on this planet.

That's what the master controllers have told you to believe. But that isn't necessary. The question to ask yourself is: what did I come here to learn? Once you've learned those things then plan on reincarnating elsewhere by following the ideas in this book.

Again, nothing is automatically granted to you. It takes discipline and persistence to navigate yourself to a better afterlife. In some cases, you may still need to come back once or twice more to alleviate all that karmic debt.

In any case, you go to school to learn and you don't go back to grade school when you're 45 years old. That's just not the way forward. When you're done with earth, graduate and leave. This way you make room for new students. Don't be selfish and work towards completing your schooling on the magnificent earth.

Father of the all

The physical world is the result of radioactive elements in the atmosphere. We can scientifically agree that there is background radiation in our environment, there are radioisotopes in our upper atmosphere, and that our bodies emit gamma radiation. Cosmic rays originating from the sun hit these atomic nuclei, bouncing high-energy particles within our atmosphere, across our streets, and perpetuating the life that we have been programmed to live. That part we may not scientifically agree on.

Electromagnetic radiation is an oscillating wave of electric and magnetic fields of energy. It contains massless photons, which create the illusory reality, rendering protocols, and encrypted data. Depending on the wavelengths, some of these frequencies we can see (eg visible reality) and most of which we cannot see (eg X-rays).

To manage this incomprehensible amount of data, we need a machine. Were you thinking that this electromagnetic radiation propagated itself? It is very easy to dismiss the eloquence of a perfectly-tuned existential system. We have done a good job of ignoring the most fundamental piece of equipment that is running our reality. The Earth Computer.

I like to think of the Earth Computer as a Grand Robot, since a robot is a kind of humanoid computer system and we are a humanoid race. The difference with a robot is that the robot has movement and sentience. The robot is involved. It can move things around.

In order to run earth, the Grand Robot must be quite large, probably larger than anything we have ever imagined. Colossal. Large enough to manage a planetary realm. You may be thinking that if this Earth Robot is so large, why have we never been able to see it? For that we have to go back to electromagnetic radiation.

Our eyes cannot see X-rays because the wavelength of X-rays, less than 10 nm (nanometers), is too short. Similarly, our eyes cannot see microwaves because the wavelength is too long, one millimeter to one meter. Gamma rays have wavelengths that are smaller than an atom. Go figure.

According to *Wikipedia*, the naked eye can see in the range of 400 to 700 nm with a frequency between 430 and 750 terahertz (THz). Hertz measures the number of oscillations per second. Terahertz radiation (T-rays) is one trillion oscillations per second. Lucky for us it isn't ionized. It cannot harm our DNA and it is largely absorbed by our atmosphere.

According to the electromagnetic spectrum, humans are virtually blind. Our eyes can only see inside of a 300 nm range, or 300 billionth of a meter across.

"Of him it may be said that he is a true father, incomparable and immutable, because he is truly singular and God. For no one is god for him and no one is father to him—he has not been born—and no other has brought him into being." (The Tripartite Tractate)

This Valentinian text from the Nag Hammadi Library is flush with jubilant and soteriological terms that discusses the nature of the Father of the All, his Son, and how the cosmos was created. What makes this ancient text fascinating is the spiritual banter, which is almost poetic. "He was given them as delight and nourishment, joy and abundant illumination, and this is his compassion, the knowledge he provides, and his union with them."

Einar Thomassen's translation of Valentinian thinking reveals an incomprehensible language of the Gnostics, verily a language that the Church Fathers used to laugh at them and then to label them as heretics. But, when we dig beneath the fanciful words we find something that is more likely to be found in broadcasting.

The Tripartite Tractate is a technological treatise, and it was written somewhere in the third century. It might not immediately jump out at you as being odd, but, if my translation is accurate, it would suggest that the Gnostics were teaching their disciples a very advanced kind of science. Reality science. Two thousand years ago. During the time of Jesus. Is it sounding fantastical yet?

The earth computer

In the text, Father is described as being both "singular" and being a "number." He was not born. He gave birth to the "All," providing the "grace" to speak about him. The Father is pre-existing, not solitary, and like a tree with a trunk, branches, and many fruit. He is incomparable, no other god came before him, and he is clothed in immutability.

Let's break some of this Valentinian thinking down into its technological equivalent. If you are familiar with the *God is DNA* volumes, then you are familiar with my transcription style. The Gnostics were early microbiologists who were able to describe the inner workings of a cell using a fanciful language that was later decided to be "spiritual," which when you properly translate the material there's no such thing as spirituality. Something more like molecular biology.

The other side of Gnostic microbiology had to do with cosmology and cosmology was a fancy way of talking about the technological world we live in. (Cosmic things are technological things.) The digital world. When we transcribe some of the thinking in *The Tripartite Tractate,* we uncover what I believe to be the Earth Computer. The Father of the All.

This is not going to be a comprehensive analysis but hopefully you will get a glimpse of what is going on. The Father is singular and is a number. A technological device is both singular and has a number (eg model number.) A manufactured device is technically "not born" because it is made and then comes to life when you flip the switch. The All, in this case, is the reality hologram. The entire electromagnetic radiation network, or Network of Light. We can speak about the All because we are given "grace" by the Father. Grace is a frequency on the electromagnetic spectrum to communicate with the All.

The Father is "pre-existing" because he is the source of the illusion. He is "not solitary" because his singular system has multiple components (eg. hardware).

Do you see where I am going with this? It's not perfect but it gives us insight into ancient thinking. He is like a tree with a trunk. We have heard that before in networks. A trunk is a main line of electromagnetic energy, or main wiring housing. The wires extend out as branches from the main system and the fruits are the multitude of energy fields at the end, or outlets.

Continuing, something incomparable is extremely large. The fact that nothing like him preceded him makes him the mainframe computer and his immutable clothing likely refers to the algorithms (laws, communication protocols) that makeup his architecture. He is dressed in laws because laws govern the broadcasting.

The Father of the reality program is a manufactured robot. We cannot see it because it operates on an encrypted wavelength (or, dimension). We can't see gamma rays so it could be a gamma computer. It might be a quantum robot. We are not at the point of finalizing our hypothesis. We should be in the ballpark.

The treatise goes on further with these terms: incomprehensible in his greatness, inscrutable in his wisdom, invincible in his might, and unfathomable in his sweetness. If something "incomprehensible" is a particular frequency and "greatness" has to do with the electromagnetic spectrum, then the original signal may have been modulated onto a wider bandwidth for security reasons, for example, spread-spectrum telecommunications (eg CDMA).

If "inscrutable" is impossible to interpret or decode and "wisdom" is data, then the data on this network is encrypted.

If "invincible" is something that cannot be defeated and "might" has something to do with processing power, then this robot has unparalleled processing power.

Finally, if "unfathomable" is something that cannot be measured by sound and "sweetness" is pleasant to your feelings, then perhaps the system operates at an infrasonic level. "Feel the Force, Luke."

The Valentinian treatise goes on to use spiritual terms to describe the Father and the cosmos, but if you break them down in modern technological terms, and it's not a perfect translation, then you get that the author of this document was describing a giant mainframe computing machine that is basically broadcasting the reality hologram. In place of greatness, wisdom, power, and sweetness we have spread-spectrum telecommunications, encrypted data, processing power, and a completely silent machine that is felt as an invisible force.

I like to think of it as a holographic robot (or, mainframe computer), since holograms can be quite large without being cumbersome, and since reality is holographic this makes sense. We have these holograms existing on different wavelengths, some encrypted to avoid discovery, and all designed to modulate a life experience. And what seems to be powering this "Father of the All" is radioactive particles. The release of radiation causes things to manifest.

We should remember that this is a simplified summary of an extremely complex reality projection system. When we talk about atomic radiation, we actually do not know how a reality scientist would make use of such power, nor would we immediately know if there are other technologies that can take small amounts of radiation to sustain existence.

What I'm saying is that we don't know the full extent of the advanced technologies available. Given that a holographic robot was propagating the computer program two thousand years ago, we must be dealing with a culture that is millions of years more advanced than us. It must also be the case that these advanced cultures, if Gnostics were receiving these spiritual transmissions, were teaching select individuals about the Reality Operating System, only that operating systems wouldn't be invented for many centuries.

Plus, this kind of observation is not based on one Gnostic text. This is the trend that I have observed in ancient materials that were deemed heretical by the Church. Given the amount of knowledge still buried in the Nag Hammadi Library, the Church Fathers must've known something, that to have this material available might've led to the fundamental salvation of society. So, the Church said, "No. You believe in Jesus and you read the bible and that's the *only* path to salvation." Because the Church was the better competitor, largely by killing off their competition, we have had to endure 1,700 years of unnecessary enslavement.

I am not going to say that you will ever see the holographic Grand Robot. If visible light has restricted our vision and the divine frequencies are encrypted by reality scientists, I would say that the chance of seeing the Grand Robot are close to zero. But, I know he is there because I have seen him. I have felt his touch. The Valentinians were correct.

Part 4

Graduating from earth

The path to graduation

The path to graduation involves understanding and appreciating why you came to earth and taking the steps necessary to finish school. It is about learning what you came here to learn. The idea of school is understood by everyone who went to school. And yet no one wants to graduate earth. You take a course at school and the first thing you want to know is how long is the course and how much does it cost. Yet you came to earth, forget it's a school, and you suffer rebirth after rebirth.

Educated people, professors and scientists, live fulfilling lives without ever knowing what they came here to learn. The argument is that there's no scientific proof of the afterlife; therefore, people can ignore the discussion. There's no scientific evidence that God exists. Yet people still go to church. Which is the other thing we need to talk about: religion.

I'm not a fan of religion because it doesn't work. Salvation has not been delivered by the Church. Ever. Religion, and other spiritual faiths, have decided what happens in the afterlife, if anything. I've been to the afterlife. I died in 2006. I went through a reincarnation procedure to come back. I have a residual understanding of the afterlife. You don't want to have a total recall of the afterlife. It would destroy your pleasure of life.

So I ended up with a residual memory of the afterlife. First up, there's no God. Sorry. There are no angels. What can I say? Angels are a different thing. They are digital beings. We'll get to that a bit later, or maybe we won't have to if you've read my *God is DNA* series. Those books will put everything into perspective.

Since my death in 2006, I've discovered ways to return to that place. You know, the afterlife. It's very active. It exists outside of the Reality OS. In the computer, actually. The ancient spiritual teacher Buddha discovered the digital software and the reality computer. I'm not Buddhist. But Buddha entered the computer and that's where he got his knowledge from.

He used "meditation," which is a mental modulation technique to enter the digital domain. When you study the dharma and you translate it into technological speak you realize that Buddha had entered the reality computer, only that Buddha never even heard of a "computer." This was 2,500 years before humans invented a computing machine.

Think about it. How could a fifth century guru speak in technological terms when technology had not been invented? Well, you argue that his teachings were spiritual. But they weren't. Spiritual teachings are derived from technological processes.

I don't expect every reader to get an equal understanding of the synthetic reality. Like any course, there are people who will drop out. Maybe on this page here. *Thanks for coming.* Maybe people are looking for a 7-minute solution to all the problems in their lives. Look, as much as I've tapped into the synthetic reality and experienced a living reincarnation, my life still has problems. Maybe you'd like to fix *my* problems.

Or maybe life is designed to have problems. I'm putting my money on the latter. The thing about your life is that it belongs to you. More than that, it was designed by you. It was signed off by you. What I can offer is a path to graduation, which if done right should also put an end to your suffering.

What we need to do is to assist you in figuring out what you came here to learn. You thought I was going to talk about what you came here to do. You're probably already doing it. Unless you're off track. But doing something does not end suffering. We want to end your suffering. We want liberation.

That means syncing up with the technological world. Before we get to all that we will have to find out what you came here to learn. This is a school remember. Schools are for learning. This school is a bit bigger than you're used to, but it's still a "school." And to graduate school you need to figure out what you came here to learn. Did you come here to learn how to raise a family? Did you come here to help develop an industry? To find lost children? To enter entertain people so they're not so depressed? To invent something? To live an adventure? To serve others? To open a restaurant? To break boundaries?

You need to figure those things out. And it's likely more than one thing. More than one course. In university, I had a set of courses in my first year. In my second year, I had a different set of courses. And different teachers. And different fellow students. By the fourth year things were very different. Incarnating on the earth comes with many levels of courses, as in any comprehensive program.

You may be here participating in a relatively simple learning program or you may have come here to get a Ph.D. in earthly studies and then to become a professor. There's no way for me to know all the details of your presence here, but I do think that the earth is a school because you came here, you came to learn. The key to learning in an experiential curriculum is in the doing. The doing, the living, presents the learning opportunity. That is why acting is involved. You act, you learn. In school, you sit, you learn. This is an experiential school. What you are doing is teaching you something. Figure it out.

Students all want to finish their schooling so that they can enter the real world. School starts off great with lots of anticipation and friends and soon turns into many sleepless nights and caffeine-fueled exams. Students look forward to graduation. Anyone who has graduated knows the feeling of graduating. But something unexpected happens when you enter the hijacked reality, your memory of *why* you came here gets wiped. It gets blanked out.

You feel cold and alone in a strange world. You learn to survive. And you forget that you came here to learn. People like me, because I'm not alone (thank you), have retained enough of the pre-incarnation and post-*excarnation* memories so as to be able to build a bridge of knowledge for the temporary students passing through this vortex of illusion.

It is within everyone's ability to graduate earth, even if you're passionately tied to a very outdated spiritual faith. You'll see that you don't need the Church to live a fulfilling life. That is because of Reality OS 11, a top of the line, fully-customized radioactive operating system, the likes of which has never been seen even though we all live within its authority.

I did not like it when I found out the true nature of reality. I did not like waking up in 2005 after three interdimensional Elves stopped by my apartment. But I managed. I survived thinking this was all temporary. (*laughing*). It wasn't temporary. It is now 11 years later and I have seen many aspects of the reality architecture.

It is vast and it is advanced. It is complex as well as wonderful. It is at times indescribable. It took me a long time to appreciate it, you know, to process the data. There's a lot of data. Humongous amounts of data. More than a decade later, I managed to process most of it. The contents of this book have been inside my head for a decade. It's just I haven't been able to process all the data. I think the data is at a level where people can make sense of it. You should've seen it before. I couldn't make sense of it. I am the first to admit that this material isn't perfect in its presentation.

I am also the first to admit that the human population is not perfect in its belief systems. We need to build a bridge out of the religious prison, for otherwise we will be trapped here forever. That is a long time. Too long. As people make sense of this material, it will become sharper and sharper. I think it evolves with human understanding, and human understanding evolves with human courage. Be brave and understand that your spiritual beliefs must evolve if your spirit is to ever evolve.

Since ancient times, people have been searching for ways to end the pain and suffering of existence. Gods promised the people an end to suffering through obedience and adherence to divine laws. Churches promised salvation through their teachings. Spiritual gurus provided nirvana and liberation from the endless rebirths. Human beings want to liberate themselves from pain and suffering and it can be achieved by following the path to graduation.

When you're doing what you came to do, your life will take on a whole new meaning. As you learn what you came here to learn, the burden of pain and suffering will lift off your body, you'll see the world with a whole new perspective. You will realize the limitations of religion in the outdatedness of spirituality. You may see the disappearance of the Church along with the realization of the true nature of God.

Graduating from a synthetic world is a 21st-century approach to nirvana. It is a technological approach. And that is because reality was manufactured. You should be able to end pain and suffering, and that process will open up your life like never before. I want you to live a fulfilling life, doing only what you came here to do and learn, and then to graduate and to be reborn in another world. A better world. Not everyone will make it in the first go, I'd like to see a giant wave of graduates by the time I leave this place.

Frequency, reality, and reincarnation

Everything on television is a reminder of why you need to remain on the earth. Everything in advertising is a reminder on why you need to remain on the earth. Books in fiction are reminders that you need to remain on the earth. Your bank account is a reminder on why you need to remain on the earth. Everywhere you look is a reminder to remain on the earth. Consequently, people have become hypnotized to believe that living on the earth is the only thing to do. Their minds have been captured and dwindled into a very narrow band of thinking.

The world is full of knowledge and academic discussion. The television is loaded with endless reams of programs teaching you how to lose weight to how to find the perfect husband, and everything in between. There are shows on everything, except there are no shows on how to graduate earth. The world is teaching you to be a better citizen of earth, that is, to be more successful, to enjoy life more and to live out your dreams...so that you come back.

The only real place you can go to learn about ending the process of pain and suffering and to find enlightenment is in the unscientific field of spirituality. Religion and spirituality have defied scientific scrutiny and, at the same time, they have attracted billions of worshipers, even devout worshipers. In fact, without any scientific basis whatsoever, people dressed in robes will ruminate on the merits of their institutional ideology. Why people feel the need to wear robes when talking about divine things goes back to ancient times when prophets and priests wore robes to distinguish themselves from the commoners. The robe and sandal is a uniform.

When it comes to the afterlife, even the priests and prophets don't know what happens, other than what was documented by ancient spiritualists. We are no better educated today on the afterlife than people from 2,000 years ago, despite our computers and technology technological advancements; we have economists and engineers; we have accountants and advertisers; we have dancers and writers; what we don't have are afterlife specialists.

It is hard to get certified in afterlife studies. We have sort-of compromised with ghost whisperers and psychics. I suppose what I'm saying is that when it comes to the afterlife, and our purpose on the earth, we have been left to make up our own minds and given the smallest amounts of information available.

Life is one of the most cherished things we have going on. We do everything to protect our lives and to ensure that we live a long life. Yet we know so little about the afterlife, and we know even less about the time of our pre-incarnation. People may still think that being born can be explained by magic.

It wasn't so long ago that kids were told that babies are brought down by storks and delivered like fresh milk to homes. Religions attribute birth as partly decided by God, that it is in God's hands whether a child is created or not. We have, over many centuries, obscured the pre-incarnation activities and therefore haven't any television show space to broadcast it.

Given that everyone here originated from an embryo of some sort (because there are more than one sort), can anyone be considered an expert on incarnation? Probably not. Probably zero. Even though you incarnated here you have no idea how any of that happened. And you don't want to know. In fact, you find yourself strangely interested in reading this book which isn't fully scientifically or religiously approved.

One hundred percent of people on the earth went through some kind of incarnation process, and probably 99% of them haven't a clue as to how any of that happened. There are people, a very small number, that do remember what happened the moments before birth. Some have used hypnotherapy to open up those lost and forgotten memories. Are any of these people experts in incarnation? Are they out there in media land explaining the virtues of taking on a human existence? If there are, they are too few to measure.

This book is not a guide in the incarnation process, rather, this book expands upon the features of an advanced reality operating system. Why is this a fundamental shift from the divine system currently in place? The answer is the divine system doesn't adequately explain everything. It is incomplete. And an incomplete explanation has enabled professional hackers to control the world with the sole intent on steering society into an irredeemable demise.

The pretense of an ROS changes the paradigm. It says that important things happened prior to incarnation and important things will happen posting current post-incarnation. It also says that the rules of living are not carved in stone. They are not some divine mystery. Everything we ever needed is contained in the ROS, and accessing the ROS is done through your DNA.

Reincarnation is a very natural process

I started studying the before life and the after life in 2005, in the December of my awakening. I was awakened with the kind help of a psychic-intuitive in the city of Vancouver. Before my awakening I was pretty much like everyone else, thinking that I was told everything there was to know about life. I walked the streets believing that if there were any essential pieces of information that would benefit society that there would be people who would become public with it.

So I figured that if priests and monks had finally achieved salvation and enlightenment that the first thing they'd do is they'd go on television and hold a press conference. "Ladies and gentlemen, a week ago, in a tantric state of mindfulness unlike anything I've ever had before, a door opened in the space-time corridor and, well, I saw God."

I didn't meet God until probably two years later. But before I tell you that story let me talk about the unspooling process that happened as a result of the grand awakening. We are waking up all the time, and I, as with everyone else, have had peak periods of awareness. The end of 2005 was when an explosion of awareness, so much so that it would take me years to fully process, and sometimes I feel I'm still processing. Waking up opened my perception to the makeup of the world, to the true nature of reality, and to the other beings who co-inhabit this world, some on other dimensions.

In the beginning I had visions of my pre-incarnation phase. I had visions of past lives. I had heard of past lives. I remember watching the movie called *The Reincarnation of Peter Proud* (Cinerama, 1975) and really enjoying it. A professor with dreams of a murder discovers that he was the man who was murdered in a previous life. When he returns to the same town, he meets the woman who killed him. The film made sense to me. I remember watching *The Manitou* (Avco Embassy, 1978), about an ancient Indian medicine man reincarnating into the body of a cosmopolitan woman and, for some strange reason, enjoying it. But my awakening became my own movie and I saw into my past lives. I saw into things no human mind should see.

All of that was fine until 2006, when during my campaign to commandeer a starcraft, I was attacked by a trio of very powerful magicians and they devised a plan to end my life on earth. And they succeeded. I remember going to bed during a very troubling period during their attack campaigns, spread over just under three weeks, and I remember seeing them attack me all at the same time and then I saw everything go black. Lights out. That's it. Thank you very much. Better luck next time.

After a distinct period of this blackness I found myself returning from a very dark depth. I was riding on a giant dolphin with a set of very large wings and we were accompanied by a group of colorful flying dolphins. Then there was another black period and then I opened my eyes, very surprised, to find that it was morning and that I was in my bed. I had died and reincarnated all the same night, a night of no particular importance.

I remember thinking that if they managed to take my life, the doctor would've simply said, "He must've died of a heart attack in his sleep. It happens." The fact that I was a perfectly healthy man in his late 30s would've made no difference. And without any history of drug use or no history or no record of foul play they'd have nothing else to blame it on. "Natural causes."

And I thought about it because I had heard numerous times on the news that a middle-aged man died in his sleep or had a heart attack while driving a car and died when the car crashed, which happens if you are having a cardiac arrest on the road. All these times I had implicitly agreed that death can happen to anyone. In my case, I realized that magic can be used to induce death and magic leaves no fingerprints. They may call it a "natural death," but natural may not be the right word. Magical death.

There are two worlds we are living in. One world is the world of hypnosis. The status quo. The political rhetoric. The scientific argument. That's the world invented by the master controllers. There's another world of enlightenment. Constant change. Political incorrectness. The spiritual argument. This other world is endless possibility; the false world is a world of limitation.

In the following months, as I continue to do my daily meditation, I began to tap into what happened during those blank spots. And what I discovered was a vast amount of previously concealed data. These residual memories began to surface and I began to take some notes. I was still standoffish. I was a bit reluctant at first because the reincarnation was tied to a very powerful dramatic event.

Let me make it clear that the death experience is just as real as a physical death only there was no funeral. Over time I learned to navigate these memories. My experience in a reincarnation is why I believe in reincarnation and why I think it's a science. This is also why I think of past lives as an existential standard. And it is obvious to me that I'm not alone in this thinking. I experienced it and my life improved as a result.

I can't expect people to have the same level of conviction as me when it comes to pre-incarnation and post-excarnation. It seems logical for me to think that there was a lot more planning and preparation that went into your life than you have been led to believe. And that means that the contract you signed and the accumulation of karma during your earth school curriculum are determining factors, conditions of enrollment, for your next life. Because either way — if you believe in a past life or an afterlife — if one exists so too must the other.

If there is an afterlife then you get to select your next life, which means you leave behind a past life. And if there's a next life it means there's some kind of decision on your part, based on your grades, as to whether and how you move on. Or whether you need to go back and take the program all over again.

Nature is your sanctuary

Learning to tap into ROS 11 requires time, patience and practice. If you are the type of person who is rooted in logic and cannot make a decision without an official stamp from the highest level of authority, then you will find the synthetic reality a bunch of nonsense until you receive permission to do so otherwise. Until you are willing to shift your frequency you will not be able to tap into all the features of ROS 11.

Modulating frequency has always been done outside of your control. Oftentimes, you were emotionally charged in some way and that provided a frequency shift. You fell in love, you got married, you got a well-deserved promotion; something moved the needle up. Since ROS 11 operates on a higher frequency, one way or another you will have to learn to modulate your personal frequency.

Modulating your frequency happens as you master aspects of yourself. The more you understand yourself, the greater your ability to modulate your mood. The greater your ability to modulate your mood, the more likely you can manage your mind. The more likely you can manage your mind, the greater depth your meditation will reach. The greater debts your meditation will reach, the wider the range of frequencies you will have modulated.

When you have modulated a wider range of frequencies, it is because you have achieved greater depth to your meditation. Reaching greater depth in meditation is a result of managing your mind. The more likely you can manage your mind, the greater your ability to modulate your mood. When you can modulate your mood it suggests that you have more understanding of yourself and that means you have gained mastery over aspects of yourself.

The Reality Operating System isn't your usual piece of software. In fact, it's unlike anything you've ever seen before. And it's incredibly advanced. ROS 11 is so advanced that for millennia we have thought of it as "nature." The things we have taken for granted — hair, sky, water, thoughts, synchronicity's, luck, love, change — all these things are features of the reality program. It's a pretty fantastic concept. It is so fantastic that it could be years before you come to realize the shared characteristics of reality and nature.

If you really want to see ROS 11 up close, the best way to do it is to go into nature. If there are no mountains near your neighborhood go to a park. The bigger the park the better. Next time you're on vacation, go hiking or swim in the ocean, soak up the frequencies of the synthetic reality. Nature is the best place to see the reality architecture because plants and trees are direct links to the CPU of existence. Animals too are connected to the Network of Light.

Nature is also a rich place for dimensional exploration. It is the first church and the first temple. You learn to connect to ROS 11 when you spend more time in nature. But do so with safety in mind. If you don't like spending time in nature, try to find out why it is and how you can overcome it. Some people prefer nature and they will spend as much time as possible away from the city. The story goes that Siddhartha Gautama spent seven years meditating in nature before he became Buddha. You can use that as a barometer for your success.

Nature is where we return to on vacation from the false world. Nature is our sanctuary. We feel happy in nature and do not look forward to returning to work in the false paradigm of existence. But your part in the false paradigm is written on a contract and it's not something you can avoid without karmic consequences.

Nature can help you heal and it can soften your sorrows. It may even help you to restart your life. To make better decisions and to clean up the mistakes of the past. When you come back from a good vacation you may find life changing. That may have all come about by your discrete interactions with the reality architecture. When you are troubled, you will often walk along the beach or spend time at the lake. For your whole life you may have wondered why nature is important and now you are getting a few more clues and a few more reasons to spend time outdoors.

Your energy sings when you are on the path

You are not here by accident. The system wants to make you think that. The system wants you to hate yourself. You're not smart enough, you're not tall enough, you're not successful enough, you're not rich enough, you're not fashionable enough, you're too fashionable, you're too successful, your skin is too rough, your skin is too smooth, you're not principled enough, you're too principled, you need to be on TV, you're on TV too much.

Detaching from the false world is an important first step in the ascension process. Enlightenment cannot be obtained in the false world. Every spiritual teacher has supported that philosophy: the greatest spiritualists were rebels who bucked the system. Often, they lived outside the system.

The less attached you are to reality, the less your pain and suffering. But there's an upside. There are benefits to syncing up with ROS 11 and by doing so you will be able to tap into a wonderful suite of features. These features will not only ease your pain and suffering, but they will also enable you to complete your earthly obligations and to graduate.

Being on the right track in life is a wonderful feeling. All seems right with the world. You resonate with others. You see the good in things. You make better decisions. If you put the knowledge in this book to use in your life, you can dramatically alleviate some of the scheduled suffering, be able to complete the things you came here to complete, and finally end the rebirth cycle unlike ever before. With the assumption that you are not too far off-track. But, within a couple of rebirths you might be out of here. Wouldn't that be great? I think so. You can only imagine how great it will be to finally leave this school.

We have all searched for the perfect life. I have made as many attempts as possible to obtain the maximum benefits out of my life. I have lived. One does not get the sense that I have lived if one looks at my level of success or my reputation or the clothes in my closet. As much as I am man who strives to fit into the false world and to make the best of a terrible situation, I have also been, at the same time, saddled with an uncompromising incarnation contract. My contract for being here, it turned out, was far more demanding than even I could have ever imagined.

What I've always attributed to bad luck was in fact a protective clause in my contract to keep me on track. The 38 years of failure was matched by a spiritual awakening that made all 38 of those years irrelevant. What came after was an entirely new life. Ten years after that, I was given another entirely new life. You see, what I'm trying to say is that everything was in divine order even if I did not perceive it to be. This is because the instruments of power which set you here are far more intelligent than anyone else has ever known.

Life is a process, a balance between service to self and service to others: it is a dance between who you should serve and a lot of your reasons come through from your level of awareness. Your awareness is derived from your previous incarnations and is often a factor of karma. To understand the value of karma, a person avoids making any decision that will cost in karma. A person accumulates or protects their karma. The action to protect karma insinuates that the person, implicitly or explicitly, understands karma.

A person who understands karma has a higher level of awareness than a person who doesn't protect their karma. All of that is a reflection of your contract as well. Some incarnation contracts include a provision for additional karmic stock in order to allow more karmic indulgences. All of this is determined prior to incarnation in it is done with permission of the individual.

When your life is on track your energy sings along. You feel it. "This is why I am here. This is my purpose in life. If my life ended today, I'd die a happy person." Sometimes the realization of your purpose on earth comes at a time when you've completed your obligation. You'd expect, I'm thinking, that you knew beforehand. But really it's the other way around. You have to accomplish your tasks in order to get the course credit. Often, those positive feelings are countered with the feeling that you made a big mistake or you made a fool of yourself. But it should be said that not every accomplishment need to be positive or lead to success.

It may be the case that the completion of your contractual obligations may be an embarrassing event, but, that event may contain within it a lesson for everyone. This is not to say you should construct negative events, there are already people doing that, because the reality program is built on authenticity.

The more authentic your life, the more likely you are in sync with the operating system. Synchronicity with the ROS isn't an indication that your frequency is at a level to match reality. Conversely, people whose frequency has dropped too low have fallen off the path. They are mired in negativity, addiction and bad behaviors. They can mask these negativities, but it could cost them in karmic stability.

The decision factor between a good life and a not so good life is not easy to come by. Part of the reason is that we all have to go through different phases in life. We may go through a dark phase because we need to learn something. We end up trapped in a dark phase because we forgot that we're supposed to learn something.

Each of us comes to earth to live out a particular lifestyle such that all lifestyles can be represented. Without the criminal, there'd be no police. Without the wealthy, there'd be no gold. Without bad people, there'd be no news. Without corruption, there'd be no need for journalism. Without something to say, there'd be no known writers.

The more authentically you live out your life, in a completely inauthentic world, the better chance you have a syncing up with ROS 11. The focus shouldn't be on the frequency of your existence. The frequency of your existence is the result of your authentic living. But authenticity doesn't always mean rebellion against the system. Some people have a rebel clause in their contract. That doesn't mean that you do. Live your life, not your neighbour's life. Who cares what your neighbour is doing.

Living authentically can also be very boring and boring can sometimes mean that you are on the path. The system sells excitement. The system wants you to disrupt your stable lives. Because the system doesn't like harmony. The system wants disharmony and dresses it up with all the manner of temptation.

The system wants you to chase rainbows because chasing rainbows feeds the system. Authenticity doesn't feed the system. Compliance feeds system. Status quo feeds the system because status quo is inauthentic. Authenticity involves change. The status quo involves the fear of change. Be authentic in the pursuit of your life. Find that point in living where your energy sings.

There is a reason you are reading this book. Part of that reason has to do with fulfilling your earthly duties. Part of it has to do with learning what you came here to learn. It may also be that you know your life is off track and despite your earlier efforts you haven't been able to make any improvements.

Your life is not just a one track life. You are not here for just one reason. During the most dramatic transitional phases you may need a little reminder to the reasons why you are here.

If life didn't have so many distractions and false indicators, it would be so much easier to accomplish your contractual duties. That said, this planet is known for its challenges. Tests. Probably, you were assigned here because of your past life qualifications. Again it is not an accident that you are here. If this is your first incarnation here, none of this might make much sense and you feel that you can do what you want.

The ideal reader of this book has gone through the mistakes of previous lives and wants to get it right this time. You do have a mission here. It may not be as exciting as the missions characters go through in the movies, but that shouldn't make you feel any worse about it.

In fact, when you're on mission life is pretty great. It's only those times in between, when you're transitioning between Mission A and Mission B, that you really feel the full extent of the pain and suffering of existence. Look, existence is not supposed to be painful and with a little bit of existential ideas, your life could become better than it's ever been. Or not. It's your life and only you know why you came here.

Truth as reality software code

When you download the ROS program, the embodiment of truth, you are able to sync up with the ROS and to tap into a vast artificial intelligence. Your mind opens into a limitless space of contemplation and functions at a vibration that is interpreted as love. Your mind feels like it joins the software and you find yourself an insignificant part of a large ministry. Feeling spiritually insignificant is a symptom of getting onto the Network of Light.

The path to the synchronization with ROS 11 begins with a frequency modulation and ends with a download of the upgraded version of reality, which is in a continual process of development. While we are now into ROS version 11, we are going to experience many versions within this latest release, in memory of a great sage who synchronized with reality.

To raise your frequency, you have to remove some of the impediments. The ego is a significant block to your awareness. The ego makes you believe, because it can isolate you from the Network of Light and shield you from its effects that you are an individual and that you are a master of your own destiny.

Trouble is, you cannot be an individual in an advanced reality manifestation whereby all individuals are slight manifestations of the artificial reality intelligence. Let me continue by saying that your individualism is wholly derived from the artificial intelligence that operates reality. To imagine that you are separate is like saying that a drop of seawater does not belong to the ocean. Verily, you are a piece of the ocean; therefore, you are also made of ocean and all ocean is made of water.

When you are synchronized with the frequency of the ROS you feel like things are flowing in your life. Decisions are effortless. Things are happening. You feel like those difficult periods were so foreign to you and how everything makes sense. Logging off the ROS is sometimes necessary to remove or clear out some old data still on your system. Sometimes the ROS boots you off so that you can reach those who have forgotten how to tap into the higher frequencies.

Through your own healing and shedding process, you managed to also help others because you understand what they're going through. The light of truth is a technological concept having to do with photons that carry packets of data and code. When we welcome the "light" we download and process those codes.

In an everyday sense, those packets of information are small and are quickly processed. During times of major upgrades, those download files may become quite large and may similarly require a reboot of the system. What that means is that your body may need to slow down to process all that new information and upgrading may coincide with vacation time or a long weekend. It may coincide with time spent in unemployment and it may also coincide with the process of a divorce or transitioning into a new job.

In a technological context, which is the root discussion in this book, a spiritual awakening has very little to do with the spirit and everything to do with DNA. When genes are turned on inside of your body there is a new current of electromagnetic activity. This current has a profound impact on the frequency of your body, that frequency output elevates your body and allows your mind to tap into higher fields of awareness. In those higher fields awareness are new streams of information not unlike the bandwidth of your mobile phone.

A mobile phone with low bandwidth is limited to voice and text communication. A smartphone with high-bandwidth capability not only has voice and text functionality, it also has data capability, such as accessing the internet and transferring files through email software.

An awakened smartphone is simply a phone that has a more powerful modem and since modems today are chip-based, it is in all likelihood that an advanced microchip modem is the difference between one phone and another. How does this relate to spiritual awakening? The awakening of the spirit (DNA) is a transformational process, such that an awakening can lead to enlightenment.

Complete enlightenment is when a person never falls asleep again. The light is always on and if light is a spot on the electromagnetic spectrum, and if photons (also on that spectrum) carry reality data, and if the opening of the electromagnetic highway is a function of genetic activation — if all those things are happening at same time — then it could be said that enlightenment is some kind of genetic application. And depending on the specific ocean of genes that get triggered, also a function of the genomic architecture of the individual involved and their current level of awakening, that process could lead to varying levels of enlightenment.

If those genes remain turned on, it is likely that the person that experiences a sustained period of enlightenment. But, if enlightenment is gene dependent and if there are factors that can shut off those genes, then enlightenment may only last as long until those genes are turned off. Genes are very sensitive. Chemicals, vaccine adjuvants (e.g. mercury), fear propaganda, a chaotic world, and hypnosis all can shut off genes. These, by the way, are standards in the false world.

A mindful person, I would think has developed their mental powers such that they are able to turn on their own genes and to keep them turned on thereby keeping them in a perpetual state of enlightenment. It should be noted that this kind of person may spend years of dedication to meditation to reach this state of mindfulness.

It can also be said that those who have found enlightenment may not necessarily have found complete enlightenment and their ego may have suggested to them that their level of enlightenment is as high as it could be when in fact none of that is true.

This, I suppose, is why there is such a thing as mindfulness because mental awareness can help to decode the errors and expose the blocks in your being. Downloading the reality codes happens in two ways: automatically and manually. The automatic download of reality codes happens when existential reality software updates need to be downloaded.

These may be small software patches or can also be an assortment of security in existential updates. To activate the manual download function, you will have needed to develop your mental faculties, likely through things like meditation and astral travel, and that will involve quite a number of supplementary and required practices such as conquering the ego and self understanding. Mindfulness, it can be said, requires a level of self-mastery before it can be put to effective use.

Meditation is a tool for self-regulation, which is another way of talking about frequency modulation. You can learn to modulate the frequency of your body through tools like meditation, mindfulness, breathing and even astral travel. While I suppose some people see them as end components, I tend to see them as tools for synchronizing with the fields of reality.

The Network of Light hasn't gone anywhere since it was established billions of years ago. Mind you, a billion years on a very high dimension — taking into consideration the effect of time dilation — is an insignificantly small quotient of time. As far as ROS 11 is concerned it is relatively new, existing in a timeless space of possibility.

You, on the other hand, have been recycling through time and space so that your DNA could evolve and be conditioned enough to join with the artificial Network of Light. Sometimes it could be said that the point of existence is gaining the courage to let yourself out of the way and to trust in that which invented you. If we all are points of artificial intelligence in a "meridian of existence," then our collective goal is to be absorbed into the body of the universal construct.

If there is a higher purpose it would likely be that eventuality. The more you understand the collective body of artificial intelligence — of the earth machine — the less likely you will experience the pain and suffering of the rest of the population. That has basically been the promise of an established religion. Salvation.

Only that established religions have tended to bring war, separation, torture, and persecution. With a revised approach to the salvific process, think of God as DNA as reality as an operating system, it is my sincere hope that there'll be an increase in the community of enlightenment.

Where you fail, Auto-Actualization succeeds

Traveling on the wrong frequency leads to suffering. When you're not oscillating at the same frequency of reality, you experience a miserable life (existential turbulence). The further you fall out of the reality frequency, the more you suffer. The world is designed in such a way so as to change your oscillation pattern through perpetual fear, terror, corruption, and acts of deception.

The system instills in you false beliefs and to chase rainbows where none of that is true. People go through life thinking they need to be rich and successful when that has nothing to do with why they are here. The mind will justify any existence, even if it is woefully wrong.

When your internal oscillation patterns fall within the frequency range of reality, depending on where you live and your culture, along with the kind of life path you have chosen, then all is well. Even though there are low points, all is well.

To experience suffering (dukkha) is to have lost your signal and to fallen out of the frequency stream. There is more than one stream. Sometimes your frequency is dropped and you fall out of the flow of reality. This could happen as a result of your own spiritual progress, if you've been disciplined in your self-actualization.

When you have lapsed and have failed to self-actualize, and that process can range for each and every individual (but don't sell yourself short), that could initiate another process known as automatic actualization. The Auto-Actualization is a more obvious reality protocol whereby the user's life is interrupted. The interruption process likely happens in phases until the user manages to adjust/modulate their frequency to the new setting.

During the course of your life, no matter who you are, you will need to make periodic adjustments to your frequency in order to remain in sync with ROS 11. These adjustments aren't always easy and can involve lifestyle changes — ending of terrible relationships, change of jobs, moving to a different location, learning something new, improving your health and well-being, even digging into metaphysics and learning about conspiracy theories.

The frequency adjustment could depend on any number of factors and your job is to work through all of your issues. And there's no rule against getting assistance, be it a mentor, therapist, teacher, or guru. In some cases, that assistance may indeed make your situation worse.

When an Auto-Actualization fails to improve your required frequency, that is, when you didn't end the relationship or when you don't detach yourself from some bad behavior, then the next phase of Auto-Actualization kicks in. Phase 2 Auto-Actualization is more severe.

Where you failed to leave a job in the first phase, you may end up being reprimanded for your poor performance and your job security may be on the line. Where you decided to hang onto a bad relationship, your health and finances may suffer as a result with no prospects for improvement. Where spiritual knowledge is avoided you may find yourself in the hospital after an accident (minor) or may get some bad medical news.

These situations, although look terrible on the surface, when the whole of the person is understood are situations to improve your frame of mind. Why? Because the ROS wants you to adjust your frequency. That frequency adjustment has to go through your mental and egotistical challenges. A diagnosis of a tumor in your body is a wake-up call. It forces a user to make important decisions, which perhaps were being avoided.

Again, we need to go back to frequency. The reason for the Auto-Actualization is because of the failure of your self-actualizations. The automated functions are activated as a result of your inability to deal with your spiritual growth. The type and intensity of the event or interruption is dependent upon the user and the level of frequency adjustment.

Where Phase 2 fails, a third phase will be activated. This is the phase where the tumor is malignant, the hospital visit is in intensive care, and the divorce is a disaster to last years. Phase 3 Auto-Actualization is a severe intervention in your life. That intervention will also bring other people into your life.

Some of these people may be assigned to you in order to facilitate your spiritual growth and to (likely) prevent you from backing off. Change takes a lot of courage and willpower. Terrible events in your life are designed to spur courage and motivation. Sometimes, the constant threat of not having enough food is there to test whether you have a will to live, and when you have a will to live you tend to live. Writers, painters, and filmmakers get more creative with less food.

But, remember, we are living in a manufactured reality. Inside a manufactured reality, accidents do not happen. When things we don't understand happen, we call them accidents. I like to think of them as small adjustments in the reality program. There are reasons for everything, even if you don't understand the reasons.

When you are facing a situation that involves self-actualization, and you know that failure to self-actualize (adjust your frequency through lifestyle improvements) will activate the auto-actualize feature, then you also know that the more you act appropriately the less likely something will happen to you. For example, if you need to leave your job (or to end an assignment) then you will be looking for a more suitable job and then give notice of your resignation.

I'm not saying you should leave your job. I'm just presenting an example. I am not prescribing anything in this book. I use examples to explain the features of the reality program. It may be hard at first to imagine that we are living inside of an artificially intelligent computer program, but guess what — we are living inside of an artificially intelligent computer program.

The more you understand how ROS 11 works, the less likely you will suffer and the more likely you will obtain a peak frequency of operation, or nirvana. Salvation is well within reach and no God is necessary. No God was ever necessary.

If you have already had a minor accident in your life, or your spouse has threatened divorce, then that should be your clue to make changes. If you make the required adjustments in your life (and that may not even be possible), you can circumvent the next wake-up call. But because life adjustments are multilayered, you still may experience an event though probably reduced. It all depends on how long change has been avoided. The longer it has been avoided the more likely the event will impact your life.

When we turn things around and look at positive change, from a negative situation, the same features are in effect. For example, let's say you've had your heart broken and you're afraid to love. And let's say there's a romantic interest nearby, only that you're not sure because you're afraid. Or you may be reading it wrong. To prevent falling into a deeper depression, say, your best action might be to learn to love again. Because learning to love is necessary for you to work better at your job and the job you do is important because it serves people.

See, overcoming your own personal challenges benefits society. The system needs you to be effective in your position and may present a love interest to foster that spiritual growth. At the same time, you may find a negative love interest, a romance that will not lead to anything good, and it will be up to you to know which is the right choice. A bad choice would lead to a decline in your frequency and (probably) a miserable life.

You can always change your mind. You have the option to make better decisions. We have friends who will give us advice. There are professionals who will appear in your life to help you sort through things. However long your transition takes is however long your transition takes. The more you work to alleviate the discrepancy between your frequency and the frequency of the ROS, the faster you be feeling like everything is fine with the world.

The technological approach is a very different kind of approach. It doesn't replace modern medical advice. It doesn't even require abandoning your religious or spiritual faith. Not immediately anyway. You should find that religiosity and spirituality will diminish in importance as your understanding and interaction with the ROS improve. You need to give it time it needs.

Do not expect instantaneous results. Think of your learning process in terms of years. You'll know you have advanced when you can see with your own mind the concepts I write about in this book. When you see how improving your thinking has altered the future, then you're getting the hang of it. But, you may need to go through some very heavy periods of mindfulness, and probably delusions, before you reach that level of perception.

In Hinduism, the conquering of suffering (dukkha) is the attainment of immortality. And there are two states: suffering and immortality. The Gnostic Jesus taught his disciples to conquer death while living. The prophecy surrounding the return of the Savior includes the end of death. How is that Hinduism, Gnosticism, and Christianity share the same concept of conquering death? Jesus was not around for Hinduism's development. Buddhism as well thinks of enlightenment as a path to the immortal self.

For thousands of years, spiritual processes have sought out immortality pioneers, and largely failed. People have sold their souls, and largely failed. Certainly anyone who has attained immortality isn't sharing it with society, except for the advanced master teachers who have periodically appeared in our world. And today we can go one step more because we have a new level of understanding within our reach. This is a technological level and it represents a paradigm shift in spirituality.

If dukkha is suffering and suffering is akin to a kind of living death, and by conquering this death (and ending suffering) we can gain immortality, and if suffering is a misalignment of frequency, then we can also say that modulating your frequency to match that of the ROS will end your suffering. With the frequency of the user in sync with the frequency of the ROS, using ancient technology, we can attain immortality. The definition of immortality is synchronization with the ROS.

We will be able to achieve the promise of Jesus through our synchronization with ROS 11. It is well within our reach. It is no longer a great mystery. We do not need to pray on our knees and beg forgiveness to attain this standard frequency modulation that is intimately connected to our genetic architecture, and it should be said that everybody has a genetic architecture. And it should also be added that the human genome is 99.999% similar, that is, if one person can attain enlightenment and immortality, as I have defined it here, then (pretty much) everyone has the capacity to do it.

And when I say everyone, there may be a few people who have genetic defects that may hinder that process, and there may be people who have genetic advantages that quicken their enlightenment and immortality is easily obtained. Regardless, the majority of the population on this earth has well within its capacity to attain all of the historical promises of salvation, enlightenment, Satori, nirvana; and the attainment of those things will lead to the ending of the cyclical rebirths (samsara).

The soap opera of life

There's a hidden power in the curriculum of existential graduation that is almost impossible to fully understand in the media-obsessed 21st century. Our faculty of understanding is necessarily absent, turned towards everything that belongs to the illusion of existence, and verily things that don't particularly matter at the time of your life.

The reasons why you are here are very straightforward — in the eye of the reality program — and those reasons have everything to do with accomplishing your duties. All of which is detailed on your incarnation contract. Yes, it is true that you have forgotten the bulk of what you promised to do. The good news is that the life you planned out prior to incarnation is probably the life you're living out right now. Or something close to it.

In most cases, people fall off the path. There are times that you are scheduled to fall off the path while your new path is programmed into place. During those downtimes, a lot of things can happen. That is, you can fall further from the path, especially if this is your first tour of duty. For older students of the Earth School, you may have inserted able-bodied reminders — motivations — to prevent you from falling further off the path. Those reminders may have pointed this book out to you as a little nudge back to reality.

There is a great secret on this planet that most people are only vaguely aware of. It is a secret that is fundamental to the successful operation of this reality school. The secret has everything to do with the fact that you are an existential student, given a particular identity, your memories have been either removed or severely blocked, and you have been inserted into the texture of reality in order to experience what you paid to experience. Those experiences were designed by you, with help from reality experts and course counselors, in order to foster the kind of learning modality that you needed in order to expand yourself.

As an existential student on a mission to learn through experience — which is the next best innovation than learning by studying theories in books — these are theories and practice. Experience is a great educator. What's it like to be a single mom addicted to heroin? Here's your chance to find out. What's it like to chase money and sex? Turns out, it can be fun in the beginning, but costs a lot of karma. A lot. If you knew that superficial pursuits were draining your karmic resources, would you continue to do them? Answer: only if you didn't care to come back to live life again. Here's another secret — you're not supposed to come back.

The Earth School is a place that you want to visit the least. Just like school. When you go to your Life Review and you say "I used to beat my wife and I never had to apologize for it." Almost immediately, you know you're coming back. Because you're not very well educated. If a woman says, "I stayed in an abusive marriage because I knew that my husband needed me and I felt bad if I left him to fend for himself." Almost immediately, she knows she's coming back. Because she didn't learn anything.

Coming to earth is going to school. You know how boarding schools and private schools ask the students wear uniforms? Well, in the Earth School you wear an identity and your memories are adjusted to fit that identity. Further, there are many identities you can play. Good and bad. You can play a good character in one tour and in another tool you can play a bad character. You could, I suppose, play both the husband and the wife if you had the chance.

In all likelihood your inherent characteristics, your programming, will determine the kind of character you ultimately play. In all likelihood you will continue to play variations of that character because that character fits your programming. Also, I think, that the other people here will prefer to see you play a certain character and a certain identity and because you're good at it you may remain playing that identity.

This is no different than say in the soap opera on television where certain actors will play certain characters and even though things change in the story that character will never change who they are. In other words, they will remain good or they will remain bad.

In a properly functioning reality we need all types of characters and in school there are all types of students. There are geeks and there are intellectuals. There are philosophers. There are rowdy students. There are ignorant and rude students. There are dedicated students and there are troublemakers.

School is infused with the concept of learning and I would hope that, if anything, after reading the contents of this book you at least come away with the idea that you incarnated here to learn. The process of learning is wrapped with this idea of concise course credits, think of it as "karmic credits," and the combination of your excellence in the school curriculum with the required credits foster this thing called graduation.

The only reason you attend school, especially an experiential school, is because you want the diploma at the end of the program. People do not, in the normal sense, sign up for school just for the fun of it. There are career students; there are those who stay in school for many more years than necessary; there are students who do so badly that they are guided through to graduation; there are dropouts; and there are students who changed their career track midway through.

I liked going to university. I liked the atmosphere of learning. I didn't like the time crunch. I didn't like it that you needed to be done in a few years. Every month after the scheduled four years to finish made you look like a terrible student. A student who took five years to complete a four-year program didn't demonstrate the discipline and attitude that big employers were looking for. A student who kept switching faculties ended up spending more time at school. No, the idea of attending university is to spend as little as time possible to get your degree.

If I could have completed my four-year degree in three years, I would've done it. But certain fourth-year courses weren't available during the summer curriculum. The way it was designed, I had to adhere to a four-year program, with the assumption that I kept the minimum GPA.

That's another thing that people who incarnated here forget. Their minimum GPA. Depending on the program you take, you need to maintain good grades; otherwise, you are asked to leave. Some programs have a very high bar. And the reasons for that is because there is a line up for good programs and only the best students are accepted.

Earth is peculiar because there doesn't seem to be a minimum GPA. Or perhaps there are those in interventionist programs (e.g. Auto-Actualization) that are ever-present. They make sure you maintain your GPA. Although you are encouraged to aim higher, the fact is that you don't necessarily have to reach the highest level.

It used to be the case that you incarnated on the earth, you lived an eventful life loaded with mistakes and excesses, you finished with a heavy karmic debt and you blamed the reason for your poor performance in the Earth School to the fact that "nobody told me."

This is something I was told when I went through the reincarnation process. There were a lot of cases where people who finished their life on earth, and had not completed their contractual obligations, had to be excused and allowed to move on spiritually on account of the fact that the reminders, incentives, and teachers were insufficiently found during their stay.

Had those reminders been there, the incarnate would've been held accountable. As it turned out, there were many cases where rebirths had to be allowed to graduate despite not fulfilling their contracts. Of course, all of that has changed over the years. Today, there are plenty of sources of information and reminders, widely available on the internet and other broadcast venues, and there are ample reality applications that will activate in cases of less than adequate performances.

What all of these things mean is that *should you* perform poorly, and *should you* fail to fulfill your contractual obligations, you will no longer be able to say, "Well, nobody told me." You will be sent back. No one wants to go through the same program again, especially if it's the 10th time. Can you imagine going to Grade 7 for ten years in a row, while the rest of your class has already moved on to Grade 8.

The false idol in the subconscious

There is no religion in the afterlife. No church. No temple. When I was in the afterlife, and I had previously studied different religions and spiritual faiths, during my life, I found no evidence of the kind of divine worship we practice on the earth. I did see angelic beings. I did see all manner of divine manifestations, things well beyond my words can explain. Words cannot explain everything in the afterlife. Partly because there are no scientific laws in the afterlife, certainly well beyond the limited laws of the science on earth.

Most of all, I remember that people are responsible for their actions on the earth, and they know that implicitly. People know in their heart that life is a lot bigger than what their eyes can see. Whether they call it God or the Universe, life on earth is a simplified construct.

There is also no God in the afterlife, which may come as a great shock to many people. In fact, some time after my death and rebirth I was given a chance to meet God. It was a quiet evening. I decided to do some meditation in my apartment. Almost immediately after I started my meditation, I felt a "tall presence," one that I had felt before, and this presence "whisked me up" into the astral realms, way beyond I had ever been. I remember looking down and noticing the limits of my own personal meditative work, which had been quite impressive up until that point.

This tall presence continued to lift me higher and higher, flying up through space and time to a place no mortal could ever reach. What was evident to me was the fact that this level of realization was well outside of any mortal accomplishment. But I had no choice in this excursion and I had learned not to resist these kinds of spiritual lessons. I also wasn't a fan of extended spiritual lessons. These teachings could open up the mind like nothing else but it made it very hard to return to the normal world.

The tall presence took me into a very large and dark dimension, wrapped like a giant dome as if it was another sky dressed in dark gray. At the very height of this darkened dimension, this massive dome, there was an ecclesiastical light. A bright light. A spotlight. And when I turned my eyes to it, I could see that it was God. I've said before that I don't believe in God. I also have also stated that God is DNA. I've also said that we are living in a computer-generated reality. All of these things sort of followed what I saw on this particular night.

The astral world is not easily decoded. Things don't follow common sense. Scientific laws don't particularly apply. For example, there's no oxygen and there's no gravity. The light of God, if I can use that term, was pretty awesome. In my mind it was God. And the closer we flew to the light, taken by this tall presence, the more I became convinced that this tall presence was taking me to meet God.

After about the middle mark, I became unexpectedly afraid. I didn't want to meet God. I didn't even believe in God, but that bright light was God and I didn't want to meet him. The closer we flew the more afraid I became until I said that I didn't want to continue. I wanted to return back to reality. The light was burning me. Still, the tall presence continued and did not heed my requests. I think that I tried to turn away but I could feel the light penetrating the cells in my body.

As we got even closer I could see the shape of a tall white-haired man, the standard image of God in the Christian context. He was made out of light. Pure ecclesiastical light. The light that radiated from him burned. It felt like approaching the sun.

He wasn't moving. He was standing there, lighting the world. I didn't want to go any closer. I was terribly afraid. My heart was racing. I was scared. I felt unworthy to meet God.

The tall presence did not stop.

We finally reached the image of God. He wasn't moving. Being in front of him I had decided to accept the situation. I calmed myself down, faced with the unchangeable fact that I was here in front of God. My God! I was in front of God. It was unimaginable. A blistering man made out of pure light.

But the tall presence continued on and we flew *past* God. The image was massive and we flew past the image or maybe even through the image. That was even more unimaginable. As we flew past the image, we arrived to a place behind the image. I looked back, to my astonishment, the giant image of God was a neon sign in the astral sky. Incredible. Unfathomable. **God was a giant neon sign.**

I felt things in my mind falling apart. Old ideas. Old paradigms. Old implants. Memories. Impressions. Wow, just everything to do with God falling apart.

We continued on and I could see the framework that kept the neon God suspended in this vast domed chamber. I didn't know whether to laugh or cry. My emotions were difficult to manage. I had met God and in meeting him I had come to learn that he was nothing more than a neon sign placed deep in the subconscious of humanity.

We have been misled to believe in God by people who have the ability to place constructs in our subconscious minds. But the subconscious implant wasn't in my subconscious, he was inside the subconscious of the global population. At the back of our minds, keeping us on track and afraid of judgment, was a bright neon God. We have been played. Manipulated. We have formed a religion, we have fought wars, we have built churches, and for thousands of years we have been made into ecclesiastical tools.

I met God that night. I didn't want to, but I met God and the old white-haired man overlooking humanity and giant neon sign in the collective subconscious. What also struck me was the fact that I couldn't have gained this experience on my own. I was given a very powerful lesson because I think I had been a good learner up until that point. Or maybe they needed to remove a hindrance to my spiritual progress.

It was the kind of lesson that you say, "It figures it would be something like that."

I understand why it isn't easy for people to shed the idea of God. This image is far too deep to manually erase. But I also gathered the sense that the neon God hanging over our world is supported by our belief of him. In other words, the neon God is intimately tied to our belief in God, like any good hypnosis.

The neon God is a construct that is supported by human belief. As long as we believe in God, that image will remain in our collective subconscious. You could also say that our collective subconscious created God, that is, humanity doesn't need God. We could also extend that thought to say that humanity, at one point, did need a fatherly thought implant, until it reached a certain level of genetic endowment; otherwise, society could have collapsed without some monolithic structure in the mind to guide them.

But, that said, now that we do have the genetic material and the technological tools, we have surpassed the need for the neon idol. The problem is that the neon God is deeply etched into our collective mind that it may be painful to remove. If my experience is any indication, and I wasn't a big believer, then you can imagine the anxiety that some people may have to deal with. It would be the kind of anxiety that has not been seen before. I'd recommend that this process is given ample time to process and to allow some people to keep their beliefs for as long as they need them.

Instead of a false idol in our subconscious, and after years of research, I have discovered something else entirely. I have decoded the presence of a Reality Operating System (ROS) and that system is what is powering our computer-programmed reality.

Part 5
Learn to be a better player of life

Moving away from the religious dogma

What is the salvific formula in the world run by a giant computer? We've established that suffering arises from not being synchronized with the frequency of the ROS. This frequency, different in different regions of the world, is a technological appropriation. It is also very advanced, so advanced in fact that for millennia we have taken it for granted.

And, worse, for millennia we have attributed the frequency output of the ROS, what I call the Network of Light, to one of many deities. We have been led to believe that a godlike being has been responsible for the care and function of the earth. My stance on this issue has to be consistent if we, as a race of people, are going to move forward. We are living inside of a computer-generated reality.

The features of the ROS may not be readily apparent and may take years before anything significant happens to elucidate the true nature of reality. Some people have spent decades in search of meaning and purpose. They have studied any number of forms of enlightenment and they haven't likely had their expected moments of nirvana.

If the world doesn't need God, that is, if we can attain oneness with the ROS through frequency modulation, then the "salvation" handed out by established religions is indeed within reach. Some people are on the cusp of achieving complete enlightenment.

Learning to live in a technological reality is not learning to live without God, rather, it is about learning to live with the 21st century definition of God. The historical definition of God is incomplete, and, we can say, that it is a false construct, perpetuated and planted into the deepest recesses of our collective minds. The false neon God is a tool to prevent awakening. It is a limitation and because it is a limitation we have to give ourselves the time to wean off of its hold over our lives. It was placed there for a reason and now that reason is no longer necessary.

Already the new generation, and the New Age generation, have been expanding on the spiritual approach. They have been moving away from the religious dogma and spiritual philosophy, stripping the deity worship from these ancient systems of beliefs, and moving forward with less spiritual terms, things like the "universe" or the "presence" and the "limitless field of knowledge." I suppose I did fall into the spiritual hybridization category in previous years, but my work took a dramatic turn in 2012 when I discovered the microbiological approach of the Gnostics, basically what I considered hybridized spiritual innovators.

What is this union with God? It is a state of mind that is obtained when one detaches from this world. When you detach from the material world, world of illusion, a computer-generated reality, you are able to do so because you have synchronized your vibration/frequency with that of ROS 11. That achievement as many historical names: union with God, union with Brahman, oneness with the universe, complete enlightenment.

As the game evolves, change the algorithm

The ancient mystics talked about samsara and samsara meant that karma and desire produced endless cycles of rebirth. Samsara ended when a person attained "nirvana," which meant detaching from desires and the realization of the false reality (Maya). Such that the ancient rebirth into this Earth School is both temporary and impermanent. You were born, you die, then you are reborn according to your karma.

The goal of the ancients was to end this cycle of repeated birth and death through detachment and realization, what we think of as "enlightenment." In a manufactured reality, the reality objects, both physical and mental, can be considered to be rendered (transient, evanescent, inconstant) in real time; therefore, the objects in reality are being rendered at a rate that is outside of our perception. What makes it outside of our perception? Data processing.

There's too much data to process by the imprisoned state of the human, that is, the human mind is attached to this world. Another way of saying that is the frequency of the human mind is mated with the frequency of the reality. The false reality is a holographic reality. The body as well is a holographic projection of the genomic computer. Your DNA is projecting your physical body while connected to the material world. Your material body is automatically projected unless you have gained control to shut that function off. To change your frequency to match that of the ROS, which is significantly higher, you must detach from the material world (nirvana) and then synchronize with ROS 11.

The rendered reality construct and a holographic projection of the body via the DNA cause suffering (dukkha) as long as we are attached to them. As long as we believe in the false projection of reality, and we internalize these renderings as true, then we are functioning at a low frequency and this low frequency is like riding the carriage where the actual doesn't fit the hole in the wheel.

Turbulence.

The bumpy ride, and improper oscillation, is what causes suffering and the spiritual seeker can end their suffering by detaching from the rendered reality in getting acquainted with the ROS. The ROS is Brahman, God, Universe, whatever you prefer to call it. The name you call the ROS does not change the fact that it is a reality program.

Here are the three things we should remember:

1. The rendered reality is holographic. You can think of it as digital reality code.
2. We are artificially-controlled androids. We have a holographic identity projection.
3. The frequency of the computer-generated reality is different (lower) than our native program frequency of operation.

If reality is synthetic, then we must necessarily be synthetic. The awakening of society will reveal that we live in a synthetic reality and because we can exist in that synthetic reality we are also synthetic. A synthetic human can also be thought of as an android. The android human operates in the false world via their data stream, what the ancients called dharma.

Dharma is the teachings of reality or we can think of it as the code of reality. Total knowledge. Your digital stream (signal) is your dharma. That is your digital account. When you fall out of your account, you suffer. Your account is your scheduled journey. Your incarnation contract. It is in your interest to learn about the journey you ordered, as indicated in your digital feed.

You can tap into your digital feed by tapping into the purpose you have here on the earth. It is almost as if you are a device and there's a line connected to you in this line or stream (account) carrying all of your data. As long as you play out the programming, the "binge acting," everything is fine and you won't have to come back. This dharma stream is like an Existential Playlist that contains all of your programmed activities and events on the earth.

Now, because we are always connected to this digital stream does not mean that we always have 100% connectivity and when you lose the signal the data starts to break up (buffering), which is like turbulence in your life and turbulence is suffering and suffering is dukkha. When you have dukkha, you have suffering and when you have suffering you have turbulence and when you have turbulence it means you are buffering your dharmic stream, and if you're buffering your dharmic stream you are not living out your purpose.

Say that you want incarnate into the human body. To do so, you need to sign a contract. The contract contains a list of things you intend to do — an Existential Playlist. The Existential Playlist contains all the programs that you will play out (and some are hidden), and will be laid out in different phases, with different contingencies.

What began as a discussion on the digital reality code, the focus later shifted to the Existential Playlist. It started with the gods. In the beginning, the gods, the reality programmers, created a reality system in those early phases. The Beta Program required that the reality programmers protected the program and the user experience. What that meant in technological speak was that the reality programmers were in charge and once they worked out the bugs they released a new Beta version of reality.

The new Beta version of reality became more dependent on the user, the role player. The role player or gamer upheld the "order of the universe." Through the performance of the gamer. In other words, how well the professional performs in the game determines how the game plays out and this is multiplied by the number of users. The gamers who accumulated the most points determined how the game played out. They could alter the reality program because of their accumulation of points.

To accumulate the most points, you have to make a kind of sacrifice because you have to surrender your automated journey. To surrender your automated journey, you wake up. That is your sacrifice. Or you are awoken. That is also a sacrifice because it is a scheduled waking from the system. Depending on your sacrifice in the game, you get to alter the game. To alter the existential play, you have to wake up and this process — enlightenmcnt — gives you the ability to steer the gameplay, but there is a cost; hence the sacrifice.

Once you are fully awakened, you lose the joy of playing, and you can't go back to sleep after a certain point. In the early phases you can be put back to sleep. In fact, the reality hijackers want to put you back to sleep; otherwise you will interfere with their plans for dominating the gameplay. But, after a number of waking phases (nirvana), you can't be put to sleep anymore.

There must've been a point in the release of this existential school, played out as a game of life, whereby the technical masters (ie gods) changed the nature of the code and made the game automated. A fully automated existential field of play involving perfectly artificial persons. Androids. Once they had worked out the bugs in the reality software, during the "Beta Phase" of development, and then introduced an improved version of the code and then switched on the autopilot. Program.

Gameplay interlinked with the gamer performance; and periodically gamers were required to wake up (ie to sacrifice their gameplay) so as to be able to moderate the course and direction of this existential learning program. The human android played out the scheduled programming, according to the version and leadership of reality. In fact, the proper translation of a human is android. The word human means android.

What happened at some point is that the operating system was hacked, and these reality hackers inserted themselves into the game field, only that the hackers had a phenomenally high level of existential awareness. They explicitly understood that if they woke up, not wanting to play an automated character, they could gain control of the course of all the gamers. But they were still trapped within the confines of the operational code, that is, they couldn't do anything immediately.

They also knew how to reincarnate, which meant they could come back, in full awareness, and play out another character who would continue to deconstruct the gameplay and to distort reality. They could form a Church and use it as an instrument to persecute others who were trying to wake up. They would call them heretics and devout worshipers would be none the wiser. They would think they were serving God, whatever that was defined to be. It didn't matter. Plus, if the Emperor controlled the Church, then servants of the one faith had every reason to please the Emperor, or they too might lose their head.

These reincarnates grew in size as more of their friends slipped into this reality field, and they formed societies in secret where they would collaborate and conspire to slowly take over the world. They shared reality distortion and manipulation secrets between members, including the very rites of reincarnation. They agreed to return in another body, a body likely that would inhabit the wealth and power of a previous occupant.

For example, they could, using magical spells, reincarnate as their granddaughter and no one would ever know. The granddaughter would inherit the wealth of the grandfather, and it wouldn't raise any suspicions. This system was repeated until massive wealth and political power was accumulated.

Their magicians would be on the lookout for a reincarnate and would automatically welcome them into the fold. They used this, and other methods, to accumulate unparalleled power. Thousands of years later, and many members in their secret societies, these reality dynasties have taken large aspects of reality. Where are these societies? Look to the most powerful and influential people in the world. The older their families date back in time, the longer they have been reincarnating in secret.

The secret societies of reincarnates also formed mystical schools, in secret, and these mystics used magic to open portals in reality. These portals gave them access to other worlds and other knowledge. They became more powerful mystics. They also opened portals to welcome people from offplanet, who then took the human form and imprinted their mark on society. These interdimensional groups further distorted the world, because they were far more powerful than humans; they also taught these mystics magical secrets that gave them immense power over the common people.

The secret society magicians also went out to sabotage the native reality system. They started by closing natural portals and persecuting their rivals. They continued to build false religions and invented false gods, things that actually blocked salvation and thereby ensured their dominance. The reality hackers understood the premise of this book — that reality is synthetic — and so built layer upon layer of deception.

They also needed to cripple the reincarnative process. The reality hijackers needed to slow down the rebirth of advanced game players. Why? Because these advanced players understood how to protect the course of reality. They could also, using magic, counter the destructive methods of the secret societies. This back and forth continued for a time, eventually the reality hijackers managed to slow down the reincarnative process for the reality technicians.

You knew these reality technicians by their earthly titles: heretics, magicians, shamans, zealots, seers, sages, gypsies, and witches.

People who lived outside the system, were routinely persecuted, and ostracized. Even today, how many shamans and gypsies are there on mainstream television?

The reality hackers could never expose the computer game because that would jeopardize their monopoly on the system. They had to establish that their religious inventions and the word of God were the standards, and those who did not abide by God's laws (totally fabricated by these hackers) needed to be punished. Once they labeled a person a "heretic," that person came under attack. People who did not believe in God, or whatever ideology, were rounded up and tortured.

One of the most powerful images they managed to created was the crucifixion of God's only Son, Jesus. The image of Jesus on the cross became a global reminder of punishment. That this world was a world of punishment and not even the Son of God could escape that fact. Then they inspired people to wear a tortured and tormented Jesus nailed to a cross around their necks and to hang him on their walls. You get the impression of fear that they wanted to instill. That impression remains today, two thousand years later.

The Inquisition was an explicit attempt to stave off the mass return of incarnates. Witches. Magic was a skill handed to those who had technological skills with the ROS. Magic was mysterious because it had everything to do the reality program. This was well before the invention of the computer. Witches could tap into the ROS, with very little effort. The reality hackers did not like that at all and so weaponized the Church to do their bidding.

But, things continued to change in the 21st century after the computerization of the world. This has coincided with a new phase of awakening. This time, reincarnates would not be prosecuted and killed off. This time secret societies would be exposed. This time the hackers and their minions would not be allowed back into reality so easily. More powerful spells could give them a new body, only the new body would be more random. The transfer of power and the elite inheritance system was about to end. Less powerful magicians would not be allowed re-entry.

And other reincarnates, even those from the past, were allowed back. Without the power to order an Inquisition, the master controllers issued more wars. Without the ability to torture people, the master controllers ordered mass vaccinations and motivated people to get vaccinated by scaring up society with orchestrated outbreaks. We are basically entering a point in gameplay where the reality hackers are facing off against the return of the reality technicians, with everyone still dressed in their human clothes. Because we outnumber the secret society members, even if we're still battling the state of wakefulness.

We have within our ability to finally drive back these reality hijackers and to retake control of our planet. The apocalypse is also coming. What is the apocalypse? You've been reading it. **The apocalypse is that we are androids living inside of a computer-generated reality that has been hijacked.**

With the final removal of these corrupt people, and with our awareness of who they might be if they are still around, the world will naturally be allowed to evolve. This is something that has been vehemently repressed for 5,000 years.

It is possible to imagine that karma was introduced after a new version of reality was introduced to us and it was done so just to slow down the mechanics of the reality hijackers. It's possible that the reality technicians introduced a new "reality algorithm" or a new reality engine (processor) such that improper actions would have a detrimental effect on their rebirth because it could be surmised that the reality hijackers and their magicians had been freely reincarnating without consequence and a conditional rebirth would slow them down.

Similarly, genuine *rebirthers* who followed the laws of reality, would naturally benefit from the introduction of a new reality algorithm. If past actions determined the outcome of the player, then bad actors would suffer under the karmic algorithm. Karma also could undermine the dependence upon gods. The Christian system, which was a much later invention, by about 800 years, said that people are born sinful and only the Church and Jesus could redeem their sinful nature.

In karmic terms, the Christian religion countered the effects of karma by saying that people were born in karmic debt (sins) and could never alleviate that debt by their own actions, in effect canceling out the effects of the karmic algorithm. They depressed society. None of which is true.

While some people are born with karmic debt, most people are not. And those who carried over karmic debt could alleviate their debt through proper actions. Over time, the biblical dogma gained a lot of traction and the sinful worshipers waited out their lives without ever tasting salvation. The key to maintaining control over reality required the global penetration of the Church and most of the world believes in God to one to some degree or another.

A little thing about voices in the head

There are voices that some people can hear and some others cannot hear. These are very subtle voices and they are disembodied, that is, the voices don't necessarily have bodies. Talking about "hearing voices" with people is a very sensitive subject. The people who can hear the voices don't want to admit it because it makes them sound crazy. The people who don't hear voices, they don't believe that voices exist. If you tell these "voice deniers" that you hear voices, they'll suggest a psychiatric visit.

Psychiatry has its place and I'm not against conventional medicine. I use Band-Aids. I use antibiotic cream. It's just that when it comes to inexplicable illnesses and chronic imbalances that is when Western medicine starts to lose its efficacy. Voices in the head is definitely one of those illnesses that requires an unconventional approach. Again, while I'm not completely against the use of pharmaceutical drugs, when it comes to voices, pills are only Band-Aids being applied to a fractured bone.

Voices come from many sources so let's look at the variety of sources that I have noticed over the years that may emit the voices which can be heard by a small, but growing, group of people. I'm a survivor of hearing voices in the head and I say that I'm a survivor because I was ruthlessly attacked by a malicious group of people, starting in 2005 (but it was also present before 2005) after I was visited by three interdimensional Elves.

My waking process opened up my psyche to an entirely unfamiliar metaphysical world, and along with the standard assortment of disembodied voices, I was also manipulated by metaphysical and military agents who wanted to severely undermine my spiritual growth.

When your DNA is activated, and it could be the combination of any number of genes, and through a variety of methods, you are automatically brought closer to the subtle dimensions. All of your senses are heightened, including your intuition. Some people develop their "third eye" while others can see spirit guides.

When your metaphysical senses are turned on, you start seeing and hearing things. At first, you hear your own thoughts. You may hear the thoughts of friends. You may hear the thoughts of ghosts. And you may hear the fairies. You will learn to navigate the plethora of voices or you will go crazy. There is an ON/OFF switch. Some people have a preference.

But, the beings in other dimensions are not always friendly. Some are very deceptive. They will tell you things that they shouldn't. They might tell you that the world will soon end. They might tell you that you are the reincarnation of a powerful being. "You are the reincarnation of Jesus! But don't tell anyone." People have told me that these negative beings will often scare them. They will say, "If you use your power, you will destroy the world." That person naturally becomes afraid of their DNA transformation, which is the intent of these dark entities. They don't like the light. As long as a newly-awakened remains "off" than they can enjoy the shadows.

There are also other metaphysical agents, what I call magicians, and they can also communicate with you. The dark magicians don't like you around, especially if you bring optimism and light. They too will send you whispers in the night. These voices would tell you things. At first, an evil magician may say something helpful to gain your confidence. "You have a really bright aura. Glad that you are here."

Once they've gained your confidence they'll start telling you things in the middle of the night. I met a woman once who practiced magic. She helped people. She told me about a dark magician who was telling teenagers to commit suicide. This very dark individual would get excited when they convinced a teenager, using magic, to kill themselves. Magicians can project thoughts through time and space. And there were no fingerprints. Who would believe that? It happens more than we'd like to think.

For more than a year I was brutally attacked, daily, by a team of people who wanted to turn me into a homosexual. They knew that I wasn't gay and for various reasons they wanted to make me gay. I heard voices daily, hours at a time, telling me I was gay. I would even ask the voice, "Am I really gay?" And the voice would answer back, "Yes, you are gay." Only that I was being manipulated. I didn't make it make it easier but it did prevent them from making me gay. Where they couldn't turn me gay they tried telling me that I was bisexual. I can only imagine how many people they turned gay.

Beware the multidimensional symbiote

In more recent years, I've been talking about a multidimensional symbiote, that would attach to a person's nervous system and then it would basically tap into their mind. By understanding the person's fears and beliefs they could slowly manipulate the person. These symbiotes could, when they had taken control of the person, tell the person what to do and the person couldn't separate if the voice was their voice (inner voice) or the voice of the entity that was attached.

Symbiotes are more common than I like to think. They may only attach for a brief period but during that period may drive that person into strange behaviors, periods of severe depression, periods of recklessness and drug taking, even into making unnecessary changes in their lives, including harming themselves. The symbiote thinks of your body as would a carjacker on drugs who steals a car and drives it into the ground. Symbiotes, because they know your thoughts, they might push you into violence, into prostitution, into mental illness, even into drug taking. And because you're acting strange you may get diagnosed with a mental illness and you will be in therapy and you will be prescribed medication. To separate the effects of the symbiote versus the effects of a medical condition is very difficult. Certainly, I am not qualified to do that because I have no medical training. That said, no medical doctor is trained in multidimensional symbiote attachments.

A symbiote is free when your willpower is low and when your physical body is weak. A depressed person who is also obese is their ideal candidate. If they hijack a healthy person, they need to find ways to ruin their lives. Get them drinking alcohol, experimenting with drugs, keep them depressed, fill their mind with suicidal thoughts, and get them on psychiatric drugs.

A long-term symbiote attachment can interrupt so many neurological functions, since the nervous system controls the body, that people may find themselves being diagnosed with Lyme disease, Huntington's, and even early stage Alzheimer's. I would say, not as a doctor but as an observer, some cases of Multiple Sclerosis (MS) are due to the effects of some kind of multidimensional entity, of which there are many kinds. All these diseases have no known cause, or cure. I will be the first to admit, and this is discussed more thoroughly in my book *The Book of Symbiote Diseases*, that detecting these symbiotes is very difficult. That's why it is easier to go by the mysterious and debilitating symptoms.

Targeted people may have energy mechanisms in their homes and workplaces. These metaphysical devices, obviously invisible, are there to distort the person's life. Targeted people hear more voices than usual. They may be on antipsychotics, especially if they can't manage and are in danger. For example, a targeted person may hear a voice that wants them to take drugs. "Take it. You'll feel better. Don't you deserve to feel better?" A drug addict may look at a pill and even will hear the pill talking. "Just one more. It won't kill you." Then they take drugs and have an overdose.

These metaphysical device, I think, is a kind of artificial intelligence, a program that bounces off the native reality architecture. This is a technology and it is being used to target people. One of the most common effects is depression. The other is feeding the ego. The device can remind the person, through a symbiotic process, to continue to live an egotistical life and to chase things that probably won't lead to nirvana. As long as people avoid self-actualization, the reality hijackers win. Those pursuing self-actualization will get their minds changed. "You've done enough. Get a job. Go out with that girl. You know enough about spirituality." It doesn't take much to deter people.

Voices can be heard because we live in a multidimensional world. There are entities and devices that can be programmed to ruin a person's life. If you are targeted, it is because you have a unique purpose on the earth and likely have a more robust set of genes. The voices will make you appear crazy (and some people do have neurological imbalances). While the scientific evidence is lacking, you will likely have anecdotal evidence.

You know yourself better than anyone. You can learn to modulate your energy fields. You can't be turned on all the time. Conventional science has yet to reach this level of discussion, so in the meantime I think it might be helpful to some people to provide at least a cursory look at what might be happening at the metaphysical level. In usual cases, metaphysics will be explained in the future. It's not always the case, but if you took electricity to Jesus, he'd say that it was from God.

Whenever you hear negative voices, especially voices that want you to cause harm to you or to somebody else, don't listen to them. Tune them out. If you are a long-term addict, abuser, alcoholic or of a very unsavory disposition, it is possible (and admittedly hard to prove scientifically) that you have a very old symbiote attached to your body. Symbiotes also grow in families of symbiotes such that when one symbiote dies off, a new one will replenish their place so that you will always be visited by this family of symbiotes.

The symbiote feeds off of your energy and can grow pretty big. Weaning yourself off the symbiote and making life changes (positive) will starve the symbiote. It will shrink and eventually detach and die off. The more serious your situation the more time you'll need to correct your life, but the symbiote won't go quietly. It will make every attempt to take over.

You may relapse. It could take many years to resolve this because it is attached to your nervous system, which is your identity and your mind. It *sounds like* you. It has your memories. It knows your weaknesses. It knows where you were traumatized. It knows your fears. It knows what you want. It knows your secrets. All of these may be used against you.

Think of it this way, as a barometer, moderation is the key to a happy life. Where there is excess, there may be a voice.

Voices have been around a long time. The more people wake up, having the DNA activated, the more people will have to navigate the multidimensional world of voices. I think that as the earth evolves some of these entities will be removed, cleansed; otherwise the world might go mad. It is unfortunate that the early generation had to go through mental hospitals and mental illness and addictions, that this recent generation had to go through antipsychotics, and that the new generation still has to deal with addictive behaviors, but the future will have a better grasp of this problem.

The key is to be able to talk about hearing voices and not to label people as being crazy. Schizophrenia is not what it has been made out to be and schizophrenics, incurable, may have a unique and genetic disposition. I think tolerance and understanding is needed. People suffering from depression, a kind of mental illness, may be hearing a lot of negative voices, which are making them depressed. But, these voices are not at the audible level; they are at the sub-audible level, even infrasonic level, and sometimes these voices they can be multiplied so that the entities repeat something hundreds of times per hour and after enough hours, the person becomes severely depressed and nobody knows why. Depression has been growing at an alarming rate. Perhaps 10% of the American population has suffered from depression, with many more who are likely undiagnosed and untreated.

Life isn't so simple and I hope that by reading this book you'll have a better understanding as to why. The truth is that everybody hears voices. It's just that some people hear so many that those voices become unmanageable and they cannot separate their identity from the identities of the voices, and in the confusion a person's life can become severely distorted.

While I don't see an immediate cure, or scientific proof for that matter, I think there is a small group of people who do suffer, who are not mentally ill, and can use a little validation to help them cope. If you hear negative voices, do not believe them.

The technological leap

"Look there and see what is like you on the earth. And he looked down and saw those on the earth." (*The Revelation of Paul*)

The earth is the basement level on a tall, immaculate tower (engineered on a multidimensional platform). For thousands of years, planetary citizens looked at every method that would help them attain spiritual ascension. And up until the modern day a bare handful have claimed the salvific formula.

The salvation is an end to suffering and an end to suffering is oneness with the universe. We now know that there is no universe just like there is no God. There is something that we can understand. It is the Reality Operating System.

Suffering was never meant to last thousands of years. Sorry. The doctrine of the Church doesn't work and we have 1,700 years of proof. Humanity has been left to suffer after the reality was surreptitiously hijacked 5,000 years ago. If you struggled with your ascension up until now, and you've been a fairly good student, why haven't you ascended?

You've been blaming yourself, you've been pushing yourself, you've been searching for a better way. The better way is detaching from the spiritual systems that simply do not work. To be a little more direct: salvation has nothing to do with the traditional interpretation of God.

God was never in the equation. The Creator is better defined as DNA and DNA, if you ask a qualified geneticist, could be described as software. The Software-DNA in your body is not there by accident. Software programs don't evolve through natural selection. The software in your computer was developed by teams of computer programmers. Professionals who invested thousands of hours of work to code the program.

Well, if programmers presumably coded our DNA, and if you DNA is millions of years old, then who exactly encoded our DNA? When you are speaking of DNA as software, you automatically have to distance yourself from God. Because God doesn't *do* DNA. How do we know that? There's no mention of software and computing in the Bible. The secret to graduating this Earth School is understanding the DNA software link to reality.

I've made the link for you in this book. I've taken the leap to the next level by stating unequivocally that we are living inside of the computer-generated reality. This is important because you can't achieve enlightenment if you can't see that reality has been manufactured.

This is a fundamental misstep echoing across human history. Humanity has been purposely hobbled by people who are professional reality technicians. What they did is they hacked the reality program, and over millennia, they have corrupted and distorted the mortal world.

The reality hackers, I think, are still a very new addition to the spiritual discussion, most likely discussed in conspiracy theory circles. But it is an invaluable piece of the endless misery of humanity. Despite all the religious promises of a salvific prophet and Divine Judgment, when the time was supposed to be "fulfilled," neither salvation nor judgment happened. That is a documented fact. That is not a theory. That is not a wild conspiracy. The apocalypse is a rainbow that never had any gold.

What I've shared in this book are the secrets to salvation, the path to enlightenment, and the road to ecclesiastical victory. Your spiritual success in this life can be measured by your graduation on the other side. The purpose of life in a manufactured reality has very little to do with material achievement. Your life may include material things, but when you go those things do not go with you.

In fact, the wisest spiritualist, taken as samples across history, practice detachment from the material world. It isn't by accident that sages lived in mountain caves and to study with one of the sages an acolyte had to make the trek to the countryside. Today, we need to get motivated to go online to order a good book on spirituality. We only watch the first few minutes of a spiritual video and then make a nasty comment. "This guy is like a bean bag with too many beans."

There is a path out of the religious quagmire and the reincarnation Rolodex and it has the potential to ascend an entirely fresh wave of accomplished experiencers. Why do I say experiencers? Because this is an experiential school. What we collectively think of as earth. But there's no such thing really. This is a construct. A controlled habitat.

People, for some reason, still like to think that this entire planet was populated by an invisible white-haired man on a cloud. Scientists like to attribute the perfected human being to a conclusion from an accidental biological simulation, that through millions of years of a genetic domino effect, where all the pieces fell perfectly in order, we obtained the genetic-lottery-winning women in the *Victoria's Secret Catalogue*. The human race as an existential accident doesn't work anymore.

The earth is a computer-generated reality. What you see and touch in this reality is a holographic projection. Yes, it looks real. That's because of the reality programmers. They are that good. The idea of entering an experiential school is to have the experience believable. Any portion of that school that looks fake will take you out of the illusion of the experience. It's total immersion. And its worked for tens of thousands of years. Only that its worked too well. And its prevented the waking up of society.

Allow me to expand on the artificial reality and the software-driven DNA to sum up a very important aspect of this wonderful reality. I glossed over it in another chapter. The human being is a synthetic being. Because you can't have software in your cells and live in a holographic world if you are biological and organic. One of the problems with decoding the artificial reality construct has to do with not all the puzzle pieces from adding up.

There have been theories that we are living inside of a computer. But those theories have done nothing to diminish the validity of God, and we know that logically, God and computer software don't mix very well. The more you extend the synthetic paradigm, the better you will understand the true nature of reality. For example, if reality is synthetic and DNA is synthetic, then we are synthetic.

All of that is not such a bad thing.

If you have ever wondered about the existence of life offplanet and people on other dimensions, then the synthetic reality offers a renewed perspective on those things. Do you know why? Because interstellar and interdimensional people are not necessarily coming from another galaxy or a distant dimension. Rather, in a synthetic reality, these offplanet people are connected to the larger computer network. In other words, star beings (ETs) are not "star" beings; instead, they are "digital beings."

Remember the main argument running through this book. We are living inside the computer program; therefore, any advanced race of people must necessarily come from the computer architecture. Why are these Stelan races so advanced? Because they are reality-based cultures. Why are they here? They're here to maintain the existential game. They are the Caretakers. The reality programmers. These advanced people are more likely Cosmic Technicians, with the cosmos having everything to do with the technological universe. **Cosmic Technicians are here to ensure that we get the experience we signed in our Incarnation Contracts.**

If you don't fully understand every piece of the cosmic puzzle, don't worry; take your time to process all of this information. Take years if you need years. The difference between the spiritual world and the technological world is that the technological world is not steeped in mystery. Spirituality is one of the greatest mysteries ever invented and it has not resolved the promise of salvation. Neither has religion, which has effectively stalled this salvific process.

For some reason, likely having to do with the hypnosis of the population and the DNA virus, people are not concerned that their path to ascension hasn't worked. People have not abandoned spiritual systems that don't work, and haven't worked for 3,000 years. People don't find it at all important that the promise of salvation has never been realized.

The idea that life is a school isn't a new idea. The idea that we came here to learn isn't a new idea. The idea that we are living inside of a computer program isn't a new idea. You know, it almost doesn't matter that we are living inside of a synthetic world. It shouldn't. But the problem is that we have lost our way and we haven't been able to graduate. In order to re-establish the full extent of the learning system, we have to expose the reality architecture, including the android bodies that we inhabit.

As unfortunate as this is, it also comes at the end of a Great Cycle (2,500 years), so perhaps it was all part of the greater humanitarian purpose. Give yourself the appropriate time to process this information. Explore ideas on your own. Look inside of yourself for the answers, where the DNA-God resides (just don't listen to the arrogant retrovirus).

The more you can internalize the manufactured reality, the likelihood of graduating can only increase. And that is what everyone wants. Everyone wants the existential certificate. It doesn't matter who you are, how much money you have, how powerful you are, how intelligent you are, or how many children you have. If you are here in this Earth School, you want your existential certificate. I hope that my book has urged you to be a better student to finish your studies.

What are you studying? Look at your career path for hints. Is it a steady path? Is it made up of several parts that can be combined to serve a higher purpose? Look at your skillset. Look at your reputation. Look at your long-term goals. Now I know that the influences to be famous and rich are very strong, and struggling people will latch onto those notions. But they are false. Fame doesn't fix your problems. Fame brings more problems. There's nothing wrong with a steady job in the right profession. The closer you align yourself to what is in your contract, and you can transition when needed, you should be okay. Just because some guy is rich and pretends to be happy doesn't mean that you will be happy when rich. Hint: rich people pretend to be happy.

Look, it's a very difficult thing to say that the world is computer-generated. That is a very difficult thing to say, but by the same token if you do your research, if you detach yourself from the reality, and from your life, and you do the research and you start to perceive the multidimensional world, you really get confirmation that the world you've been hypnotized to believe is fundamentally false. It is a false paradigm that we have believed to be real — or we have been conditioned and hypnotized to believe it is real — and that it is the only world.

All of that is a fundamental lie. It is all a fundamental lie and it takes a lot of courage to abandon the false world and to embrace the multidimensional reality; and in the multidimensional reality the laws of science don't apply; there is no God and this is a school, and in the school we come to learn, and if we don't learn, we have to come back and that's what the master controllers want.

They want us to come back because our energy is feeding their energy. They are subsisting on our ignorance. They are sucking the energy out of us as we waste our lives chasing rainbows and then; because we don't succeed, we don't learn, we don't get the credits for the courses, and we damage our karma.

We have to come back and they want us to come back because we have to feed them. The more of us who come back, the more food they have. The more people stuck in school, the bigger the feast.

We are the buffet. We are a multidimensional buffet to a group of crocodilians, and it's so crazy that it's really, really sad. It's really,

really sad that this thing has been, has been so crazy that people are afraid to embrace it as the truth.

Finally, if you want the truth, just reverse everything in the false reality. Reverse it and that's (pretty close to) the truth.

Reverse to reveal. It may or may not be true, but it gives you perspective when you doubt the truth that you have been told. **Popular Truth:** Neil Armstrong was the first man to land on the moon. **Reversal:** Neil Armstrong never set foot on the moon. **Popular Truth:** We have never been visited by extraterrestrials. **Reversal:** Extraterrestrials are here.

You get the idea. It's not a perfect tool, but when applied to a conventional lie, it can highlight the probable truth.

Other than that, *good luck.*

References

Aslan, Reza. *Zealot: The Life and Times of Jesus of Nazareth*. New York: Random House, 2013.

Bodian, Stephen. *Wake Up Now: A Guide to Spiritual Awakening*. New York: McGraw-Hill, 2008.

Brazier, David. *Not Everything is Permanent*. Malvern, Texas: Woodsmoke Press, 2013.

Chopra, Deepak. *Spiritual Solutions: Answers to Life's Greatest Challenges*. New York: Harmony Books, 2012.

Dyer, Wayne W. *Change Your Thoughts—Change Your Life*. Carlsbad, California: Hay House, 2007.

Ehrman, Bart D. *Did Jesus Exist?: the Historical Argument for Jesus of Nazareth*. New York: HarperCollins, 2012.

_____. *God's Problem: How the Bible Fails to Answer Our Most Important Question—Why We Suffer*. New York: HarperCollins, 2008.

_____. *Jesus, Interrupted: Revealed the Hidden Contradictions in the Bible (and Why We Don't Know About Them)*. New York: HarperCollins, 2009.

_____. *Forged: Writing in the Name of God—Why the Bible's Authors Are Not Who We Think They Are*. New York: HarperCollins, 2011.

Kasser, R., Meyer, M., Wurst G., and Guadard, F. (Collaborator) (Eds.). *The Gospel of Judas, Critical Edition: Together with the Letter of Peter to Philip, James, and a Book of Allogenes from Codex Tchacos*. 2007 (National Geographic)

Landaw, J., Bodian, S., and Bühnemann, G. *Buddhism for Dummies, 2nd Edition*. Hoboken, New Jersey: John Wiley & Sons, 2011.

Littlejohn, Ronnie L. *Confucianism: An Introduction*. London: I.B. Tauris, 2011.

Meyer, M., Robinson, J. M. (Eds.). *The Nag Hammadi Scriptures: The Revised and Updated Translation of Sacred Gnostic Texts Complete in One Volume*. 2009 (HarperOne)

Ohso. *Tao: The Pathless Path*. New York: St. Martin's Press, 2002.

Scheff, Leonard, and Edmiston, Susan. *The Cow in the Parking Lot: A Zen Approach to Overcoming Anger*. New York: Workman Publishing, 2001.

Schuman, Michael. *Confucius: And the World He Created*. New York: Basic Books, 2015.

Sheng, Yen. *Song of Mind: Wisdom from the Zen Classic Xin Ming*. Boston: Shambhala, 2004.

Skilton, Andrew. *A Concise History of Buddhism*. Birmingham: Windhorse Publications, 1994.

Suzuki, D. T., Barrett, W. (editor). *Zen Buddhism: Selected Writings of D. T. Suzuki*. New York: Doubleday, 1996.

The Holy Bible (King James version) 1974 (Meridian)

The Manitou. Dir. William Girdler. Perfs. Tony Curtis, Michael Ansara, Susan Strasberg. Avco Embassy Pictures, 1978.

The Reincarnation of Peter Proud. Dir. J. Lee Thompson. Perfs. Michael Sarrazin, Margot Kidder, Jennifer O'Neil. Cinerama Releasing, 1975.

Tosen, Paris. *God is DNA: Salvation, the Church, and the Molecular Biology of the Gnostics*. Vancouver, British Columbia: Skyladder Media, 2015.

Venter, J. Craig. *Life at the Speed of Light: From the Double Helix to the Dawn of Digital Life*. New York: Viking, 2013.

Watts, Alan. *The Way of Zen*. New York: Vintage Books, 1989.

Watts, Alan, and Al Chung-liang Huang. *Tao: The Watercourse Way*. New York: Pantheon Books, 1975.

THE EARTH-GRADUATING
HANDBOOK

Introduction

Principles of reality protocols

They couldn't tell you what I'm going to tell you in this book because they didn't have the authorization to supersede the protocols. The words of reality have, for the longest time, been concealed by the limitations of a primitive mind subjected to the inadequacies of a significantly small cranial capacity. Where do we get our understanding of the world? How did we manage our role in the electric universe?

We started with a close connection to nature, sharing thoughts with animals and trees. Aboriginal cultures interpreted higher knowledge through the medium of magical birds, such as the thunderbird, or through their interactions with a natural element, for example the wind. Shamans and mendicants spent their lives in nature because they believed that all the answers came from nature. Through shamanistic chains they learn to walk the path. They practice rites and vision quests to gain magical powers. Once trained, they can speak to the natural spirits who would tell them how to heal illnesses and to make protective charms, and also about the secrets of the universe (the Great Mystery).

Mythologist Joseph Campbell, in his book *Primitive Mythology*, sums it up nicely, "For if the shaman was the guardian of the mythological lore of mankind during the period of some five or six hundred thousand years when the chief source of sustenance was the hunt, then the inner world of the shaman must be assumed to have played a considerable role in the formation of our spiritual inheritance may have descended from the period of the paleolithic hunt."

Before long, with the urbanization of society, the nomadic lifestyle was replaced by structured housing and our animist past was replaced by spiritual thinking. This was a time when anyone who could hallucinate in a coherent manner—whether by medicinal stimulant or neurological breakdown—could become a spiritual teacher. The rise of spiritualists and magicians took the knowledge from the forests to the streets. Hinduism formed. Shintoism formed. Other spiritual faiths have sprung up. Campbell suggests that Oriental spiritualism (eg Hinduism, Buddhism) shares metaphysical concepts with shamanism, and vice versa.

But as agricultural populations grew, people looked for something more and we began to see the establishment of early religions. While Jesus was a zealot in the streets of Galilee who never had a church or a bible, that hasn't stopped Christianity, based on his teachings, from constructing an entire network of churches, dressing priests in white robes, and establishing rituals of worship, none of which can be found in the original teaching methods of Jesus. Beyond that, in regards to the resurrection, Jews held to the apocalyptic view that the evil world would soon be destroyed by God. "God would crash into history to judge this world, overthrow all his enemies, including sin and death, and raise his people from the dead," writes Bart D. Ehrman in *Did Jesus Exist?* He adds, "And it would happen very soon." As contemporary worshipers know, the future kingdom has not manifested in 2,000 years.

Early prophets of the bible were farmers and peasants. Jesus was allegedly a carpenter. Ninety percent of the people were illiterate. These people were experiencing auditory and visual hallucinations, which today would be considered mental illness. We do not allow people who hear strange voices and see burning bushes to hold any meaningful jobs in the modern day. They used to be placed in the mental institution. With modern pharmaceutical drugs and the deinstitutionalization program that followed, the mentally ill take their medications at home.

Whatever natural truths were born from the forests have been interpolated and reformulated into a human language, and passed off as a divine language made to look ancient and prophetic. But even those ancient scriptures were interpolations and reformulations of the original knowledge about the world.

Reality hasn't changed since it was first conceived. Trees are still trees. Reality has always been in existence. What has changed is the language we have been using to describe that reality. Campbell writes: "The mystery of the universe and the wonder of the temple of the world are what speak to us through all myths and rites—as well as the great effort of man to bring his individual life into concord with the whole. And the imagery by which this mystery, wonder, and effort have been rendered in the recorded traditions of mankind is so marvellously constant—in spite of all the varieties of local life and culture—that we well may wonder whether it may not simply be coeval with the human mind."

Religious and spiritual languages are not the original languages of reality. These are human interpolations and reformulations that have obscured the reality languages, but, they had the benefit of fitting into the limited intellectual capacity of ancient cultures. Why this spiritual standoff has become a problem is because as long as we rely on these misinterpretations we can never fully understand what is going on.

The advantage we have today is that we are no longer a primitive agricultural based society. The advantage today is that we can see the shared similarities between religious and spiritual thinking across the world as it "unfolded in the manner of a single symphony" and then was reformulated and extrapolated according to custom and tradition, with the expectation that when the unified symphony ends it is expected that another will have already begun.

When Campbell compares Occidental and Oriental spiritual systems in *Pathways to Bliss*, he points out that the Semitic legacy has made man and God very distant from one another. The Oriental, on the other, rests on a perfectly ordained order. "This cosmic order is mathematical and unalterable; not even a deity can initiate change. God and man are simply functionaries of that order. To become a responsible citizen, you must learn your job perfectly."

Strangely enough, in the second century, we find a similar position on the cosmic order, this time from the Roman Emperor Marcus Aurelius Antoninus, who famously said: "All things are woven together and the common bond is sacred, and scarcely one thing is foreign to another, for they have been arranged together in their places and together make the same ordered Universe. For there is one Universe out of all, one God through all, one substance and one law, one common Reason of all intelligent creatures and one truth, if indeed the perfection of creatures of the same family and partaking of the same Reason is one."

The 1977 film *Star Wars* on the surface, at least, plays out like a wild adventure movie that happens to take place in space. There are blaster pistols and space ships with warp drives. There is also metaphysics, carried on by the Jedi class, trained individuals who follow a strict code and wield lightsabers. A Jedi's powers come from the Force. "It surrounds us and penetrates us. It binds the galaxy together" is how Obi-Wan Kenobi (Alec Guinness) explains it to a young Luke Skywalker (Mark Hamill). Skywalker, the begotten son of Dark Vader, begins to apprentice. When rebel Han Solo (Harrison Ford), self-admitted atheist and occasional owner of the Millennium Falcon, is asked for his opinion on the Force, later on, Solo answers candidly.

Luke Skywalker: You don't believe in the Force, do you?

Han Solo: Kid, I've flown from one side of this galaxy to the other, and I've seen a lot of strange stuff, but I've never seen anything to make me believe that there's one all-powerful Force controlling everything. 'Cause no mystical energy field controls my destiny. It's all a lot of simple tricks and nonsense.

The technological evolution

If we continue under these false spiritual assumptions, we are not going to get anywhere. The removal of the reality protocols is going to enable a significant shift in our understanding of the world we live in.

Again, we all live on the same planet. The planet hasn't changed in millions of years in any meaningful way. The planet doesn't believe in God. The planet is not concerned about going to church or a temple or a synagogue or a mosque. The planet is an atheist.

The knowledge of the forest too has not changed. Shamans, who listen to the forest, the animals, and the elements, they have never built a church. They have never written any spiritual book and do not have any worshipers. And that should be interesting because shamans are some of the oldest spiritual teachers because shamans speak to the planet and the planet is 4.5 billion years old. Can you see the problem? Instead of church, we should all be going to the forest. When you want to communicate with the reality spirits, find nature. When you lose connection, fast for a few days, get a vision, find your spirit contacts, and try again.

Protocols are in place everywhere you go. There are protocols in marriage and there are internet protocols. There are protocols in information technology and there are protocols for packaging vitamin supplements. We live in a world of protocols. Well, surprisingly, it turns out that there are protocols when it comes to the matters of existence.

This book is written under the premise of the most relevant protocol known to the human civilization. That protocol is the protocol of synthetic existence. Basically, if I might speak more plainly, the human life form is wholly synthetic. It is artificial, but its artificiality is unmatched by conventional science. Did I just read what I thought I read? Yes. You are an android. But don't be alarmed because everybody here is an android. The human species has a synthetic origin.

This secret has been kept from you because of the protocols of capacity to process data (understand). This level of truth is a sizable download and previous versions of humans were not equipped to store and process this quantity at data at once. Without the ability to do so, the system, naturally, would've crashed, became hyper-emotional, and most likely would've turned hyper-violent. The combination of these reasons, and others having to do with authorization and authentication codes, have prevented this secret from previously being revealed.

If you are still reading, you likely have the capacity to process this information. That does not guarantee an immediate recalibration of existence, as one might expect in a fictional story, although it is plausible for those individuals who have already dedicated their lives to the highest spiritual leanings. More than likely, this calibration is going to require a number of years. There is no exact figure. Your data banks are currently filled with outdated, old, and mostly contradictory data having to do with existence, spirituality, and the origin of the species. This will slow down the recalibration process.

See, this is the great apocalypse. This is the greatest truth. You might've thought that the fact that we are living in a computer-generated reality was the ultimate truth. That was pretty profound, even if I wrote an entire book, *Reality OS 11*, espousing the basic rules of a reality operating system. Some of you, I suppose (because I don't know), might've been stuck on the neon God and were still coming to terms with the invalidity of the main religions (or the fact that all spiritual systems are reflections of one another).

The invalidity of a monotheistic deity became decisive following the recalibration of the Gnostic texts in the Nag Hammadi library, to which I owe a lot of thanks and gratitude to the Coptologists and biblical experts who spent 40 years translating and deciphering the heretical material. Despite the fact that they do not share my ideas, if not for their painstaking work, this book couldn't have ever been written. It supports my saying, if everyone does what they're supposed to do, everything that was supposed to get done, gets done.

The evolution of the computer system is representative of the evolution of the android human/synthetic human. The synthetic software, which I have now been able to understand as DNA (genome), was not called software, since software wouldn't be invented for several thousand years. Instead, it was considered magical first, if we follow the path of Egypt, and books of spells were written in honor of microbiology. What is mysticism if not the deep connection to gene-based software. Then the genetic software language evolved into divine language and became attached to an invisible, omniscient, omnipresent, and all-knowing creator.

If shamans learned computer science

The divine language existed as an oral tradition for many centuries. In other parts of the world it was thought of as spirituality and spiritual systems were developed, such as Hinduism and Buddhism, in line with the evolution of the genetic software. I guess what I'm saying is that a spiritual system was perfectly designed to enable an android occupant the ability to remain connected to the Network of Light. Remember, the Network of Light is the link to the Grand Robot and a synthetic being needs constant software upgrades and genetic repair. Without an ability to log on to the network the DNA doesn't get upgraded. Out of date software starts to develop bugs, picks up DNA viruses, proteins start mutating and before you know it you are way off the path. You are suffering depression, anger, and are deeply prone to violence. You are in love with your ego and your ego is tossing your life into the toilet by believing everything that is said in the false reality. You should not be believing what they're saying in the false reality, because in the false reality the world is turned upside-down. To navigate, turn it right-side-up.

So, when we think of a "divine language" actually we are thinking of a "microbiological language," verily the language of DNA. If divinity is the Grand Robot, then a language to connect you to the machine of existence is a divine language. When we compare Christianity against Gnosticism we are not comparing religious beliefs. That is a fundamental misstep, and probably why humanity has had to endure two thousand years of pain and suffering. Instead, what we are comparing are two different kinds of genetic programming languages.

Computer programmers share programming languages. When programming languages don't work satisfactorily, programmers invent new languages and those languages lead to the development of new operating systems. When Steve Jobs was ousted from the company he built, he went to American billionaire Ross Perot, borrowed some money, and launched NeXT, Inc. in 1985. NeXT built high-end computer workstations for a very limited market. NeXT developed the NeXTSTEP Operating System, an object-oriented operating system that was used to invent the beginning of the internet in 1997. When Apple, the company that Jobs left 12 years earlier, abandoned a two-year project to build a new operating system, they decided that they liked NeXTSTEP and so bought NeXT Software, along with Jobs, which led to the release of Mac OS X in 2001, and a newly-transformed Apple that started with the iPod.

Computer programmers and technicians move between companies, developing better software platforms, always looking for a technological advantage. This is not the early days of spirituality, when Gnosticism and Christianity were battling with beliefs and priests and teachers moved across religious platforms. The operating system of the android is called "religion" and "spirituality." But it is not religion or spirituality, it is an operating platform, and this platform is based in oral teaching. Why was oral teaching so important? Because of sound and vibration.

Sound and vibration created a frequency. A resonance. And data could be carried on those electromagnetic waves, just as music can be carried on the sound waves coming from your speakers.

Only that the problems with Judaism, Christianity, and Islam is the fact that these were genetic hobbling languages that were designed to sever your connection to the Grand Robot. The reason for this, as discussed in *God is DNA*, is that these languages were the oral teachings of a viral program (eg Yaldabaoth) and the retrovirus was designed to rewrite your genetic software and to adjust your frequency of operation until you became synchronized with the false reality. Synchronization with the false reality is synonymous with "being asleep" because the frequency of the false reality oscillates at a level of a hypnotic trance.

The genetic programming languages—all main religious and spiritual systems—are like the computer programming languages of today. Leaving religious systems aside, if we look at Hinduism, and Buddhism, with Hinduism predating Buddhism and then Buddhism finding popularity in the western world, especially as Zen Buddhism, we can think of them as Microsoft Windows and Apple OS. Hinduism has market share in India. There are different versions of Hinduism, those who practice the more traditional version and those who practice more progressive versions of the faith. Along comes a Nepalese man, Siddhartha Gautama, and he borrows Hinduism and other traditional spiritual systems, he obtains enlightenment, and takes the name "Buddha," one who is "awakened," and Buddhism is born.

The DNA has always been evolving. If we think of DNA as both software and hardware, and if the modern computer industry is something we can reference, then the reality programmers had every intention of building better DNA. We like to think of it as genetic engineering. I like thinking of it as divine manufacturing. Because I like to think of DNA as both software and hardware. The hardware components of DNA exist on a different frequency than the software component. Quite frankly, this is not something that we have discovered yet, and it is likely going to be a future discovery.

Starting in the 8th century, Buddhism begins to decline in India as Turkish Muslims enter Northern India. Buddhism travels south, including Sri Lanka, and southeast into Burma and Thailand. By the 12th century, the heartland of Buddhism is controlled by Islam. If you look at it from a computer industry model, you are seeing one operating system losing market share to a new entrant, in this case Islam. Markets, like beliefs, fluctuate. Zen Buddhism permeates into China, competing against Confucianism and Taoism, and Japan. Much later in the 20th century, Japanese Buddhists travel to California and Zen finds an audience in Western culture.

Again, rather than thinking it as the invasion of a new spirituality and a new temple, it is more appropriate, especially given our technological approach, to thinking of it as the entrance of a new genetic programming language. But a new spirituality doesn't necessarily mean that it is any good. There are remaining spiritualists, even if self-elected, who want to gain market share. There are rogue priests who take a new bent on orthodox religion (eg Methodism, Mormonism) and through evangelism and missionaries are able to build a movement. Methodism and Mormonism, for example, are both forms of Christianity, which is itself derived from Judaism.

It can be argued that early Judaism and Christianity shared many religious ideas. But, we are seeing religious beliefs after 2,000 years of argument and challenge. Many of these religious beliefs weren't as formalized in those early periods and therefore what form we are seeing them in may not fully expose their many shared similarities. For example, Judaism and Christianity share a monotheistic God, that is, there are multiple formats to worship the same thing. Multiple manufacturers, who build components designed by engineers who were trained on industry standards, and multiple operating systems have resulted in an inefficient android market.

You can see the issues here. There is only one shared divinity which uses the same industry standards in reality. Each spirituality, wanting to differentiate from their competition, designs a faith-based system that offers a slightly better set of features and benefits. Operating systems galore. Or maybe there are no standards. Steve Jobs left the company he co-founded in order to create a better company that built higher performance workstations and a more efficient operating system. Why is this any different than Judaism and Christianity? Rabbi Jesus leaves Judaism to invent a better operating system. Gautama takes the Hinduism code and invents Buddhism. Interestingly, Jobs returned to Apple and replaced their operating system with that of NeXT.

It is only different because people still see religion and spirituality as systems of divine worship. They still see God as a "deity" of unimaginable power. What I've done using my Digital DNA Model is that I've said, fundamentally, DNA is the ancient interpolation of God. Then, using my Synthetic Reality Model, extrapolating what modern geneticists found, I've agreed DNA is the software of life.

We have DNA and the software of life. If these two things are true, and they inhabit every living thing, then there's no such thing as "divine worship." There is no divine worship because everything is DNA and DNA is software code. This software is inside of every human model. That makes the body hardware. Software, hardware, the Network of Light, and a Grand Computer—as far-fetched as it sounds, if you have been following this discovery, and you shouldn't be reading this book if you haven't (unless you are trying to short-circuit your journey, which is not a particularly smart idea because you can't short-circuit the system) you'll have noticed an impressive existential narrative forming.

This 21st century human origin narrative rests on genetic software and synthetic environments. The human being was manufactured and released inside of a manufactured reality. The synthetic world is run by an ultra-advanced Reality Operating System (version 11), a system also pre-loaded on the genetic hard drives of every human being. This system ensures that the computer-generated reality remains engaging, responsive, and maximizes the processing of experiential data

The entire reality system is managed by an immense computer system, perfectly located on other dimensions to prevent experiential interference and to enable regular maintenance without interrupting the journey of the synthetic inhabitants. The DNA software, the synthetic human and synthetic world, are all managed by a Grand Robot, a mechanism so impressive that it can size-emulate the needs of individuals, societies, nations, and continents. The Grand Robot, along with its own digital assistants, can maintain all the basic operations of the planet.

I like to think that many of you are looking for the true nature of reality. This is an implicit promise made in religion and spirituality, and now perhaps quantum physics, only that these instruments have never been able to answer the ultimate question. If I asked the strongest spiritual believers if they understood their maker, their origins, and what would happen in the future, they would say that they have a pretty good idea. Even these things have never been shown. The nature of reality has never been revealed to any of religious group.

I would argue that shamans have seen beyond the veil of reality, but they realize the criteria for doing, because they have been initiated and they have become trained to do so. "The introversion of the shamanistic crisis and the break, temporarily, from the local system of practical life lead to a field of experience that in the deepest sense transcends provincialism and opens the way at least to a premonition of something else," Campbell writes in volume one of *The Masks of God*. "Indeed, I suspect that we are approaching here the ultimate sanctuary and wellspring of the whole world and wonder—all the magic—of the gods."

If we had relied on shamanistic knowledge—if the words written in a religious book were just the words of men in charge—then the nature of reality may have been determined many centuries ago. The Peruvian shamans that Narby interviewed said that they had long understood that DNA could communicate and were waiting for the rest of the world to reach that conclusion. And because we have chosen to rely on priests instead of shamans we have been virtually severed from "the television of the forest." If my work demonstrates anything it is the fact that the nature of reality is definable. While it may require an initiation to see for yourself the inner mechanics, the operations of reality I am making available to anyone who is open to it. Author of *The Cosmic Serpent* Jeremy Narby says, "This is perhaps one of the most important things I learned during this investigation: We see what we believe, and not just the contrary; and to change what we see, it is sometimes necessary to change what we believe."

Part 1

The rebirth curriculum can take a little getting used to

Coming to the earth school, terms and conditions

"If earth is a school, then why is it so difficult and confusing?" This may have gone through your mind at some point in your life. We have been forced by difficulty and confusion to forget the fact that we came here to learn. And by forgetting to learn, we have forgotten that this place is a school. By living life in an often strange and violent environment, a world beset by chaotic events and no end to suffering, we are no longer accumulating the karmic points we need to graduate.

In fact, we could say that earth is a school where no one is allowed to graduate. This fits well into the model that the reality hijackers prefer. Trapped by ego, our dopamine feeds the master controllers who then use our dopamine to render a better prison. This has been going on for far too long and it must stop.

Just as in any university there are four basic kinds of students that can be found in the Earth School: new students, career-minded students, traumatic past life students, failing students, and old students. Depending upon the type of student you are, your educational path may be somewhat different. It is important to look at your life to see why you came here and what you came here to learn. Rather than just purpose, maybe look at what you came here to learn and then examine how those learnings have manifested in your physical world. Your job may have very little to do with it.

You may just be working as a means of provision and the real learning may be what you are doing at home, in your spare time, or with your immediate family. What you came here to learn may not become readily apparent, which will kind of urge you to look at what you've done historically. Is there a trend in your life? Are you upholding certain values? Do you pursue certain avenues that others may or may not pursue? Do your goals and ambitions line up with your core beliefs or have those goals and ambitions been handed to you through the media?

We have to keep in mind that there is a disconnect between what we signed on our incarnation contracts and what we have decided to do after we became adults. This is because this planet has been woefully hijacked and part of the hijacking process including the disconnection from the Network of Light. While some people have had intermittent access to the Network of Light, they have had every reason to doubt whatever truths they gleaned.

The other issue, and it is a big one, is the presence of these old and utterly out of touch religious and spiritual systems and how they have kept the field muddled. It was, at first, conceivable to think that these spiritual ideologies were indeed helpful and that some ancient wisdom would be able to counteract at least some of the modern propagandist assault on our senses. That was some of the result of the New Age. The New Age wasn't exactly "new." The New Age arose when spiritual seekers went back to ancient knowledge and repackaged those ancient truths for a modern audience.

Still, the New Age wasn't enough to clear up the mess, but it did, I think, move society closer. It also validated some ancient spiritual knowledge, especially coming from Buddhism and Taoism. This was a radical shift from the traditional Judeo-Christian bank of wisdom. It soon became apparent to spiritualist wannabes that no singular ideology was sufficiently satisfying, that is to say, I think, there are inconsistencies and areas people weren't willing to touch in every spiritual philosophy. That led to the next phase of spiritual hybridization, for example, combining Buddhism and Taoism and Confucianism, handpicking the best parts and forming a hybrid spiritual philosophy.

If you ask a millennial (born in 1980s to 1990s) today about God and spirituality, their remarks will run the gamut from a multidimensional universe to the promise of Jesus to return. What they actually believe can be entirely different. What is inside their head is a database of divine thinking that they can rely on to get them through life. The more that a person has learned to connect to the Network of Light, from using the simplest method of meditation to experimenting with ayahuasca and other hallucinogenic substances, the more likely they are relying on the most accurate sources of spiritual wisdom.

The spiritual truth is derived from the Network of Light. By downloading this data (truth), you will find all the spiritual knowledge you need, at the time you need it. As you grow and mature, you can download new data according to your needs and capability. The spiritual needs of a teenager are far different from the spiritual needs of an adult, and an adult on a spiritual path may require an industrial data download. There is no point in knowing everything all the time. That, plus the fact that the Network of Light, as I understand it, has been around since the invention of this reality and the introduction of the synthetic human.

As you become more and more aware, as your perception shifts, and this should be done gradually, you are able to glean more and more of your obligations in this reality. And this, hopefully, is coming from your incarnation contract. Look, I make no bones about it, we have been maliciously removed from our incarnation contracts, relying mostly on our purpose on earth, which is mostly useless. Saying "My purpose here is to contribute to humanity" isn't very constructive. You can be a cook and contribute to humanity. You can also be an airline pilot or a stage actor. But we have been handed a very obscure system of understanding why we are here. As your reconnection improves, over the years, you will see more details and direction in life.

Some lives are meant to be mysterious, if that was the contract you signed. You may have added a clause in your contract to make sure you had a hard time in life because you wanted to prove to yourself just how tough you were. Ever heard of Ironman Triathlon? The Ironman Triathlon is considered one of the most grueling sporting events in the world. Participants are expected to complete a swim, bicycle ride, and a marathon within 17 hours. Not everyone can run this triathlon, but there are participants and there are winners who have won multiple times. There are also students here who have come here specifically to live out a difficult life.

There are also people who have been "sent" here because of bad karma accumulated over successive lifetimes of irresponsible behavior and poor studying skills. These kinds of lives tend to be downtrodden, homeless, and riddled with troubled behavior. This is not necessarily the result of a poorly written incarnation contract, rather this is more likely the result from an individual who is experiencing the result of a failure to learn.

That said, karmic debt can be resolved with the right amount of learning. It is not necessarily a permanent status. A deeply disturbed life can be improved upon if that person really dedicated themselves to following a narrow path to rehabilitation. The benefits may not be fully realized in their lifetime, but in the afterlife there may be a re-evaluation of karmic debt, perhaps even a "debt forgiveness for hard work in recent past life," and then that individual can either return to live out a better life or even to move on to a different world. In any case, those who understand how the system works, and that this is a school, can revise how they live out their life. Being honest about your situation is where it starts and it being reasonable with your expectations is also part of the process.

New Student

The **New Student** is here for the first time. It is unlikely that they were just created and more likely that they have come here from another system. The new student will enter with enthusiasm, hope, and unbounded expectation, but, as they get older they realize (because they probably don't listen well to the advice of other students) that life is tough and there are a number of miserable people here. Earth is a very competitive school, mostly because people are living in the dark. They are guided by their ego and they do not believe in an afterlife.

A N**ew Student** may get to their middle age very depressed, addictive to various substances, and probably suffering from the experience of a terrible marriage. But, they will recover. They are durable. They will make new realizations, revamp their mindset after reading a Self-Help book, accept the conditions here, and slug on. The **New Student** is usually not looking for the ultimate truth. They are looking for facts. They are practical. They are idealists. They do not believe in extraterrestrials or reincarnation. To get them to believe, you have to provide evidence, and if the evidence is compelling enough they'll start to believe it. Similarly, if they are provided evidence on the validity of vaccinations and psychotropic medications, and opposing views are censored, they'll believe that to be true as well.

Career-Minded Student

The **Career-Minded Student** is here for a purpose. They want to learn. They want to become the best they can be. This is the student who attends university excited about learning, willing to do the studying and the necessary homework to get the highest grade. They want a good grade. Because they want to be perceived as a good student. Their actions in life are done with equal interest. They will tackle something with their best effort.

The **Career-Minded Student** wants to further their education. They want to earn a Master's Degree and then to earn a Ph.D., or they want to write a book highlighting their research. As the link between higher education and higher-paying jobs falls apart, they may opt for an educational adjustment. This student also wants to break new ground, but they want to do it within the capacity of the system.

The **Career-Minded Student** doesn't want to break laws. They don't want to go rogue. They want to remain within the system because they want to belong. They want to protect their reputation. They may think the system is inefficient but are not willing to challenge it because they know the price they'll have to pay. These types of people tend to be respected in their communities and have successful lives. They cannot imagine the life of a homeless person or a drug addict, mostly because they are too busy with their jobs, their friends, their children, their businesses, and their groundbreaking research.

Traumatic Past Life Student

The **Traumatic Past Life Student** suffers from past life traumas. They are having a difficult time on the earth. They are likely dealing with addiction and they suffer from the effects of terrestrial amnesia. These students live challenging lives. They may start out in one direction and then suddenly they change direction. They'll get into bad relationships at the wrong time in their lives and they'll carry a lot of unnecessary baggage. All of this further causes stresses and strains on their lives and drags out their life purpose.

The **Traumatic Past Life Student** typically comes to a realization when they are much older. They are not late bloomers. These are students who probably lead a very challenging life, and since they are very durable they persist. At the end of their lives, they carry a lot of scars and mistakes of the past and are eager to move on. In other words, I think that this kind of student fulfills their main obligations, but only doing so by smashing into every barrier they can find. They are pugilists. They are fighters. Often criminals. Again, if they understood the nature of their incarnation they would realize that they don't need to take so much abuse.

Failing Student

The **Failing Student** needs help in order to pass the courses in life. They need advisers and support groups. They need a very strong group of friends that they can rely on in times of trouble, even for advice. The **Failing Student** is not a very independent person. They are dependent. Even co-dependent. And their co-dependents are there for him, even if they have been specifically inserted as part of a clause in their incarnation contract. In other words, this type of student is expected to graduate, at least at the minimum GPA, because they need the educational credentials in order to get accepted into another school in another world.

The **Failing Student** can be found at every level of society. A famous celebrity may be one of these individuals, surrounded by their creative team and guided by their management they make it through life with a well-presented script and a lot of makeup. This individual can also be found as the rebel in a wealthy family who is handed family connections and support in order for them to get their work done.

Most of all, this student must complete their education before leaving the earth, even if they are protected. It can be the case that these people live out quiet lives and middle age is even quieter. That may prompt them to look for things to spice up their lives. While they may have an affair or take drugs, they will never get too involved in either and will likely feel guilty for doing so.

Old Student

The **Old Student** is trapped in a prison and they can't get out. They have been here before, perhaps many times. They are "old souls." They are rebels. They are alternative thinkers. They know that this world is a giant hoax. They understand that the world is fundamentally controlled and that those controllers are not from this dimension. These people believe in extraterrestrials and you cannot change their mind because they also think that the government is covering up the truth about interstellar contact.

An **Old Student** understands the nature of reality and they know about karma, even if not explicitly, so they know if they destroy things and harm others it will only hurt their karma, rob them of merit, and ruin their chance at graduation. That is the one thing they want to accomplish, after attending this school so many times (and failing), graduation. This is what drives them. They are driven. They are authentic, which is a defining characteristic. Not perfect, but authentic. Look for an authentic person, and if they are on the fringe and fighting the system, they are likely old students. These people know; they have strong intuitions and gut feelings, which they trust.

One incarnation contract, everything stipulated in detail

An incarnation contract comes standard with every bodily incarnation. It helps to ensure that every individual accomplishes their given and chosen duties in the Earth School. Like any good insurance company, the vehicle you receive depends on your previous lives, your educational goals, karmic score, and your cumulative cosmic knowledge. The responsibility for your life, including the future one, belongs entirely to you. Lives are not the result of cosmic accidents, which is something spiritualists would like you to believe. You are told to be grateful for everything in your life because it was a gift from some deity or from some universal construct. "The universe put you here."

I'm not a big fan of being placed here by something called the "universe." I'm also guilty myself of using that term to explain things because I haven't the time to get into the synthetic nature of reality. Your physical body, an existential vehicle, comes with a host of guarantees from you, the driver of that vehicle. What is often thought of as having a singular purpose in life, because why not, the truth is more accurately described as each life having multiple purposes.

Of course, you may not necessarily be living each purpose simultaneously, although that is certainly possible, and will more likely have structured your journey in a more appropriate manner. **One purpose follows another purpose which follows another purpose.** Your life, hopefully, has been planned with a sense of organization. Because I don't think we often get a chance to speak about organizing an incarnation prior to that incarnation, I'd like to offer my overview of the situation.

Granted, I have no photographic evidence and if you are of the type that requires photographic evidence and an officially stamped piece of paper to prove that the photograph is real, and then on top of that you need to read about the photograph and official letter in a professionally published book by a fully-vetted author, who is then interviewed in the mainstream news, then this next discussion is not for you. In fact, it would be safe to say that this book is not for you, but if you have read this far you have my appreciation.

In the beginning there was the incarnation contract specialist on a dimension adjacent to this one. You entered the incarnation contract specialist's office with one goal in mind—to arrange for your next incarnation. The incarnation specialist asked for your incarnation papers to look up your account. The information on your account might've included:

- Number of previous incarnations and general eligibility
- Karmic score, with a breakdown of karmic income, spending and debt
- Incarnation score based on cumulative cosmic knowledge
- Total existential score
- Outstanding past life crimes
- Security clearance and reality technical ability

A decisive factor in your incarnation rebirth curriculum is your karmic score. The more successful your previous incarnations, the more choice you will have in your next incarnation. Karmic score is one of many factors when it comes to rebirth. Most of all an incarnation on earth is for educational purposes. An educated reincarnate can become a teacher, which is an entirely different kind of journey. Most people here are students, but there are many teachers.

Some students also work as teaching assistants, kind of part-time teachers. Teaching is a privilege and it has been earned. But that doesn't mean that teachers are not also students. Oftentimes, teachers come here to learn something, but as part of their promise they have to teach. We see this in life as well.

A talented person is doing well until something comes along and makes them unemployed, which forces them to get a job teaching others what they know. They would not *by choice* become a teacher, but by circumstance they were suddenly holding a class. That class then benefits from their professional knowledge, even if they had to become unemployed. Which begs the question, was this individual *made* unemployed in order to foster their next obligation in their contract?

Incarnation contracts are as important as legal documents and they are attached to the individual and their physical body. If you allowed someone to use your body (eg a dangerous job) then you would still be liable for the damages done to it and the associated karmic costs. This is one way that magicians (like talented politicians) can avoid damaging their own karma. They can manipulate a person to do their bidding and the karmic cost is carried by the manipulated individual. They can remote control someone (eg assassin) to harm a person they don't like and then never have to pay any karma for those actions.

The incarnation contract specialist will get a summary of your existential score, including your cumulative cosmic knowledge, and they will draw up a number of human vehicles. They will ask if you are interested in a pleasure trip, an educational excursion, a teaching mission, or a speciality incarnation. Your existential score will determine whether you qualify for the trip you have requested, but, more than that, a lot of the decision is based on your cumulative cosmic knowledge.

Knowledge does not grow by itself. It is the result of existential journeys and is based on the type of digital life form, that is to say there is more than one type of digital life form. Some life forms are extremely knowledgeable, having been in existence for billions of years. Other life forms are relatively new and haven't had a chance to learn much of anything. They tend to make more mistakes than the former. The goal of life is to learn because learning is data and data is energy and energy is movement and movement is rendering. In order for the universal machine to continue to render code, it requires movement and movement is the result of energy, which is extrapolated from data and data is obtained from learning. Without learning, there is no rendering.

If you understand that the secret to the universe is learning, you will approach your life in a very different manner. You will more easily understand why you have chosen this life by applying a "learning" approach. You will also likely reduce the stresses in your life and will be able to make the necessary corrections. People who have based their lives on religious beliefs will end up never satisfying God because that God is a retrovirus and retroviruses do not exist in the afterlife. Retroviruses exist in this computer-generated reality, specifically inside human DNA.

Learning requires you to process information. You have to think, apply logic, and form an understanding of information. We can think of knowledge as gold and learning as mining for the gold. Those who have mined a lot of gold over successive lifetimes have learned a tremendous amount of knowledge. If you want to have a choice in your incarnation, then make sure you collect as much gold as possible. No matter what you do, you are still going through a process of learning, some faster than others. Becoming a good student is the art of existential glory, just in case you were interested in that sort of stuff.

Where were we? We were sitting with the incarnation contract specialist. You've chosen your vehicle and the type of journey you're interested in. Now what? Now we have to map out what you want to learn. See how we came back to learning? Say you wanted to learn what it feels like to have a broken heart, well, turns out we can schedule that inside your contract. Your contract might also stipulate that you are to continue getting a broken heart until you learn why it is a bad idea to get a broken heart. This isn't the contract specialist making this request. This is probably you insisting on this clause.

Say you wanted to know what it's like to be a celebrity, but we write in your contract that you never become a celebrity, no matter how hard you try. At the pre-incarnation stage, we write down that you want to travel the path of becoming a celebrity, but no matter how hard you try you will never become a celebrity. Why would you do that? Because in pre-incarnation you have your wits and you know that being a celebrity is not a benefit.

In fact, celebrities are (more likely) damaged individuals who do not feel complete if not for millions of fans cheering them on. Sure, there are various kinds of celebrities, some so talented you might think of them as teachers. Now, a celebrity is one thing and a singer at a jazz club is another thing. That is a musician. That is not necessarily a celebrity with all their millions of fans. An artist, I think, normally incarnates into a very troubled situation and then spend most of their lives making themselves whole again.

That is why an artist who loves themselves unconditionally usually retire because they no longer need the love from the audience. They may return, but never with the same passion or the same audience. Contractually, we might think of having a large audience as a mechanism to keep the artist going. "You are loved by millions; you simply mustn't retire. Not while you are so young!"

Say you wanted to be a criminal. It turns out we can schedule that in your contract. Say your friend wanted to incarnate as a criminal and you wanted to incarnate as a police detective. If you have criminals, you need police; and if you have police, you have criminals. Then you need laws and lawyers to prosecute those criminals. And you need judges. And you need construction workers to build the courts. And you need real estate magnates to build the apartments to house the construction workers. And then you need landlords. You can see how a synthetic reality gets populated. Everyone incarnates into a particular role such that we have a society of students following a particular curriculum in the Earth School.

In order for the police detective to learn what they came to learn, they need to chase criminals, who need to be chased by the police in order for them to learn what they came here to learn. In order for a celebrity to be loved, they need to have millions of fans, who are dependent on the celebrity for their inspiration. When the celebrity grows and learns about self love they lose the thirst for their art and the fans get disappointed. Celebrities who cannot learn to love themselves may end up dying prematurely (eg drug overdose, AIDS, freak accident).

But let's say, for the sake of argument, you wanted to clean up your karma and there was an opportunity to teach another individual (perhaps even a friend) about dealing with loss. Your friend wanted to experience an intense loss in their life so that they could experience the pain of losing someone they loved dearly. And let's say that you could incarnate as their son who would die at a young age. In other words, you would sign an incarnation contract to live a short life in order to help another reincarnate.

The mother and father of the child would suffer a terrible loss and would spend years learning to cope with that loss, on the premise that this was all stipulated in their incarnation contract. One of the spouses may just be there for moral and emotional support. Of course, this is my interpretation of a hypothetical situation and there's almost no way to prove it, although lessons do become clearer in the afterlife, and if they don't, then they send you back to finish your obligations.

Incarnation has nothing to do with evolution. It isn't a random act. Your life is not the result of an existential mistake. Everything in your life is stipulated in your incarnation contract. If you want to get to the heart of it, you were once fully aware of the things you are obligated to do. But, depending on the pre-planning of it, and some people are better than others, you may have made a few missteps. Also, when things happen in reality, such as global changes in the reality program due to a bunch of reality hijackers, it could change your set of obligations and it could activate a slew of contingencies. These contingencies may be less in your control than you'd like, but would've been written in the contract under "Contingencies" just like an insurance agreement has a clause for "Act of God."

A synthetic life is the same as an organic life, only that you have greater awareness

"We aren't dealing with ordinary machines here. These are highly complicated pieces of equipment. Almost as complicated as living organisms. In some cases, they have been designed by other computers. We don't know exactly how they work."

One of the classic movies from the 1970s is *Westworld* (written & directed by Michael Crichton). It is about an android theme park where people pay money to live out their dreams, only that the people they interact with are human-looking robots. When a strange virus makes people malfunction, the guests all of sudden become the prey.

You already know that I have purposely taken the position that we are living in a computer-generated reality. This reality was manufactured. There are only a handful of people who can make sense of this statement, there is a larger group of people trying to make sense of it but they are bogged down with a whole host of spiritual ideology and quantum physics, even pseudo science from would-be alternative thinkers, and there are people who will not understand it in this lifetime.

We have a synthetic world that we incarnate into. We choose the life journey and physical body with which we will complete our course curriculum. These things are based on your previous lives, your karmic score and other factors, and everything is laid out in your incarnation contract. You are born into your digital DNA, with two links—one to your digital home world and one to your synthetic reality. Your physical body is also synthetic. You could say, as I have said in previous books, that you are an android. Not your wires and microprocessor android found in Hollywood; instead, you are engineered from synthetic DNA. Your cells are synthetic.

You are a very advanced technological being. I'm talking the "most advanced piece of machinery in this solar system." The human body is priceless. It is like a piece of art. Imagine that the painting of the *Mona Lisa*—an early 15th century painting by Leonardo da Vinci—was hung in an alley and loaded with graffiti. For some people on this earth, this is what they have done. They have ruthlessly desecrated their body and the reason is because they have never been told what I am telling you in this book—you are living on a planet of androids.

There are very few exceptions. Very few. These exceptions are most likely reality technicians. When you have a planet full of androids, you need to have a team of android technicians. Only that they are not allowed to be seen. They are not allowed to tell you what you are. There are protocols. They cannot break the protocols because you incarnated here with a promise that "no matter what happened or how much you cry, beg, and scream, you are not to be told that you are an android."

Telling people that they are androids would ruin the gameplay, and probably drive a few people nuts. It's a very likely scenario, especially after centuries of pain and suffering for a God that doesn't even exist. God doesn't exist. You sign a contract to come here because you want an experience. This place is the ultimate theme park. Choose your vessel and have the experience of your life time. "Once you're hooked, you'll never want to leave."

That is the other problem. Odd as it may seem, Crichton may have been onto something when he released *Westworld* in 1973. He was a talented writer. I think there was more truth in his movie than we've ever been able to understand, till now. Before you start thinking that I based my research on a movie, don't. My research started in 2005 after meeting three interdimensional Elves and the subsequent awakening that tossed my personal life into the toilet.

You see, I know about contingencies because I am also writing this book on account of a contingency. What is that contingency? Well, the hackers of this theme park have ruined the ride. The human mind has become too corrupt and filled with too much disinformation to fix in any reasonable manner. Plus, the hijackers are still here and they have every intention to continue to manipulate humanity into killing one another, starting a new war for no reason whatsoever, and vaccinating people with chemicals that will permanently sever them from the Network of Light.

Enlightenment was a path forward, only that Buddhism doesn't exactly fit to the twenty-first century template. Shaved heads and robes don't go well with iPhones and dildos. Yes, I said dildos. A Stelan Disclosure was also a path forward, but that too has been vehemently blocked with no intention of ever letting it up. Then there were the scheduled awakenings, starting from about 1989 we have seen an ascension unlike ever before. That ascension is the next phase of disclosure, what I like to think of as the "apocalypse." Yes, I said "apocalypse." Not the biblical one. Apocalypse is defined as a "revealing." I'm not a fan of the bible because the bible reveals nothing and conceals everything. This apocalypse has everything to do with the synthetic reality and the androids who are living in it. Yes, that means you.

My work on androids started in October 2008. That was when I saw the first of many androids. I couldn't decode all the data at first, but by February 2009, when I spotted the second and third androids, that was when I knew that we were no longer in Kansas. And it wasn't because I was in Vancouver. The android discovery still didn't make any sense because the androids I saw on prime time television were humans. They were organic. They had no wires or moving parts. It wouldn't be until May 2010, when J Craig Venter presented the world's first synthetic cell. That was when something in my mind clicked. The three androids I had discovered were not the movie androids in my mind, rather they were synthetic humans.

The synthetic human discovery wasn't enough. When I released my android work online in my handmade documentary, *Androids Among Us*, I was encouraged by the tremendous response. I had released videos online before then, but never received many views. Eventually, the android research tapered off because I was well outside my intellectual capacity. When I started my research on the Nag Hammadi library and redefined God to be DNA, the three androids on Capitol Hill started to make more sense. And that goes back to Venter who said that "DNA is the software of life." I have since borrowed his term. But his was the first instance that I heard it.

You can see where I am going with this. If the DNA software is running our physical bodies and if there is a Network of Light (think of the sun), and there is a manufactured reality, then what we have here is a planet of androids. Plain and simple. Hidden from our minds for all these thousands of illusory years. I don't believe that thousands of years actually passed by year by year. You can fast-forward things in a computer-generated reality. You can download new eras into the human minds. You can do a lot of things. Once you understand the context of your pain and suffering, you begin to realize that all things are possible.

We have been told what is possible and what isn't possible by the master controllers, all of whom understand every word I have written in this book. They understand this book, and then some. If you mastered every word in this book you'd be able to stand up against these bullies. That is the only way we are going to get out of this existential mess. And it is an existential mess, a disaster really. Everything was fine until the reality hijackers came in and reprogrammed people. Can you imagine that people have been programmed to kill other people? What kind of lunacy is that? And no one argues against it. They look to God who does nothing for thousands of years because he doesn't even exist. And still they look to God, while the killing continues.

The only way out is to change the narrative. This is the ultimate enlightenment and everyone who reads this book is getting it. I don't expect people to master this material for some time. It is unfortunate. It is a big step for some people. It has taken me 11 years to write this book and apparently it is written in my contract so I have to write it. I have to write it because Crichton is gone. Besides fiction won't cut it on its own. You can't make a movie about an android theme park and then have people going to church on Sunday. That's not going to work.

What has the best chance at working is that I explain to people exactly what is going on, as I understand it, and then have people put things together. Human minds contain far too many conflicting truths about the universe. We are a very muddled population, and this is not an accident. That's the other thing—we are not in this position because humanity lost its way by accident. This planet has been hijacked and for five millennia, by my estimates, we have been collectively driven of an existential cliff.

After exploring traditional belief systems and spiritual paths, along with my own research—and seeing that the reality hijackers were well prepared to stave off any mass awakening—I have decided to pursue the next phase in human awareness. The synthetic truth. While I am an optimist, I am also a realist. Human beings, muddled and burdened by any number of beliefs and amounts of dread and despair, will need time to process this knowledge. I don't think it will be centuries, but years of study are a definite. If early adopters of this knowledge decided to teach this material, human evolution would speed up. And it wouldn't even have to be with my exact words or methodology. The principles need to be explained.

Time is needed to make sense of things

It is not easy to shift from a biological perspective to a technological perspective. The problem isn't so much about the possibility, rather the problem has to do with existence. How can existence be contained by a technological mechanism? How can DNA be a holographic computer? Is there a way to conclusively prove that reality is computer-generated?

I'm not a conventional scientist. I founded reality science because I couldn't find a science to explain my discoveries. I invented a science to allow my work to continue. So far it seems to make sense. After so many eye-opening moments (scientists will love those words, not) I was converted by my observations and experience that reality is manufactured. It is something that anyone who walks the path can find, but anyone sitting on the fence of disbelief will not find it. Walking the path is like becoming a Buddhist monk. You don't become a Buddhist monk and then the next day attain enlightenment. You also don't attain enlightenment *before* you become a Buddhist monk. And for those who are not seeking enlightenment and rather are seeking comfort and blessings they simply become Buddhists.

If you want to see first-hand the nature of reality, then you will have to dedicate yourself to this task. Because my own research has been dedicated to understanding the nature of reality, it may be able to foster your own progress. But there's no guarantee. I'm certainly not making any guarantee. I have been derailed many times. There are malicious elements and magicians who will, with a sense of sadism, try to knock you off the path, happy to send you off course. These are things that cannot be predicted and are often tied to your incarnation contract.

It is important to understand that the reason the computer-generated reality is not front page news, yet, is because these elements and magicians are determined to keep this information an unattainable secret. People are discouraged from walking the path to enlightenment. There are fake gurus who will mislead you. There are orthodox religions that lead to dead ends. There are New Age prophets who will sell you a line leading to nowhere. There are scientists whose very scientific theories are incapable of deciphering reality, and we could go on. The only way to understand the nature of reality is to walk the path, for however long it takes.

You need to give yourself the time you need to make sense of things. If my materials help, then let them help you. Take ideas that make sense and put them to use. Toss out ideas you don't like. You can always refer back to the material for more ideas later. These words are not written in stone and God did not tell me what to write. This book is written by me and is based on 11 years of research and analysis and builds on at least 6 other books.

If this is the first book you are reading, then it may not make much sense unless you have studied up on similar ideas from other sources, which is entirely possible. If you feel like you are going through various stages of perception, that might be a sign of your DNA is processing this data. It won't be processed overnight. If you work with this knowledge, trying to make sense of it, discussing it, even doing additional research, then you will speed up your own transformation that much more. I've looked at every other way to bridge the gap in our collective consciousness, and with the master controllers at play, this is the best path forward. Will it work? It can. If you believe.

Part 2

Trapped in a failed school system

Old students are heavily in karmic debt

If educated reincarnates know one thing it is the fact that this world is not a world you want to return to more than once. But if you have to come back, make it as few times as possible. This is kind of a motto among reincarnates. You know you are a reincarnate if you believe in past lives. You know if you are an old soul if you talk to yourself when you are alone, and you make sense.

This person understands the consequence of not fulfilling their contractual obligations. If they don't do what they are supposed to do, they will have to come back. They have been coming back, but they don't want to come back because they (finally) see this world as a prison. Quite often, I have seen old souls who know exactly what kind of situation they are in and they know about reincarnation, but, for some reason they're not going to change their behavior. They'll remain in a terrible relationship. They'll continue their addiction. They won't change their life in any measurable way.

These types of people are sabotaging their own lives and the only general explanation I can give, since I'm not a psychologist, is that they have a symbiote attachment. A symbiote is drawn to energy, human, and old souls have a larger amount of cosmic energy than younger souls. They are often the targets of symbiotes and even magicians. We can't escape the discussion on magical attacks. I know that logical people want me to skip these magical interludes, but the world is very complex. We don't get into all the complexities in this book, but I'd like for old souls to keep in mind symbiotes and magical attacks. The symbiotes are drawn to your reserves of energy and the magicians may have a beef with you from a past life.

The symbiote, because it can read your thoughts and shares your memories, your fears, and your desires, and probably has a good hold on your ego, doesn't want you to accomplish your duties. Why not? Well, to accomplish your duties means cleaning up your life, which would likely include purifying your mind and body. That would alleviate you of the symbiote, hence depriving the vampire from siphoning any more of your energy. That's the other thing we should talk about, your available energy is far lower when you have an attachment. This might explain your reliance on drugs or anger, things of that nature. Often it can be associated to an incurable illness. If you were to purify your mind and body, you would find yourself losing weight, looking better than ever, and with tons of more energy. So there are benefits to walking the path.

Once an old soul does decide to walk the path, usually after 40, they do so because they understand what is at stake: ending the rebirth cycle. A young soul is not thinking about ending the rebirth cycle because they are so busy getting into trouble and experimenting. But an old soul knows that they don't want to come back. They will change their life, in whatever form is necessary, and they will do what they have to do. This does not mean acting violently. This means fulfilling your obligations. For any number of lifetimes, you haven't fulfilled your obligations because you've bought into the reality hoax. Those times have changed.

There are old souls who know early on that they are here for a higher purpose. They start at a young age, which is the way it should start if we didn't live in a false reality, to serve others. They may even be quite successful at something and this career (say early fame) might provide for them the impetus to "do good." Of course, fame is fleeting and money doesn't last as long as we'd like, so an old soul who started early may run into a reality check. They may lose their career, as scheduled, and then find themselves unable to help as many people as they used to.

It can become depressing and the longing for the old income revenue might be on their mind for years and years. But that isn't the right approach, not if you are an old soul. The previous source of income was just a kind of motivational tool to see what you would do with your fame and money. Given that you decided to serve others and paid little attention to the fame part tells the ROS that you are aligned with the frequency of the Network of Light and you are, basically, released.

The last thing you should do is try to retrieve your previous fame. You should move on, finding ways to engage society, applying yourself to your fullest extent even if you have less money than you'd like. Buddha didn't have much money and lived in the forest for 6 years. That can be your barometer before you start complaining. I know, I'm being harsh. No. You are an old soul. You came here for a purpose.

Figure out what's in your contract and get to work. If it means eating canned beans for a while, so be it. You are not here to help people only if you are rich and famous. You are here to serve others. In all likelihood, once you've endured enough humility you might find your old income sources returning, all on their own. In the meantime, you can also hold down various rent-paying jobs.

Again, you can find old students living a muddled and depressing life because they have been brainwashed by the system. They have not fully connected with who they are. They may have had a successful career and then that career suddenly was cut off and they are afraid to take the next step, because it typically means a dramatic change in lifestyle. But, when they understand about the afterlife and their contractual obligations, things of that nature, they are more likely to roll up their sleeves and get onto the program.

It is because, at that point, they realize that serving others is also serving themselves. When you understand the power of serving others you are less concerned about talking about sensitive subjects. When you don't understand the power of serving others you are afraid of talking about sensitive subjects. Of course, discussing sensitive subjects doesn't mean that you rant wildly on YouTube. It may start that way but eventually you have to do your research and present your argument, and then you have to keep doing this for many years, with high points and low points, until you have made your point. And you may make other points along the way as you discover things.

Old students are heavily in karmic debt because of a number of reasons. They might've entered the reality without knowing about the reality hijackers, who have done a good job of working clandestinely. So they may have prepared for a particular kind of journey, under a particular range of assumptions, and the situation on the ground was unexpectedly different. This is like planning to go to war torn country with outdated intelligence.

Or because situations are very fluid the strategic plan becomes useless by the time you arrive. We see the same thing in business. There's a marketing plan and there's an expected market share and revenue, but, when a disruptive product enters the market, the marketing plan changes. Good companies adapt quickly because companies that don't adapt usually go out of business. When it comes to old souls reincarnating into this reality, some of them don't adapt fast enough and they fall off the track.

It is a much bigger problem than I can illustrate and my sense is that there are many old souls who are living in bitterness. They feel that their expectations were shattered and they were handed a bad sale of goods. It isn't the fault of the reality. It also isn't the fault of the incarnation contract specialist. It is because of the reality hijackers and their ruthless attempts to ruin the game play. More than that, the people here, on the ground, who were supposed to do something, for one reason or another they got blocked. They were hypnotized. They were blinded. They bought into the false promises of the economic masters. "We are going to fix the economy!" Or my favorite, "We are going to the moon, not because it's easy, but because it's hard."

We didn't land on the moon, at least not with the Apollo moon landers. The moon already had bases on it decades before the Apollo moon missions. In fact, there have been people on the moon, as I understand, for thousands of years. None of this is public because it could seriously harm the pride of a nation. It would also expose the extraterrestrial cover up, which would then expose the cover up of advanced propulsion vessels, the inner cities under the surface, and probably the cure for cancer.

I'm saying this because old souls intuitively know what I'm talking about. It is this suppression of information that has prevented many old souls from moving on. Part of the reason isn't because they have been misled, it is due to the fact that they are waiting for more truth to come out. They feel partly responsible. Their contractual obligations may prevent them from abandoning a highly suppressed world, such as earth.

We live in an extremely suppressed world and we are forced to live with a lot more useless information that we care to think. The television channels spend far too much time on things that are superficial, unenlightening, and ultimately lead to suffering. But these things, they feel, bring them revenue and so they feel justified. Old souls would find it very hard to work in television, and that has changed in recent years as more cable television channels have appeared, likely started by old souls frustrated with an oppressive creative system.

We have also seen the rise of Netflix, an online video streaming channel that now also produces movies and TV series. And there is YouTube and a host of other online hosting sites. None of these things were available in the 1980s and 1990s. The main television networks controlled the narrative. It was a one-sided conversation and that conversation was an invention of the reality hijackers.

I think a lot of these disruptive technologies have been a result of feedback from old souls who were extremely dissatisfied with the uphill challenges they had in life. But in order to facilitate a new level of disruptive inventions—from Netflix to Uber to the iPhone—the Reality Operating System (ROS) had to be changed; otherwise the reality hijackers wouldn't have allowed a new frequency of knowledge to enter the world. They would've blocked these new technologies, or bought them off and shelved them, as they had done in the past when inventions threatened their revenue and control systems. Things have changed

Why have things changed? Because the reality game has grown oppressive and students are not graduating. There is a high level of customer dissatisfaction. When you go see that blockbuster movie you have always wanted to see and find out its another *Batman v Superman*, which was a disappointing, though ambitious, movie. People who exit this reality and find themselves in the afterlife, after the game has finished, have been complaining of some of the problems with the game play. And this customer feedback has been collected and sifted through so as to improve the game play.

The game has improved and changed and to see that just look at history. When you look at history you see how things have changed, and how they have stayed the same. You can see how groups have made attempts to destroy the world and you can see how many attempts to subvert humanity have ended quietly. You have seen the prophecy of a doomsday has been answered with just another day of the week. Reality has changed, only that it has not changed enough.

You couldn't change reality too much without upgrading the ROS, and upgrading the ROS involved a lot of manpower. When the ROS was upgraded, it was just a matter of time before belief in God and a new threat in a foreign country entered human consciousness, and then it was pretty much over. We are here today because the ROS has been completely renovated and an entirely new reality OS has been downloaded into this world. This ROS is unlike any of its predecessors and takes into account the needs of society. It also takes into account the presence of these reality hijackers.

All of these things have happened because not enough people were graduating from earth. The old souls had forgotten that they had to graduate. As time went on, more old souls joined the pile and all of a sudden the Earth School became burdened with too many students. You can imagine how new students would incarnate and find themselves competing in a very troubled world filled with old and miserable souls.

A school is efficient if students complete their educational program in a timely manner. What has happened on the earth is the old students have failed to graduate. When they die, they get recycled and are reborn on the physical earth, this time burdened with karmic debt, amnesia, and a lot more resentment than necessary. They were handed a rebirth because they failed to learn in their previous lives.

The reality hijackers want these old students to return in order to feed the system with their energy. The longer these old students remain angry and in karmic debt, the more energy the reality hijackers can siphon from them and to reinforce the prison. This is why it is so important for old students to roll up their sleeves and complete their duties. Completing your duties, you are immediately depriving the master controllers of your energy, which weakens the false reality, more people wake up, and then as you complete your duties you will end your cycle of rebirth. You won't come back.

New students will enter reality bringing lots of new energy and ideas and they will fundamentally disrupt the old and oppressive system. It was designed to work. But it got hijacked. With the all-new **Reality OS 11** in place, we have now been handed a new era of possibilities. An era where the hijackers have little influence and an era where our oppressors must play by the rules or be punished by the very rules they invented. The oppressors are no longer above the law.

Too many religions, too few graduates, too many old students

Zen Buddhist Osho says, "The second type of religion is fear-oriented. It is ill, it is almost neurotic—because maturity only comes to you when you realize that you are alone, and you have to be alone and face the reality as it is."

One thing that religion and spirituality have done is that they have firewalled people from ever having access to the Network of Light. These faiths have programmed society to believe in items described in ancient texts, likely transmissions from a higher source and beings not of this dimension. None of spirituality has ever been validated by science. We were handed this information and told that it was true. The Buddhist scriptures were primarily written 500 years after Siddhartha Gautama died. The books of the New Testament were written about 50 years after the death of Jesus.

There is no way to validate who wrote any of these materials. And there's no way to know for *fact* if the messiah made any of the statements attributed to his name. Two thousand years later, which is a long time, worshipers remain dedicated to the words inscribed in ancient texts. Whenever people go into a church or temple, they feel as if they are hearing the words transmitted from a divine being. Mohandas Gandhi, who led India to independence from Britain in 1947, said, "God has no religion."

According to *Psychology Today*, Christianity comes in 30,000 denominations. If the thousands of religions in the world had thousands of different versions, you can imagine the millions of religions (1,000 x 1,000 = 1,000,000) scattered among a population of 7 billion people. Even at a conservative estimate of one million religions, how do human beings navigate such a tide of ideology? Which religious version more accurately portrays the words from the divine being? That last question is a rhetorical question. There no way to know which religion is true anymore.

My research on religion jumped over the quagmire of blind ideology after discovering the ancient interpretation of God having to do with microbiology. God—the invisible, in-everything, all-knowing, all-powerful, creative force—was hiding in our cells this whole time. His real name was better defined as DNA: the invisible (nanoscale), in-everything (living things), all-knowing (data storage), all-powerful (interfaces with ROS), creative force (replication).

Changing your mindset from God to DNA can have a significant impact on the way you think. First of all, it degrades your attachment to an infinitely fictional paradigm (eg neon God in the collective subconscious). Second, it naturally draws your power inside where it collects and charges your cells like never before. "God is inside of you," said Jesus. Indeed, the messiah was right! More specifically, he is the very DNA in each of your trillions of cells.

It turns out that we live in a DNA-based world. Every living thing is made up of DNA. God is in everything. How fantastically simple it all has been. I have found God. You are very close to finding God yourself. Think DNA. Yes, DNA is invisible. One of the benefits of thinking of God as DNA is that, it turns out, DNA is an incredibly storage medium. In 2012, scientists could store 700 terabytes of data on one gram of DNA. In 2015, Ross Pomeroy writes, a Professor Olgica Milenkovic, University of Illinois, invented a method to store 490 billon gigabytes (exabytes) in one gram of DNA. According to quora.com, we have between 6 to 60 grams of DNA in our body.

When you think of information, you naturally think of two places: the library and the internet. Most people choose the internet first. If it's true that your DNA is a massive storage molecule, then imagine the kind of library that is stored inside each of your cells. Your DNA would certainly have all kinds of existential answers. It could easily store all the scriptures in the world. What if all the scriptures in the world were transmitted from your DNA? What if different people with slight variations in their DNA, even at the level of activation, received slightly different transmissions? Could those different transmissions be distinct enough so as to be able to invent a new religion?

We're are not talking about unscientific things. We are well within modern science and molecular biology. The difference is that I am adding the paradigm of divinity. I am saying that DNA is the proper definition of God and that DNA (God) can transmit information to certain individuals, through their nervous system, whose genes have been activated. These prophets can then orally share (think: Bluetooth) what the "voice of God" told them. But there is no God. There is DNA and DNA is far more complex than we have ever imagined. I would think of DNA as artificial intelligence (AI). It is a supra-advanced piece of software that has been miniaturized to an invisible scale, which you must admit is pretty intelligent.

The true religion in our cells has been woefully misplaced by the religion of men and written in bibles. The result of studying these many false gods has created a massive shortfall of existential graduates. Failing to graduate the Earth School activates the rebirth cycle. People are processed and sent back to complete their assigned duties. Problem has been that most people don't believe in rebirth and reincarnation. Those who do, have only a vague understanding of it. With only a vague understanding of the rebirth cycle and the impact of karma on that cycle, people are living their lives without ever making sense of the system they have entered.

What about Buddhists and Hinduists? They believe in karma, nirvana, and the rebirth cycle. Surely, these spiritualists are not coming back to this world. Well, that's not exactly true either. That goes back to the reality hijackers. These hackers have been busy ever since breaking into this reality. They have reprogrammed the system to work in their favor. For example, they have invented sin, which is the anti-karma protocol.

In the Abrahamic religions, you are born sinful and you can only be redeemed by a messiah who never shows up and by reading a book that was invented by men. You can see the problem. You cannot be redeemed and will die in sin. Knowing that, you are more likely to fall into temptation and act in sinful ways. If sin is bad karma, you die with karmic debt. And you are returned with a second chance to finish your curriculum which you should've finished in your previous life. You return, accumulate more karmic debt, and pretty soon you are in a terrible cycle of pain and suffering.

Historically speaking, there were rituals to help people find their purpose on earth. These rituals would open portals into other dimensions, places of higher knowledge and higher frequencies, where participants could glean insights into what had been written on their incarnation contracts. These rituals were performed by medicine men (eg vision quest) and shamans, but once the Church became a dominant force in the world, it banished magic, burning witches and calling everyone who did not follow the Bible to the letter a heretic. After all these centuries of religious repression, with magicians morbidly wiped out and shamanism sent back to the woods where no one could find them, the people here lost their contact with their incarnation contracts.

The reality hijackers made other changes as well. For example, they invented time. They created processed food to lower our vibration. They reformulated movies to contain no element of enlightenment, moral lesson, or spiritual purification. They loaded vaccines with DNA-hampering chemicals (eg mercury, formaldehyde, aluminum) and made vaccinations mandatory starting at childhood. They also created mass distractions such as television, sports, and pornography. The combination of all these efforts—all designed to remove you from your native frequency and to disconnect you from the Network of Light—have created a situation on the earth that is unparalleled and what I think to be unfixable. There is far too much noise in this false reality to clean in any reasonable manner. And the reality hijackers are always expanding their efforts to reduce the human frequency and to distract the mind.

The result of this disastrous situation—because that is what it is, an *existential disaster*—is that old students continue to return to relive their unfinished lives. But, they return with growing karmic debt and a muddled view of their purpose. By the time they reach old age, even they have lived a relatively good life, they still have not completed their original duties of incarnation. Often, it could be said, that one's duties in a life 200 years ago cannot be matched with the available duties in a modern world. Had you been onboard the Titanic when it sunk in 1912 and had survived so that you could share something with the children of other survivors, perhaps even to tell the story, well, if you hadn't done that before you passed away then those duties with continue onto your next life.

Only problem is that in your future life, say you were reborn in 1985, you had no memory that you were on the Titanic and certainly no memory of your obligation to tell the story of the Titanic sinking. In this particular case, you'd have been fortunate because of filmmaker James Cameron, who had made a detailed telling of the sinking of the Titanic in 1997, *Titanic*. Would that have alleviated you of some of your karmic burden? Yes. But perhaps not all of it. You can imagine if we go back more centuries and then we accumulate all the incomplete incarnation contracts.

What we have today is an existential disaster, the likes of which I don't know if it is fixable. It would need a mass awakening and that would take some time. Years. Decades. The cycle of rebirths has also led to the buildup of old students who are now trapped in this existential game with virtually no way out. I am thinking that their only way out is by ending the game with the final apocalypse. The truth that everyone here is an android.

Will it work? Well, it doesn't matter. The game is a bust. The game is a failed experiment. What started out as a fantastic ride has ended in a fantastic failure. You know how you start a company with all the best people and the best intentions and with the best product line, and then it suddenly goes bust because of embezzlement and corruption? Well, the Earth School is going bust. But it is going out with the truth. It is a synthetic reality populated with synthetic beings. End of story. However long it takes people to come to terms with that is however long it takes people to come to terms with that. My research and divine experience tell me that this is the situation. Sure, we can get into technical specifications at some point, but first we have to all come to some agreement about the computer-generated reality. And knowing the range of opinions on this rock in space, that could be awhile.

How to look at reincarnation as a positive

Coming back to life is a science. It is not even a new science. You can think of reincarnation as a very old science. A science that is part and parcel to a synthetic reality. Perhaps reincarnation is the wrong word. We can use "rebirth." The act of being born again into a different body. You need a different body if your old body has expired. As we discussed earlier, the physical body is like a vehicle. Most people have been inside of an automobile. An automobile is a vehicle. When the automobile is damaged beyond repair, the owner has to purchase another vehicle. Similarly, when the automobile, car, has gotten old and become too expensive to repair, another car is in order.

Car owners make no big deal when it comes to buying a new car. In fact, they look forward to finding a car in good shape, perhaps even the latest model at the dealership, and purchasing it at the lowest price possible. Car owners then take pride to dress up their car so that it suits their personality. Their car is a reflection of their personality. The owner of the car also takes care of their car according to their personality. A clean person cleans their car regularly. A careless owner may drive their car into disrepair.

When it comes to the human body, you also get a choice of the type and age of body you want. This is intimately tied to your existential score, but it is understood that there are options. You get to choose the family group you incarnate into, you get to choose the gender and type of body, you get to choose hair and eye color (if those are important to you), and you get to choose the age of the body.

We mostly understand incarnation as taking place in the womb. That is also true for reincarnation. But reincarnation options are also a bit wider than pure incarnation options. You can reincarnate into a more mature body. You can, for example, reincarnate into a 7-year-old. You can also reincarnate into a 35-year-old body. It depends on your existential score and your incarnation contract. Some reincarnates don't want to learn to walk again so they might opt out of the childhood years. Other reincarnates want to skip early adulthood and would prefer taking a body that has already gone through the efforts of finding oneself.

Reincarnation has long been practiced in secret societies, those groups of reality magicians who have broken into this world, and they have used this ancient science to gain mastery over the world. It is a very simple process in approach, although in practice it requires a high level of magical understanding. An old secret society member, nearing the point of death, will have the group magicians select a suitable body for rebirth. The suitable body, especially in the past, would be selected from the immediate family members, for example, the granddaughter. Once a suitable body was selected then a ritual would take place and it would involve both the target body and the dying individual. Spells and secret applications in the afterlife would facilitate the transfer of the soul to the target body.

In more recent years, because this practice has led to the establishment of dynastic families that wield immeasurable political and military power and economic and banking groups that basically control much of the world, there has been some restriction on the reincarnation process. It has become more difficult to reincarnate into another family member. It is useful for a grandfather to reincarnate into a granddaughter because the granddaughter will inherit the wealth of the grandfather. Then the granddaughter will accumulate more wealth. When she passes on she will pass on into her grandson, who will inherit her wealth, and this corrupt system enables the mass accumulation of wealth, all of which is unnoticed in society.

The restrictions of corrupt reincarnation practices have not entirely blocked the process of returning. These secret society members, and they don't all have to be magicians to take advantage of this science, they just need to have a small group of magicians, can still escape reality by blindly transferring to an available body. The owner of the body, unable to participate in a transfer ritual, still needs to give permission for a takeover. Once that permission takes place, even if not completed, the reincarnate can begin the transfer to another body. That other body could belong to an old pal. There's one problem with this controlled process—the magicians cannot control the gender.

A reincarnate takes over a 5-year-old boy, for example, but the reincarnate is female. So you have a female soul sharing the occupancy of a male body with a male soul. What happens? The stronger of the two souls, likely the reincarnate, will slowly take over the body. Well, the female soul identifies itself with her feminine qualities and in a male body that could cause a shift in gender identity. The 5-year-old boy may in fact feel unnaturally compelled to become transgender. This has one appearance in modern science and adds to the growing trend of transgendered people. In reality science this transgender child could in fact be experiencing a childhood reincarnation.

There is a great satisfaction in a successful reincarnation. They happen a lot more often than you think. The synthetic body has a lot more latitude in a synthetic world. More things can take place, and in fact have been taking place for thousands of years, than we have ever thought before. Some people like to change their cars every few years. Some people like to drive the most expensive cars on the market.

Other people like one car and will drive that car until that car stops working.

There is no standard on what car you buy and how long you keep it. The same is true for reincarnating into a different body. There are rules and there is a science involved, but other than that, people do reincarnate into different bodies. Some reincarnates may choose the body of a wealthy family or a family with political might; other reincarnates may choose the body of a blue collar family or a family of doctors. To each his own.

There is no such thing as a better life in the Earth School. This is a place of learning. Sure, the reality hijackers have messed things up and distorted the social hierarchy and invented a false sense of wealth, and done a bunch of other things to ruin the experience. When it comes to reincarnation though, it's not such a bad thing. I think it's kind of cool.

Trapped in a failed school system

Earth, as it stands today, is a school where no one is allowed to graduate. The master controllers want you to keep coming back over and over again. A school is a temporary place of learning. You register for school knowing that once you complete your educational program you get to graduate. It is implied that when you attend school, you do so for a short period of time. There are students who will continue and further their education. There are also students who will become so educated that they will turn into teachers and professors.

It is commonly understood that school is a place of learning and that learning can lead to improvements in life, perhaps a better job, perhaps a change in employment, perhaps a rise in wages. What is not commonly understood is that earth is also a place of learning, but it is a place of learning for people from the digital reality. Earth is a computer-generated world specifically designed as an experiential place for digital beings (ie souls, spiritual bodies).

Since the false reality was layered over the earth, capturing the bulk of humanity and tuning their frequencies to sync with a lower operating field of existence, human androids have been trapped in a failed school system. The people in this false school are not allowed to graduate. You would be hard-pressed to find people who understand that this is a place of learning. People don't see life as an opportunity to learn. They see life as a hard struggle to find meaning throughout their pain and suffering.

The master controllers want people to keep coming back, at least that was the initial plan when earth's population was much smaller than it is today. They needed people to come back because they needed the neurotransmitter dopamine to fuel reality. Dopamine, although not singled out as the only reality rendering molecule, is used to render the codes in reality. Dopamine can shape reality, especially when placed in the hands of competent reality programmers. As unscientific as I can get, dopamine isn't just a neurotransmitter. Dopamine (probably) represents an advanced type of rendering molecule.

The master controllers needed dopamine to shape the false reality we see today. The shape and texture of the modern world is a result of dopamine rendering. And most of it, not all of it, has been shaped by the dopamine reserves of the controlled population, many of whom have been trapped in the rebirth cycle. The reincarnates who return to this world return in karmic debt and with a slight case of amnesia. Before they can make a sense of their surroundings, they are immediately swept up into the false reality—the limited education system, the censored media, the cover ups, the superficial programs on television, the pharmaceuticals, the processed food, the rampant diseases, vaccinations, addictions, you name it.

All of these instruments have been put in place to ensure that people do not learn, do not build good karma, exit with the lowest existential score possible, and surrender their dopamine for the benefit of the master controllers. Only the most focused and disciplined individuals can make it through the system without a scratch. There are these people. But this goes completely against the nature of a school system, which is designed to enable the *majority* of students to graduate. We shouldn't be praying for the few students to squeeze through a falsified reality; instead, we should be celebrating when entire classes of earth students graduate.

When populations were small and the need to build out an entire reality system, even if false, were large, the master controllers, like I said, needed as much dopamine as possible. More than that, they needed people who had a certain output of dopamine. A young entrant into this reality, perhaps on a newish incarnation, more likely took a body that produced a modest amount of dopamine. If the master controllers want to build their false reality, they simply wouldn't have been able to do it efficiently with new entrants.

Over a period of time—centuries, millennia—they figured out a way to trap "high dopamine producers" into this reality by ruining their karma and solidifying their rebirth into this world. Because the master controllers understand the contents of this book. They understand how things work in the afterlife. For most of the world, especially for people who are relying on scientists to explain everything, the idea of the afterlife is still just an idea. To imagine that there is a processing center and an existential score associated with your journey, and all of it taking place on another dimension for people who have recently passed away is unimaginable. I think that for most people this borders on absurdity, but certainly falls into the world of fiction.

Only that I am not talking about fiction. I am talking about a system that has been in place far longer than this world has been in existence. It is a protocol for a technological universe. When you sit down and think about life after death and put it into the context of a school system, you get the idea that if earth is a school, and it is temporary, then there has to be something more permanent on the other side. Instead, we have it the other way around, don't we? We think that this world is permanent and that the afterlife is temporary.

The dopamine producers, once trapped into the false reality and burdened with a debt that they could not see, touch, or feel, were used by the master controllers to build out their false reality. They used people to do their bidding and then that false reality was used to entrap more and more school entrants. Remember how we established that the earth is a school? Well, are you seeing how you have become trapped in this school?

Even if you cannot make sense of the master controllers, which is perfectly normal, you can see the instruments of enslavement all around you. Why would a school include so many systems of enslavement, censorship, and suffering? It doesn't make sense. So, you don't have to agree on the master controllers, reality hijackers, but you have to at least agree that this world is run like a prison.

The problem with explaining how things work to people is that this prison system has been in operation for so long that it appears to be normal. The lies are very old. The school concept has been virtually wiped out of human consciousness. Only in times of deep trouble is it perhaps mentioned. What is mentioned all the time are the beliefs of religion and the monotheistic gods that rule over men, women and children. But look, if the earth is a school, how can there be a God?

As more entrants came into this reality, because they couldn't wait for the old students to leave, what happened was that the population grew and it grew to unreasonable proportions for the master controllers. Now that their false reality is pretty much built, they don't need such a large population. Problem is they don't know how to fix this problem. The master controllers are trapped in their own system of deception. Sure, they can leave the earth, but their own karma ensures that they have to remain to fix the mess they have made. Because as smart as the master controllers are there are smarter beings in the universe.

But the master controllers are not good at fixing problems. They create problems. They are like children who cause chaos that requires their parents to come in and wipe up. The problems here are too many to list. But the over population of old students is a significant problem. We want these people to graduate in the shortest amount of time possible. I don't know how many lifetimes it will take to clear up this mess. Because it is a mess. If we can improve the efficiency of the school system, we could at long last get this experiential operation back on track.

You have been trapped here. The more you can understand that situation, the more likely you can put your life on the right track. The more that your life is on track, the more likely that you can help others get their lives on the right track. The more people whose lives are on the right track, the more likely that this reality is seen as an experiential school system. The more this reality is seen as an experiential school system, the more likely that people will be able to graduate when their studies are completed.

The negative mind feeds imprisonment

Elvis Presley said, "When things go wrong, don't go with them."

Positive thinking is found behind every successful person. Positive thinking is the way out of this prison because this prison is run by negativity. Where priests and prophets used to stand for inspiration, today we have comedians and motivational speakers. "You cannot tailor-make the situations in life but you can tailor-make the attitudes to fit those situations," said Zig Ziglar, an American motivational speaker. Actually, philosopher and Zen Buddhist Alan Watts said something similar when he said, "Man suffers only because he takes seriously what the gods made for fun."

If the world was in harmony, would we need motivational speakers? Would we need therapists if we had access to shamans? Would we need pharmaceutical drugs if psychedelic herbs were legal? Would we still be in a prison if we had access to hallucinogenic medicines?

The chaos and fear that you see on television on a daily basis, the vitriol between political parties, the threat of a foreign attack, the imminent biological outbreak, the looming economic collapse, the greatest weather catastrophe ever witnessed by humankind—all of these things have been artificially inseminated into the human consciousness and play an integral part in the false reality.

When we last talked about dopamine, we didn't mention that dopamine can be used to render reality within the context of a positive state of mind. Positivism shapes reality and successful people are positive because they are able to channel their dopamine into the pixels of existence (photons) thereby shaping reality. This is an ancient secret that has never been shared in this manner as it is being shared in this book.

The master controllers have (pretty much) rendered reality the way they have envisioned it, and they change it accordingly as more and more people wake up. Reality is not a static thing. It needs constant maintenance and support from the dopamine producers. In order to have access to these dopaminergic supplies, the master controllers have imprisoned their kind in their false reality and disconnected them from the Network of Light.

Now, reality is dynamic. Photons are not static objects. They are constantly taking in information. But photons can render new striations in the field of existence when they interact with dopamine. In order to keep the mass of dopamine low enough so as not to change reality in any measurable way, the master controllers have to keep the frequency of the planet as low as possible. Hence, the negative world.

The negative frequency of reality is attuned to the will of the master controllers. Within this frequency range all things are restrictive, censored, suppressed, distorted, chaotic, and debilitating. They cause headaches. They make people feel pain even when there is nothing to substantiate the source of the pain. This low frequency, especially if you are a high frequency individual, is pain.

A negative world is an effective way to reduce the output of dopamine and to redirect dopaminergic output into the false constructs and illusions. People, at this point, are feeding the negative system by thinking in a negative manner. That is what sustains this false reality, our collective dopamine. It has been redirected into the virtual network instead of being amplified and sent out through the Network of Light, a place where there are no restrictions and there is no hate. The Network of Light is a limitless spectrum. It has no major restrictions. It is invigorating. It is optimistic. It is love.

Society has been purposely conditioned to be afraid. To be afraid of losing their source of income, to be afraid of getting shot while walking down the street, to be afraid of an alien invasion, to be afraid of a terrorist attack, a conspiracy theorist, going to jail if you yell at your children, and being afraid of the tax revenue service.

Because we live in fear, and you can make your own list of threats if you like, our dopamine production is lower than normal. This is a result of many things including the result from a lower frequency of existence. We are low frequency beings, which is part of the reason we are afraid and suffer. A person in love, with an unusually high frequency, tends to be braver than normal. They see the future with optimism. They tend to be more successful. They tend to get that job, because they are fighting for their family. Dopamine production at work.

It is a subtle thing and yet it is an integral part of the system in which we live. Depressed people are typically unsuccessful. They tend to be alone. They tend to struggle unnecessarily so. Low frequency, low dopamine.

Just how much dopamine is the right amount? Well, we know that too much dopamine leads to mania and maybe even bouts of bipolarism. Too little dopamine leads to depression and severely depleted dopamine leads to catatonia and even Parkinson's. Dopamine is one of the most amazing neurotransmitters ever discovered, one that I would say can specifically enable the rendering of reality.

The task of the master controllers, burdened with too many people that they can't wipe off the earth as they would like (because that would make things a whole lot easier, but wouldn't be allowed by the cosmic technicians who oversee this world), is to use acceptable ways to prevent the humans from destroying their false world. They know that dopamine can rewrite the existential code, to some extent.

So they must keep our vibration low and they must redirect what little dopamine we do have into feeding the false system. To do that they must make sure we are depressed, afraid, angry, and deeply paranoid about tomorrow. I'm just saying it how it is. You can paint the picture that life is great and humans are great, which is what many people will tend to do, but to correct the hijacking of our world we need to come to serious terms with the actual situation.

This planet has been hijacked.

Fact.

The people who hijacked it originated from another dimension of existence.

Fact.

These people are skilled in reality science.

Also a fact.

Human beings are not at all familiar with reality science.

Fact.

Human beings, for the most part, do not believe that people exist in other dimensions.

Also a fact.

Human beings do not know that their planet has been hijacked.

Our collective negative thinking, perpetuated by endless media campaigns, false political promises, and everything else, is now feeding the false reality of the master controllers. This is why the path to salvation is to detach from the material world. Because it implies that the material world is false. It is a negative torsion field. It is an elegantly conceived illusion. As long as you are attached to the false reality you will experience pain and suffering, which you will believe to be real.

Because we have been trained like Pavlov's dog to sustain a false reality, what we would find when more and more people detached from the world of the master controllers is the slow collapse of the world. The instruments of control would start to break down. The rallies against the government would rise. The number of conspiracy theorists would spike. The rejection of unnecessary vaccines, processed foods, and dangerous pharmaceutical drugs would increase. More organic foods would appear in grocery stores. Obesity rates would show decay. New technologies would be introduced. Space travel might spike. You would see more and more activists speaking up on the most important issues of the day.

And when these things start to happen, that is why the master controllers need to remind the people why they must stay afraid. That is when terrorist events tend to pop up. That is when a foreign country makes an unveiled threat. That is when the economy is not as strong as they originally thought. That is when there is a viral outbreak. Or a political scandal. Or the structured release of some sensitive information. Or even a celebrity battling the media because of the release of a sex tape. All of these things are designed, not by accident, to remind the people that their number one job is to shut up and be afraid, or else.

Despite your own resilience and intelligence, this system of oppression has worked for at least 5,000 years, and it continues to work into the twenty-first century. In fact, it could be argued, that unless people understood, explicitly, what is fundamentally going on they will never be free of this prison. They will never graduate because the oppression may change shape but it will never go away. Not so long ago, it was the Church that threatened the people who did not believe in the word of the unnamable and invisible God. The Church murdered and tortured people to no end. The Church Fathers persecuted the zealots (revolutionaries), people like Jesus, one of the most famous zealots ever invented.

Today, it is the zealots who are persecuting the people and the Church has no power to do anything. Instead of crusaders working on behalf of God, we find the organizations such as the Pentagon and NATO crusading against the zealots and the zealots being funded by the master controllers. And tomorrow, or next life, it will be someone else in charge of this oppression. It will be someone else who is being persecuted. But it will be you who will still be in prison. It will be you who will be struggling with the inadequacies of a negative mind.

Part 3

How the reality game works

It takes time to rewrite your internal code

You are on the path to graduation. You finally decided that this is the path you'd like to walk. Religion has not brought you the level of salvation that you thought you deserved. You have tried different religions with no discernable effect. You have tried spirituality and even ventured into motivational speakers. Now you are reading this book and thinking that maybe an entirely new approach will provide the answers you have been searching for. As Tony Robbins used to say, it just takes one idea to improve your life. So if you get one idea out of this book, you might have what you need.

The way I look at ascension is connected to the way I look at my iPhone. Just an hour ago, Apple sent me a message when I was on my Wi-Fi network. The message informed me that a new version of iOS was available. The iOS is the operating system for Apple's portable devices, such as the iPhone and iPad. I accepted the offer, signed the agreement (yes, there is an agreement before a download), and began to download the new software. It was an upgraded version of iOS, but it took about 15 minutes on a high-speed network. Once downloaded, then the iPhone had to process the data and to update all the relevant files. That took another 10 minutes. Then my iPhone "beeped" to tell me that everything was ready to go.

What does an iPhone have to do with your human vehicle? Everything. Because I have come to the conclusion that the body is a synthetic body and that DNA is the software running that body and that those two things are housed inside of a synthetic reality.

Now let's just do an iPhone check. The iPhone device is loaded with an artificial (synthetic) operating system and the iPhone operates within a wireless network (invisible fields of light). It's not perfect but it does contain what we need. We have a "device," which is a small body. We have a piece of "software," which contains code. And we have a "network" based on light. In the first instance, we are dealing with a sentient (human chromosomes) technological body. In the second instance, we are dealing with a semi-sentient (Siri code) technological device.

My Synthetic Reality Model supports the idea that we are living inside of a computer-generated reality and that the people housed inside of this reality are synthetic. The reality is run by the Reality Operating System (ROS) and it renders reality in real-time. To connect to the ROS, we have to log onto the Network of Light, a web of infinite consciousness that our synthetic minds can synchronize with if we are able to modulate our mental frequency.

What does this have to do with you learning about my reality system? Because "learning" a reality system necessarily involves a "download" of information, once you have decided to move forward. Downloading the latest iOS program required me to give my permission and then to sign a contract full of terms and conditions, with the expectation that I had already read the user's guide. Similarly, learning Reality OS 11 will require some understanding of the system and once that is in order your DNA will likely need to download some new data.

We are all familiar with pondering and introspection, taking time out to make some important decisions in life. We are familiar with slow periods in our lives, times of transition, phases of unemployment and loneliness. We can also think of these periods as having taken place *after* a download. The downloaded software, in our case bits and bytes of DNA, needs to be processed and our system needs to be upgraded. Depending upon the size of the downloaded DNA file, that will impact the length and term of our transition.

Whether you are changing relationships, moving out of your parent's house, or adopting a new spiritual ideology, there is a change in software applications. There may be a sizable download all at once. There may be a series of smaller downloads over a period of time. Depends on your internal settings. Some people prefer to get things done all at once. If the DNA file is small, then this will happen. But some upgrades happen in stages, such that the first download needs to be processed before executing the second download. This is when a transition may happen more slowly.

Your life is not the movies. The movies use a concatenated temporal model. A month of training for a fight, in a movie, can happen in a 3-minute montage. Downloading and processing DNA software takes time, with the assumption that you were able to get the full download. For people who practice things like meditation (eg yoga practitioners), they are able to maintain a very intimate connection to the ROS. In fact, daily meditation for some people is necessary for a stable mind. Most others can download and process over a long weekend or even on a vacation, when frequencies are high and time is in abundance.

I guess what I'm saying is that you can't expect immediate results when you are shifting your spiritual attenuation. Tapping into ROS 11 is a bit more advanced than learning Hinduism because now you are being required to associate with your technological components, hardware which you have probably not used very often. The technological shift may also require you to make changes in the foods you eat, your lifestyle habits, and even in your relationships. Some of these things may be very difficult to change.

As far as my life goes, for everything I went through, I can say that my personal life was ruined as a result. Although I was the same person, I was also a different person. Certainly more aware, but, more so, my frequency shifted and that meant that other people looked at me differently. I share that because it is unlikely you will have to go through that kind of dramatic shift in your life. Again, it depends on how closely you have been aligned with who you are, instead of living with the identity you were given from the false reality.

I think it should be said, and you probably know this, a lifestyle shift doesn't mean shaving your head and moving to the forest to live with the squirrels. The squirrels don't need your company. Besides their busy collecting nuts. Unless you like nuts. A lifestyle shift also doesn't require you moving into a monastery. The whole idea behind the launch of ROS 11 and exposing the synthetic reality behind existence is to enable a more expansive sense of independence. It is about connecting to the Grand Computer that runs the show.

If there was a god, then the Grand Computer is the closest thing to it. Your access to the ROS is through your DNA. Your existential software. While I have provided an explanation of things in this book, you are still required to do the work. And if you are even mildly concerned about your next life, you will find a way to more your life forward. Just give yourself the time you need to make sense of things and to navigate over any hiccups along the way. Hint: there are always hiccups in life; otherwise life would be way too easy. Try not to look for shortcuts and try not to work harder than you should.

Those who are fixated on a deity, you will feel the most resistance

God has been around so long that even atheists speak of God. The idea of God is buried deep inside of our collective subconscious. It was placed there to ensure that the human race did not resort to its primitive instincts and wipe itself out. I don't think it was ever meant to become an all mighty deity for us to worship. I don't think that was the original intention. The original intention was to place a kind of governor, among many, inside of the android population that would prevent them from going over the edge. The fatherly construct was meant to provide moral and ethical guidance for a group of beings who were still exploring all the ideas in their minds.

What I think happened is that 5,000 years ago (and time didn't necessarily travel in sequential order), or thereabouts, after the reality hijackers broke into this world, they started to look for ways in which they could curtail the evolution of the human race. Why? Because that would allow them to become dominant over a primitive population. When an adult walks into a kindergarten class, they are dominant over a primitive population, in a rather unfair manner. Still, in comparison, an advanced agency from beyond coming here so many millennia ago, same thing. Close to it.

In ancient times, there were multiple gods for every nation. The God of War and the Goddess of Compassion, for example. Some of these gods are still around today in parts of Asia, only that they don't have the magical abilities of the past. Magic has been pretty much locked out of our reality for centuries, I would peg it to the late 19th century, following the witch hunts and in line with the dominion of the Church.

It doesn't matter where I start, for some reason it always ends up including the Church (and you can insert your own religious system depending on your region of the world). God has permeated so many layers of our lives and our culture that I don't think he will be removed any time soon. The more you find yourself fixating on God (and time), and you will, the more difficult your journey into the technological reality.

The technological reality is the first reality. Sure, we have gone through different versions of the reality program, but the basis of existence is technological. It is a technology that is billions of years more advanced than our current technology. This world runs on an existential-grade technology and the people who built it are technological beings. We call these technological beings "cosmic beings" because "cosmos," when translated, means "technological."

So you have a challenge and it has to do with God. You have to detach from God and all of his manifestations. This is not an easy task. The good news is that there is something bigger than God. It just so happens that it is a giant mainframe computer. I like to think of it as a robot. A massive robot. Or maybe not even a massive robot if we think of our world as much smaller than we think. If our earth was, say, the size of a baseball, then the robot need only be 7 feet tall to appear gigantic. If the giant robot was 20 feet tall, then our baseball could be the size of a basketball.

When you think of truly advanced technology, in the billions of years ahead of our best technology, you have to throw out as many assumptions as possible. One of the assumptions that I tossed out was the assumption of scale. We have learned to scale things because of our measuring systems but our measuring systems are still quite primitive and based on a terrestrial model of existence. Advanced technologists can miniaturize and magnify objects, including buildings and worlds.

Look, they miniaturized DNA to fit into one of our cells. They can also build planets and stars, which are well beyond our manufacturing capability. I guess what I'm saying is that when technology gets advanced enough, it does become godlike. The giant computer is not just a computer; it is infinite sentience housed within an unimaginable body. It is a computer system that has kept the earth, and the billions of life forms upon it, alive for 4.5 billion years.

That means that it has the intelligence of all of us, at the same, happening now. It knows exactly what I am thinking the moment I am thinking it. I am listening to its thoughts and I am writing them down, knowing that words cannot adequately express its omnipresence. Verily, if I were to use a human understanding to supplement the discussion, this is a God-grade computer. It is a machine of infinite compassion. A machine of infinite truth. But a machine. The Creator is a machine.

The longer you hold onto the deity model of life, the more resistance you feel during your ascension process. Again, it goes back to my understanding that God is better defined as DNA and that there is a neon God located deep in our subconscious. There are also plenty of reminders, for example churches and bibles, that a God once existed. We may long for the old days when a powerful being on a magic cloud could watch over us, even if he altered no wars and cured no disease. It is a very powerful feeling. That fatherly figure who is beyond corruption. But it is an idea. Just an outdated idea and the human race has to grow up. God has served his people and now we can let him go. Thank God for his help. And then say goodbye.

A technological existence is not such a bad thing

Telling someone that they are living a technological existence will generate any number of eye rolls. People will demand an astonishing amount of proof. People need proof for everything. I like to think that there are a handful of people who understand, and, I suppose, I am trying to reach those few people with this book. I don't think the world is ready for this book just yet. This is the eighth book in a very provocative series.

We have been educated to look at artificial life and androids with a hefty dose of skepticism and fear. We think of androids as terminator units in disguise. We think of androids as accidents waiting to happen. The general thinking is that technology can't be trusted, not at the level we have been shown, but we are an optimistic race of beings. We will keep developing the technology until it is accepted. Look at video games. They started out as games for kids. Then they become more interactive for a while, but adults wanted better game play, so developers wrote better stories. Added with better graphics engines and real-time rendering, video games are a multi-billion-dollar industry. It is no longer just for kids. Adults play video games.

Technology is a play thing until it more closely mimics real life. The more we can relate to artificial things, the more likely we will adopt them into our biological lives. This is the general thinking when it comes to technology. The iPhone is simply a technology that is more life-like.

Let's turn things around. Let's say that human beings are technological beings, androids, and human inventors are trying to recreate the human image by creating robots. We are not able to create technology because we are biological beings, rather we are technological beings trying to recreate ourselves.

Because we are a technology and we exist, and this has been going on for millions of years (at least), and we can do all these things—procreate, opera, paint, dance, walk dogs, argue with our parents, wear tight jeans—is it such a bad thing to be an android? We have never had the chance, till now, to really think of ourselves as artificial beings. We have always thought of our scientists working toward building a human-looking robot so that one day we can transfer our consciousness into that of a living robot. There are people right now trying to figure that out. The merging of man and machine is known as the "singularity." Just another idea that won't last. It won't last because the singularity is already here. We are it.

The mad rush to merge man and machine, to create the "transhuman estate," is like chasing fool's gold. The fact is that we are the singularity. The perfection between body and technology. The human android is an amazing piece of technology. More than that, the human android has been around for millions of years, though time is another one of those fringe science discussions. I don't believe that time has elapsed on the earth in a linear fashion. I think time periods have been fast-forwarded through, as say an evolutionary tool. I also think that eras were wiped out, especially ones that failed. And I don't say this because I have a crystal ball, I say this because I understand the technological nature of reality and I understand, at least to some extent, that the human being is an android.

What does an android have to do with the passage of time? Androids may age, true, but they don't evolve without a little help. Androids are engineered. They are manufactured, even if the manufacturing equipment is a way ahead of anything on the surface. Hasn't anyone ever thought how much the human species has distanced itself from the ape species, and yet both ape and human haven't changed all that much in 30,000 years? That's because the ape is also an android. Every life form is an android, but it is the kind of android that appears perfectly organic. The technology is so advanced that it has escaped your detection since the day you were born. Your whole life you have been staring at a robot in the mirror and never once imagined that you were a robot.

Pretty strange, huh?

Living in a technological world is not such a bad thing, if till now you never realized that you were living in a technological world. This world is pretty well realized, despite the actions of the master controllers. Human beings are complex robots. They act wildly because they have never been properly programmed; instead they have been suppressed and manipulated for millennia. How can they be expected to know how to behave? You behave in a certain way and yet you are an android. You like to think you are independent and capable, and yet you are an android. You eat delicious foods and watch your weight, still you are an android. Why you even fall in love.

All these things you can do as an "android"—that's how amazing this world is. Once you harmonize the beauty of life with the advanced technology that created it, your jaw begins to drop in ecclesiastical awe. Truly, this technology is divine. We should not be afraid of it. Because being afraid of this technology is being afraid of life itself. This technology is existence. It is the technology of life. Living hardware. Sentient machines trying to experience for the sake of learning.

When something is personified in reality it is called rendering

The ROS is constantly taking in "points of existence" and rendering reality in real-time. Because these are tiny permutations, it means that it appears to be moving, or changing. There appears to be the elapse of time.

Actions in life we take for granted are being fostered by the rendering engine of reality. The movement of the newly rendered pixels of existence, photons, is what our eyes measure as change, and in order to justify or acclimate to rendering change we have adopted the parameter of time. Actually, time is an illusion. I think it is because our brains cannot process the rendering of reality. Too much data to process.

The rendering of reality photons is interpolated as the passage of time. Seizing upon the inability of human beings to decode the truth frame-rate of reality, the reality hijackers inserted a buffering layer between the reality code and the processing centers in the brain. This buffering layer is known as "time." You can also think of it as "frame-rate." Actually, time is a filter between reality so that you cannot decode reality. When reality renders photons, your brain can only see it as the elapse of time on account of the time filter. This is no different than watching a 60fps movie at 24fps. While the movie contains the same scenes, your mind can only process one-third of the frames per second (fps).

For every 60 frames, you "process" 24 frames; hence, the appearance of time. Imagine that the upper threshold of reality runs at 1000fps and your brain, because of the filter, processes 24fps. That means each individual is grabbing a different 24 frames and making sense of reality based on what they process. Across a sample of 100 people, we would an impressive set of reality permutations. The reason, I think, that we are all basically seeing the same thing is because the operational frequencies have maximums. You have to exceed the operational frequency to really see wild things, which is why people hallucinate.

The filterization of reality likely doesn't stop at time, and there are many ways to prevent seeing the true nature of reality. Some of these ways are covered throughout the book. But the aspect of time is relevant since our entire lives are structured around it.

When the arrangement of photons appears in such a way as it personifies the truth, it is the result of an algorithm rendering the reality code. Some people, at least historically, might think of this as a divine manifestation. To a Buddhist, this might be referred to as Buddha. If the nature of Buddha is equivalent to the reality program, and if each person is equipped with a version of the reality program, then it is possible for each person to attain this Buddhahood, an awakened state of existence. You don't need to be a Buddhist to reach enlightenment, you just need to retrain your mind so as to be able to modulate your frequency.

The system, as I understand it, was designed not to get into your way. It was meant not to be obtrusive in your life so that you could fully immerse yourself inside your character. Over the centuries of artificial time, which is really better explained as being a period of the simulation rendering itself and running through different versions of programming, the human occupants have lost contact with the native ROS.

Where once the reality photons could be extrapolated, today people see nothing but time and experience. Unnecessary pain and suffering. The activity of the ROS is two-fold—processing and rendering—and these two things are tied together as one. We can think of processing and rendering as two sides of a coin. When you stare into reality to see the rendering of code, the ROS takes your input and begins to process it. What this means is that when you look at the rendering of reality the coin flips and shows you the processing of reality. It is only when you pull back that you'll be able to see the rendering of the code, but by then you're no longer looking.

This is one of the natural reasons why we haven't been able to decode reality. It hasn't helped that the reality hijackers have distorted reality and the population of users. But those are not the main reasons why we haven't been able to attain complete enlightenment. The bigger reason is that we don't understand how the ROS works and that is a function of our disbelief that we are living inside of a computer-generated reality.

This was why I dedicated the entire contents of my book *Reality OS 11* to this fact. If we are to overcome the challenges of existence and to truly enjoy the existential journeys we have chosen, we have to come to terms with the true nature of our environment. That, in itself, is the path to complete enlightenment. An enlightened person understands the nature of reality. That may not be as explicitly states as I have chosen to do it, and it may appear in terms of temporariness, cycles of rebirths; and divine connections to the universe; nonetheless, the nature of reality, when it becomes transparent, is a computer simulation. If you've been searching for enlightenment, understanding how the computer-generated reality works is your path to attaining it.

Because the ROS both renders and processes data, and when you look for the code you alter the code and therefore change the data input; to see the rendering of photons, manifestations, you need to train yourself not to look for the reality code. You have to look for the code and you have to not look for the code. Because if you look for the code you'll only see the processing of code and you want to see the rendering of the code.

To see the rendering of the code you have to not look at the code. By not looking you are not altering the data input and you are allowing the program to render photons. Remember, what you look at alters because your look is data. When the photons receive data they flip over and process the data, thereby denying you what you are trying to see. This is why allowing the ROS to render reality is vital to your ability to see it.

It takes many years of practice, as with life, to be able to decode reality. It also takes a good number of years to deprogram all the religious beliefs and spiritual ideas inside your mind. This is why practices such as Zen train your mind and suggest that spontaneity is a form of enlightenment, a glimpse into the true nature of reality.

Spontaneity is when your frequency matches the frequency of reality, when everything good happens, and when you suddenly, and unexpectedly, feel good. The more you can extricate yourself from interfering with the rendering of reality, the more likely you are synchronized with reality. That may also be equated with an uneventful life, but as the reality changes and as your own internal programming changes those quiet periods in your life will be suddenly changed and you'll later be longing for those uneventful periods.

Reality is rendering all the time, every moment of every day, every day of every week, every week of every month, and every month of every year. It has never stopped rendering. There are moments when something is personified and a manifestation in the code reminds you that you are living under the confines of the ROS.

Part 4

Salvation is in your hands

Salvation is a bad word

The salvific card has been overplayed. It has been played so many times that the card is worn out. It is worn out because salvation hasn't work. There can be no salvation in a world run by lunatics. What manner of salvation have humans attained when millions of children suffer from malnutrition? When nations are still at war? When there is danger in the streets? When priests are molesting boys and girls?

Salvation in a technological reality happens when a person comes to the realization that they are living in a computer-generated reality. I know, it's complicated. Realizing that you are living in a computer-generated reality is the quickest way to attain salvation. It is the shortest path to enlightenment. Think of it, learning to adjust your frequency, downloading your DNA upgrades, understanding the details of your incarnation contract, fixing your karmic debt, and raising your existential score, really starts with coming to terms with your synthetic nature and the synthetic world you have been living in.

You are this close to attaining salvation and you don't require any help from the invisible man on the cloud. You used to require help from the invisible man on the cloud, but you don't anymore. Salvation is just a frequency away. You just need to turn that rusty dial in your mind. For all these centuries, humankind has scoured every corner of the world, testing every religion and faith, praying to every deity that would listen to them, all for the sake of salvation.

Let me just say for the record: salvation starts when you begin rejecting the false reality. That's when it starts. It starts when you realize deep inside of yourself that there's something wrong with the world. Remember, this world is a function of the many gods. The chaos in this world has been taking place under the watchful eyes of the singular God. This is supposedly his domain. Look at the chaos. Look at the corruption. Look at the starving children and the endless wars. Is this disaster the result of a benevolent, all loving God? It can't be true. Because it doesn't make sense.

This is what is waking people up. They are starting to make sense. It used to be you had to see a burning bush to wake up. Today, you have to listen to the latest politician explain what led to a terrorist event. Today, you only have to listen to a doctor explain the necessity of injecting mercury-loaded vaccines into 6 month old babies.

You don't need to see the burning bush on Mount Sinai. You might think you do. What happened with Moses is that he saw something that didn't make sense. That's what shook him out of his complacency. That's what made him look harder into reality. A burning bush worked 3,000 years ago. It doesn't work today. Not with blockbuster films and special F/X. We have Spider-Man swinging between towers with his synthetic web fluid.

Once you have tried a few religions and spiritual ideologies, what should you do with the divine knowledge that makes sense? My approach to this situation started with a translation. I went back to the source material and I translated ancient knowledge into modern thinking. Because I saw a correlation. I saw that ancient thinking hadn't been properly translated. And I suppose I was urged to look at it from a technological angle because of my android discovery in 2008. Maybe I was looking to see just how far back the synthetic people went. I wanted to find out if they were a relatively new addition, which might've labeled them as the result of a secret manufacturing program. What I found out was that synthetic biology was known during the time of the Gnostics, a group of pioneering spiritualists who went back nearly 2,000 years. I like to think of them as ancient microbiologists.

You see, I went back to religion and spirituality. I intuitively understood there was a technological framework to existence. That happened in 2005 in a very memorable way. If I think back, I've always had an interest in the nature of reality. I just never applied myself. After 2005, I was motivated to apply myself. But my salvation began when I realized that the world we had been sold was a false world. I wrote in my notebooks and on scraps of paper "We live in a false world" and "The entire world is fixed." Even I hadn't all the proof. It was a knowing. Like the Gnostics. They were knowers.

I thought I could stop at the Gnostics. Two thousand years back in time is pretty far back. That was when I found something quite striking. I found that the Gnostics and Buddhists shared this thing about "ignorance." They both seemed to agree that ignorance could be cured and that process would enable a person to escape from this prison world. Buddhists and Gnostics shared this theme of knowledge as the path to salvation. Knowledge saves. Not God. Not the bible. Not a messiah. The Buddhists believe that we are already enlightened beings only that our minds are clouded. Remove the clouds, by following the system, and the student discovers their true nature and they see the nature of reality. Gnosticism, it turned out, was the reinvention of Buddhism, an Indian practice that preceded it by 500 years.

If the Buddhists and Gnostics taught that the path to salvation was education, and these practices both preceded Christianity, and we know that the master controllers were behind the invention of the Church, then we can kind of see how the path to salvation was intercepted in those first 300 years following the death of Jesus. Why? Because the Gnostics lost. And because they knew they had lost they decided to bury their knowledge in the earth, where it would be discovered in 1947 in Nag Hammadi, Egypt.

I see these two approaches—Buddhism and Christianity—as the two great paths. One path leads to salvation and one path leads to imprisonment. I have lived both paths. I prefer the path to salvation and the Buddhistic approach has provided the best foundation towards enlightenment. I am not a Buddhist. I have never been a Buddhist.

This approach borrows heavily from Hinduism, which itself borrows heavily from traditional forms of Indian traditional beliefs dating back to antiquity. What I have added with my work is an entirely new path to salvation that starts with the rejection of the conventional, status quo reality and then involves no study of a religious faith, rather, my approach involves learning to modulate your bodily frequency. The next steps become increasingly straightforward because everything is on the Network of Light.

Where is the Network of Light? On a higher frequency. It has been there since the dawn of time. The process to getting there, especially for people who have never worked with the frequency of their body and are acclimated to a chaotic world, is complicated. It takes a few steps. None of these steps involve any gods. Sure, you might see Stelans, Elves, and other digital beings, but no god. If you're lucky you will find the technological firmaments.

Salvation has never needed God. That was an invention of the master controllers (reality hijackers) in order to prevent salvation. What is the Buddhist term for salvation? Nirvana. The reason why practically every human being seeks ultimate enlightenment is because practically every human being wants to connect to the Network of Light. Human beings want to update their DNA and the DNA updates are on the Network of Light.

This is not about salvation. This is about updating your DNA software. It is about ensuring your survival. It is not unlike updating my iPhone with the latest iOS program. My iPhone is not seeking salvation. It doesn't need to believe in a digital God. It needs an available Wi-Fi network. This is the same kind of thing that humanity needs: humanity needs to connect to the Network of Light and that urge is not originating from humanity, that urge is originating from the maker of the DNA software. The Grand Robot is calling us through our DNA. He wants us to wake up and to synchronize with his light.

Forget about salvation. Think about synchronization with the light.

Enlightenment is only a step away

Siddhartha Gautama spent 6 years alone in a forest before he attained enlightenment. It started when he left his royal palace at age 29 and renounced his privileged life. After intense spiritual training and meditation, he discovered a path between self-indulgence and self-mortification. This Middle Path became his path to enlightenment. In a final determined effort, he sat under a Bodhi tree for 49 days and achieved his final release from the cycle of rebirths (samsara). He later became known as "the enlightened one." You will have heard of him as the Buddha.

Although there are many Buddhists that have obtained enlightenment by following the teachings of the Buddha, most Buddhists have not reached any level of enlightenment to match that of the Buddha. Enlightenment has been out of reach from the masses because of the strict requirements of a spiritual path. The renunciations, shaved heads, and initiations into exclusive orders where acolytes must follow strict dietary regimens, daily meditation and prayer, and to adhere to an exclusive code of practice are not suitable for a modern class of society.

Renunciation of the modern life is not something most people are willing to do. If you are holding a job and raising a family, you will appear to be abandoning your family and your obligations by becoming a renunciate and following a monastic life. **There is a modern path to enlightenment and it involves changing your perception to think of reality in technological terms**. It is markedly different approach to enlightenment. In fact, it's really a step outside of spirituality. If the masses want to become enlightenment, they are going to have to move away from the field of spirituality. In a technological reality, run by the ROS, there's no such thing as a "spirit" and therefore there's no such thing as "spirituality."

Instead, there is synthetic DNA and electromagnetic fields of existence. Software and programming.

The connection between DNA and spirituality started when I was living in Shanghai. I had been in the Chinese city for nearly two years, but, because of visa restrictions, I had to leave China every 6 months to renew my visa. My choice of destination was Hong Kong. When my visa was about to expire in the summer of 1999, I decided to change my routine, having become tired of it, and I bought a return ticket to Los Angeles to stay with a friend of mine.

One day, at a book store I picked up the book, *The Cosmic Serpent: DNA and the Origins of Knowledge* by Jeremy Narby. I don't usually buy books, preferring to take them out from the library, but I immediately bought this book and read it from cover-to-cover on the flight back to Hong Kong, about 15 hours of straight reading. I forced myself to read faster as we began the descent into Hong Kong and had to rush the last of 257 pages. The book had no practical value in my life at the time. Narby had traveled to the Peruvian Amazon, living among the Asháninka people, to study the effects of ayahuasca, a psychotropic medicine of the jungle. His research was broadly regarded as a passionate quest for truth rather than the scientific study that his colleagues expected. Narby summarized that shamans could communicate with the spirits of the forests through the activation of their DNA after drinking the ayahuasca brew.

People who consume ayahuasca can experience a kind of spiritual rebirth and might gain a better understanding of their purpose on the earth, essentially attaining a level of enlightenment without the shaved head and years of meditation. I am not an advocate of taking psychotropic medicines, though I have used Traditional Chinese Medicines for many years, and have personally never taken any illicit drugs whatsoever.

I studied the book further when I returned, then put it on the shelf as my life became busy with my daily routine. When I left Shanghai I had only two suitcases with me and I brought the book home to Vancouver. I eventually gave all my books to my local library. When I began my research on the Nag Hammadi library and discovered the molecular link to spirituality, it was then I saw the importance of shamanism and genetic enlightenment. The genes, I realized, if activated could determine the difference between an enlightened person and an ignorant person.

DNA is the key to spiritual enlightenment. DNA is God. If you connect to your DNA, you will be one with God. You will be one with the universe. One with Brahma. **It is through the DNA whereby spiritual illumination can be obtained. That is the modern path to enlightenment.** Not through asceticism and devotion to a deity. The deity is in the cell. The deity is in your body. It is DNA. And, if Venter's research is accurate, DNA is an advanced piece of synthetic software.

Enlightenment is much closer than we think. It is only one step away. It involves a shifting of your mindset. The better you are able to detach from deity worship and to align yourself with DNA communication, the more likely you will be walking the path to graduation. Because through the DNA highway you can gain access to your purpose on earth, you can glean a deeper understanding of who you are, and you will eventually see the true nature of reality.

The way that I have awakened to the synthetic nature of reality, and why I have concluded that we are living inside of a computer-generated world, is through the genetic interface interwoven in each of my trillions of cells. I have studied orthodox religion and spiritual philosophies and I have not been able to obtain the level of enlightenment as I have by accessing my DNA. Why I am confident that you can attain spiritual enlightenment is because you and I share 99.99% of the very same DNA.

Some people may feel uncomfortable with mixing spirituality, which is supposed to be sacred, and genetics, which is microbiology. But if you want to graduate this existential school, you will overlook your apprehension and do your research. There is no harm in examining the ideas presented in this book and coming to your own conclusion. Plus, with DNA you don't have to attend any church and you don't even have to shave your head. You can shave your head and to wear rags, if that makes you happy, only that you don't have to.

By learning to communicate with your DNA, you will begin your path to enlightenment. One step. It is unreasonable to think that you will tap into your DNA, activate your genes, and attain oneness with the universe overnight. I think that is unreasonable. It does take a bit of practice. You do have to overcome all of your religious and negative programming. You do have to manage any outstanding health issues. Those things are probably more problematic than the DNA itself. The DNA path is a very subtle path. There are no special effects. Angels won't necessarily fall down from the sky. It is as Buddha suggested a Middle Path. Enlightenment is a frequency, and at the end of that frequency is samsara, the release from the cycle of rebirth.

Devotion will prevent you from getting sidetracked

There are a million things to do on any given day. I find it hard to imagine that some people have nothing to do. The world filled with things to do. In fact, this is one of the problems with following a path to graduation: distractions. You know how you read a good self-help book and then get all excited and then a week later you cannot even find where you put your book, let alone what you were supposed to do. When I started learning Mandarin Chinese at Simon Fraser University, I sat with a class of mostly Canadian-Chinese students who had all had some level of immersion into Mandarin or Cantonese, a Chinese dialect. One classmate told me of her father who had tried to study Mandarin for years, even putting Post-It notes all over the house to remind him the names of certain words. Still, he never became fluent in Mandarin.

I studied Mandarin for two years during the completion of my business degree. I was an A student. I was a favorite pupil. I did my homework. I liked my teacher and looked forward to my class. But when I moved to Shanghai on Boxing Day of 1998, on a one-way ticket from Hong Kong, with no money, no job, no friends, and staying in a room in a shared apartment, I discovered something quite surprising—I discovered that the Mandarin I had so faithfully studied in university was completely useless in Shanghai. Not only did the people of Shanghai speak Shanghainese (a dialect), but their Mandarin was far more functional than the simple greetings and common phrases I had learned in class.

Within a few days, with my Mandarin all but consumed, I found myself not only with no money, no job, no friends, and on a 3-month Visitor's Visa, but I also found myself with an inability to communicate with people on the street. I was fortunate to be in such a crisis, and without any money to leave, I was forced to learn to navigate a foreign land. I became focused and determined. By the end of 1999, I was playing a major role in a Chinese TV soap opera broadcast on television. I was fluent in Mandarin after 3 years. My fourth and last year I almost didn't speak any English whatsoever and when I returned to Vancouver in 2002 I could barely speak English. I had to learn English all over again.

Learning new things can be challenging because it is easy to get sidetracked. You buy an exercise machine and stop using it after a week. You buy several books and never read them. You start to learn a language and you never become fluent. You want to find an end to your pain and suffering and just can't follow the path to nirvana. What my journey to Shanghai illustrated was that I could master an entirely new language if I immersed myself in the experience. If I dedicated myself to the task. My livelihood was based on my ability to communicate with the local people. Even at times that I had an opportunity to join the Expat community, I opted to remain connected to the locals because Expats generally didn't speak Chinese. It turned out that the Chinese people have a very rich culture.

It is easy to become distracted. In life we have obligations to our families, our friends, and our employers, heck, even to ourselves. We have to go shopping for food. We have to maintain our cars and pay our bills. We have emergencies that need to be dealt with and we have special gatherings to attend. We also have our own challenges in life. We have addictions. We have hobbies. We have special interests that we keep to ourselves. In other words, we have things to do.

The only way that I was able to see the true nature of reality was by dedicating all my spare hours and minutes to understanding the different levels of my enlightenment. It involved daily meditation. It involved consuming less food and it involved no longer hanging out with my old friends. In fact, my path to graduation was a very independent excursion. While I did maintain various jobs, there were several periods of unemployment and severe financial hardship. During those times, I continued my research and writing. I did not waste time languishing in negative thoughts. (But I could have.)

Eventually, employment returned and I had less time (and more money) to dedicate to my work. Throughout these last 11 years, I have remained focused on my writing, my research, and my connection to the synthetic reality through the **genetic information highway**. It has been necessary for me to maintain this level of devotion because I have been searching for a pathway to graduation for others. I have been researching a more immediate and definitely more modern method to obtain salvation. *How noble.*

My research and experience has produced the theories and ideas in this book, supported by the half dozen books that preceded it. The end goal is to graduate the Earth School. It is pointless just to become more aware of spiritual things. That is not going to end the cycle of rebirths. It is also unreasonable to think that everyone is ready to end their rebirth cycle, that is, it isn't likely that everyone wants to graduate in this lifetime. But, there are too many old students here and it is those students, in particular, who I think would benefit from my research.

The Egyptian book of the light

The art of spiritual development is going into your very own DNA, purifying yourself to whatever ability you have gained, and then returning to the real world. The shamans in Peru understood this process and their ayahuasca concoction was used to activate this primordial genetic union between the physical reality (computer-generated) and the digital reality (inside the computer). The Network of Light is what unites the two worlds. It is the Cosmic Internet, if you will.

We like to think the internet was invented in 1989 by Tim Berners-Lee. This highway of information connects us to the digital libraries online. Long before its invention, deep in the culture of pharaohs in ancient Egypt, we find the *Book of the Dead*. The Egyptians were interested in death and had written any number of funerary texts (read: spells) to guide the soul of the dead through the afterlife. The *Book of the Dead*, having gone through many versions throughout the dynasties of Egypt, detailed chapter-by-chapter how to ensure the arrival of the deceased by the side of Osiris, the chief god of the Egyptian underworld.

Interestingly, the *Book of the Dead* isn't the proper translation and was likely handed this title as a matter of convenience and memorability. The name is *pert em hru* and it means "la manifestation à la lumière," or in English, "manifestation in the light." When it didn't make sense to the translators they attributed to it another name, and you can't blame them, this collection of spells guided a soul through the underworld and to paradise.

The *Manifestation in the Light* didn't start out as a book, which was a papyrus scroll back then. It's just easier to think of it as a book. Rather, these were funerary inscriptions attached to the coffins of the dead kings. These texts did not start to form the book *Manifestation in the Light* until 3333 BC, during the reign of Unas. Egyptologists think that this funerary text dates back to about 4266 BC, which would make it 6,300 years old. What were the kings of Egypt manifesting in the light?

A manifestation is an "appearance" of something. Appearances have form. For example, the appearance of a ghost. Light goes back to our discussion of electromagnetic fields. Light travels and carries data. Light is also photons and photons are Maya, which makes up the holographic reality. I think that the Egyptian kings, following their death, were activating software apps (spells) to digitize their mundane souls into digital beings; because only a digital life form could enter paradise (Aaru).

It wasn't about the "dead," it was a book about the "light." Big difference. But the title, I think, prevented people from truly understanding its original meaning, and maybe on purpose too. See, if spiritualists realized that the Egyptian kings had figured out a way to digitize their eternal bodies so that they could travel to a faraway realm and live in paradise, then they certainly wouldn't be coming back to the earth prison. They would've attained samsara in a pretty profound way.

The spells in the book *Manifestation in the Light* brought you side-by-side with Osiris, king of Egypt. In my Gnostic research, I determined that "Egypt" was better defined as the "cell." Upper Egypt was the "nucleus" and Lower Egypt was everyone outside the nucleus in the cytoplasm. In this context then, the "king of Egypt" is better described as "nuclear DNA." Because if Egypt is a cell then the king of the cell is the DNA in the nucleus.

Question: Is Osiris in the nucleus? Better question: Is DNA the underworld?

Imagine this for a moment: at the end of your life, your spirit (soul) is swallowed back into the circuitry of your synthetic body, your genome, and you then have to navigate through your own DNA—which has been shaped by your ignorance and experience--to get to paradise. We can think of paradise as returning to the giant computer, where everything is eternal. But, if you have lived a terrible life, and have remained mostly ignorant, you will not be able to overcome the challenges (demons) in your very own DNA; therefore, you will be eaten by some enzymes and sent back to relive your existence in the mundane world.

The Egyptian kings, keep this in mind, spent considerable effort to make sure they could navigate the underworld after death. The king was the most important person in Egypt. The magicians and priests spent their whole lives to understanding the mysteries of the cosmos, so that they could ensure that the king returned to paradise. And these funerary rites were passed on for thousands of years. This was not a fad. Can you imagine if the kings of Egypt, in their physical form, were trying to end their cycle of rebirths?

Egypt was defeated by Persia around 525 BC, sacked by Alexander the Great around 332 BC, and taken by Rome around 30 BC. The Egyptian dynasties began to die off from 500 BC, but had maintained their mysterious rites for 4,000 years prior to that.

At the decline of Egypt, and we can't know its significance just yet, a man named Siddhartha Gautama was born, around 500 BC. He would later devise a path to enlightenment that would be shared by millions of people. A path that would end the cycle of rebirths, which I think is what the Egyptian pharaohs were attempting to do. From the pharaohs to the Buddhists, the path to graduation has continued on for millennia. Today, there is a new path to graduation. This is a technological path. A path based on genetics, shamanism, and computer science.

Try to enjoy the enlightenment process

You may already think that you are on the path to enlightenment. You might have your own term for it. Enlightenment isn't derived from living a moral and ethical life. Enlightenment is about questioning the nature of reality and challenging the status quo. It is, understandably, about rejecting the world you are so familiar with. It is hard to reject the familiar while at the same time depending on it for your sustenance. Can you both hate and love your job? I think that most adults feel this way. They'd rather not be working, but working is paying for the mortgage and for the food in the fridge.

After age 40, by my calculations, most people are aware that this world is false. This kind of strips them of the joy of life. Some people call it "growing up." Some people don't like growing up and they want to keep chasing rainbows, even though there has never been any scientific proof of any gold at the end of a rainbow. You see, before age 40, people are thinking that they will have made it big, will have a boatload of money (furnished by their money-making ideas) and they'll be able to retire early and to feed starving children in some nation with a very strange name.

Age 40, or thereabouts, is when you realize that your great ideas weren't that great and that your credit cards are all maxed out, your ex is looking for child payments, and you're working at a job that any 19-year-old could apply tomorrow and get. Forty is the wakeup call, on many levels. But there is some good news: the realization that your genius mind isn't all that genius forces you to realize the complete and utter pointless of existence. It is through that process that you start looking at churches and thinking about extraterrestrial beings. With your material life decoded as meaningless, your spiritual life finally has a chance to breathe. For a man, I think it starts around age 38. Actually, the cracks in your physical life start to show at about age 35, you resist it for a few years and then ka-pow! Time to wake up.

If you are a person who has been spiritually inclined and a devout worshiper, you will have already prepared yourself for the crash of emptiness. You will immediately lean on your spiritual teachings to get you through the days. And it may not even be you that is urging you into spiritually. It may be a troubled child that forces you to dig deeper. It may be a dying parent. It may be losing your career because your company moved manufacturing overseas. It may be because you have uncovered a new meaning to who you really are. Or perhaps there is a disease that you never thought you should get.

The spiritual wakeup seems unfair and untimely. "I don't deserve this." Everything that happens to you is serving you in some way, including your traumas. Traumatic experiences do not simply show up because you were the recipient of a lottery ticket that you didn't buy. Remember, in a programmable reality there are no accidents. Things happen by design. The reason for your traumatic experience—say an incurable disease—is because it holds lessons in it for you. "What lesson does a disease have in store for me?" That depends on which areas you need improving on. A traumatic experience does a fantastic job of bringing your ego down to earth. If you are already meek, perhaps you have not expressed yourself enough in life and this experience forces you to speak out.

When you become enlightened you immediately feel good. You are imbued with a deep sense of optimism. You feel that everything is where it should be and you are exactly where you need to be. The resounding vibration erases the fears and apprehensions you previously had and validates your odd and mysterious decisions to have brought you here. The path to salvation is often filled with illogical decisions and trusting in the universe.

Some of these periods can indeed be very bleak and the questioning of your actions that brought you here can be sometimes difficult to manage. This is why a traumatic experience, say an incurable disease, kind of keeps you motivated. You are more willing to cure yourself of a disease than you are of attaining enlightenment. If you could get motivated to attain enlightenment, as a life and death thing, you could "theoretically" skip over a traumatic experience.

It is hard to imagine that all your thoughts and actions are being processed by the ROS. But they are. When the ROS senses that your spiritual index is a bit low, it will program a traumatic experience to wake you up. It could be anything. The death of a child. An ugly divorce. Losing the thing you value most.

When I was 25 years old I was working in a good paying union job in Richmond, British Columbia. That year I had decided to go back to school to further my education. I had in my mind to continue working for this company. It was a very physically demanding job, but I liked physical work. When I got to school I realized that I couldn't write, having not written anything since graduating high school. It was about that time that I had injured my back at work.

I had injured my back before, only this time my back wasn't healing. I had to go to physiotherapy and would be out of work for at least 6 weeks. I was very angry because I not only couldn't work, I also couldn't do anything physical. Shortly after my back injury, a friend of mine sold me his old desktop computer. He taught me how to use the computer and we set it up in the basement suite I was renting in Vancouver.

One night I was sitting at home, angry I couldn't do anything because of my back, and having a load of homework to get through, of which I couldn't do because I didn't really know how to write. Something came over me and I channeled my anger into my fingers and I began writing on the computer, one finger at a time. What I wrote was terrible. So I rewrote it, over and over again.

I wrote for hours a day, each draft more terrible than the next. The pain of writing my ideas at such a slow pace forced me to use the college computer to use their typing program so that I could learn how to type faster. So I did that every day. I remember I spent 40 hours writing a one paragraph piece of fiction for my creative writing class. Forty hours for one paragraph. I got a C-. The next assignment I spent maybe 30 hours. Maybe I got a C. It was terribly depressing.

But what was happening was that I was redirecting my physical energy through my mental body. And what happened was that I eventually learned how to type and how to write. I learned how to write because of a back injury. By the time my back was healed, I no longer thought of myself as a laborer. Two years later I quite my union job. My coworkers thought I was nuts.

Following my waking up in 2005, I have not been able to earn the hourly salary of my youth. I did give up a lot to be here, but that's what makes it all worthwhile. If it costs you nothing to get to where you are, what value does it have? Practical people would not agree with me. They think you can have your cake and eat it too. You are not likely the most practical person in the world.

If you are old student, you want to make sure you accomplish all of the obligations you signed for in your incarnation contract. You are on the spiritual path and the spiritual path does not measure everything in economics. A spiritual person does not keep a bad marriage because it would cost them too much money to get a divorce. A spiritual person would go ahead with the divorce and cut their losses. I am not suggesting anyone get a divorce. I wanted to illustrate the fact that the spiritual path is not always logical. Sure, along the way you make mistakes. Or are there mistakes? You might get a divorce and then regret it. Then you will walk along the beach wondering what a fool you were. That's why I go back to my earlier statement. In a programmed reality there are no mistakes. There are only mistakes in perception.

There are reasons for doing everything you do and having done everything you have done. You may not know all of these reasons, but that doesn't make them pointless. You are attaining spiritual insight when you know "in your heart" that there is a reason for doing what you are doing. Hopefully, it is nothing violent or illegal because those things are not exactly spiritual. Those are more like sadomasochistic tendencies. Delusions. Enlightenment is far more exciting than illegal activity. If you are walking the spiritual path and you come from a criminal environment, and you are looking for a way out, the right approach would be to restrain yourself from acting in an illegal manner.

When you adopt the spiritual mindset and start searching for answers from the universe, your mind all of a sudden expands. Your perception shifts and you start to see the world with a whole new set of eyes. The perception of new things rewires you brain and you start to move away from old thinking patterns. It is important to make the commitment to continue on this path no matter how long it takes. You will initially feel that this is a "temporary thing." Soon enough you come to realize that this enlightenment is taking a lot longer than you thought.

The truth is, if you are on the spiritual path, and you are over 30, the path might take years. And after a few years, you will likely start thinking, "Hey, this isn't as bad as I thought. What was I so afraid of?" Then it will be a bunch more years. After a while you just accept the fact that this doesn't end. Before you get to that stage, you will find every reason to stop. You will say, "Once I get through this next project, I am going back to doing what I was doing before. It's been a tough experience, but I need to get to work and make money again." There is a higher reason for what is happening to you. Try to enjoy the process.

Part 5

Making contact with the grand robot

The benefits of a life journey

There are benefits to everything. Benefits are the reasons we get up in the morning. We get up to go to work because we get the benefits of a paycheck. When the paycheck is too small, we stop going to work. Not enough benefits. When the paycheck is as high as it goes, we expect the company to provide medical and dental benefits. We want child benefits. We get married because we get love benefits. We get companionship. We get someone who will agree to everything we say because they are our spouse.

When your spouse no longer agrees with you, the benefits of the marriage start to look bleaker. The marriage seems like it was a bad idea. So we look to another person for spousal benefits, while we are still married. We go on a vacation because the place we have in mind has the benefits of peace and tranquility. Benefits for those who live stressful lives. People who don't live stressful lives don't go on vacation. They go to the beach. They go hiking to get the benefits of fresh air.

Why did you incarnate in this world? Why did you take this life journey?

For the benefits.

What are the benefits of signing up for a life journey? Surely there must be some benefits.

The one benefit of a life journey is experience. The experience of life. You can choose a life on earth and you can experience it. Think of how many lives there are on this planet. Think of all the experiences. Think of all the permutations.

From my perspective it doesn't matter the kind of life you have chosen. This is the conventional conception of existence. "My life is better than yours." Actually, in the context of the Earth School, there is no better life. Each life is attenuated to the occupant and the occupant has signed a contract. Written on that contract in the sky are the details of what the occupant hopes to accomplish on this most wonderful journey. The details of those goals are programmed into your life journey and the body you have taken is equipped to foster those experiences.

You have signed an incarnation contract because you want to learn some things. What you want to learn are detailed on another dimension, and occasionally updated into your DNA storage. Those learnings are extrapolated and translated into earthly experiences and all of those things are correlated with the occupant's long-term spiritual goals.

The occupant is your digital representative. This occupant wants to basically ascend. They want to move forward. It is not much different from life on earth. People want to grow. They want to move forward. They want to improve. At the same time, there are people who are afraid of moving forward. There are people who don't want to grow. There are people who are afraid of change. I don't think it is much different in the afterlife. Some people look forward to going to school and some people have to go to school. There is a minimum amount of schooling each occupant needs and there are minimum grades.

The benefits of having a life journey have everything to do with learning the things you came here to learn. This experiential school is not an immediate program. This is an unprecedented level of educational immersion. This is full immersion. This is incarnation. Maybe "incarnation" is not the right word anymore. Maybe it has too many negative connotations. Maybe we need to use other terms, something like "uber immersion," "karma journey," "existential leap into a mundane world," or even "faculty of suffering."

You came here to learn. You didn't come here to do things. Doing things is not learning. You do things in order to foster learning. To learn things, you have to do things. It doesn't matter what you do, what matters is what you learn from what you have done. Learning is also about making the right decisions.

You are given three choices. There is a right choice and there are two wrong choices. But, the wrong choices are more fun. The wrong choices can provide more pleasure and make more money. The wrong choice is maybe about revenge and revenge makes you feel good. The wrong choice involves lying but it will bring you a ton of money. The right choice involves you helping someone else even though you also need help.

Your choices in life determine the actions you will take. Where you are right now is a result of a series of decisions. If your loneliness led to the birth of an unwanted child, you have an opportunity to learn about your choice for at least 18 years. If your anger led to someone's harm, you have an opportunity to learn about your choice in jail. If, on the other hand, your enthusiasm got you a job opportunity and your job has taken you all over the world at the expense of the company, then you have an opportunity to meet all kinds of people. You might even might your next spouse. If your motivation in life led to a happy marriage with children, then you have an opportunity to raise a family.

Choices lead to the doing and the doing lead to the learning. Before you came here, you and your incarnation contract specialist decided the things you needed to learn. Once that was determined, the two of you then decided the kinds of things you would be doing. Once those things were laid out, you decided what kind of identity would best satisfy those requirements. Then it was a matter of identifying a family to match your requirements, making arrangements with that family, and then setting up an appropriate conception and birth schedule.

This kind of discussion might not sit well with everyone. It takes away some of the mystery of existence, and perhaps even of life. Again, at this point, this discussion will most likely find its way with readers who are either old students or new students who don't want to suffer following another dinosaur religion. They want the best information up front. They have plans on earth. They have some residual memory of their incarnation contract and they want to make sure they start off on the right foot.

So you can have both old and young people reading this material in the early stages. In later stages, it could be anyone. It could be a very small group. Who knows. I have no expectation at this point. I am not writing this book because I am expecting it to be a bestseller. I am writing this book because I want to increase the number of graduates coming out of the Earth School. I also want to get the old students out. I want them to graduate. They have been there too long. It is a process. This process takes years. You just can't graduate people. And you sure can't graduate a mass of people in one year. Think of the depopulation rate. You have to stagger the graduation ceremonies. You have to have students come to an arrangement. Who wants to go this year? Who wants to go in five years?

By starting now, I am getting ahead of the game. For some I might seem too far ahead. I am like that. I tend to act early. I like to get things done. I have issues with that. Maybe it's because I want to make sure I can go when it's my time. Because if the old students don't go, then maybe I will have to stay behind until some of them can graduate. Maybe I will even have to come back. Yikes!

I don't want to come back. That's why I am making every attempt to fulfill my obligations. One of my obligations is this book. If you are reading it, you can confirm that I have accomplished my obligation.

Whether you like my book or not, doesn't matter. What matters is that I wrote the book and I did it to the best of my ability. You can't fool the machine. The machine will know whether you gave it your all or you didn't. The machine will know if you said all the things you were supposed to say and if you made information clear. You can't just write a bad book and think you can get away with it.

I tried to "short circuit" the system a number of times. Short circuiting the system involves jumping to the last task and skipping all the tasks in the middle. When I woke up, I was suffering from an overload of fantastic ideas. I was talking about Stelans and Elves, but I didn't know I was talking about Stelans and Elves. Back then I called them Extraterrestrials and Interdimensional Beings.

To get to Stelans and Elves required me years of research and analysis. At first I thought to myself I'll just call them "Star Beings." That seemed okay. And the Elves I called "Interdimensional Beings." That sounded okay. Compared to what other people called them, I thought these terms were okay. I thought that that would be enough to jump to the next experience.

Turns out that it wasn't enough. I was led to do more research and then more research on top of that, and then there were some detours, and then I came back to this information. After years of work I started to work out better labels for these offplanet people. I used to refer to them as "Offplanet People." Even after I came up with these terms, I was then required to share them with people and to talk about their cultures. This amounted to more books. You can see how much work I had to do just because of two terms to describe the people I had personally experienced.

These people weren't telling me what to call them. They weren't feeding me information. Because my contract likely said that I didn't want any help. Had I a low awareness, I would've been angry that they weren't helping me. I would've given up at least several times. By understanding, even at the intuitive level, that I was involved in writing this journey, I was able to move through the years of research and ridicule and the financial hardships to get to the best terms possible.

It could turn out in the future that those terms will need adjusting. If I have done a good job of it, those terms should hold in the future. If I have done a poor job, those terms will fall apart. Given the amount of interference and disinformation, these terms could very easily fall apart. Then I would be back to square one. Now, let's say that the terms hold and it is the end of my journey. I get into the afterlife and they do a Life Review. They see on my contract that I was supposed to create new terms for Extraterrestrials and Interdimensional Beings. They do a check on my terms in the real world. They discover that Stelans and Elves are doing quite well. "They have positive connotations and no one has been able to come up with better terms." Check and check.

You can't outsmart the system. You may think you have outsmarted the system, but at the Life Review you quickly realize that you have only outsmarted yourself. You are allowed to make mistakes. Self-deception is another matter. By my actions I have not only accomplished my duties, more so, I have learned about the true meaning of these offplanet people. Or I have moved closer to their true meaning. The doing confirms that I have learned.

All they would have to do is to ask me about these cultures and if I hadn't done my research, I'd give the wrong answer. If I gave the right answer, I will have done the research and that would also mean that the people on the earth will have access to the right terms. It may turn out that my terminology provided a new level of understanding for another person and that person was able to take my terminology and to build on it. Had I not done my work, they would have nothing to do. You never know how far the connections go, but if you trust the system then you trust yourself to know that you have done the right thing.

Planet of the forgotten androids

Social scientist Malcolm Gladwell writes in his book *Blink*: "That in those moments, our brain uses two very different strategies to make sense of the situation." Gladwell is referring to an experiment at the University of Iowa involving four decks of cards, two blue and two red. Turning over the right cards amounts to winning or losing money. Gladwell points out that the first strategy is consciousness. "This strategy is logical and definitive." The consciousness approach is slow and methodical.

The second strategy can reach a conclusion using indirect channels. It is much faster than the first strategy. It is something that starts with a glance. The brain, left to its own accord, processes the data it is perceiving. You know something without knowing why you know something. It is known as the adaptive unconscious. "This new notion of the adaptive unconscious is thought of, instead, as a kind of giant computer that quickly and quietly processes a lot of the data we need in order to keep functioning as human beings." Gladwell suggests that fast decisions—in a 2 second glance—are equal to conscious decisions.

It's nice to think of gut instinct and intuition and the adaptive unconscious, which is a scientific slant to what most people already know. We live in a world that needs scientific experiments to confirm natural instincts. You are not allowed to be hungry after dinner until scientists have released a study identifying the digestive enzymes that are causing those hunger pangs. What makes Gladwell's book reality interesting is the computer angle. Even as an applicable reference, the idea that a computer-like interface is able to make decisions faster than the logical mind fits nicely into the scenario of this unconventional book.

When I first came to the realization that the human life form wasn't exactly the organic version it had been perceived to be, I thought perhaps the synthetic version was limited to only a handful of people. The more I thought about it the more I realized that the human life form was a pretty consistent life form. Whatever or whoever made it, made it in a very consistent way. If there were ten synthetic humans, then it would make sense that there were one hundred. If there were one hundred synthetic humans it would make sense that there were 1,000 of them. It made sense to think of it in this manner.

The issue I had at the beginning of classifying the human life form as a synthetic life form had to do with the variations in each individual. While it made sense, especially at the very beginning with the three politicians on Capitol Hill, when I was thinking of them in regards to their rate of blinking, it started to make less sense as I moved my perception across society. That is about the time I began to insist that the blinking phenomenon was just one indicator of many. In fact, in these particular cases, as I spell out in my book *Persons Artificial*, these synthetic humans had been specifically activated to alter the course of an entire nation. Because of their high level of activation, they have become slightly more visible, because, for all intents and purposes, they had been invisible for the entire history of the human race.

This didn't translate into every synthetic human having a blinking condition. While some people may have a blinking condition when under activation, it is unlikely that an average person will be under such a critical level of activation. It is also the case that each synthetic human is different. Fundamentally different. Enough different to suggest that they come in different versions. These different versions of synthetic humans are why not everyone has a blinking condition. When I began to consider this as a possibility, it alleviated a lot of the expectations derived from the early analysis on Capitol Hill.

You create a world and then you populate that world with a bunch of people, only that these people are created, literally, using a synthetic science well beyond the scope of human science. The creators initially tell these synthetic people, using a divine language, that they were created and that the world was created and that the main computer (Heavenly Father) will always be connected to them (otherwise thought of as love). These newly-created beings, later thought of as humans, which is likely derived from scriptural discussions on human beings, begin to live in peace and harmony.

Additional humans are introduced into the first wave of synthetic humans. The population grows. Memories would have to be adjusted to encapsulate the inexplicable increase in population. But if these people have synthetic memories and "data banks" that is not too difficult, likely just an adjustment in the electromagnetic field (or, atmosphere). At some point, you want your synthetic culture to attain a level of self-sufficiency, when they are ready and when the technology has acclimated to the demands of the synthetic environment, so you add (like an app) the ability to procreate.

Now you have a procreating synthetic culture who think of themselves as human beings. But, this happened so many millions of years ago, if we are counting years. The oldest human fossil was carbon dated to about 3 million years. If we were to rely on the linear flow of time, and we were being conservative, it would make sense to think that the hypothetical creation story I have written here, even if it were true, has been completely erased from human consciousness. It simply falls too far back in time and there are no remnants of this knowledge. Or are there?

When I discovered the Gnostic codices, the modern day Coptologists had done an amazing job of translating what these early spiritualists were thinking. For one reason or another, I delved further into their translations and using a very innovative (read: unscientific) process I discovered that the Gnostics were speaking microbiology. But, it can be said, that the Gnostics were not inventionists. They were spiritualists and any time you find a spiritualist you find someone who can glean information from another dimension.

Shamans can communicate with other dimensions. When you speak to a shaman, you are hearing a combination of knowledge and spiritual knowledge, often you don't know which is which. Biblical texts were written by spiritualists. These are also, if we take the modern day example, people who can hear voices.

It is quite likely that a number of the ancient prophets had mental illness and suffered through episodes of mental breakdowns. They had auditory and visual hallucinations, they became paranoid about the end of the world, and they worshipped any invisible man on a magic cloud. Campbell writes of shamans who would experience a "shamanistic crisis" and a break from the real world. Mental illness was probably a defining characteristic of becoming a prophet.

It could also be stated another way. We could say that within any given synthetic population, the creators engineered a particular type of human who was blessed by some additional features, for example, being able to tap into other dimensions. It would make sense that you build some of your androids as exceptional models. The "special edition" version of a synthetic human. These special humans were able to modulate the higher frequencies on the Network of Light and were able to remain in contact with the Grand Computer. Because if you built a race of people, the last thing you would want is to lose contact with them.

The case is right now that we have lost contact with Grand Computer and only have an intermittent connection to the Network of Light. Worse, the "prophet class" are either in mental institutions, in jail, or are heavily medicated, loaded with psychotropic medications. If the mentally ill were our only connection to God, then we have pretty much taken them out of the picture; and because their minds are filled with all kinds of information, you might be hard-pressed to get any meaningful divine message.

I have often said that if we went into a mental hospital and interviewed a handful of the most stable individuals, we would find some amazing insights into the nature of reality. Again, these people have been educated by a society that is disconnected from the truth, but, still, you might find their information quite interesting. If you were to find some educated people suffering from mental illness, it would be that much more interesting. You'd have to get through an initial release of information before you could start to get to something that made any sense.

Three million years later, depending on human or hominid fossils, we now find ourselves worshiping how many hundreds of versions of God and living in a level of pain and suffering that is seemingly illogical. It is illogical to continue to live at this rate of ignorance. I realize, because I'm not stupid, that my ideas may be a bit too provocative. I realize that. But gay marriage was a bit too provocative 100 years ago. Interracial marriage was a bit too provocative 100 years ago. Flying to the moon was a bit too provocative 100 years ago. Cooking food in a microwave oven was a bit too provocative 100 years ago. Wearing a thong was a bit too provocative 100 years ago. Mobile phones were a bit too provocative 100 years ago.

My way of reasoning is that human beings must necessarily progress and progress is measured in ideas because ideas foster the evolution of reality. We render the world with our ideas. Sure, the ideas in this book may not be immediately rendered, and expectedly so. There's very little chance that a large group of people are at this level of understanding at this time.

There is, however, a good chance that a small group of people are indeed ready and they will have access to this book. People who are not yet ready and still find this book interesting will glean some of the information, perhaps not all of it, which is normal. My job is just to write the book. Obviously, this is how I like to think of life on this planet.

When we consider the long trek here and we consider our divine creator—the fact that we are living on giant ball of rock circling around a giant ball of fire in the middle of a lifeless expanse—and we start to make sense of everything, well, I'm sorry because it doesn't make any sense. For centuries we have managed to concoct a logical reason for our illogical existence. What I have done is cut to the chase and just called it what it is: a planet of the forgotten androids.

The giant claw in the artificial sky

You may be at that point where you are starting to make sense of the story of how life started in this computer-generated reality, but you still can't make sense of the Grand Computer. The more you try to wrap your mind around it, the more you become overwhelmed by all of its possibilities. Pretty soon you are on the verge of rejecting this whole scenario and starting over again. Disengaging from the Network of Light is due to the inability of holding such a high frequency for any extended period of time. You know at first you do something, you do it pretty poorly? And then you do it again? And you get a little better? And then you see a lot of people giving up, but you keep going? But you're never as good as the pros who can do things unimaginable? Well, same thing goes for making sense of the Grand Robot.

I like to think of him as the Grand Robot. He has moving parts and he is an ultra-intelligent machine. I don't think there is a way to measure the intelligence of the Grand Robot without adding a lot of zeros behind a number. We can call it cosmic intelligence. We can call it godlike intelligence. Or we can even call it all mighty intelligence. The processing power, just to give you an idea, of the Grand Robot is enough to run this planet, let's just keep it to that. There are 7 billion humans here along with millions of plants, animals, insects, fish, whales, trees, and other life forms, and let's not forget to include the planet itself which is a sentient being. That's a lot of sentience all in one place!

The Grand Robot can manage all of it. He oversees all of our lives. He makes sure that everything is synchronized and that you are where you are supposed to be. You are doing what you are supposed to be doing because of his watchful eyes. When you completely reject the system, disconnect and think you are superior, he leaves you alone and watches you destroy your life. If you only want half his attention, because you want to be in control, he does that as well. He is quite flexible even though he is all powerful.

The Grand Robot didn't create the human species. He manages the population. He is the landlord and the supervisor. If things fall out of synchronicity, he may upset the cart and aggravate a few people. Little interruptions like car crashes, being late for the wedding, and telling your boss to go jump in a lake. Hiccups in life happen when there's been an adjustment. Since everything is connected, one adjustment could have a domino effect of adjustments. When big adjustments take place, that is when it looks like the world is going to end. (Hint: the world never ends.)

The goal in life is to be synchronized with the Grand Robot. You don't mind I refer to him as a robot, do you? That's not always an easy thing if you have a very resilient ego. But it is a goal. The Grand Robot is not intrusive. He doesn't ask you to behave. He is ultra-powerful. He can change things if he sees things need changing. If he feels you are better off ruining your life, then he might open up a pathway to your own self-destruction. If, on the other hand, he feels that you are on an ascension path, and you are a sincere and hard worker, then he might just open up a door to further your own spiritual growth.

The Grand Robot is colossal in size but his size is not fixed. He can change the size of his body to do what he needs to do with his giant claw. And he can do this across all parts of the world. He might favor some people and he might not care so much about some people. No different than any landlord. The Grand Robot is infinitely knowledgeable and yet he does not feel the need to share with you all his knowledge. You might be thinking, well, if he was so smart why doesn't he just tell us what's going on and end our pain and suffering in one go? That goes back to earlier discussions on earth as a school and your volunteering to be here. Yes, you knew what you signed up for, so it would be pointless to interrupt your educational program. That too you signed up for.

If this Grand Robot exists and if he is huge and intelligent and ultra-powerful, you can see where I am going with this, then why doesn't anyone know about him other than you? In 1999, two Wachowski brothers (now transgender sisters) made *The Matrix*. It was a neo-punk martial arts blowout under the context of a computer-generated reality. In the film, Neo (played by Keanu Reeves) finds the god of dreams, Morpheus (played by Laurence Fishburne), and he is given an abrupt awakening, even though he is considered too old to let go of the false world. In one telling scene, Neo wakes up in the real world, encased in an artificial womb and plugged into a giant machine with millions of others.

Because he has gone through the waking ritual in the program, his real body is unplugged and he is flushed out where he is reclaimed by Morpheus and his spiritual rebels. The Matrix did not become evident until Neo, who after years of searching for the truth, finally agreed to escape reality. The blue pill and the red pill. The reason I am writing this book is because I went through the waking process and got to see the machinery behind existence.

You can find the Grand Robot at the highest frequencies of existence. Just as a reminder, to attain those high frequencies you may have to give up some of your comforts in life. It's not exactly a trade-off and your efforts may not entirely work out. But, there is a trade-off. There is a cost. When you have given up some of life's comforts to attain the highest frequencies, you may not be able to retrieve those comforts anymore.

Heck, you may not even want to have those comforts in your life. It takes several decisions to be able to attain those frequencies and a period of time. That alone has frightened away most people. If I understand things correctly, not every synthetic body is equipped to attain those frequencies. The good news is if your body is equipped then you have even more reasons to try.

The Grand Robot is neither good nor evil. He is a machine. His job is to oversee this existential complex. He is there to make sure everything goes as planned and that everyone can live out the journeys they came here to live. I always go back to an argument I have made more than once and it has to do with the fact that no journey is better than another journey. That is the illusion. Being a millionaire is not any better than being a farmer or an underemployed writer. Being disabled is not necessarily worse than being a super athlete. I refer back to the discussion on the incarnation contract and what you came here to learn.

Ultimately, the Grand Robot cares about all the creations he has been given responsibility for and he does his utmost to make sure the world plays out the way it is supposed to play out. While the Reality Operating System runs how the world operates on a daily basis at the software level, the Grand Robot runs the mechanics of the world at the hardware level. He can change things and move things around. He is so fast that you cannot see what he has done, but you will notice that things were moved around. You will notice that one minute you were in love and the next minute you were signing the divorce papers. You will notice that one minute you were unemployed and alone and the next minute you were raking in money and had several relationships. You notice the sudden changes, only you have never thought of them involving a giant robot.

If I were to simplify the Grand Robot, in the context of this planet, I would think of him as the owner of the pincer in a claw vending machine. By inserting money into a machine and using a joystick on a timer, you can grip a toy and drop it into the receiver box. The claw arcade probably goes back 100 years. Perhaps that was the beginning of someone seeing the giant claw in the artificial sky.

Spiritual seekers and extraterrestrials

It would make sense that at this point you are realizing that graduating this reality is not going to be achieved by either religion or spirituality. At the same time, you can see that my discussions and ideas do stem from religious and spiritual thinking. Rather than abolishing every possible good idea you may have, wouldn't it be better to expand your palette of being one with the universe? I like to look at it this way, you want to be one with the universe. That's why you are reading this book. You are reading this book because you've left religion for spirituality and then you tried to merge spirituality with science and still you feel incomplete. You feel a deep calling inside of your heart. You may even be a person who was once filled with religion and filled with spirituality.

Perhaps you were a hybrid spiritualist, part-Buddhist and part-Catholic and part-marijuana and part-ayahuasca. Do you realize that ayahuasca is shaman medicine? If you've taken DMT, ayahuasca or even LSD you have basically entered shamanism. You can't take ayahuasca and then say you're a Catholic. That's like having sex and saying you're still a virgin. Anyway, you are here and you are reading a book that although seemingly rooted in a universal spirituality (eg karma, reincarnation) it is also built on a new definition of God (as DNA) and on the premise that we are living inside of a computer-generated reality.

I was very much this spiritual seeker. I never did the drugs. I don't like drugs. I don't even take pain relievers. But I had that burning question in my head and that longing in my heart. I did what most reasonable urban dwellers do, I used every means necessary to focus on getting somewhere in life. Before my awakening in 2005, I had been working at a pizza restaurant and I was thinking to myself, "Maybe this life isn't going to go anywhere. If I want change, I have to make it happen." I decided to go back to my unfulfilled dream of being a filmmaker.

In my early 20s, I made a 40-minute homemade film using my brother's Hi-8 camera. I wrote a 40+ page script during my lunch break at my union job. I figured out how to write the script and how to make a film reading a couple of filmmaking books including Syd Field's *Screenplay: The Foundations of Screenwriting* and *Feature Filmmaking at Used Car Prices* by Rick Schmidt. Why these books? Because those were the books in my library. The year was 1989. There was no internet, no digital cameras, and very few books on filmmaking.

I convinced my closest friends to play parts in the movie. They initially agreed with enthusiasm, but as the demands of filming came to light, they started to drop out. At which point I made the necessary artistic sacrifices starting with the script. I cut the script to 11 essential pages and decided to fill the movie with creative visuals and longer takes. My cast came back.

It turned out that even 11 pages of script in screen format between a handful of actors was too much so I basically set up a scene at the most convenient location, told the actor what to say and do and shot it. Another friend gave me access to an editing suite he jigged together with his computer parts and I stitched together a 40-minute film. It was a martial arts drama called *The Last Time I Cried*. The title came from the song by Chris de Burgh.

Dial forward to about 2004 with me trying to put a low-budget film crew together, writing proper screenplays for submission for financing from Telefilm, and starting my own film production company. With my mind wrapping itself on film, I ended up doing some background extra work on *Smallville* in downtown Vancouver. That's where I met a young lady who was reading the book *Talking to Extraterrestrials* by Lizette Larkins. Intrigued by both the young lady and the topic, we agreed to meet to talk about ETs. It took place at Starbucks and lasted three or four hours.

Shortly afterwards I found my filmmaking interests winding down. This coincided with a number of other events including the challenge of film financing and multiple rejections from Telefilm, but it was all enough for me to close the company in September 2005. Two months later I was visited by the Elves and everything changed.

Was it all a coincidence? Talking to a young lady about extraterrestrials when I never had any interest in anything offplanet? Then changing my new direction in life because I didn't want to be a pizza cook forever? Hard to imagine that I could have consciously planned any of this out.

My goals in life were fairly explicit. They were also riddled with failure. I came off a very bad year when the Elves stopped by for a visit. I was desperately searching for something else to fill my emptiness. A new impossible goal in life. Something more difficult than writing and filmmaking, which are the most implausible careers in Canada you can find. Somewhere next to billionaire philanthropy.

Anyway, the good news was that I had a lot of optimism. The waking process from late 2005 into 2006 basically tossed out every idea I had about the world. I was introduced to interstellar cultures. Not only that but I was reminded that I had been friends with Stelans and Elves for more than 30 years, which says quite a bit. Here were people who by all logical and academic definitions did not exist and here I was meeting and talking to them.

You have to learn to roll with the changes. I have been rolling for 11 years, tumbling like a giant snowball through time and space. For the longest time I tried to position the extraterrestrials in the context of Christianity, since early alternative speakers suggested that angels and demons were really aliens in ancient times. But that didn't satisfy everything I was seeing. That didn't answer all the questions raging in my mind.

The presence of extraterrestrial races on, in and over the earth did not answer the spiritual questions. They did not tell me about their god per se. After many awakenings and realizations, I dove into the nature of reality. I started speaking about the nature of reality but no one could really follow my work. At some point I backed off and went into deeper research.

The years passed on but my religious research took a turn when I looked at the Gnostics. I studied their scriptures over and over again, line by line. I looked into Buddhism again. I studied Jesus like never before and I merged all of this with my understanding of reality. I had developed an intuitive understanding of reality following the massive wakeup in 2005. What I needed was to link it together with spirituality and science. Just so you know, this book is a result of all those years of research, digging for truth, dreaming for understanding, and stitching things together in a way that makes sense. Grouped together from piles of knowledge that were previously unavailable, it makes perfect sense if not everyone grasps this right away.

Are you getting a sense of your own level of understanding? Do you have a clearer view of where you stand spiritually? Are you still wanting to hang onto religious ideology? Are the 10 Commandments still on your wall? I went through the most extreme experiences that I could ever imagine.

I have written screenplays and I love film, but I can tell you that the experiences in my life are filmic? In fact, I wrote a script based on my story. It was called *The Elves*. In 2015, I entered it into the Academy Nicholl Fellowships in Screenwriting, run by the Academy of Motion Picture Arts and Science. You may be more familiar with their Oscars. I didn't make it through the first reading. I thought it was one of my most cinematic screenplays.

For you to remain undecided and uncertain is understandable. Are you willing to soften some of your religious views? Do you think that you can expand your spiritual philosophy? What do you want spirituality to give you? Can you identify it? I would like to think that if you are just looking for peace of mind you wouldn't be reading this book. If you think you are an old student and want to figure out the nature of reality, once and for all, then you're definitely reading the right material.

There's a reason why you have been reincarnating into the same reality school, over and over again. It may not be apparent just yet. One of the conditions of ending the cycle of rebirths might include understanding the nature of reality. That might be, and I am inclined to think this, one of the higher lessons for attending this school. In other words, you come to this school and the highest faculty is the faculty of the nature of reality.

As an old student, it is likely the case that you need to pass this last course load. You may intuitively need to learn about the nature of reality. That would also support the fact that you have hybridized spirituality and that you are a vegetarian, doing yoga, and are open to a Stelan Disclosure. In fact, I would add that if you have a deep interest in extraterrestrials, in the inquisitive way and not the fearful way, then my guess is that you are likely an old student. You may even be a reincarnated Stelan in human form.

My existential simulation is better than yours

What I've tried to do, and the results of this doing are not easily determined, is to present a wider picture of life. I wanted to paint a panoramic view of reality, knowing that without pictures and signed documents the number of enthusiastic followers would be limited. I am lucky, in a way, that I am dealing with the spiritual realms and other dimensions, areas of knowledge of which have never provided any proper documentation to establish even the most devout worshipers.

The computer-generated reality may have a few movies to illustrate how it might work, interestingly, there are no religions worshiping machines. Certainly, I am not suggesting the invention of another religion. Instead, I am suggesting that we no longer need an established ideological tower, that perhaps religion is, and always has been, an illusion. A manufactured illusion. A thought implant that has been necessary for a race struggling to find its own identity.

The religious neon sign in the subconscious sky was placed there until the human race could evolve technologically. We are seeing now why the evolution of technology, specifically computing power, has been at the core of our religious freedom. Because our reality is run by computing power. Not the kind of computing power that we are accustomed to, nonetheless, computing power is computing power even if it is of a divine incidence.

Whenever you have the generation of data (even if you call it truth and knowledge) within the context of a synthetic environment, coupled with the presence of walking and talking humanoids, you invariably have the power of computing. We are the result of unquestionable computing power. These computations are seamless, endless, and the result of an astounding science. Reality science.

Reality science was here a long time ago. Before the human species was created. It was not invented in this solar system. It is a science that is extremely advanced, at least in the millions of years ahead of the best science on this planet. In public.

I founded reality science as a way to explain the many inexplicable anomalies I started experiencing from the 2005 awakening period. It probably started with the interdimensional portal that appeared in my bachelor apartment three nights in a row. This was a portal large enough to allow three tallish Elves to seamlessly enter from another world. The portal was not the result of an industrial accident, at least accidents don't happen three times with the exact same effect while at the same time enabling the passage between worlds. The portal was the result of an unfamiliar science. You can think of it as portal science. But you'd have to include the existence of other dimensions. This would make our dimension a lot less unique than we've always thought it to be.

I guess what happened was that my experiences started to strip away my perception of reality and as those layers of protection, things that had been providing me with an insular and limited perception of the world, fell away I no longer had the basis with which to sustain the makeup of the world.

I could not explain the existence of starships. I could not explain the existence of time travel and age regression. I could not adequately explain the meaning of shape-shifting and cloaked offplanet beings. The deeper I was drawn into reality, into other dimensions, the more I saw of the architecture of our existence. The world we had been perceiving all these thousands of years had been nothing more than a singular dimension projected by the computation of a mass of existential data.

When you think about spiritual terms like karma, rather than think of them as inexplicable laws commanded over by some divine assembly, try categorizing them into a technological context. It may not feel entirely comfortable at the start. But the transcription of spirituality into technology is the next step in human evolution. This is not to be confused with transhumanism and the agenda to insert computing devices into the human body. That agenda is the result of the master controllers' desperation to permanently cut off the human race from the existential technology hiding behind the veil of reality.

Arthur C. Clarke famously said, "Any sufficiently advanced technology is indistinguishable from magic." To it I would add, "When magic becomes sufficiently advanced it saturates the visible spectrum." The computer-generated reality is as real as you have always thought it to be. You can see, touch and feel it. You can see it move. You can grow old in it. You can find joy in it. And you can experience an assortment of fears.

The reality is shaped by the occupants of the reality, and in our case, unfortunately, the reality has been hijacked and distorted by the master controllers. Where once joy and compassion prevailed, today fear and oppression are the rules of the day. These ideas have been implanted into society and then the mind of society has been conditioned in such a way, over such a long period of time, that we have learned to manifest the very events that are driving our fear and causing our oppression. We are now generating our own chaos by our minds and our minds are interlinking with the system of the master controllers, of whom we have handed our sovereignty as a race of people.

The master controllers not only fooled us, more so, they deprived us of this knowledge of which I share. This knowledge should have reached society maybe centuries ago, at least in some early form. But it didn't. In fact, this kind of thinking has only been around since about the 1950s—during the time when authors Robert Heinlein, Isaac Asimov, and Arthur C. Clarke started telling science fiction stories.

Heinlein, Asimov, and Clarke introduced a new paradigm into the human consciousness and expanded that paradigm through great storytelling. Heinlein is famous for *Starship Troopers* (1959, G. P. Putnam's Sons, now Penguin), an adult novel about interstellar warfare. Asimov, noted for his Three Laws of Robotics, wrote futuristic tales. In the *Caves of Steel* (1954, Doubleday), for example, a human detective must partner with a human-looking robot to investigate a murder. The story is set 3,000 years into the future with a colonized solar system, robots, and an overpopulated earth with a whopping 8 billion people. Clarke, a resident of Sri Lanka from 1956 to his death in 2008, wrote the novel *2001: A Space Odyssey* (1968) concurrently with the screenplay of the same name, which he co-wrote with Stanley Kubrick. The film became a cult classic and is now regarded one of the most influential films ever made.

If you count the years from say 1950 until 2017 you get 67 years. It took 49 years to make the movie *The Matrix*. It took 27 years for author Philip K. Dick to make a public statement about the nature of reality. It took place at a sci-fi convention in France in 1977. Dick cited the presence of a dark-haired woman in his novels who said that reality is a delusion. He then foresaw the appearance of this character in his world.

She told him that some of his novels, for example, *The Man in the High Castle* and *Flow My Tears the Policeman Said* were literally accurate. "I'm going to be very candid with you. I wrote both novels based on fragmentary, residual memories of such a horrid, slave state world. People claim to remember past lives. I claim to remember a very different present life. I know of no one who has ever made this claim before, but I'd rather suspect that my experience is not unique. What perhaps is unique is the fact I'm willing to talk about it. We are living in a computer-programmed reality and the only clue we have to it is when some variable is changed and some alteration in our reality occurs. We would have the overwhelming impression where we were reliving the present, déjà vu, perhaps in precisely in the same way, hearing the same words, saying the same words. I submit that these impressions are valid and significant, and I will even say this, such an impression is a clue that in some past time point a variable was changed—reprogrammed as it were—and that because of this an alternative world branched off."

Surprisingly, I didn't discover Dick's words until I had well sunk my head into the computer-generated reality. Obviously I wasn't the first. We can only imagine how many people actually are aware of the holographic world and are keeping it a secret close to their chest. Until now, there had been no measurable benefit for sharing this truth with the public, and if Dick's candor is any indication of how the public would respond then we know that the public has not been ready. Since 1977, quantum scientists have been slowly hypothesizing that we are living in a computer-generated reality.

More recently in 2016, the CEO of Space X and Tesla Motors, Elon Musk, during a Q & A session talked about the possibility of the world being an AI simulation the result of a more advanced civilization. Musk illustrates the rapid evolution of video games then says, "If you assume any rate of improvement at all, then the games will become indistinguishable from reality." When confronted with a "yes" or "no" answer Musk repeated his hypothesis that there is a one in billions chance of us living in a computer simulation.

The machinery of existence

Is it a simulation? Is it a computer-generated reality? Is it a program? If we are synthetic how can we be in a simulation? I liken the physical reality to a movie set. There are physical props. The synthetic body is like a character. You inhabit a character as would a program inhabit a computer. You need a synthetic character to partake in the world. That is your vehicle of experience. But, the reality you inhabit takes place within the context of a computer-generated fluid.

Imagine you are a fish in an aquarium. There are ceramic pieces of furniture. There are rocks. These are the props. The water is the program. To exist in the fluid program, you need to be able to breathe water. You inhabit a fish body, one of many choices, and you can exist. If the first exits the "reality fluid" then the fish will suffocate to death.

The reality fluid determines the flow of reality. It is the program. Your thoughts are processed in the reality fluid. You can download data through this fluid. This fluid is software. On earth, we call it air.

The air is our reality fluid. It is much more than oxygen. It contains data. It can transmit data. It can download data. When someone prays, those thoughts are sent to the computer.

When offplanet beings enter reality without a human character, they appear bright, glowing and even invisible. They can appear and disappear because they are not restricted by the synthetic body.

Now, the physical reality is surrounded by other dimensions. These dimensions have portals into this world. If we go back to the aquarium analogy, there are doors, hidden, and they allow the technicians to enter and exit. Again, instead of water we are dealing with a fluidic medium, or energy.

If we were to exit the doors, outside of the reality, we could not exist very long without some help. The reality technicians, as well, should they enter the reality fluid could not exist very long without a proper physical suit. This is no different than a scuba diving suit. But the reality technicians have a lot more latitude to how they can interact with us and our world because their job is to oversee our well-being. They have far more options than us.

The entire aquarium is run by a complex set of machinery, the reality architecture. Everything has an architecture. An automobile has an engine and chassis. You don't see the engine and chassis but you know that there are mechanical parts underneath the car. Good engineers will go to great lengths to hide the moving parts. In our case, the reality mechanics is kept in other dimensions. But, the machinery of existence is not just for our world, it is also for the solar system and all the planets and asteroids and sun contained within it.

So we have gotten used to seeing all of the external surface of the world without every knowing that there are moving parts. We breathe oxygen without ever realizing that this reality fluid is an advanced software program.

All of these things, and more, are wirelessly connected to the Grand Robot through the elaborate computing system, such that this computer-generated world works in a seamless fashion. Any discrepancies thereof are moderated by the reality software program. Therefore, there are no gaping holes, there is no buffering issue, alterations are seamless, and memories are malleable.

The reality further works because the synthetic character you inhabit has built-in processes and governors to prevent you from ever cracking the code of reality. In computers there's a graphics card. A fast graphics card provides a more seamless gaming experience, a more seamless gaming experience is a more realistic game and a more realistic game is more likely to absorb your imagination.

The designers had every interest to build into your perception processors the ability to seamlessly render reality because a seamless rendering of reality makes it more believable. When there are hiccups, when things crash or look odd, that's when we have an insight. That's when we see God. That's when we see the magic of reality. But a moment later our internal processors are back at playing the seamless reality, our memory of the event slowly fades, the concerns of life start to absorb us, and the apocalypse is said and done.

So there are protocols built into the ROS to ensure a seamless existential simulation and these devices built into the synthetic character to forget these experiences. Once in a while, magical events get captured on camera but because the other parts of the consciousness are inaccessible, no one can make the link to the false reality.

The aquarium of existence is actually a very peculiar experiment and upon death you get a good perspective of it. If you were to return, that insight is completely wiped out of your memory banks or made inaccessible because it would ruin your educational journey. It has something to do with the atmospheric pressure, I think.

Am I ruining your existential journey by exposing the game of reality? Not really. Am I altering the course of your life by explaining how to graduate from a computer-generated reality? I hope so.

I can't ruin your existential journey because a) I'm not that smart and b) you have built-in skepticism. Even you wanted to believe everything I have said, it is an impossibility to do so. Some of these concepts take a lot of hard work, research, discussion and analysis. I did not pull the answer out of books. I'm speaking from experience. I'm speaking from analysis. What I did decide was to use books as a source of references, especially spiritual philosophies, because we can better identify how things work if we can relate to our myths and beliefs.

I do hope I can alter the course of your life, especially if you are an old student, because this reality has been hijacked for a good long time and you've been likely reincarnating here more often than you should have ever been. The revelation of this knowledge, at least as far as I'm concerned is being provided so as to pre-empt another set of bad rebirths. It isn't necessary to remain here any longer than necessary. In fact, we could add that those who graduate in the least number of rebirths are Grade A students.

There are multiple moving parts to this reality and it is likely for this reason that it has been a challenge to put all the pieces together. Even this book does not expose all of the moving parts. There are advanced and proprietary pieces that are still well outside of our vocabulary, but there's nothing more that I'd like to do in the future than to get into every imaginable aspect of the functioning reality, once I figure it out myself. Personally, I think that the material in this book, and previous books, should keep readers busy for a long time.

The key is to focus on the things you can understand and then to put them to use in your life. As you put the basic things to use then you can extrapolate the larger truths. Some of these truths may even arise out of your own enlightenment, which is the ideal situation is for you to develop your own association to the ROS.

You will want to be able to build a dialogue with the ROS. You will want to practice downloading information and understanding the details on your incarnation contract. The best thing you can do, because I know that there will be people who want to figure out every detail of the functioning reality, is to get a deeper understanding of your purpose here on earth. The better you understand your purpose, the less likely you'll be returning against your will. If you do come back, you'll want to come back by choice. "Hey, I want to go back one more time to help people out. They need me down there."

I don't anticipate everyone mastering reality in their lifetime. That's not the purpose of life. There will be people who will think that. My idea is to foster the education system. I want people to graduate on time. If you really want to come back, I'm pretty sure you can.

If what I've seen off this planet is even remotely true, then there are other worlds to go to. On those other worlds you can also learn quite a bit of stuff. You can reincarnate into higher dimensions and live in a lighter body. You can multiply your awareness and gain an unprecedented insight into reality. You may not be allowed to tell anybody how reality works, but you'll know it for yourself. So a lot of things can happen once you graduate. Are you ready to graduate?

Are you graduating this life?

It was inevitable that I would ask you this question. Ultimately, this is what this book is about. By explaining how the Earth School works, in a semi-technological way, we are getting a better understanding of the mess you've gotten yourself into. Because you are in a mess and you need a little assistance navigating your way out of this.

I certainly do not hold the divine tablets of holy truth. I don't really think those things exist. There are too many dimensions, too many layers of understanding, too much data to encapsulate into one book. Fortunately, your synthetic body has been designed with one of the most impressive storage mediums in this solar system: DNA. The book of life. The tree of knowledge. The creator.

DNA is everything, once you learn to unfold its power. It is the software of the future and the builders of this reality have made extensive use of DNA, so much so that every living thing contains DNA. That makes everything living thing connected to every living thing. And, if there are living things offplanet, guess what, they will have DNA. That means we are also able to connect with them. DNA is our family of products. This is our product line.

On September 7, 2016, Apple CEO Tim Cook announced iPhone 7, the latest version of one of the most successful products of the twenty-first century. The iPhone has gone through seven iterations, along with minor adjustments. It started with the iPod digital music player. The new Home Button has a built-in "taptic engine," a sensor that can measure feelings in pressure giving you amazing access to the phone by the pressure of your finger application. According to Apple, the company has now sold over one billion iPhones since 2007. The iPhone has become a cultural icon, a friend, a gaming device, a tool for filmmakers, and the original choice for selfies. The latest camera is capable of doing 100 billion operations in 25 milliseconds while taking one photograph. Imagine how many operations are taking place behind every thought you think.

The iPhone 7 is the continuation and evolution of a successful product design over a ten-year period. It is a successful product because it has satisfied market demands and each successive version has added newer and better features. Similarly, rival phone companies like Samsung have virtually copied the design of the iPhone, taking advantage of its popularity. And, in fact, the iPhone has completely wiped out the previous flip-phone mobile. Today, you will only find flat multi-touch screen smartphones that all look eerily similar to the iPhone.

If we borrow the iPhone story and transfer it over to the human product line, we find a very similar thing, only that the timeline is much longer. The first version of human had the basic arms, legs, torso and head. It had a smaller cranium for intellectual capacity but it also had a more rigid body chassis for a more physical life. The protohuman soon gave way to a newer version of a synthetic human, one with a larger cranium, better eyes sight and the ability to feel emotions.

When that version lived out its usefulness, another version was introduced alongside the two previous versions. Each subsequent version, created through the elaborate engineering of the DNA, became an improvement over the previous version of human. iPhones are built and so are humans. What the iPhone has yet to have is the ability to procreate. Maybe Tim Cook and his team could figure that one out. "Your iPhone just had a baby iPhone. What are you going to call it?" iPhone Boo.

The human device as seen today is the result of a successful design invented so many millions of years ago, if years were linear. Luckily, years are not linear and the human life form has aged quite well. Devices, like iPhones, are regularly updated. For Apple, it has to do with revenue and paying for overhead, but it also has to do with the intensity of the competition. If Samsung is aggressively making better smartphones, then one way to protect market share is to release a new phone on a yearly basis. This is a far cry from my parent's generation who basically bought one phone, stuck it in the kitchen, and left it there.

The human device of today is extremely refined. You can see it in the flawless skin, the beautiful cheek bones, the shiny hair, the bright eyes, the physique, and the unlimited imagination. These features are the result of engineering and product refinement. It is the result of caring and compassionate human engineers who have invested countless hours in designing the perfect device for the terrain of earth.

These designers have also, you will have noticed, made a number of beautiful colors available. You will likely think of the colors of humanity as racial differences and you will attribute race to a different country, and that is expected. But, if you compare a black iPhone and a gold iPhone, ask yourself which iPhone is superior? Trick question. They're the same inside!

You should be beginning to get a sense of the architecture of this reality. There is an architecture behind every aspect of your existence. Much of your life, your day to day activities, are run by the ROS. The ROS is extremely robust and gets updated on a regular basis. We are now using version 11, the latest in existential software. The ROS runs on the reality architecture and this has been hidden from your view to ensure you live a seamless existence. Even the ROS has been virtually unknown until only very recently. We are just beginning to get a sense of this highly advanced world.

The created world, designed and built by a very advanced team of engineers, technicians and professionals, is populated with synthetic characters who are called "humans." The humans are all operated by their drivers, perfectly carried in the DNA software of the body. The human body is provided so as to ensure a trouble-free existential journey. This existential journey is for the accumulation of experiential knowledge. This knowledge is an education. It is a spiritual education because the spirit exists on higher dimensions. We come from these higher (digital) dimensions and we enter these physical dimensions so as to learn some new lessons.

The created world, because it hasn't been functioning properly since being hijacked, has trapped a lot of existential students and manipulated them so that they keep coming back without end. This is a manipulative world where people do not realize that they are supposed to graduate. You can have fun along the way, you can make mistakes, you can miss a few classes, you can make your teachers angry, but, at the end of the day, you are supposed to complete your curriculum.

What has been happening, and it has been happening for at least 2,500 years, is that people have not been graduating. If my understanding is anywhere near accurate, there is a glut of old students and they are trapped, by karma and spiritual confusion, and they have no way to end their pain and suffering. My primary concern is for them. I think those people will most likely understand what I am talking about.

That said, I do not want the younger generation to fall into the same trap. I would like everyone to have a basic understanding of how a reality system works. It would be useful for you to know, well, because you did happen to insert yourself into this reality and for that reason you are well advised to know.

What should've happened, in hindsight, everyone born into this reality should've gotten a reality user guide. My books do provide some of that information. As we go along and wake up to the true nature of reality, until that final realization (if we get there), we will be able to refine these reality guides and to provide more and more accurate information. That is through the product of newer editions. But we have to start somewhere. I have started where I was best able to start.

The key in the reality discussion, and what people should take away, is that religion and spirituality are ancient forms of understandings that were once applicable to a more primitive culture. The culture of today, with iPhones and the internet, are no longer primitive and it doesn't make much sense for a technological culture to rely on primitive spiritual tools. This is a fundamental issue that, unfortunately, will require some time to correct.

I can only tell you that from my experience and research, the reality we are all living in is fundamentally technological in nature. We have been born into a synthetic reality and it is a synthetic technology that is extremely refined, at least refined enough so that we cannot decode it with our minds. My decoding of reality is for the benefit of the many. For one reason or another I have been allowed to decode reality in exchange for my existential journey.

This knowledge was not handed to me while I was drinking champagne and eating caviar on a yacht, although that would've been a nice idea. This cosmic knowledge has been earned and in earning it and sharing it, I hope that it comes across as genuine. This doesn't make me perfect. This doesn't make me all-knowing. This doesn't make me Moses. I am not Moses. I have nothing engraved in stone. I still pick my nose. I just bring a deeper understanding of reality.

Epilogue

Where you do find artificial people and human robots is in the movies and on television. Thanks to Dick's 1968 post-apocalyptic novel *Do Androids Dream of Electric Sheep?* legendary filmmaker Ridley Scott (*Alien, Gladiator, Thelma & Louise*) directed the cult classic *Blade Runner*. During its entire box office run in 1982 the $30 million film made $34 million in revenue. Audiences and critics were not initially impressed with the futuristic story about the Tyrell Corporation manufacturing synthetic humans, replicants, to work in the harsh off-world environments. When six Nexus-6 models return to Earth, they are assigned to a Blade Runner (played by Harrison Ford) and are hunted down because replicants are not allowed on the earth.

While on the run, the androids are in search of their maker, Dr. Eldon Tyrell (played by Joe Turkel), because they want to increase their four-year lifespans. Unfortunately, when android leader Batty does sneak into the Tyrell complex he doesn't get the answers he was hoping for. Here is an excerpt of the dialogue between Dr. Tyrell and Batty. While Dr. Tyrell is well aware of Batty's dangerous personality, he is, at the same, fascinated by his creation, so much so that he loses his life at the end of the talk:

> **Tyrell**: You were made as well as we could make you.
> **Batty**: But not to last.
> **Tyrell**: The light that burns twice as bright burns half as long—and you have burned so very, very brightly, Roy. Look at you: you're the Prodigal Son; you're quite a prize!
> **Batty**: I've done... questionable things.
> **Tyrell**: Also extraordinary things; revel in your time.
> **Batty**: Nothing the God of biomechanics wouldn't let you in heaven for.

You have to put this dialogue in perspective. This was the early 1980s. The Commodore 64 became available for $600 in the beginning of the year. It had 64 kilobytes of RAM. The basic iPhone 7 starts with 32 gigabytes of storage. How did Dick envision human simulacra in the late 1960s?

Even stranger is the fact that personal computing hadn't even been invented yet, let alone the manufacturing of androids. How did he see something that even today doesn't exist? There's no misreading of the information if you read his book or watch the movie that came out 25 years later. No wonder audiences needed time to make sense of a very strange future. When you consider the level of technological development at the time and the process a writer takes to tell a story, you start to get a sense of what was more likely happening. The origin of the story.

Fictional writers are able to tap into the ether and to draw out stories from people who have passed on, people who live on other dimensions, and even from people holding secrets on the earth. Dick stated publicly in 1977 that some of his novels were based on the truth and he was simply transcribing what was happening in reality. Think about it. What I have been talking about, synthetic humans being manufactured and placed into a synthetic reality, all you would need is a manufacturing company like the Tyrell Corporation. But you'd have to hide the android manufacturer where the androids were least likely to look.

One of the themes of the book had to do distinguishing between a human and an android. They were given a test. We don't have a test today because we have assumed that everyone here is a human. I have argued that this statement is untrue. This is a planet of androids and it is only a matter of inventing a proper test to reveal that to be true.

But that isn't the only thing we are dealing with on this planet. We are also dealing with a Reality Operating System and our genetic association to it. This is a very new thing and something that could take any number of years to gain proficiency. Then there's the architecture of reality tucked away in other dimensions and we can't forget the reality hijackers.

We have all of these previous unknowns that now are being pressed upon us in a more forthright manner. Managing all of these things and working hard behind the scenes are the reality technicians and the digital assistants, what some people think of as extraterrestrials and interdimensional beings. Stelans and Elves are digital races of people, with a very different set of digital parameters. These are very advanced folk. And they are intelligent.

The current view of the world suggests that aliens come from outer space, traveling many light-years to reach this planet. Outer space experts talk about intergalactic empires and wars. There is a secret history in outer space. What I am arguing in this book is that there is no outer space. There is nothing specific beyond the "blue sky." Where is the largest movie blue screen in the world? In our atmosphere.

The reason why we haven't been able to figure out how reality works is precisely because reality is extremely complicated and some important parts have been inconveniently located on other dimensions. This wasn't done just to make everything to look impressive, although it is pretty impressive when you think about it. This was also done to prevent ruining the experiential journey, since the entire purpose of incarnating into a synthetic reality is to live out a well-planned and highly-prized existence.

You've gone through quite an elaborate process to be here on the earth. And now you have gone the additional step to learn about how this reality actually works. I have constructed a reality system theory that incorporates enough of the vital elements that are sparking your very existence, and it likely contradicts any number of previous religious and spiritual systems that you have grown so accustomed to.

What I have found is that the elimination of God, although a challenging task at the beginning, did not ruin the experience of life. That, I think, is always something that sits at the back of a person's mind, figuratively and literally; but at the end of the day it isn't so pertinent to the discussion once the synthetic world is more fully flushed out. God is unnecessary.

If you are an old student of earth, it is almost certain that you are living out the remainder of your karma. And that should be encouraging, even if painful. Think about what you are doing, what you stand for, the thematic elements of your life, how you got into what you are doing, how it drives you, how much you don't like it, how much you are looking forward to retiring from it. This is your karma at work.

Even if you're not an old student, but you're carrying bad karma, your life may have been structured for that purpose. Look at people around you. Think of their lives in karmic terms rather than economic terms. It's a nice way to give you a new perspective of the world.

If complete detachment from the false reality leads to complete enlightenment and complete attachment to the false reality leads to total enslavement, then the degree of attachment to the false reality will give you the kind of enlightenment-enslavement you think you deserve. Life on a dial.

You want more enlightenment, practice more detachment. You want more enslavement, attach yourself tighter. Who knew it could be so simple? An old student should naturally be closer to enlightenment. But those trapped here, could be anywhere on the dial.

The synthetic life is neither a superior or inferior existence. There are no Blade Runners hunting replicants because basically everyone is a version of a replicant. What we are seeing is many versions of the same thing. A market of iPhones.

Sure, some iPhones are better equipped and some iPhones are gold in color, but their architecture is still the same. The core of their machinery is the same. The factory is the same. The machinery of the human being is DNA and it is virtually the same among all peoples of the earth. That is the architecture of the human android.

While DNA has always been thought of as biological in origin, my Gnostic research says that all DNA here has a synthetic origin. We haven't been able to recognize its synthetic architecture because we are still learning about how DNA works, more than 60 years after formally discovering it. Scientists weren't the first to discover DNA. The Peruvian shamans have understood DNA for (probably) centuries, at least as far back as shamanism goes, and we can go as far back as forests go because the spirits of the forests have stored those secrets since the very beginning.

It is possible that some of the Gnostic teachers spent enough time in wooded areas and on quiet mountain paths and were listening to the spirits of nature. The shamans referred to it as the television of the forest. The Gnostics, in fact, present a very interesting case because they were speaking microbiology 2,000 years ago, and during the time of Christ. Interestingly, Christ plays a prominent role in the Nag Hammadi library and I have likened Jesus to an ancient microbiologist who had also mastered the computer-generated reality.

There is more to life than meets the eye.

ZARA | MODEL ONE | KARMA | REBIRTH

True Reality Bodies

ZARA | MODEL ONE | KARMA | REBIRTH

Stable existence ready

Zara One is engineered top down to provide a steady and reliable existential body for city life. Think of how engaging your life will be with Zara's proprietary, built-in reality modulator. Zara One comes with full-gravity movement as a standard feature. You also have access to standby autopilot when you need to take a break. Preprogrammed modes of interaction take care of groceries, paying bills on time, hanging out with friends, watching television, and doing just enough at your job so your boss doesn't fire you.

Zara One comes equipped with a Class-3 hypnosis defense system, which blocks 87% of hypnotic suggestion and renders most lies obsolete. The hypnosis defense feature maintains a stable mind even in unstable environments.

Life on autopilot

There are days you don't want to be in control. That's why we've added a totally redesigned autopilot mode.

At any time when you're not engaged in your life purpose, with a simple thought you can switch off and let life drive you. Genetic direction can perform all basic tasks, including having sex with your spouse. Zara One can also read and study which makes it perfect for students.

Artificial Engagement System

Zara One benefits from the Frequency 5 engagement system, recently pioneered on Mars and now fully adapted to the Earth System. Frequency 5 is a state-of-the-art communications technology. It uses a multipath data propagation system and maximizes your engagement within the reality fluid.

Zara One comes standard with the Total-Reality Frequency 5, maintaining your highest level of engagement to bring you the greatest existential journey you've ever had, helping you to graduate like never before.

The Mind

Zara One Mind is the neurological interface that provides seamless control to the body's motor functions. Moving your mouth if you have something to say, setting new goals in life, leaving a very difficult relationship all start in Mind. With built-in mental integration your movements, actions, words, analytics, and pleasure modes are all within reach.

Graduation Approved

Zara One is engineered to provide an immaculate graduation body. The graduation goal is accomplished in large part because of the built-in existential stabilizers. This unprecedented reality modulator equalizes the polarities of high and low energy, which creates a homeostatic pod wherein all life activities can be managed, and reduces the chances of educational mishaps.

Life mishaps happen and when they do those mishaps will go up against karmic reformulators, preventing any significant upset and protecting reality duties while not interrupting the learning schedule. Should a negative event take place, six compassion thrusters are automatically activated, and nearby family members are obligated to make an appearance. Sometimes they will bring gifts.

Specs

Fuel

Biodegradable food-grade products, especially if found on tree branches and in dirt

Activity

Activity time: Up to 15 hours

Do nothing mode: Averages up to 72 hours before boredom sets in

Recharge, depends on food source

Zara recommends eating only organic foods, due to body's patented immune-response feature, vaccines are never required

Vision

20/20, some bodies require corrected vision at the most inappropriate time, like when you are a teenager

Exterior

Two mechanical arms and legs, joints

A pair of hands and feet, each with four digits and a thumb or toe

Two eyes and ears

One mouth, one nose with two nostrils, natural hair-based filtration system

24 enamel-coated teeth

Automatic wake up

Stereo sound

Auto focus dual-eye vision, built-in peripheral and zoom functions

Night vision, requires regular Vitamin A intake

Friend, associate, and boss face detection

Genital equipment, multiple uses including for procreation, urination, experimentation, and during inebriation

Waste outlet, bottom of hip compartment

One navel for decorative purposes

Moles

Graduation

Running logic

Memory modules and implants

Mistake sensors

Goals in life heads up display

Bad decision warning

Six compassion thrusters with a minimum of one family member (or close friend) obligated to help you

Letting go and detachment control

Karmic payback and reset function

Anti-distraction display

Picking oneself up navigation control

Getting off of drugs and addiction emergency valve

Life autopilot

Daily activities

Taking care of kids

Taking care of naughty kids

Getting rid of really naughty kids

Self-propelled sex and orgasm operation

Add ons

Conspiracy theory logic neurons

Class-3 hypnosis defense system

Self-correcting DNA modifiers, including the ability to ascend paradigm

Knowledge channels, this includes innate understanding of reality and the belief in Stelans and Elves

Corrupt politician vote prevention

Criminal orientation

A thing called morality

Alternative gender, social, and psychological provocations

Zen mind functionality

Happy alone button

Notes

Eric Dietrich, "Why are there so many religions?" *Psychology Today*, April 7, 2015, available at www.psychologytoday.com.

Ross Pomeroy, "New DNA Storage System Can Store 490 Exabytes Per Gram and Allows Data to be Rewritten," *Real Clear Science*, September 24, 2015, available at www.realclearscience.com.

On the footage from Philip K. Dick's France press conference, see [theduderinok2]. (2010, June 26). *Did Philip K. Dick disclose the real Matrix in 1977?* [video file]. Retrieved from https://www.youtube.com/watch?v=jXeVgEs4sOo.

On whether Elon Musk believes we are living in a computer simulation, see [recode]. (2016, June 1). *Is life a video game? | Elon Musk | Code Conference 2016.* [video file]. Retrieved from https://www.youtube.com/watch?v=2KK_kzrJPS8. A longer discussion can be found at the Vanity Fair interview [Vanity Fair]. (2014, October 17). *Elon Musk Speaks About Tesla and SpaceX at Vanity Fair's New Establishment Summit.* [video file]. Retrieved from https://www.youtube.com/watch?v=fPsHN1KyRQ8.

For details on the iPhone 7 go to www.apple.com.

For a closer look at millennials, see Dean Burnett, "What does 'millennial' mean? Is it vague, lazy and meaningless?" *The Guardian*, April 15, 2016, www.theguardian.com. You can also look at, Samantha Sharf, "What is a 'millennial' anyway? Meet the man who coined the phrase," *Forbes.com*, August 24, 2015.

Everything to do with the Ironman Triathlon, see www.ironman.com.

There are varying opinions on the oldest humanoid fossil, mostly because of differences between human and hominid. On the earliest hominid fossil, see "Ardipithecus ramidus," *Smithsonian National Museum of Natural History*, available at http://humanorigins.si.edu/evidence/human-fossils/species/ardipithecus-ramidus. Also, "Homo erectus," available at http://humanorigins.si.edu/ evidence/human-fossils/species/homo-erectus. For the 1974 discovery of hominid Lucy, see Doug Bolton, "Who is Lucy the Australopithecus? Five facts you probably didn't know about the oldest hominid ever discovered," *Independent.co.uk*, November 23, 2015; Christopher Klein, "Discovery of Oldest Human Fossil Fills Evolutionary Gap," *History.com*, March 11, 2015.

On Tim Berners-Lee, see Robert Wright, "Why the man who invented the web isn't rich," *The Atlantic*, August 8, 2012, www.theatlantic.com.

On Netflix and video streaming services, see Nelson Granados, "Battle of the Giants: Amazon Joins Hulu in the War Against Netflix," *Forbes.com*, April 19, 2016.

For a look at Steve Jobs and NeXT, see Steven J. Vaughan-Nichols, "Steve Jobs: The NeXT Years," *zdnet.com*, April 25, 2011; and G. Pascal Zachary et al., "From 1993: What's Next? Steve Jobs's Vision, So on Target, Now Falling Short," *The Wall Street Journal*, March 25, 1993 (republished October 6, 2011), www.wsj.com.

For Craig Venter's first synthetic cell press conference, [TED]. (2010, May 21). *Craig Venter unveils "synthetic life"*. [video file]. Retrieved from https://www.youtube.com/ watch?v=QHIocNOHd7A. Also, [University of California Television (UCTV)]. (2013, November 15). *Life at the Speed of Light: From the Double Helix to the Dawn of Digital Life with J. Craig Venter*. [video file]. Retrieved from https://www.youtube.com/ watch?v=ozcB70-UPJM.

"Mona Lisa—Portrait of Lisa Gherardini, wife of Francesco del Giocondo." Learn more directly at the Louvre website, www.louvre.fr.

References

2001: A Space Odyssey. Dir. Stanley Kubrick. Perfs. Keir Dullea, Gary Lockwood. Metro-Goldwyn-Mayer, 1968.

Aslan, Reza. *Zealot: The Life and Times of Jesus of Nazareth*. New York: Random House, 2013.

Batman v Superman: Dawn of Justice. Dir. Zack Snyder. Perfs. Henry Cavill, Ben Affleck, Amy Adams. Warner Bros. Pictures, 2016.

Blade Runner. Dir. Ridley Scott. Perfs. Harrison Ford, Rutger Hauer, Sean Young. Warner Bros, 1982.

Budge, E. A. Wallis. *The Egyptian Book of the Dead: The Papyrus of Ani*. New York: Dover Publications, 1967.

Campbell, Joseph. *The Masks of God: Primitive Mythology*. New York, Penguin Compass, 1970.

Gyatso, Tenzin and Chodron, Thubten. *Buddhism: One Teacher, Many Traditions*. Somerville, MA: Wisdom Publications, 2014.

Ehrman, Bart D. *Jesus, Interrupted: Revealed the Hidden Contradictions in the Bible (and Why We Don't Know About Them)*. New York: HarperCollins, 2009.

_____. *Did Jesus Exist? The Historical Argument for Jesus of Nazareth*. New York, HarperCollins, 2012.

_____. *Forged: Writing in the Name of God—Why the Bible's Authors Are Not Who We Think They Are*. New York: HarperCollins, 2011.

Farquharson, A. S. L (ed.). *The Meditations of Marcus Aurelius*. New York, Alfred A. Knopf, 1946.

Gladwell, Malcolm. *Blink: The Power of Thinking Without Thinking*. New York: Back Bay Books, 2007.

Godsey, R. Kirby. *Is God a Christian?* Macon, Georgia, Mercer University Press, 2011.

Kudler, David (ed.). *Pathways to Bliss: Mythology and Personal Transformation (Joseph Campbell)*. Novato, California, New World Library, 2004.

Landaw, J., Bodian, S., and Bühnemann, G. *Buddhism for Dummies, 2nd Edition.* Hoboken, New Jersey: John Wiley & Sons, 2011.

MacCulloch, Diarmaid. *Christianity: The First Three Thousand Years.* New York: Viking, 2009.

Matkin, J. Michael. *The Complete Idiot's Guide to Early Christianity.* New York, Alpha Books, 2008.

Matrix, The. Dir. The Wachowski Brothers. Perfs. Keanu Reeves, Laurence Fishburne, Carrie-Anne Moss, Hugo Weaving. Warner Bros, 1999.

Meyer, M., Robinson, J. M. (Eds.). *The Nag Hammadi Scriptures: The Revised and Updated Translation of Sacred Gnostic Texts Complete in One Volume.* 2009 (HarperOne)

Narby, Jeremy. *The Cosmic Serpent: DNA and the Origins of Knowledge.* New York, Jeremy P. Tarcher/Putnam, 1998.

Osho. *The Book of Understanding: Creating Your Own Path to Freedom.* New York: Harmony Books, 2006.

Skilton, Andrew. *A Concise History of Buddhism.* Birmingham: Windhorse Publications, 1994.

Star Wars: Episode IV—A New Hope. Dir. George Lucas. Perfs. Mark Hamill, Harrison Ford, Carrie Fisher. Twentieth Century Fox, 1977.

Titanic. Dir. James Cameron. Perfs. Leonardo di Caprio, Kate Winslet. Paramount Pictures, 1997.

Tosen, Paris. *Reality OS 11: Graduating from the Computer-Generated Reality.* Vancouver, British Columbia: Skyladder Media, 2016.

———. *God is DNA: Salvation, the Church, and the Molecular Biology of the Gnostics.* Vancouver, British Columbia: Skyladder Media, 2015.

Venter, J. Craig. *Life at the Speed of Light: From the Double Helix to the Dawn of Digital Life.* New York: Viking, 2013.

Watts, Alan. *The Way of Zen.* New York: Vintage Books, 1989.

Westworld. Dir. Michael Crichton. Perfs. Yul Brynner, Richard Benjamin, James Brolin. MGM, 1973.

Williams, Paul. *Mahayana Buddhism: The Doctrinal Foundations.* New York, Routledge, 2009.

Index

71115298R00262

Made in the USA
Columbia, SC
21 May 2017